Learn Desktop Graphics
and Design on the PC

Donald Jenner

ADDISON-WESLEY PUBLISHING COMPANY

Reading, Massachusetts · Menlo Park, California · New York
Don Mills, Ontario · Wokingham, England · Amsterdam
Bonn · Sydney · Singapore · Tokyo · Madrid · San Juan
Paris · Seoul · Milan · Mexico City · Taipei

Many of the designations used by manufacturers and sellers to distinguish their products are claimed as trademarks. Where those designations appear in this book and Addison-Wesley was aware of a trademark claim, the designations have been printed in initial capital letters or all capital letters.

The authors and publishers have taken care in preparation of this book, but make no expressed or implied warranty of any kind and assume no responsibility for errors or omissions. No liability is assumed for incidental or consequential damages in connection with or arising out of the use of the information or programs contained herein.

Library of Congress Cataloging-in-Publication Data

Jenner, Donald.
   Learn desktop graphics and design on the PC / Donald
Jenner.
     p.   cm.
   Includes index.
   ISBN 0-201-40788-4
   1. Computer graphics.   I. Title.
T385.J45 1995
741.6'0285'4165--dc20   94-16261
                                        CIP

Addison-Wesley books are available for bulk purchases by corporations, institutions, and other organizations. For more information please contact the Corporate, Government and Special Sales Department at (800) 238-9682.

Sponsoring Editor: Philip Sutherland
Project Manager: Sarah Weaver
Cover Design: Barbara T. Atkinson
Text design: Sonia Hale
Set in 11 point New Century Schoolbook by compuType

1 2 3 4 5 6 7 8 9-MA-9897969594
First printing, November 1994

To my wife, Shu-Huey Yen Jenner

Preface

Prefaces are where authors do something fundamentally at odds with the notion of authorship: They express humble thanks and a sense of their own imperfection.

This book is not the product of a single effort. It is a collaboration of many people, with substantial understanding of what a book like this should be. Addison-Wesley's Trade Computer Books division, under the guidance of Kathleen Tibbetts, brought that team together. It has been my good fortune that Kathleen thought to call me with her idea for a book of this nature, and some really good ideas of how it might come to be—just at the moment when I was thinking much the same thing and was wondering how to get the project under way. Clearly, I owe thanks to these folks, and I give it, heartily.

Say perhaps, the gods smiled on this project. If you read this and buy the book, we know the gods are still smiling— or is that chuckling?

I also owe thanks to the magazine editor who brought me into this end of computing. Brad Schultz, sometime editor of (the late, lamented) *Computer Graphics Today,* convinced me to try my hand at writing about computer graphics. It was the beginning of an adventure that, quite literally, changed my life.

This adventure took on new dimensions through my association with the then-publisher of *Computer Pictures,* Richard McCarthy. Dick's career has spanned all phases of marketing, and working under him to understand the significance of computer graphics for different groups of users was perhaps the most educational aspect of the adventure to date.

Computer software is never finished—take that as an axiom. New and better ways to do things are always discovered as hardware becomes more able and programmers more sophisticated. Books about the use of computers and computer software are equally unfinished; there is always more to say.

Nevertheless, I think this effort goes a long way toward defining current computer-graphics capabilities and related design issues for most people. As a takeoff point, it should be a good foundation for further development. I've been fortunate in having the advice of a number of talented designers—notably, Bruce Wasserman, who reviewed this manuscript. If there are any flaws in it, they reflect only on me, and the fact that my own adventure in computer graphics and design is still unfinished.

Donald Jenner
New York
May 1994

Contents

Introduction: More Reasons to Read This Book

You picked up this book for a good reason. Let me augment that reason with a few more.

Buy this book; it's not just that I need the royalties.

While you were out thinking about computers and business and all the things that keep you occupied, a change has taken place. Pictures have become a part of the lifeblood of communications again.

Nowhere is that change more obvious than in basic desktop, business-oriented computing. In the mid-1980s, serious desktop computing meant green or yellow letters on a black screen. Maybe an adventurous soul would design some graphs on the screen and print them out on the laser printer or maybe even a color plotter.

Serious graphics was the province of a separate department, or perhaps a service bureau. Folks over there—if they used a computer at all—used strange things: color displays, fancy (and expensive) graphics workstations, and even Macintoshes with little black-on-white screens and a mouse. Those folks were, of course, either techy-nerds or artists, and by definition, weird.

The Mac is the delight of the techy-nerd.

Things have changed! First, almost every business-oriented computer sold today is, for all intents and purposes, a graphics-capable machine. In fact, an Intel 486-based computer with upper-midrange graphics display is hands-down superior to the best workstations of five or six years ago. Almost 25 percent of these powerhouse machines are purchased for small businesses run from a home office, and a lot of the ones going into home offices are second stations. These machines are capital investments substituting for costly or unavailable labor. A nimble PC commonly outperforms a comparable Mac—and does it at a lower cost. These are machines for everyone.

Second, that PC graphics capability is not latent. The enormous popularity of Microsoft Windows (some 50 million copies sold, and most are not shelfware) has brought most people into the graphics world one way or another. For example, classified ads for secretaries commonly specify not only word-processing skills, but also desktop-publishing skills. Office administrators are learning that designing a business form is not just a matter of drawing lines and typing words on a page. Database design no longer takes place in some Information Systems glass house, and the database front-end is expected to have a snazzy designer look. Business graphics—the heart and soul of PC graphics from the beginning—has progressed from a few slides or overhead-projection foils generated by a spreadsheet, to sophisticated, computer-managed support systems, frequently including animations and sound.

The people doing these things are not artists or designers. Art school was a few classes at college or in the deep past of high school. These people use computer graphics because it is expected of them and because it serves a host of needs—and frequently because it is fun. Computer-produced graphics have become ubiquitous, in short.

There is a good reason for this pervasiveness of computer-generated pictures. Pictures tell the story people want told better than words. Combine pictures and words, and the impact is substantial, if not completely irresistible.

Take presentations: Many of us make lots of them. In my case, I am either talking to undergraduates (who would rather be elsewhere), or computer-graphics professionals (who would rather be elsewhere). I have 8 seconds, according to most accounts, to make each point hit home. After that, if I don't have their attention, my students start thinking about other things—like, mauve would have been a more effective color for my tie, or something.

Effective graphics will secure the attention I want. The point will be made. If attention wanders as I talk around that point, filling in the details (a presenter has to do *something*), at least the basics will be there. The images tell the story, and they can be integrated with written text in a leave-behind piece, which stretches my access to that audience from minutes to hours. (See Project 4 for more information on effective presentations.)

Another obvious example: the resumé. Go to someone's office during a search to fill a job. You'll see *piles* of the things. Some are perfectly awful (you'd be surprised to see how many are still produced on typewriters with worn ribbons). Some have come from small-time service bureaus ("Your resumé laser-set on special resumé paper; 20 copies plus disk, $40") and will all look the same. Add in a few strange pieces (the resumé on a CD-ROM) and what you have is something that inspires dread in many potential employers. I have recently taken to sending something different: a small, #10-envelope-size folder with my resumé in it, along with some work samples. In fact, the whole thing is a work sample, and it has garnered some new opportunities. (You'll learn how I produced it in Project 10.)

My new resumé is a "brochure cover" with step-up inserts.

This is more than desktop publishing, as that term has commonly been used. It is a design job, above all. Part of the design involves the use of tools commonly associated with desktop publishing; a large part of the job uses text as one design element. But the heart of this folder is design, pure and simple. The idea is to use design to tell the story I want told, in a manner eccentric enough to attract notice, without being so eccentric as to put the reader off.

The point is simple: Images are an effective communications tool, if—the *if* has to do with the way the images are put together in a package. That is what design is about.

A certain level of excitement accompanies the creation and use of images. Clearly, the person on the receiving end is excited; if not, the images are not effective and the sender trots back to the drawing board.

The excitement in the creation process can be even more important. It is easy to get lost in detail or become bored with something, or any number of other things can happen to lose the thread of the story you're trying to tell. Distilling a concept into a design, creating images to tell the story, and fitting the whole thing together in a project often restores vigor to an almost moribund idea. That energy tends to stick. The pride you take in the project—presentation, poster, flyer, whatever—rekindles your interest each time you work with it. The danger that the project will overwhelm the story it is supposed to communicate is real, but it is less often a problem.

What This Book Is About

In a word, this is a *cookbook*. It is long on practice and less concerned with theory. Basic tools and techniques of design are presented, using PC-based computer-graphics software included on the accompanying disk.

That's *logos* as in business emblems, not λογος as in Greek theology.

Rather than deathless prose on design, most of this book is a series of projects. They are *live* projects, in a couple of ways. Each teaches design concepts and, at the same time, introduces computer-graphics tools used to execute the design. Each project can easily be modified to suit your special needs. For instance, Project 2 gets into a discussion of logos;

the designs in the book are things I've done for myself and for clients. You can use the same techniques and concepts to create a new logo or implement a computer-graphics variant on your present one. In fact, you *should* do that; it's a good way to practice.

After you have done these projects, you will have a good foundation for routine design using computer-graphics tools.

The software that comes with the book has been carefully selected. It is power enough for a wide range of graphics chores. It is easy to use. It will see you through this book and beyond. But other things are out there. As you become more adept at using the tools, you may want to graduate to software capable of more sophisticated effects. The same goes for hardware—the foundation on which the software runs. There's no reason not to think about these things, and the appendixes present some of the hardware and software options.

This book is a comprehensive introduction. It covers the basics, and that's plenty for most people. If you really want to get into the subject, I also provide some guidance throughout the book on where to go next.

How to Use This Book

This is a book for people who most likely already have a graphics-capable PC-family computer (sometimes called an IBM PC-clone—no longer an accurate term). This means a computer based on the Intel 386 or 486 processor, normally; other compatible processors are supplied by AMD and Cyrix. It has a color display of at least VGA resolution, a mouse or other pointing device, and a graphics-capable printer. To access the supplied software, you must have a CD-ROM drive (the good ones are now attractively priced at the cheap-computer stores). A good CD-ROM drive (double speed, XA-compatible, and using a SCSI interface) costs about $350.

I also assume you have Microsoft (or IBM) DOS and Microsoft Windows (version 3.1 or later) installed on that machine.

I do *not* assume familiarity with computer-graphics software and its uses. The projects in this book provide both a way to consider some design issues and hands-on training in the use of graphics software. Throughout the book, I give suggestions on system settings and options to tune your system for graphics.

Desktop computing is more like tennis than philosophy. It's a matter of learning to respond almost automatically— a skill.

If you are really new to this—getting your first machine, or just moving up to a graphics-capable one—that's all right. There is no better way to learn your new machine than to work through projects like the ones in this book. Using a personal computer is a skill, not an intellectual enterprise; "practice makes perfect" is the byword. Moreover, the skills this book develops translate well into other uses of desktop computers. You will use word processing, spreadsheet, and database applications (the most common business computing chores) more ably and more creatively!

Following this introduction, this book is organized into projects. Starting with some simple exercises to introduce the basic tools, these projects progress to fairly elaborate productions.

Marginal comments are asides—places to emphasize a point, stick an icon, show rather than tell—or simply make a comment.

In sections like these, you'll find fairly lengthy digressions from time to time. This is where variant procedures—either in the provided software, or in other popular graphics software you may choose to use—come up. It's also a good place to look for things such as tune-up suggestions and other related ideas.

At major points in a project's design process, illustrations—screen shots or other pictures of the project—will show you more or less what should be on your screen. See Figure I.1. The "more or less" reflects a couple things. First, you will almost certainly be working in color, but the illustrations for the book (except for the color insert) are grayscale.

The other reason has to do with graphics display systems. Your computer may display somewhat less information on the screen than mine does. A basic graphics-capable computer may be equipped with VGA display; that means it shows 640 picture elements (*pixels,* or dots of color) across and 480 pixels from top to bottom. It can accurately render 16 colors; other colors (or shades of gray) are simulated by a pattern of lighter and darker dots using a process called *dithering.* More sophisticated display systems can display more colors (*high color* or *true color*) at higher pixel resolutions (commonly 800 × 600 or 1024 × 768). More is better, generally; you don't need more to use this book, but if you get hooked, one of your first upgrades will probably be your display system.

A practical graphics display uses a 15-inch or 17-inch monitor, showing "high color" at 1024 × 768-pixel resolution.

If you have any doubts, or if you are still shopping for your computer, you should probably turn directly to Appendix B,

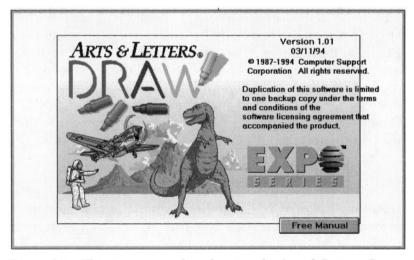

Figure I.1 This is a screen shot showing the Arts & Letters Draw opening screen. This is what you should see when you start the program.

where you'll find a fairly complete consideration of the options, including reasonable guesses about what the future holds as this book is being written.

Installing the Software

Most how-to books come with a floppy disk; this book comes with a CD-ROM. The kind of floppies used these days usually store somewhat less than one and a half megabytes (1.5Mb). The CD-ROM stores 400 times that, but it is as cheaply (and perhaps more reliably) manufactured. The graphics software packages included with this book would take at least a dozen floppy disks; a CD-ROM is lots easier to manage. CD-ROM is increasingly the distribution medium of choice; that is why CD-ROM drives are becoming standard features on desktop computers.

Each of the major software packages has its own installer, custom written to go with this book.

You need 6Mb of free disk space to install A&L Draw.

To install Arts & Letters (A&L) Draw, place the CD-ROM in your CD-ROM drive. From the Windows Program Manager, use the Run command in the File menu. Click on the Browse button; a File Search dialog opens. From the drive list (the one-line box on the lower right of the dialog box), select your CD-ROM drive letter. When the directory list (the box just above the drive list) changes, select the DRAW directory by double-clicking on it. In the file list to the left of the directory list, you should now see a program called INSTALL.EXE. Double-click on the file name, and it will be copied into the Run command-line box. Click OK, and the A&L installer loads. This installer is self-guiding; simply follow the step-by-step procedure.

Installing Micrografx Picture Publisher follows a similar procedure, except you start from the PICTPUB4 directory on the CD-ROM.

The CD-ROM directory, SAMPLES, includes all of the .GED work files used in making this book. Copy these to the A&L Draw directory so you can refer to them as you work.

Three comments: Picture Publisher is supplied in a time-out version. That is, you may use it for a certain amount of time, and then it will lock itself out. This is a top-of-the-line product, not an entry-level version, and the reason for choosing it is that top-of-the-line products are easier to use. Anyway, you have some options.

First, since Picture Publisher is introduced in Project 5 (after you should be comfortable with A&L Draw), you can delay installing it until you reach that point.

Second, the Micrografx installer (one of the more elegant members of the breed) offers some options. If you are short of hard-disk space, choose the option to run from the CD-ROM drive. Using this installation option, only a small number of system-dependent files are written to your hard disk; all the big files stay on the CD-ROM. You pay a slight speed penalty in this option; CD-ROM drives (even the fast ones) are generally slower than hard-disk drives. You will not notice this unless your system has the speediest class of hard disk, though.

Third, if you like the program, you can upgrade to an unlimited version. I have used most of the major bitmap editors around; I use Picture Publisher for production work.

Picture Publisher is big! You need around 28Mb on your hard disk to install the full program. Or you can run it from the CD-ROM directly.

The Nickel Tour

A&L Draw is the junior member of a family of drawing programs developed by Computer Support Corporation (CSC). CSC, in turn, has been doing graphics on PCs for about as long as that has been possible. Although it is an entry-level product, Draw has a sufficiently generous set of features that many people don't need much more. Where a top-drawer drawing program might offer a special tool for making a special effect, Draw offers this as a canned effect, ready to use.

This section describes A&L Draw in detail. To keep life simple, the introduction to Picture Publisher is in Project 6.

I think you are going to like using graphics, and eventually you will want a more powerful set of tools. You will still find this book helpful.

By and large, the high ground in PC drawing programs has been held by three products: CSC's A&L Editor, Micrografx Designer, and Corel Draw have each owned the market at one time or another, and each has merits. Most serious designers use at least two of these—one is used most of the time, and the other for special effects the favored program doesn't offer. The also-ran programs are Aldus Freehand and Adobe Illustrator; Illustrator is also available on Macintoshes and is a stronger player on that platform, but it has never enjoyed the same popularity on PCs.

Draw delivers, one way or another, about 85 to 90 percent of the capabilities of these top-drawer programs; the remainder is specialized stuff.

The Big Picture

Draw's work area is typical for drawing—and, for that matter, painting—programs. See Figure I.2. In addition to the standard Windows menu bar, a toolbox on the left side of the screen shows the most frequently used tools. The drawing area visible on the screen varies, depending on several factors.

The General Tools

The general tools control what happens in the workspace. See Figure I.3. Arts & Letters programs do things a bit differently from other drawing programs, and this is reflected in the kinds of tools shown in this part of the toolbox.

The top tool—and the most typical of all graphics-program tools—is the Picker or the Pointer tool. Use the Pointer tool to select objects on the screen. With this tool selected (indicated by a darker gray color), click on an object. Immediately, the status of the object as *picked* (or *selected*)

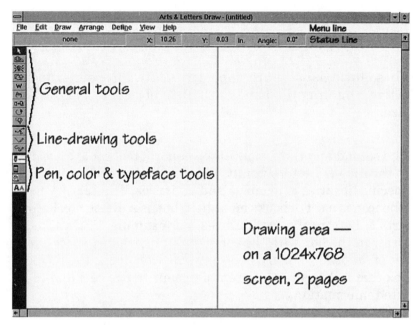

Figure I.2   This is your drafting table and the set of tools you will use to execute most of the projects in this book.

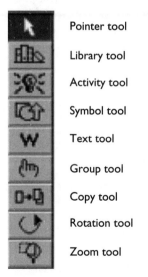

Pointer tool

Library tool

Activity tool

Symbol tool

Text tool

Group tool

Copy tool

Rotation tool

Zoom tool

Figure I.3   General tools

shows. The picked objects grow *handles*—little black control points.

Those little handles are important. With the Pointer tool active, you drag the handles to scale objects to the correct size.

Handles

The second and third tools in the general tool set are specific to the Arts & Letters family. These tools are used to access specific libraries of symbols and activities. The Library tool (the icon is a set of books on a shelf) opens a dialog box listing Arts & Letters clip-art libraries. For example, CSC tucked Draw in the box with the company's remarkably successful set of dinosaur clip art; choosing this icon opens the dialog box that indexes the different dinosaur image sets and related information.

The dotted line indicates the scaling operation.

The light-bulb icon, denoting the Activity tool is also special. Draw does not have some of the special-effects tools a more advanced graphics program offers, such as text on a curve or blended colors. But you can still use these effects. Draw provides them as canned effects; you choose them from the Activity Manager menu and mix and match more or less at will. The projects in this book will apply some of these effects, and they will also explain how to create the effects using more advanced software.

The fourth icon in the general tool set, called the Symbol tool, shows several *geometric primitives,* or basic shapes. Arts & Letters drawing programs approach basic shapes in a special way. Most drawing programs have special tools for drawing circles and ellipses, and squares and rectangles, and they have another tool for special symbols. Arts & Letters drawing programs treat all of these as symbols. To add a rectangle, click on the Symbol tool and select the basic shape from the scrolling visual-selection box. Press the add button, and place the new shape. See Figure I.4.

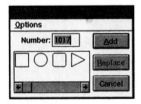

Symbols dialog

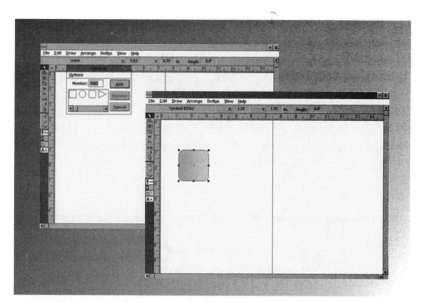

Figure I.4   Pick an object type from the Symbols dialog box, and place it in your developing drawing. Color is applied based on the colors you have already chosen.

Practice this. It is a basic function, and you want it to be almost as natural as breathing.

Arts & Letters drawing programs all use the same process to add clip art, and CSC has one of the most extensive collections of clip-art symbols around. Some of it is very good, and in some ways it is the most general-purpose collection available. A good selection is included with this book; you can add more. Each clip-art symbol has a number, so you can call it by typing the number in the symbol-number space in the Symbols dialog box.

Clip art saves time, and it can be very effective if you take the time to modify it to suit your needs. Since most clip art is simply a drawing, it is easy enough to edit it. In this book's projects, you will learn how to use clip art to enhance designs.

The Symbol tool places both graphics primitives and other clip art; it supplements the Library tool.

The fifth general tool, with the letter W as an icon, is called the Text tool. Again, Draw does things a bit differently from other graphics programs. Click on this tool, and Draw opens a dialog box. Type in your text, and choose either Add (if it is new text) or Replace (to change old text). Essentially, you are adding an object to the drawing. You can size, color, or alter the text object by changing the selected typeface. *Typeface* refers to a style of letter; *font* refers to a set of letters in a particular style and size.

Most other graphics programs manipulate text differently. In those programs, you choose a text tool and enter text directly into the work area, rather than into a dialog box. That method is more direct, but not essentially better. The key item is that text can be treated as an object using either method. In fact, text can even be made into a true graphics object by converting the text to curves—that is, true geometric shapes, no longer recognized by the program as text. Don't do that, though, unless you are at the end of your design process, because it is irreversible and you lose easy text-editing in the process.

The pointing-hand icon is Draw's Group tool. Select this tool, then drag a *marquee* (a box indicated by a dotted line) around the objects to be selected. All the groups inside the marquee are selected. They are, effectively, temporarily grouped; they can be moved as a unit, colored as a unit, and so on.

You can also use the Group command on the Arrange menu to make a temporary grouping permanent. The Arrange menu is discussed later in this chapter in the section "Menus—For Good Measure."

Another way to select several items at a time is to hold the Shift key while pointing and clicking on each of the objects to be selected. Use this technique to select objects when a marquee selection would include too much. Or, if you have used the pointing finger to pick a whole group of objects, and you wish to deselect one or more of them, hold the Shift key and click on each of the items you want to deselect.

In many Windows applications, including Arts & Letters Draw, you can select several objects by holding down the Shift key while clicking on each object to be selected.

The next tool, with the one-object-to-two-objects icon, is the Copy tool. Select this tool, then point and drag on any object to create a copy of it.

The tool with the circular-arrow icon is called the Rotation tool. Select the tool, then click on the object you need to rotate. You get handles and a center target. The target is really cool—it's actually the pivot point for the rotation. Drag it where you want it, then drag one of the handles, and the selected object (or group of objects) rotates around that point. A little window in the status line at the top of the work area tells you how much rotation has been applied, in degrees.

Anchored Pivot Point

Grab any handle and rotate around this fixed point. It need not be inside the symbol.

The Zoom tool, with a magnifying-glass icon, lets you focus on a part of the drawing. The best way to use this tool is to select it, then drag the pointer to show a marquee around the area on which you want to focus. Release the mouse button, and the picture snaps to that area.

Line-Drawing Tools

The line-drawing tools are used for drawing different kinds of lines. See Figure I.5. In Arts & Letters drawing programs, the first tool is the Line Editing tool. It is automatically selected when either of the others is chosen, or you can select it manually.

Basically, there are two kinds of lines: straight lines and curves. The second tool is for straight lines, and the third tool draws curves.

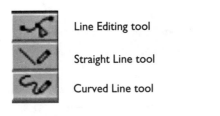

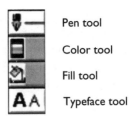

Line Editing tool

Straight Line tool

Curved Line tool

Pen tool

Color tool

Fill tool

Typeface tool

Figure I.5 Line-drawing tools

Figure I.6 Pen, Color, and Typeface tools

Like all quality drawing programs, Arts & Letters drawing software draws curves using Bézier formulas. That means the curve can be adjusted in several different ways, with great precision.

Pen, Color and Typeface Tools

The tools in the next group let you specify a range of options at the click of your mouse (or other pointing device). See Figure I.6.

The Pen tool opens the Line Control dialog box. This dialog controls line width and type. See Figure I.7.

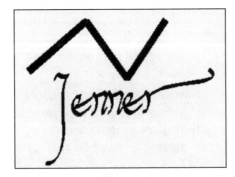

Figure I.7 The straight line has been drawn with flat corners, and a calligraphic line, with penlike thicks and thins, was used for the imitation handwriting. (The "jaggies" are the result of changing this to a bitmap—more on that later.)

The Color tool picks fill and outline colors for your objects, and the Fill tool (the little paint bucket, almost universally used as a fill icon) lets you choose how the color is applied in a range of patterns and shadings.

The Typeface tool at the bottom accesses the Type Attributes dialog. See Figure I.8. In Arts & Letters drawing programs, you have choices. The company includes its own typeface outlines—which are scalable graphic objects, for all intents and purposes—or you can choose to use printer fonts. Effectively, you can use any typeface outlines your selected output device supports. Since you can use all your Windows True-Type fonts (or Adobe Type 1 fonts, if you have Adobe Type

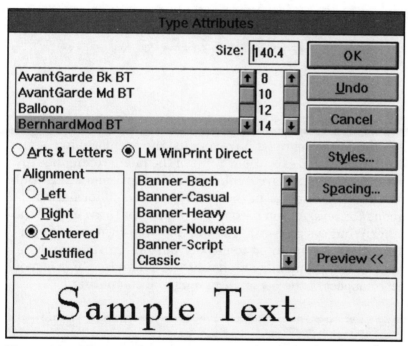

Figure I.8   The Type Attributes dialog box lets you select either Arts & Letters–supplied typefaces or the typefaces installed for use with your printer. It also controls a range of special adjustments.

Manager), and they are legion, it means you have a virtually infinite selection of typefaces.

A&L Draw retains a capability from early desktop graphics days. It used to be that each program came with different typefaces, and there was no uniformity. When Microsoft specified TrueType technology (it was trying to compete with Adobe's PostScript—an attempt that has failed for the time being), this forced a degree of uniformity. It became simpler for all software vendors to simply access the TrueType fonts and let Windows handle the printing chores, including getting typeface data to the printer. Adobe— never easily outdone in matters of this sort—advanced its Type Manager tool, which effectively added universal access to Adobe Type I typefaces. Designers can spend hours arguing the merits of one scheme versus another; you needn't, since the real issue is that you can use just about any typeface you can get, in any size you want. Oh, rapture . . . !

Menus—For Good Measure

All Windows programs have menus; they conform to a standard. Draw is no exception. Some of the menu commands are special, and others are duplicates of toolbox commands. But menus serve another purpose: They provide information about *hot keys*. As you become familiar with Draw and all the other Windows software, you develop your own way of operating them—combining toolbox or button-bar commands with menu commands and hot-key commands. This is another aspect of the *personal* in personal computing.

Micrografx Designer is an exception to this rule, by the way. In the new version of the program, most toolbox options invoke special button bars, and menus are minimal. This makes for a somewhat steeper learning curve for this advanced program.

File Menu In the File menu, pay particular attention to the Printer Setup command. Make this an early stop in your design process. Arts & Letters drawing programs design for the screen by default. By setting the drawing for your intended output device, you gain access to whatever special features it offers, especially available typefaces.

File menu

The Import and Export commands let you bring in images from other programs, or export them in forms that can be used in other programs. In Draw, the import/export list is limited but practical, and sufficient for the projects discussed in this book.

Edit Menu The Edit menu shows the command overlap. Block Select is the same command as the little-hand icon (the Group tool) in the toolbox. Notice the ^B beside the command? That is a hot key. That makes three different ways to issue this command: Use the tool, pick from the menu, or hold down the Control key and press the letter *B* (uppercase or lowercase—Draw does not distinguish). The Select All command highlights all the objects in your work area. This command is useful especially when you are copying a complex drawing.

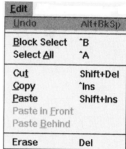

Edit menu

The grayed-out commands, Paste in Front and Paste Behind, are unique in my experience. When you are importing through the clipboard—for example, moving a chart from Windows Excel or some similar spreadsheet program—you may want to paste the object behind other objects. Select those objects (foreground text) and use the Paste Behind command. Paste in Front pastes things on top of *selected* objects. This is a shortcut for the Arrange menu's Front and Back commands.

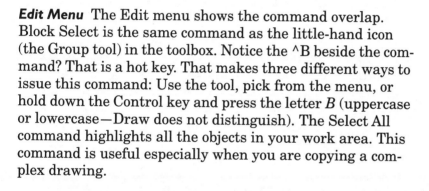

Draw menu

Draw Menu The Draw menu duplicates the functions found in the toolbox with hot keys as well as menu options. My guess is that you will rarely use the Draw menu.

Arrange Menu The Arrange menu, on the other hand, will be almost as constant a companion as the toolbox.

Arrange menu

Arrange	
Group	**˘G**
Break Apart	˘U
Align...	ˆN
Bring to Front	ˆF
Send to Back	ˆK
Duplicate	ˆD
Flip Λ V	
Flip < >	
Correct Shape	

Arrange menu

The Align command on this menu is a wonderful example of how much even the simplest computer drawing tool brings to the design process. Alignment seems like a simple-minded task—until you do it manually. The computer makes alignment a snap, and it is as close to perfect as can be.

The same is true of the Group command. As you add design elements and make their position final, you can lock them together in the same relative position. For all intents and purposes, you can treat this group as a layer on a clear acetate sheet. You can then position other objects and groups, and you can move each layer around relative to the others. Use the Break Apart command to separate groups.

The Flip commands are used to tip objects upside down or backward. These commands can be very useful when you are creating symmetrical shapes. You make half the shape, duplicate the line, flip it (horizontally or vertically), and join it to the first line. Use the Draw Close Shape command (F7) to weld the object together.

The Arrange commands can vary in appearance (but not functionality) from program to program. Draw provides basic utility; more powerful players (Arts & Letters Editor, Micrografx Designer, Corel Draw) offer advanced functionality. In alignment, the differences include the ability to fine-tune positioning with a nudge. In horizontal and vertical mirroring, the options include combining the duplication and flipping actions. Another arrangement option—rotation—shows up in these programs with a way to input a precise angle. In short, arrangement of objects is a major feature in a drawing program.

Define Menu Like the Draw menu, the Define menu is basically an alternative way of getting at the functions of the Pen, Color, Fill, and Typeface tools. It adds one neat feature, the two sides of which are the Save and Recall commands (grayed out in the illustration). Use Save to save the color, fill, and pen styles of a selected object; use Recall to apply that same style to a new object. Think of this as a rudimentary style sheet, and you are not far off.

Define menu

View Menu The View menu is vital. Among other things, it offers the corollary to Draw's one-way Zoom tool. Use the hot key ^V to zoom back to the previous view, or use the various other commands (or hot-key equivalents) to see your work area the way you want. Generally, I prefer to work between a Zoom In area and a Current Page area (on my screen, effectively, two pages show), and I move between them using the ^V hot key.

View menu

The Control Points command is also essential. Click on it so that it is checked off, and leave it that way; Draw should remember your choice for future sessions in the same file. When Control Points is checked, you can adjust curved lines using full Bézier controls using the line-editing tool.

The Preferences command opens a dialog box. You set various options—units of measurement and so on. The most useful of these options in Draw is the Ruler command. Generally, you want the ruler on, if you have a display with more than minimum resolution. If you are running with basic VGA (resolution of 640 × 480 pixels), you may want to leave the ruler off to allow the maximum amount of space in your drawing area.

A grid option appears in the Preferences dialog box. In other drawing programs, grids are very helpful for precise drawing; you can set a grid, then set a Snap to Grid feature. Lines will snap to points on the grid, and objects will snap to grid points. You get the idea. This snappiness does not seem to be available in Draw. But the grid remains useful as a drawing aid.

Help Menu The last menu is the Help menu. This is standard Windows help, which means it is a species of hypertext, and CSC has done a fairly good job with it. Use it if you forget something, as a refresher. The Contents command gives you the basic screen, and the Search button takes you to a list of all indexed terms. The How to Use Help command tells you more about this.

I am entitled to be professorial; I teach university-level stuff, after all.

Now, it seems about time to stop with this boring, professorial stuff, and get to the good stuff. In short, let's create a drawing.

Project 1: Org and Systems Charts

This first project has two purposes: First, it gives you a chance to test most of the tools in A&L Draw, the drawing program used with this book. Second, it introduces some fundamental design concepts in the context of a couple of basic, common business graphics.

Before beginning, you must have installed Windows and the graphics software used with this book (or your own graphics software, if you choose to use that instead). If you have not already done so, turn to the Introduction for complete installation instructions.

If you are completely new to Windows, spend some time with the Windows manual, and play around with basic Windows functions. The standard procedure is to play one of the two games (Solitaire and Minesweeper) included with Windows a lot until you are comfortable with the graphical interface. (I prefer Solitaire; I never do well with Minesweeper.)

Making an Org(anization) Chart

OK, so this is not a thrilling drawing to make, but it gives you a chance to test the software's various features. It is also a real project; businesses use graphics software to produce org charts for inclusion in all sorts of presentations and reports.

Setting Up Your Work Area

Obviously, the first thing to do is to start Draw.

If you've been fiddling with Draw, checking out the tools and the menus, use the File menu's New command to clear the screen.

The program should come up and fill the screen completely. See Figure 1.1. If it doesn't, use your pointing device (mouse or whatever) to click on the up-arrow in the upper right corner. (If you see a double-headed vertical arrow in that corner, you are already maximized and ready to go.)

Set up your work area. Use the Preferences command in the View menu to access the dialog box and turn on the rulers. Then use the Printer Setup command on the File menu to select the printer you will use. From this dialog box, use the

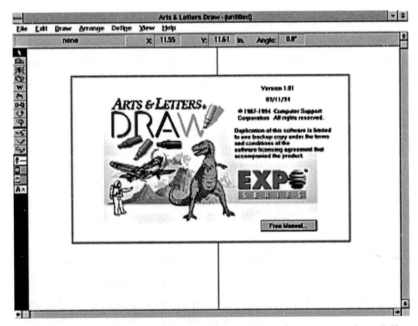

Figure 1.1   The Draw opening screen. After the program has fully loaded into the computer's live memory, the sign-on message goes away. This two-page view reflects the use of a 1024 by 768 display.

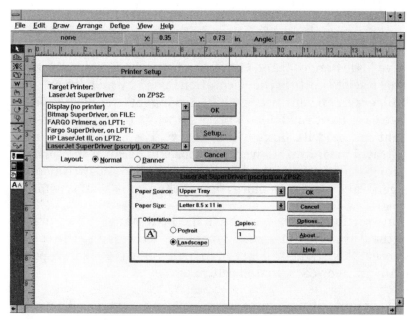

Figure 1.2   Select the output device and set it for landscape display. Draw reads this information and adjusts the work space accordingly.

Setup button to set your printer for landscape (sideways) printing. See Figure 1.2. Org charts tend to be broader rather than longer, so a wide format is appropriate. I've chosen a black-and-white printer (my laser printer, controlled by Zenographics SuperPrint and Zscript, Zeno's Post-Script interpreter).

Charting the Administrative Hierarchy

The organization to be charted is a small college similar to those where I have taught from time to time. The purpose of the chart is to show the administrative hierarchy and its internal relationships.

Let's begin by entering some labels. This chart should have more than one use (in a report, and in a presentation later on). This dictates a typeface style.

Times Roman is a typical serif typeface, as is **Century Schoolbook.** Both are very readable.

Serif and Sans-Serif Type Here's the general rule: Use serif typefaces for blocks of text, and use sans-serif typefaces for words that stand alone in a larger type size. Serif typefaces have little flanges (called *serifs*) on the ends of major strokes. These serifs imitate the decorations used by monument builders in ancient Rome when carving letters. Serif typefaces are most readable in black on white (or other dark-on-light spaces) with large blocks of text. The human eye tends to travel from word to word, supposedly because the serifs help it move in the right direction. Serif typefaces are also, in a general sort of way, more *elegant* than sans-serif typefaces.

Arial, a Helvetica look-alike, is a common sans-serif typeface.

Sans-serif typefaces don't have the little flanges; they are without (*sans*) serifs. Such typefaces, according to the conventional wisdom, are more readable in larger sizes, especially in color-coordinated schemes.

Arnold Böcklin is a decorative font, as is **Eurostile.** Used carefully, they tell a story.

Lots of fonts fit neither of these general categories. They can be lumped together as decorative typefaces, and they frequently reflect a calligraphic style. Choose these decorative typefaces for special effects in design. Avoid them if you are the least uncertain about the effect they may have.

The other major rule is, don't use too many different fonts! Use one or two fonts, and think of them as contrasting elements.

If you look at printed material, you will notice something. The conventional wisdom is to use a clean serif typeface, in a 10-point or 12-point font, for body text and a sans-serif typeface, in a larger and perhaps bolder font, for topic heads. This works for printed text, but it has limited application in other graphics enterprises (such as slides or multimedia screens).

Nor is the rule absolute. When designing reports for arts organizations, I have frequently used Optima (which is a sculpted typeface, but essentially sans serif) for body text, and contrasted it with Times Roman or some similar serif face—usually emboldened—for headings.

Entering the Text For this project, let's use a sans-serif type-face. For a chart, where there isn't a lot of text in each block, the clarity of sans-serif lettering is useful. I am choosing a printer font, commonly available in all Windows systems, called Arial. Choose the font by clicking on the Typeface tool at the bottom of the toolbox. In the dialog box, click on the little round radio button by the name of the selected printer, and then select Arial from the list of typefaces. Set the size to 10 points—readable enough for a chart to be enclosed in a printed report. See Figure 1.3. Then select Centered from the Alignment options.

Click on OK, then move to the Text tool (the W icon). In the text box, on separate lines, enter the following name and title.

Murray Hill, Ph.D.
President

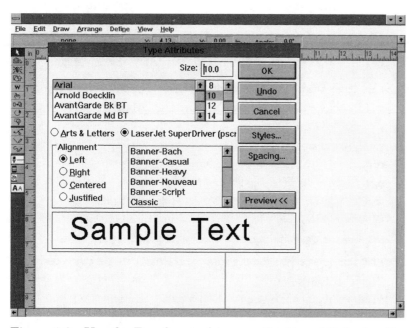

Figure 1.3   Use the Typeface tool to open the Type Attributes dialog, then choose the typeface and font size.

Note: I have already told Draw to center lines of text, so I don't fiddle with that in the text box. Click on the Add button, and Draw's place-an-object cursor appears. For the moment, stick this text to one side, and go back to create some more titles and names.

This is a very small and very informal college, let me tell you.

C. Ima Decan	Academic Dean
Everard Friendly	Dean of Students
Worthington Market	Chair, Business Administration
C. Icahn Cutemup, D.Sc.	Chair, Natural Sciences
I. M. Literate, D. Litt.	Chair, Humanities
I. C. U. Dewitt, Ph.D.	Chair, Social Sciences
Cash Osgood	Bursar
Iris Bookkeeper	Registrar
Dorothy LeGrande	Administrative Services
"Bulldog" Molloy	Security Chief

Use the same procedure, once for each name and title.

The " and " are proper quotation marks, but all your keyboard offers is ". If you use special characters like this a lot, consider adding Character Maps to your Windows Startup Group. This will work with *printer* fonts, but *not* with standard A&L Draw fonts. Use Character Map to get the correct special-character codes.

I used a nickname for the security chief, and I put it in quotation marks. Now, this is a problem, because the keyboard doesn't give you real "66" and "99" quotation marks. These count as special, or extended, characters. To add them, hold the Alt key and enter the code for the character using the numeric keypad (with Num Lock turned on). To add left-quotation marks, hold Alt and enter 0147; to add right-quotation marks, hold Alt and enter 0148. Sadly, Draw's text box can't display these characters, and substitutes a bar. But the on-screen type will contain the correct marks.

Aha! But how do you find out about all the other special characters? Windows comes with a little program, usually installed into the Accessories group in Program Manager, called Character Map. Run this program, and select the typeface you want to know about. You are shown a diagram of all standard and special characters. Click on the character you want to see its code. Character Map lets you copy one or more characters to the clipboard, for pasting where you want it, or you can use the Alt-*number* procedure instead.

Using proper characters this way lends polish and professionalism to your design.

Creating Boxes You have the main names for the chart. Now you need some boxes—because all good org charts have names in boxes. It's a convention, and it is wise to use conventions in something like this. It's a matter of getting the right psychological response. (Still, you might find a way to jazz things up a bit, later.)

Do yourself a favor. If you haven't done so already, press the F9 function key or use Save on the File menu to save your work. Nothing is more discouraging than to have something happen, so that your computer goes away, losing your work in progress. Do this with some frequency—like, after every major step in the design process.

Choose Save on the File menu or press F9 after every major step.

To add the basic boxes, use the Symbol tool (the icon with basic geometric shapes). Pick the square, not the symbol with round corners. (Draw won't let you edit a round-cornered square very much, and during scaling, the round corners get badly distorted.)

Ah, but the box comes up in the default color—cyan. And this is for a printed report—black and white. What you really want is a solid, white fill. Choose the Fill tool (the one with the paint bucket). Click the Solid radio button if it is not already selected, then OK. Then use the Color tool, and choose white. While you are at it, thicken the line. Use the pen tool, and change the number in the Width box to 2—or click on the 2pt Wide Line in the list of line types at the bottom left. Click OK. Now the box should have a white fill and a bold outline.

Your next task is to scale the box. Select the Pointer tool, and click on the box so it is selected (if it is not already selected and showing handles). Drag it up to the ruler so it is adjacent to an inch mark. Drag the handles in the middle of the right and bottom sides to obtain a box two inches wide and three-quarters of an inch deep.

The arrows point to the handles used for this scaling operation. I've used the upper left corner of the work area, where the ruler's zero points are.

There are 11 names on the list, so you need 11 boxes. Select the Copy tool from the toolbox, and click-drag on the first box to make a second box. Do this until you have all the boxes you need. When you have all the boxes drawn, select them all (either with the Group tool—the little finger—or by holding the Shift key and clicking on each one, so that it shows handles). Use the Send to Back command on the Arrange menu to move the boxes to the layer behind the names.

Putting Text into Boxes Move the college president's name to the first box. Now, while the president's name is still selected (still showing handles), hold the Shift key, and click on the box. It should also show handles; both objects are selected. From the Arrange menu, select Align, and click the Center radio button, then OK. Next, use the Group command on the Arrange menu (or the ^G hot key) to group the two objects (now neatly aligned, text centered in the box) into a single object. You will also see one set of handles, instead of two. Do the same for each of the other names.

What happens if you have not moved the boxes to the back? When you move the names to the boxes, they disappear (they are behind the solid white box). To make the names appear in the boxes, simply select the boxes and use the Send to Back or ^K command.

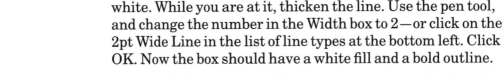

This business of centering and grouping may prove a bit bothersome in the next use of this chart, but it makes things infinitely easier in the job at hand. This is called a trade-off.

By the way, this process goes a lot faster if you use the hot keys ^N (Align) and ^G (Group). Simply select both objects—no need to move the name into the box at all. ^N calls the Alignment box (which remembers the previous centering operation), and pressing Enter executes it; ^G groups the objects.

Speed up the process by using ^N (Align) and ^G (Group).

Finally, you need to move the boxes into place to show the hierarchy of all these brilliant scholars and teachers and college supernumeraries, as shown in Figure 1.4. Click on each grouped box and drag it into place.

Because Draw does not have a bulletproof snap feature, use Align to check your work.

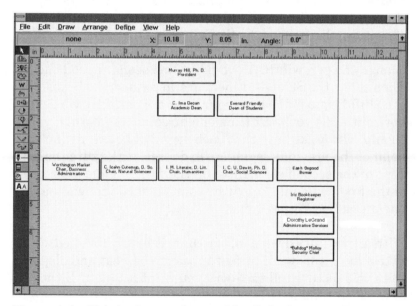

Figure 1.4   This is the org chart, with all the boxes and names grouped and put into place. The rule along the right is Draw's page-edge marker, not one of the temporary lines used to line up objects.

It would be helpful to have some lines on the screen to help line up the various hierarchical levels. Some graphics programs provide for *guidelines*—nonprinting lines that can be

To draw perfectly
straight lines: Select
the Straight Line tool,
hold down the Shift key,
and draw.

dragged into position for this purpose (effectively, the blue-ruled lines on graph paper). A&L Draw doesn't have these, but it is easy enough to draw in lines for the purpose, then delete them later. Use the Straight Line tool; if you hold the Shift key as you draw, the line is constrained to a vertical or horizontal axis—perfectly straight lines, the easy way.

The Align-Top or Align-Bottom commands can be used to place the boxes precisely. For example, draw a vertical line along the left side of Murray Hill's box and use it to line up the dean's box. A horizontal line can be used as a mark for aligning the row of staff boxes in mid-page.

Connecting Lines What remains in this version of the org chart is to add lines indicating the working relationships. This is another job for the Straight Line tool. Since you used some hairline-width rules for alignments, first you want to change the pen width. A two-point line seems a good choice. Then select the Straight Line tool and connect the boxes. Use the Shift key to make sure your lines are perfectly vertical or horizontal. As you shift from one direction to another, you should also make sure that each segment begins at the end-point of the previous segment. To do this, make sure the first click of the second segment is on the little handle at the end of the first segment. This way, your finished line will be all one piece. See Figure 1.5.

With all the lines drawn in, the chart is nearly finished. Stop, take a look, and see if things appear to be neat and elegant. Does this picture tell the story you want it to tell? If the answer is yes (and for the moment, let's make that assumption), then it is time to do some straightening up.

Finishing Touches

First, use the ^A hot key (or the Select All command from the Edit menu) to select all the objects. Then move the (temporary) group so it is more or less centered where you want it on the page.

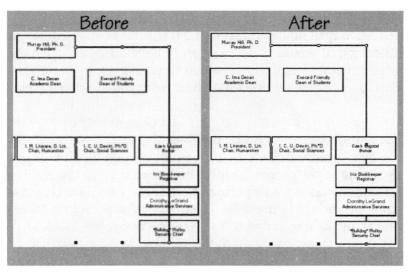

Figure 1.5   Drawing lines can be simple or complex. Here, I drew a two-segment line, and then moved it to the back layer, so my opaque boxes cover it. That's lots simpler than drawing little lines, then aligning them between those boxes on the right. Notice, by the way, I can adjust the position of the lines by stretching the object handles that represent the area they cover.

Then, a title is in order. You *could* put a title at the top . . . but notice that large white area in the lower left quadrant? That might be a better place, don't you think? It's not that *white space* (a common term in graphic arts for open, unused space on a page) is bad, but *that much* white space is rather silly—not a bad place for a title at all.

Let's call this the "Smallville Community College Administrative Structure" org chart. At this point, you have yet to set up a logo for Smallville Community College (next project), but you can easily add the type in two blocks of different sizes.

Use the Typeface tool (at the bottom of the toolbox). Choose a suitable typeface—something fairly expressive. Simply because I think Smallville is a fairly informal place, and at this point, I have some discretion, I have chosen a Draw typeface called Wyeth. A variation on typeface called Brushscript, Wyeth has a nice informal feel to it. (If this were an established operation, it would almost certainly have an established organizational look, and you would have to stick to it—or risk real displeasure for mucking about with the approved style.)

Using the Text tool, enter *Smallville Community College* in the dialog box, press Add, and place the text. Finally, adjust the size—manually, not using a predetermined point size. Grab one of the corner handles and drag it up to the right size. "Look" is more important here than precision. Use the same procedure to make an *Administrative Structure* label, and then scale that down. To align the two labels, select them both, then use the Align command to apply vertical alignment.

This is a good time to check your work in hard copy. In a word, print it! From the File menu, select Print, then hit the OK button. When you get the printout, check things. See Figure 1.6.

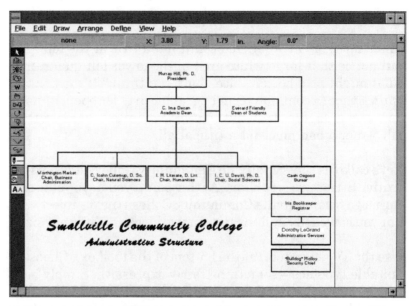

Figure 1.6   This is what my final version of the chart looks like as I go to make a test print. Yours should look more or less like this, depending on changes or variations you may have tried.

So. At this point you have used every important A&L Draw tool except the Curved Line tool. You have set some type, and you have drawn objects. You have filled objects and moved them around and grouped them. Everything you do, in every project from here on out, simply expands on the uses of these tools and procedures.

The Org Chart in Portrait Mode

The org chart is *beautiful*. It is ready to be included in the report to be handed to the trustees. But the boss doesn't like it; "Make it vertical, like all the other pages," you're told.

If this chart had been made the old-fashioned way, you would either have to labor long for no more money, or you would throttle the boss. Since this chart is merely a bunch of charges in a computer's memory, however, changing it is a piece of cake!

If you have closed the file and turned off Draw, call up Draw again and use the Open command on the File menu to get the file back on screen. Use the Printer Setup command on the File menu to get at the output device's setup dialog (access it with the Setup button). Change the orientation in the Printer Setup dialog from landscape to portrait. OK your way out of this (that is, press the OK button at each level until all the dialog boxes go away). Draw automatically resets your pages in portrait mode.

Pick up the title items with the Group tool, and drag them off to one side out of harm's way. Select the various lines and delete them; you can do this one at a time, by clicking on each and then pressing the Delete key, or you can select all the lines with the Shift-click procedure, then use the Delete key. Both procedures take about the same amount of time and have the same result.

In fact, the only real problem to be solved is how to represent the hierarchy, and the only special difficulty is that long horizontal group of academic department heads. There is only one choice: They must be grouped in a cluster of four, and

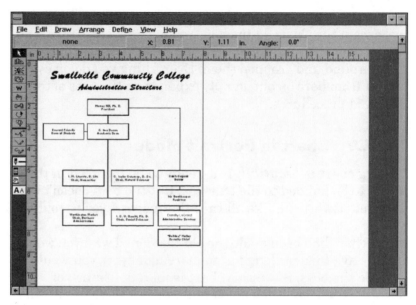

Figure 1.7   Here is the revised portrait-format org chart (note again, my screen is showing two pages side by side). I simply moved the boxes around, redrew the lines, and moved the label to the center at the top. I left a bit more margin at the left side (about a half-inch; a bit more would be better) for binding into the report.

their inherent equality indicated with a different line pattern. See Figure 1.7.

The Org Chart 3—The Colorized Version

"My friend," says the boss, "that is really great. Now, I need to discuss this organization chart with the board. Can you make something I can use as a chart?"

Life is full of challenges—and one rises to them lest one become employment-challenged.

Actually, this is not so difficult. There are two possibilities, and frankly, the revision you just did will make both of them easier to execute. For the sake of discussion, assume that President Hill is going to use an overhead projector with a whole bunch of images.

Actually, you can simply pop a piece of laser-printable (or laser-copier-type) overhead-projection film in the printer and print out the same black-on-white chart. I don't recommend doing this. First, the chart that results is boring. Second, I gain no opportunity to tell you about using some of the fancier color options. The overhead-projection foil of this org chart will, therefore, be a masterpiece in full and glorious color. It is suitable for printing to a modestly priced Fargo color wax thermal-transfer printer, a Hewlett-Packard color inkjet printer, or any of that ilk of low-cost color printers.

Colorizing may or may not ruin old motion pictures, but it is almost without exception a plus in computer graphics. People like color better.

The main thing to do is to add in a colored background to fill the entire page. Do the printer-setup routine: select the color printer of your choice, and make sure your printer is set for portrait mode.

You can do this part of the project even if you don't have a color printer. Leave things set up for your standard printer, but work in color on the screen. You won't print in color, but you can send the image to a service bureau when it comes time to do something for real.

Use the Symbol tool to get a new square. After placing it, stretch it using the handles on the sides, so it fits the entire page. You will cover up the chart, but don't worry about that. Once the background is finished, you will move the whole thing to the back.

Selecting Colors

The symbol you've just created is going to be colored—and A&L Draw gives you lots of options as to what that color might be.

First, there are solid colors. Look at the range offered in the Color-tool dialog—don't forget to scroll the palette box. Add to that the various shading options from the Fill-tool dialog (raster options that lighten the solid-color choice, and sweeps from chosen color to white). Add to that the color patterns available in the Magic Color Cubes collection. These are the simple possibilities. There are others, involving patterns.

In short, it seems it is time to begin (but not exhaust) the discussion of color selection. There will be lots more on this, especially in Project 4 on presentations, where some of the psychology of color comes into play.

The fundamental rule for color selection is to choose according to the circumstances. That seems obvious. Sure—if it is so obvious, then why is it so often violated?

Colors on Slides Take slide shows. Slides are projected in darkened rooms. People sitting in darkened rooms tend to get sleepy. If you put a slide on the screen, and the slide's background is dark, it simply blends in with the dark room and folks start snoozing.

The precise technical term for choosing dark backgrounds for slides is *stupid*. But it is really surprising who chooses this kind of combination: demonstrators of slide-making software, major executives

Learn Desktop Graphics and Design on the PC

of companies like Microsoft, and the like—including, on more than one occasion, Bill Gates himself. What happened? In the early days of PC graphics—almost entirely a matter of presentation support images, often created on systems with a monochrome display—folks were told that this was a conservative choice, and anyway, it was a safe choice (the slide-making companies were less likely to ruin it). The error has simply been perpetuated.

The proper palette choice for a 35mm slide set, then, is one that uses a fairly light-colored background, with darker lettering.

Colors on Overhead-Projection Foils Your current job is to make an overhead-projection foil. Overhead projection is used in normally lighted rooms. Appropriate color choices are, therefore, different. In fact, you have substantially more options.

When doing overhead foils, consider whether the foil will be generated on an inkjet printer or a wax thermal-transfer printer. If I am using the inkjet printer, I normally choose a clear (white) background, which uses ink more sparingly—I tend to be niggardly like that. On the other hand, the wax thermal-transfer printing process uses the same amount of the color ribbon regardless of whether I choose a rich-colored background.

Color-choice issues:
- The presentation medium
- The presenter
- The audience
- The material
- The desired effect

General Color-Choice Issues Another factor—more involved—is how much attention you want to draw away from the data. The more elaborate the design, the less attention is paid to the information on the screen. (Sometimes that is useful.)

Much the same applies in considering the presenter. If the presenter is really hot, you do a better job if you do not distract from his or her spiel. On the other hand, if the presenter is like the character in Benchley's "The Treasurer's Report," you have to help out—a lot!

So, what is at work in this case? Murray Hill, Ph.D., is a college president. His job description includes being able to take candy from babies—without inciting a crying jag! It also means he is expert in lulling trustees at board meetings into trusting acceptance. On the other hand, he is dealing with a sensitive subject, and it impinges to some extent on Worthington Market's turf. He needs a strong image that soothes trustees' minds into the realization that he has shown the best possible approach.

Blue and colors rich in blue are soothing. Colors that add a touch of red with the blue can also help create that fuzzy-puppy feeling. So the background should be rich in blue, and maybe have a touch of red or a deep violet.

But this is the boss and conservatism is perhaps wise—at least at this point.

Applying Color

So let's apply color—first, to the background (which for the moment, is a foreground object—that large rectangle). Make sure the rectangle and nothing else is selected (it is the only object with handles).

Background Color Choose the Color tool (third tool from the bottom) to open the Color dialog box which has a scroll bar on the bottom and a bunch of color chips. This box can also break these color options into groups, displayed with names—effectively, numeric formulas for producing the color from process (CMYK) colors. Use the Options pull-down menu in the dialog box to display these named colors.

A&L Draw reflects one unfortunate decision by Computer Support Corporation, its producer. There are several standardized color systems, of which the most popular in this country is the Pantone Matching System (PMS) and its process-color companion. Part of the way in which a print job is specified to a printer is to give the standard name or number of a color, which is used as a check on the final color. CSC has so far chosen to avoid paying a license fee for PMS, and it is therefore compelled to use its own color system. As it happens, this is not a tremendous problem, but it means you need those CMYK values so you can convert CSC's proprietary color system to a standard one.

After trying some combinations, I chose a blue shade that is heavy in magenta. Select this color (050-100-000-025) for both fill and line color (and make sure the appropriate boxes are checked in the Named Colors dialog box). The color name shows that this color is heavy in magenta (100) and cyan (050), entirely lacking in yellow (000), with some black (025). See Figure 1.8.

You could lighten this color a bit by applying one of the raster options from the Fill dialog. In this case, the full, saturated

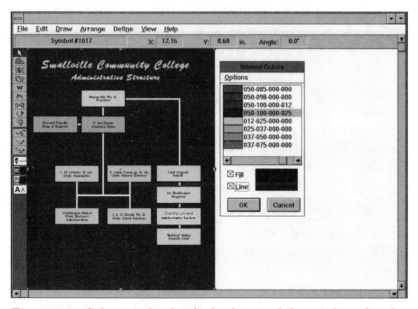

Figure 1.8   Select a color for the background (here it has already been moved to the back, using the ^K hot key).

color is going to be more effective, and lightness is not really an issue (the room will not be darkened).

Foreground Color Having set the color for the background (and with the background object only selected), move the background object to the back, using the ^K hot key. Now you can turn to adjusting the colors of the foreground objects (the chart boxes themselves). You could leave them white on the dark foreground, but to do so is to miss an opportunity to make the whole business clearer.

There are some options at this point. First, you might want to drag the background object to one of the other pages while you are working on foreground objects. If you are using a higher-resolution display, the adjacent page will be visible; just drag the background over there temporarily. If your display does not show adjacent pages, use the All Pages command on the View menu to see the adjacent pages, drag the background over, then use the ^V hot key to go back to the current page.

There are advantages both to having the background in place (you see the developing design) and to moving it out of the way (you will avoid mistakenly selecting the background while working with foreground objects).

If you do work with the background in place (my preference), and you do mistakenly select the background object, hold the Shift key down, and click on the background object someplace away from the foreground objects to deselect it.

Click on each of the foreground boxes in turn to select them, and use the ^U hot key to ungroup the box name groups. See Figure 1.9.

Careful! Make sure you select only the box and not the lettering or the background object.

Select the president's box. Use the Color tool to open the Color dialog box. Pick a very pale color (normally, a color

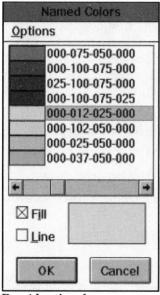

Named Colors

Options

000-075-050-000
000-100-075-000
025-100-075-000
000-100-075-025
000-012-025-000
000-102-050-000
000-025-050-000
000-037-050-000

☒ Fill
☐ Line

OK   Cancel

President's color

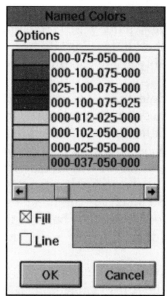

Named Colors

Options

000-075-050-000
000-100-075-000
025-100-075-000
000-100-075-025
000-012-025-000
000-102-050-000
000-025-050-000
000-037-050-000

☒ Fill
☐ Line

OK   Cancel

Deans' color

Named Colors

Options

100-050-025-012
100-068-025-000
025-012-000-000
037-012-000-000
050-025-000-000
068-037-000-000
100-050-000-000
100-075-000-000

☒ Fill
☐ Line

OK   Cancel

Faculty & Staff Colors

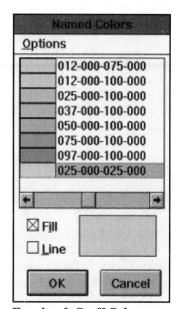

Named Colors

Options

012-000-075-000
012-000-100-000
025-000-100-000
037-000-100-000
050-000-100-000
075-000-100-000
097-000-100-000
025-000-025-000

☒ Fill
☐ Line

OK   Cancel

Faculty & Staff Colors

Figure 1.9   Named Colors dialog boxes

name with 000 in the last group—that is, no black). I chose a very pale, yellow-rich shade for this box and changed only the fill, leaving the line color black (in this instance, it probably makes no difference, though). Press OK.

Select the two deans' boxes (use the Shift-click combination to select each object). Open the Color dialog again. Again, a pale shade (to have the lettering show up well) works; I chose one a bit deeper into the magenta range than the color chosen for the president's box.

So much for the honchos. For the department heads, I selected the four boxes and chose a very pale blue. For the supernumeraries, I picked a pale green.

With all the boxes nicely colored, what remains is to make the lines visible. Select the lines, and use the Pen tool to change their width to 5 points—that should be wide enough. Then use the Color tool to change them to white. Remember that you are changing the line, not the fill; uncheck the Fill box and check the Line box in the Color dialog box.

Title Colors Finally, change the title. To do so, select it. Use the Color tool to pick a color. I chose basic yellow, but white would do as well. Be sure to change both the fill and the line. You may also want to check the Pen dialog, to make sure you still have the *Use for Type option selected.

Finishing Touches

Last step: Use the Group tool—the little finger—to select the chart elements as a whole (all the boxes, names, and lines). Using the handles in the lower left and lower right corners, stretch the chart elements to fit as close to the sides as possible. There is no special merit to wide margins in this chart, so this will let you make the text as big as possible. It will still be too small to read (by and large, anything much smaller than 24-point text is hard to read in a situation like this). That is not vital, since President Hill will be talking about the chart, and the black-and-white version is available as a handout for the trustees. The key information—the structure—will be visible, and in this case, that is sufficient, if not perfect.

Finally, print the overhead-projection foil on your color printer.

At this point, you have had your first introduction to the special benefits of computer-produced graphics.

The initial chart has been quickly changed in several ways. First, the original landscape design was shifted around to a portrait format. Then the same information was turned into a colored presentation-support tool. Only once did you enter data; everything else was simply a matter of playing with it.

I've spent some time introducing elements of good design— typefaces, color selection, and so on. I've suggested decorative type where that was useful, and starkly utilitarian type where that was appropriate. And I've discussed some of the things that make color work in a design.

If this reminds you of kindergarten collage-making, well, it's not a bad analogy. What is important is the time factor. This is fast!

The Systems Chart

I know, you are heartily sick of charts. But there you are. Once some basic concepts are on the table, you can breeze through the rest of the book (at least, that is the theory).

In this next chart, you will use the Curved Line tool, and you will create some symbols of your own.

In a more powerful drawing program, you would probably already have the symbols you will create here. And, if you made a bunch of special symbols, you would then create a library of one kind or another from which to select the symbols in subsequent sessions.

That option isn't in Draw (it uses libraries created by A&L Editor, CSC's flagship program). But there are some little things you can do.

Systems charts are used by programmers to plot procedural logic. But a systems flowchart is also a useful tool for understanding the way an organization works. Some of the standard flowchart symbols are useful—about eight of them—and others are not. Some are part of the standard A&L Draw library; some it is easy enough to make.

Creating a Shapes File

Start by setting the fill color to white, and the pen width to 2 points. This gives you defaults for the library of shapes. Next, use the Symbol tool to get a square. After it is on the screen, drag it up to the corner and size it so it is about two inches wide and an inch deep. Drag that rectangle off to the side—perhaps even onto the adjacent page. Rectangles like this are the main building blocks of the systems chart.

Do much the same thing to get a circle symbol, but make it a half-inch across. Small circles serve as node indicators for various kinds of branching in the system.

Making a Diamond To make a diamond, which is used to indicate a decision nexus, you could simply bring in another square, rotate it 45 degrees, and scale it. But the proper shape for this diamond is more properly a sort of lozenge on its side. So, let's make one.

First, use the Preferences command in the View menu to turn on a quarter-inch grid. Select the inches units (that's the default, and it should already be checked). Select the ¼ radio button, and check off the grid (and ruler) items, then press OK.

Use the Zoom tool (the magnifying glass) to zoom in on an area in the upper left corner of the work area—about 3 inches down the side, and 4 inches across should be about right.

Select the Straight Line tool. Pick a grid point right under the 1-inch mark, and draw a line (hold the left mouse button and drag) from there to a point about three-quarters of an inch to the left, and about half an inch down. Release the mouse button, and then immediately press it again, to begin a continuation of that line in a different direction—down another half an inch and back to the right to the 1-inch mark. You should hit grid points at each of these places. Figure 1.10 sketches the steps involved.

This is one side of the lozenge. Use the Copy tool (the one-object-to-two-objects icon) to drag a copy of that side over a quarter inch or so. Then, with the new line still selected, use the Arrange menu's Flip <> command to make that copy into the other side of the lozenge.

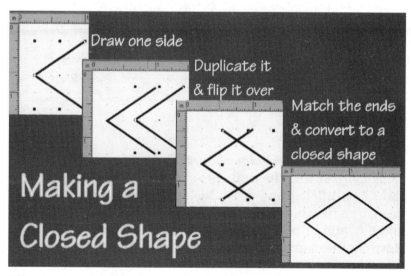

Figure 1.10   These are the steps in making a closed shape—in this instance, a lozenge.

Drag the right side up against the left side, so that the ends match up. Select both objects by double-clicking on the left side. The right side should also be selected and show handles.

Use either the Close Shape command on the Draw menu or the F7 hot key to close the shape. The left box in the status line (the gray area below the menu bar, just above the rulers) should now say Closed Shape. You should have one set of handles showing for the whole item. Check it by clicking someplace else in the drawing, then clicking on the new shape.

If the box doesn't say Closed Shape (in which case it will probably say *Open Shape*), don't worry; the endpoints of the two lines were not perfectly matching, and there is an open spot someplace. This is easy to fix.

Make sure the new shape is selected. Choose the Line Editing tool. The shape should now show as hairlines with little clear handles at the points in the drawing. Look closely. At one of the intersections, do you see two little boxes, pretty much overlapping? That's the problem. Point to one of those handles, and drag it so it is perfectly on top of the other (they will sort of snap together). The box at the left of the status line will now say *Closed Shape*.

Making Other Straight-Line Shapes Make some more objects, using more or less the same procedures. For example, to make a parallelogram, draw the top and left sides, duplicate them, and flip them vertically and horizontally (using the Flip V ∧ and Flip <> commands on the Arrange menu). Move the two parts into conjunction, and convert them to a closed object.

Make a trapezoid by drawing a longer top line and a shorter bottom line. Use the Align command to center these lines

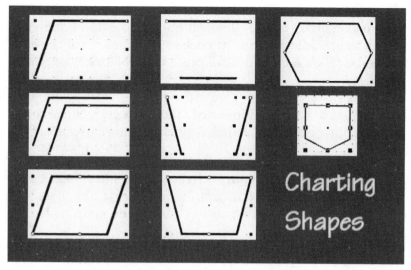

Figure 1.11   These are the charting shapes using only straight lines. The construction techniques are suggested for parallelograms and trapezoids.

vertically, about 1 inch apart. Then connect the endpoints of each side with a line. See Figure 1.11 (middle column).

A couple other shapes are useful for system charting. They get made more or less the same way as the ones described, with one exception that needs some curved lines.

Making a Curved-Line Shape   Start making this shape by drawing three sides of a box. Use the techniques that you have learned to create the three straight sides.

Go to the Curved Line tool (just under the Straight Line tool). Draw a curve—sort of an S on its side. Don't worry too much about how pretty it looks; you're going to edit the line to take care of that problem.

First, make sure you have turned on the Control Points switch on the View menu (the hot key is ^4). Then click on the Line Editing tool to turn it off and create the line, and (with the line still selected and showing handles) click on the Line Editing tool again. A few small, clear handles appear; these are the line-editing nodes. There will probably be five or more of them. Clear all but three of the handles—one in the middle and one at each end. To get rid of the extra nodes, click on a node and press the Delete key on your keyboard.

Now adjust that curve. Move node points by clicking on them and dragging them as needed. Adjust the curve in one of two ways:

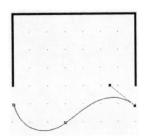

These are the lines for the next shape. The curved line is being edited, and a Bézier line can be seen on the right node.

- Click a second time on any selected node, and a dotted line with another handle appears. Move the extra handles to adjust the way the line passes through the main node.

- Use the Line Editing cursor (a small clear triangle) to push against portions of the line; it moves and reshapes smoothly.

To complete the object, select the curved line and the three-sided box, and use the Close Shape command (F7). If *Closed Shape* doesn't come up in the status line, use the Line Editing tool to fix things. You can also adjust the curve if you need to.

Saving the Shapes Move all these shapes to the second page of the file, and save it under some name like CHRTSYM. See Figure 1.12.

There is another way to save these symbols for subsequent use. Select each object in turn, and use the Export command on the File menu to export each as a Windows Metafile (.WMF). Make sure you have chosen the Selected Object option and specified the directory where you want to store the file.

A&L Draw lets you import these Windows Metafiles and lets you scale them. You cannot edit them, however.

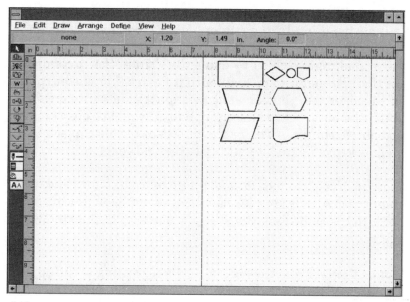

Figure 1.12   The Systems Chart shapes file constitutes kind of a library.

Creating the Systems Chart

Start by making a copy of the CHRTSYM file; use the Save As command on the File menu to save the library file under a new name. Effectively, this preserves the basic library in a pristine form, and you work with copies of the symbols you made.

Setting Up   For the sake of the exercise (which is by nature of a review), let's go back to Smallville Community College, alma mater of famous superheroes and so on. President Murray Hill has decided to include in his report to the trustees a chart on the system by which students are recruited.

The steps to be displayed start out with the student contacting the college, or Dean Friendly contacting local high schools to locate potential warm bodies. This is followed by sending an admissions kit (catalog and application forms). The student completes the form and sends it in with a check.

If this seems like a simple system, well, of course it is. But I really do use charts like these to study clients' businesses and how they work.

The application is reviewed, then passed to the admissions committee. Finally, the student is notified of the decision.

Start making the chart by using the Printer Setup command on the File menu to pick an output device. For the purposes of this exercise, you can stick to a black-and-white device—but if the boss wanted another slide, it would be easy enough to change things. Also, for the purposes of this project, it makes sense to stick to portrait (vertical) page orientation.

Use the Typeface tool to select a typeface and font size—again, use Arial's simple, clean sans-serif lines in a 10-point font. In the same dialog box, select centered as the alignment option.

Action Boxes From the palette of shapes sitting in the adjacent second-page window, use the Copy tool to drag over a rectangle. Place it more or less a third of the way from the left edge of the page and near the top. Use the copy tool to drag a couple more of these boxes into a line beneath the first.

Zoom to the top of the page to easily add some text to the top box:

Student contacts college.

In the second box, add

College sends admissions kit.

In the third box, add

Student completes and returns application.

With A&L Draw's Text tool, you add text into a dialog box, then place it. Since you can see the text in the dialog box, you really don't have to zoom in to add the text. Just add the text item and place it

Learn Desktop Graphics and Design on the PC

> temporarily about where it needs to be; later, come back and use the Group tool and the Align command (^N) to match things up neatly.

Decision Boxes The next step involves a decision. Decisions are represented with lozenges, so zoom back out (with a ^V or ^2, the Current Page command hot key) and use the Copy command to drag a lozenge into place. The decision is based on the question, "Is the application complete?" Each option— yes and no—each gets a box. So drag over a couple more rectangles, one to the right of the lozenge and one directly below it. In the box to the right, add the text

> No. Forward fee to bursar and return application to student for completion.

In the box under the lozenge, add the text

> Yes. Forward fee to bursar and application to admissions committee.

This leads to another decision point. Copy another lozenge, and add to it the text

> Is the student accepted?

Drag over two more boxes, again one to the right of the lozenge and another under it. In the right-hand box, add the text

> No. Student sent polite rejection letter.

In the other box, add the text

> Yes. Student is notified and deposit requested.

Neatness Counts Time to make things neat. Use the Group tool to select each box and its text in turn. Then use the Align command (^N hot key) to align the text to the center of the box; follow this with a ^G (the Group command) to lock text and box together.

Do a bit of manual adjustment on the positions of the boxes for vertical distance between them. Use the grid (I set mine for quarter-inch increments) to help get the position about right.

Then, use the Group tool to select all the boxes on the left—a long vertical line—and apply the Align command's Vertical option to line them all up. Do the same thing to the two boxes on the right. Finally, select each of the lozenges, and the No boxes to their right, and use the Align command's Horizontal command to correct that alignment.

Showing the Connections What remains is to add lines to indicate the flow. First, draw a single straight vertical line from the top box to the bottom box, using the Straight Line tool. Deselect the Line Editing tool, and use the Send to Back command (the ^K hot key) to move the vertical line to the back of the boxes. This line should pass through the top and bottom angles of both lozenges.

Draw other straight lines through the points of the right-hand angles of both lozenges, to the adjacent boxes on the right.

Now draw a line from the first No box (adjacent to the first decision point) straight up, until it is even with the Student completes box, then continue the line to the left to connect with that box.

Putting the Flow in the Flowchart

The chart is finished, but it could be made better. Flowcharts should have arrowheads every so often, to indicate the direction of the flow. Since A&L Draw has no arrowhead symbol, you can make one.

Making an Arrowhead Zoom in on a blank area of one of the pages—about 2 inches square is good.

Use the Straight Line tool, as before, to draw a solid V about a half-inch across, then continue the segments to draw a smaller v inside it. Deselect the Line Editing tool, and use the F7 hot key to turn it into a closed shape. Fill it with black, and then scale it down to a quarter-inch (about a quarter of the original size). Zoom back out using the ^V hot key.

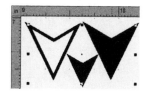

The steps in making the arrowhead

Positioning the Arrowheads Use the Copy tool to drag copies of the arrowhead to each line between boxes. (You may want to scale the arrowhead down later, but this is about as small as you want it now; any smaller, and it gets difficult to grab with the pointer.)

Don't forget to move arrowheads to the lines connecting the boxes on the right. Obviously, these arrowheads need to be rotated (using the Rotation tool) to orient them in the correct direction. You may also want to use the Align command to handle the alignment of arrows and the lines they sit on; for example, use the Group tool to select the entire long vertical line and the arrowheads on it, then use the Align command's Vertical option to line everything up.

Finishing Touches

Dress the whole thing up a bit. First, use the Group tool to select the entire chart, and move it more or less to the center of the page. Then enter some text to identify this chart as the Admissions Procedure Chart for Smallville Community College. See Figure 1.13.

There are lots of ways to use this chart. It can be printed. It can be output to the clipboard or a Windows Metafile (use the Group tool to select everything on the page, then use the

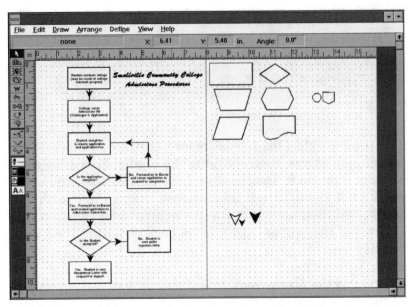

Figure 1.13 The completed flowchart is on the left-hand page.

Copy command or the Export command, as needed); you can use these commands in any Windows word-processing file. It can be colorized for live presentations, as the org chart was.

A Quick Review

At this point, you really have seen all the tools, and you have seen them applied—and if you have been following along, you have used them all yourself.

You have actually made a couple of typical business graphics, and you have learned about some design elements involved in these graphics.

You have learned to work around some program limitations. A&L Draw is a simple graphics program; it does not have the latest bells and whistles. And you have learned that this makes no difference for many graphics chores. Doing these projects would have involved pretty much the same work even if you used the highest-end drawing package. The lesson is simple enough: It is not the software, but the conceptualizing, that is most at stake in getting an effective design out of the PC.

Save your files. Go away for a while. Have a cup of coffee. Then come back and get on with another project.

Project 2:
The Logo

Smallville Community College needs a suitable logo—something that conveys the dignity of education and all that. It needs to be appropriate for both color and black-and-white applications.

Symbols and Seals

A good logo involves text, inevitably. Sometimes—most of the time, in fact—some kind of an emblem that tells the story of the organization is appropriate.

The useful skill associated with creating emblems is called *iconography*. Literally, it means "writing about symbols," and it covers the associations that obtain in a given culture about symbols and what they mean. The word *symbol* is also interesting. Literally, it means, "that which is thrown together." So think about it this way: A symbol brings together the disparate elements in an organization.

Please notice that symbols vary enormously from culture to culture. There is potential quicksand here, and you would do very well to develop sensitivity to the culture of the organization being symbolized. *Culture,* in this context, is used in several senses.

There is a rich literature on iconography, and if you get involved in illustration, you may want to add appropriate volumes to your library.

Another good source of iconographic information is to look at symbols used by other participants in similar cultures. In the case of a college, what kinds of symbolism do various colleges employ?

The academic world is rich in established icons. Among other things, universities exist under charter and are proud of that fact. Part of the ancient charters of universities established the seal under which they might grant rights and privileges according to the authority vested in them by the chartering authority. Ancient universities have elaborate seals. More modern institutions almost immediately adopt a seal—usually rich in additional symbolism. The Smallville Community College logo will look like a seal.

Books are symbolic of learned study, and an open book suggests the availability of learning to all. The open book is a common symbol for colleges; it appears in the seals of many venerable, prestigious colleges. Using a book in the logo makes sense. Good sense also suggests that something be done to distinguish the book used by Smallville from similar images used by other colleges.

A torch or lamp is commonly used in designs for academic institutions to symbolize the enlightenment knowledge is supposed to bring. As it happens, a torch is a simple thing to draw, and it solves some other design problems.

Finally, there needs to be some text: Smallville Community College. The decision made in Project 1 to use A&L Draw's Wyeth typeface turns out to be a good one, and there is no special reason to change it. But it needs to be fitted into the rest of the design—to become a design element.

Making the Smallville Community College Logo

Seals are usually round (there are exceptions—notably, Chinese seals [square] and ecclesiastical seals [sort of a vertical football shape]), but text entered into A&L Draw is on a straight line. Draw has an unusual way of solving this problem.

Positioning Text in a Circle

To access this special technique in Draw, open the Activity tool (the tool with the lightbulb icon). In the left-hand box (Selected Activity Libraries), choose the activity called Special Effects—Words. In the right-hand box, scroll down to and pick the activity called Spiral. See Figure 2.1. Click on "Add," and use the Symbol tool to place this activity anywhere in the work area.

What comes up is a group—a set of instructions and a string of text coiled up like a snail shell.

Ungroup the whole thing, and either move the two text blocks off to one side, or simply delete them.

Be careful! The spiral itself is another group, and it must stay that way! Don't break that group apart, as Draw lacks the tools to put it back together.

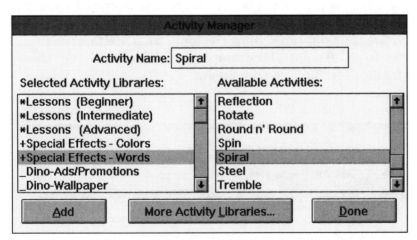

Figure 2.1   The Draw Activity Manager is set up to select the Spiral option of special effects using words.

This is text on a path. It is a nice effect, and more complex graphics programs allow its creation in several ways. A&L Draw provides it as a canned effect, and it works nicely, with some minor peculiarities.

Clearly, you don't want that whole spiral, but the bottom curve would make a nice shape for the Smallville Community College label. With the spiral selected, get the Text tool (the tool with the W icon). In the dialog box, the spiral text is already entered and highlighted. Simply type in its place

Smallville Community College

Use the Replace (not the Add) button to complete the change to the new text.

At this point, the text is not all that useful. It is not in the right typeface, and it looks miserably lopsided. This is easily corrected. With the curved text still selected, pick the Typeface tool at the bottom of the toolbox. Scroll the typeface list to Wyeth and select it, and set the font size to 26 points.

I checked that size on my system and it worked well; look at Figure 2.2 to see if your result matches mine. If it doesn't come out with the ends of the curved text more or less even, then repeat the process, changing the font size until it does. Notice that you can change the font size in decimal increments—15.8 points, for example (which looks silly, but there you are)—for precise adjustment.

This is not perfection; this spiral text effect has some severe limits in the way A&L Draw presents it.

First, the curve is not quite a perfect arc. It is slightly squashed on the right side—an artifact of the inward curving of the spiral (which is still there in its entirety, even though you can't see it).

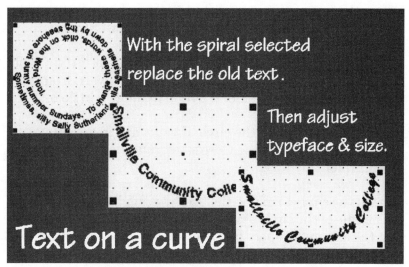

Figure 2.2 A&L Draw lets you position text in the lower half of a circle.

Second, this technique is fine for text placed at the bottom of a curve. Putting text on top is not possible using this technique, though.

The advantage, of course, is simplicity—as flexibility entails complexity, simplicity entails limitation.

Creating the Seal's Border

The next step is to create the seal, in the outer border of which this text will be fitted. A seal is sometimes a plain circle (sometimes it has fancy edges, but let's keep life simple). So, use the Symbol tool to get a plain round shape. Use the Color tool to change from the default cyan to white. Finally, move the circle to the back with the ^K hot key.

The black-and-white version of the logo comes first, then you get to color it.

Inserting the Text To fit the text inside this circle at the bottom, drag one of the corner handles on the circle until it is big enough, roughly, then either drag the circle under the letter-

ing, or the lettering on top of the circle, and adjust the circle until it just accommodates the text in the lower half.

Immediately, you'll see the problem with this spiral text. The circle is perfectly round, and the text pulls inward from the edge a bit on the right side. It's time to fudge a little bit.

Zoom in on the text in the circle if you want to see things more clearly—though the closest tolerance is probably not essential for this task.

Squash the circle to match the text by dragging the handle in the middle of the circle's right side ever so slightly inward, so that the amount of space between the baseline of the text on the right is fairly close to what it is on the left. See Figure 2.3.

Adjust the position of the two objects manually (the Align command can be a little eccentric in this kind of situation). What you are aiming at is an even baseline for the text, as much as possible matching the curve of the slightly elliptical seal.

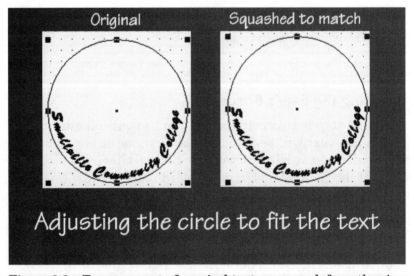

Figure 2.3   To compensate for spiral text, you can deform the circle slightly so that it matches the curve of the text.

Adding the Inner Rim The next chore is to create the inner rim of the seal border. Use the Copy tool to drag a copy of the first circle up just far enough so its base is inside the tops of the capital letters of the text. Slowly shrink that circle by dragging the corner handles down and in, and adjust the position of the smaller circle so it stays approximately in the middle of the bigger circle.

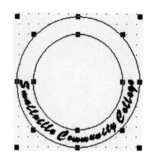

When you think you have it more or less on target, hold the Shift key and select the larger circle, too. Then use the Align command to center the two objects.

Punching It Up This is coming along nicely, but it is boring. Time to punch it up. Make sure only the larger of the two circles is selected. Then use the Color tool to pick a nice 40 percent gray fill for the outer circle. While you are at it, select the text, and use the Color tool to change it (both fill and line, this time) to white for better contrast.

Gray increases in 10-percent increments, with white being 0 percent. So 40 percent gray is the fifth color box down. To see for yourself, turn on the color names from the Color dialog's menu bar.

A hint for a color-changing session: The other option in the Color dialog box's Options menu, the Stay command, keeps the Color dialog box on the screen even after you pick and OK a color. When you are changing lots of colors, this is convenient; when you are working on a drawing, it is more convenient to close the Color dialog so more of the work area is visible.

Drawing an Open Book

The next part of this logo is the book. This would be a great time for a piece of clip art—and there is a book in the A&L Draw clip-art collection. However, that one is a religious book, and this is a publicly funded college. So now's your chance to draw a nice, open book.

Select the Curved Line tool. Begin with a shallow recumbent S curve. Deselect the Line Editing tool and pick up the Copy tool. Drag over a copy of the first line, then use the Flip ⟨⟩ command on the Arrange menu to make a mirror image of the copy. Match up the adjacent endpoints, select both lines, and use the F7 key to connect them into a continuous whole.

Again, use the Copy tool to drag a copy of this compound curve down a good distance (you know what a book looks like; eyeball the drawing until you have the top and bottom compound curves about the right distance to suggest the top and bottom edges of a book). Use the Align command to dress these curves up; select both lines and align them on one side (left or right—your choice).

Use the Straight Line drawing tool to connect the left and right edges of the two compound curves. Then deselect the Line Editing tool, and holding the Shift key (to keep the last-drawn line selected), select one of the compound curves and press F7 to connect it to the side. Continue around until all the lines are connected. If the whole thing doesn't change to a closed shape (indicated in the status line at the top left), use the Line Editing tool to find the unconnected points, and snap them together. Finally, if it isn't that way already, make sure the fill for this shape is solid white.

I have no idea what the precise metric equivalent of a smidgin is, so don't write in and ask.

The next step is to draw a sort of shadow behind the open-book shape. Go to the Symbol tool, and from the Symbols dialog box, pick a square. Place it in the work area, then drag it over to the developing book. Place it so it is a smidgin to the left of the left side of the shape you just made. Drag the handle in the lower right corner of the square so that it reaches about the same smidgin below the bottom of the lowest point of the shape, then drag the handle in the middle of the right side so that it extends to the right side of the book shape—again, about the same smidgin. Fill this rectangle with black. Last, use the ^K hot key to move this rectangular shape to the back of the book shape. See Figure 2.4.

Figure 2.4 Here are the steps in making a book for the logo.

One more step: Draw a straight line to connect the two dips in the middle of the compound curve, top to bottom. Use the Group tool to select all these elements and the ^G hot key to lock them together. This is not a bad image of a book.

It is not a perfect image of a book, either. For example, the thickness of the book has not been suggested. The spine of the book is missing. And so on. You may want to come back to this book and gussy it up a bit after some of the later lessons. However, our culture finds abstraction an adequate expression (it was not always so), and for the purposes of the present exercise, this simple, abstract image of a book should be all right.

This is a somewhat modernized seal design, so the book will be placed so it sort of spills over into the band around the outside. Start by scaling the book down so it just fits the inner circle. Move the book image to the center of the circle. The trick is to place it somewhat above the center of the inner circle, so the corners of the book overlap its edges, but the lower corners don't seriously impinge on the Smallville Community College text. This will take a couple tries, adjusting position and size.

Heh...
Heh...
Heh...

There is method to my madness, Igor.

The vertical triangle

The trapezoid proper

The trapezoid is moved into position with the base. After adjusting position, group the two together with ^G.

Drawing the Torch

The next element is a torch. Why a torch, rather than a lamp? The developing design suggests the virtue of the choice.

First, that space at the bottom of the inner circle is uncomfortably bare. Then too, the top part of the outer rim is also bare; that is, in part, an artifact of the way you do curved text in A&L Draw.

The lamp that is normally used in seals like this is the sort of thing that would comfortably accommodate Aladdin's djinn. Its lines are horizontal. But a flambeau (a nice heraldic term for a torch) is vertical, without much relative breadth. Using the torch, in short, solves a design problem. It fills those spaces while serving the concept of the school seal very nicely.

Then too, drawing a nice flambeau is much simpler than drawing a lamp.

Start by using the Symbol tool to get a triangle. The vertical triangle is the one you want—the fifth symbol in the scrolling window. Use the Flip ∨ ∧ command from the Arrange menu to turn it upside down. Make it fairly skinny, using the handle in the middle of one of the vertical sides to squeeze it down. Use the Color tool to change this to a solid black fill.

Pick the Straight Line drawing tool and draw a trapezoid (that's a four-sided figure with a wider top line, a narrower parallel bottom line, and slanting sides).

You should be able to create the trapezoid in a single set of strokes (across the top, down on the right or left, across the bottom, then up on the opposite side). You may want to use the Shift key while drawing the top and bottom strokes to keep them absolutely straight.

If the shape doesn't automatically close when you have deselected the Line Editing tool, press F7 to close it and make it a solid black.

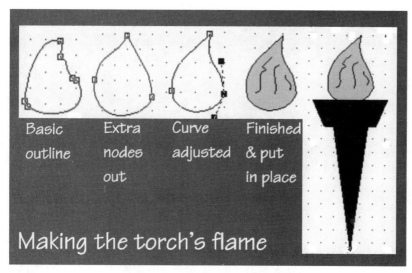

Basic outline Extra nodes out Curve adjusted Finished & put in place

Making the torch's flame

Figure 2.5   Here are the steps in making the flame.

Now to make the flame: This is a curved, sinuous shape, round at the bottom and pointy at the top. See Figure 2.5.

The flame is a bit easier to draw if you have a tablet and a stylus, but it's doable even with a coarse mouse. In either case, you need to do some editing to get it right.

All that remains is to place the grouped flambeau in place along the vertical centerline of the seal and adjust it for size. See Figure 2.6.

Colorizing the Seal

The black-and-white version of this seal has lots of virtues. It can be cheaply printed on stationery. In fact, it could be exported to Windows Metafile format and used in a Windows word-processing program template, then printed out on a laser printer with any letter or other document.

In that exported format, it could be used with other design software, such as the cover-page designer in WinFax Pro, to make a professional-looking custom fax cover page (or a whole series of them).

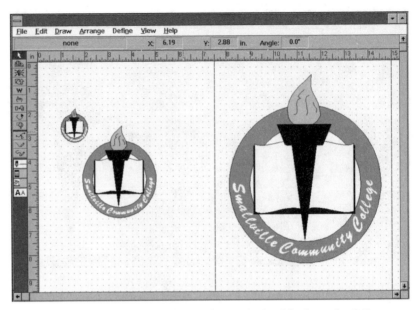

Figure 2.6   The finished seal is shown in its black-and-white form, in several sizes. There is some merit in checking the scalability of a design; sometimes what looks good at one size looks awful at another size.

You can use the seal to create business cards and all sorts of other things, then print them out and take them to an instant-print shop for duplication. It is very useful.

But a color version would be nice, and it's simple to do. So why not?

Use the Group tool to collect all the pieces, and make a copy next to the original using the Copy tool. For the sake of this exercise, assume the college colors of Smallville Community College are yellow and blue (they are good scouts all—and being a *junior* college, they're at the cub-scout level).

Select the outer circle—the one now filled with gray. Use the Color tool to change it to blue. Select the text, and change both the line and the fill to yellow.

Select the torch and ungroup it. Selecting only the base and trapezoidal flange, change them both to brown (a nice woody color).

For the flame, something special is called for. A solid gray may be OK for a monochrome flame, but in color some shading—a *blend,* in the language of computer graphics—is preferable. This is another canned effect in A&L Draw. Select the flame.

Use the Activity tool to open the Activity Manager dialog box. This time, select Special Effects—Colors from the left-hand box, and select Magic Color Cubes from the right-hand box. See Figure 2.7. Press the Add button, and place the resulting image in the right-hand window of your work area. Ungroup that whole image.

Under Magic Color Cubes, the color patch in the second column of the fourth row is a diagonal blend, shading from yel-

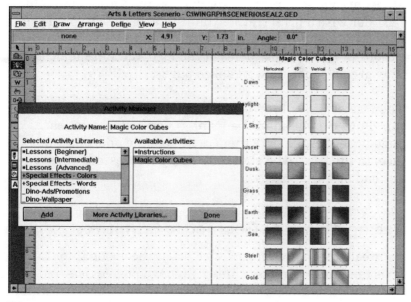

Figure 2.7   To get the Magic Color Cubes in A&L Draw, use the Activity tool.

low in the upper left to red in the lower right. Select it. Use either the Save command on the Define menu or the ^Q hot key to copy this color scheme to the Color and Fill tool indicators in the toolbox.

Select the flame shape. Apply the blended colors to the flame with the Recall command in the Define menu or the ^R hot key. Voilà! The flame is now a lively colored image suggesting the play of colors in a real flame.

Check the work as before. Does it look OK in small and large formats? (*I* like it, anyway.) It is time to save the file, and then do a couple prints to show the boss.

Printing the Smallville Logo

To do the printing, use a color printer, if you have one. Select a printer. (You did not specify a printer earlier because it was not clear at first what kind of output was needed.) I selected the Fargo wax thermal-transfer printer (the crayonlike vividness of colored wax is irresistible). I might also select a film recorder with a print (rather than slide) back (a colored print with its photolike richness is also irresistible). Adjust the locations of the various copies of the logo in different sizes so they are on separate workspace pages.

Then, select any object on each page, and use the Print Current Page command in the Print dialog box to print each page in sequence. Take them, with a smile adorning your face, to the boss, who should be fairly impressed. These are not bad at all!

Seeing Things as Geometric Primitives

Before doing another logo, let's discuss the vision thing. Most of us tend to see things as integrated wholes. Artists and others who make their way in the visual world see things differently—as composites, the integration of which may even be somewhat arbitrary. This is certainly true for those who work with computer graphics, and it is something that can be described and that you need to learn to do. (If you don't believe this is true, go to an art-supply store. Take a look at the standard jointed-figure models sold in such stores. The models, utterly neuter, are composed of geometric solids.)

The trick, if it is that, is to see things in terms of their geometry. This has two components:

- The easy part is to see things as a composite of plane-geometric primitives—circles and squares and the like.

- The hard part is to see things as geometric solids—spheres, cubes, and other three-dimensional figures.

Getting the hang of seeing things as plane-geometric shapes is essential. First, this helps with understanding composition. Second, the computer can help, to some extent, with the solid-geometry issues such as lighting.

The more advanced the software, the more help with solid geometry you get—up to photorealism.

As I have became more involved in the use of various graphics tools—and this has changed my life—I found the ability to look at something and break it into a group of geometric primitives useful.

For example, a book is basically a rectangular cover. Sure, after binding, the spine of the book is actually a section of a sort of squashed cylinder (and that can be represented). Or, the bulk of the pages can be represented in several different ways (depending mostly on how much time you are willing to spend). But even the abstract book used in the Smallville seal seems to do a good job, because the primitive shapes gathered in that way are familiar to the eye for one reason or another.

A more elaborate book: A spine and some thickness is suggested, and a picture has been stuck in and skewed to suggest the topology.

Some commentators have suggested that this ability to perceive things from their abstract shapes is a relatively new phenomenon. They believe that as late as the end of the 19th century, an abstract view of things was not recognized as a map of perceptual reality. Certainly, abstraction as a commonplace seems to be fairly recent.

Three-dimensional perception—seeing things as complexes of geometric solids—is at once more familiar and more obscure. Clearly, sculptors have been doing this for millennia. At the same time, it is axiomatic that teaching people to use three-dimensional graphics software is harder than teaching the use of two-dimensional graphics software. In part, this is reflected in the substantial effort that goes into making the application of three-dimensional techniques more completely automatic.

Whatever. This ability *does* seem to be something most people can learn, and it does seem to be independent of physical capability to some extent. For example, I know some competent artists whose vision is impaired in one eye. Although the stereoscopic effect is not part of their experience, they still manage to represent things as three-dimensional.

Practice looking at things and seeing the geometry in them. See doors and windows and books and paper as geometric shapes—either in a single plane, or rotated in three-dimensional space. Looking at things this way will help you in figuring out how to apply the geometric primitives that are at the heart of using computer-graphics software. It will also help you understand some of the skewing that shows up in some projects.

Recreating a Complex Logo Using Geometric Primitives

A logo should tell a story. It should also be easy to use in a variety of contexts. Take this example.

St. Mark's Church in the Bowery is the second oldest Episcopal parish in New York, and its site is the oldest site of continuous worship in Manhattan. (Apparently, the Native Americans in the area didn't live in Manhattan; they commuted from Brooklyn.) Originally, old peg-leg Peter Stuyvesant, the Dutch governor, had his personal chapel on the property (adjacent to his farm house). He and several succeeding generations of Stuyvesants and collateral relatives are buried in the churchyard, along with lots of other prominent Yorkers.

This church has a history of being a center for social activism and the arts (dance, theater, and poetry are housed in the church buildings). The church itself is a landmark and has survived intact despite fires and the decay of centuries. It is a center for the community it serves.

Not surprisingly, it has a well-established logo: a line drawing of the church's elegant facade and steeple.

On the other hand, making that logo accessible for a spate of badly needed publicity materials presented a problem.

Naturally, it would be foolish—and perilous—to change an effective logo.

St. Mark's in•the•Bowery
10th Street & 2nd Avenue

Ways of Capturing the Logo

It was certainly possible to scan the logo. Using a high-resolution scanner and a variety of enhancement techniques, it was quite possible to make a computer-storable and usable image. But such an image is not flexible. Changing its size is possible only within narrow limits. Scale it up too much, and it gets fuzzy; scale it down, and detail is easily lost. Any imperfections in the original are captured and magnified in the scanning process. And the file can be *enormous!*

Of course, the scanned image could be traced. Several drawing programs have powerful automatic tracing tools. They track the map of dark pixels in a scanned image and produce an accurate translation into images. The trace may be automatic; the cleanup is not automatic—and it is often more bothersome than manual tracing (the other tracing option—a laborious and usually unrewarding enterprise).

In fact, a glance at the St. Mark's logo reveals it is made up of geometric primitives. See Figure 2.8. The easiest way to capture this logo is to draw it.

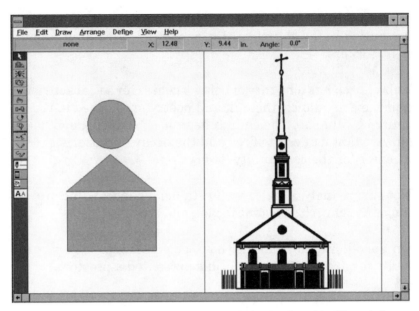

Figure 2.8 Most of the picture part of the St. Mark's Church logo (on the right) is composed of three basic shapes.

In fact, there are *two* ways to draw this image.

- Use the line-drawing tools, which would make a pen-and-ink facsimile easily enough.

- Construct the image from plane-geometric shapes, grouped appropriately and layered on top of each other.

Both techniques have advantages, and I eventually did both versions, but the one that has proved most useful has been the constructed version.

Creating a Constructed Version

Having made the decision to create a constructed version, it will be easier to apply this construction to making some kinds of posters (see Project 7). There are also some advantages to using a constructed version when you want to create faded and colored versions of the design.

Here's the method for constructing a logo. White shapes are mounted on black shapes to show a black border. Object outlines are neutralized—made to be the color of the shape itself—to make them invisible, where need be.

Among other things, this means using the Color tool a lot to adjust line and shape colors. It makes sense to keep the Color dialog open and on the screen. Use the Color tool (or the Color command on the Define menu) to open the dialog box, then choose the Stay command from its Options menu. The dialog box changes from static to sizable (it grows a different border). You may want to resize the box so that only the first three or four rows and columns show. You can use the little arrowhead in the upper right corner of the dialog box to shrink the box to its name tag and menu and back (which makes this a roll-up menu).

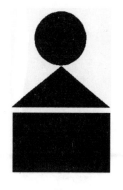

Setting Up the Building Blocks To begin, then. The first step is to put a square, a triangle, and a circle in the work area, using the Symbol tool. Size them more or less the way they are in the marginal illustration, then move them off to one side. Call up the Color dialog box, and set it to stay on the screen. Change each of the shapes to black.

The next step is to create some basic building blocks for the church building and the tower. See Figure 2.9. Each of these blocks consists of a black shape and a white shape. Move them in place, align them, and then group them.

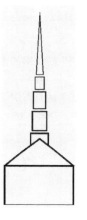

Arrange the various blocks in order. The big rectangle is on the bottom, capped with the triangle. One medium-size rectangle, moved to the back of the drawing with a ^K hot-key command, is tucked under the triangle to make the base for the tower. A series of three graduated, vertically oriented rectangles sit one above the other; these are the various sections of the tower proper and the "lantern" at the top. Finally, a long, skinny triangle forms the steeple.

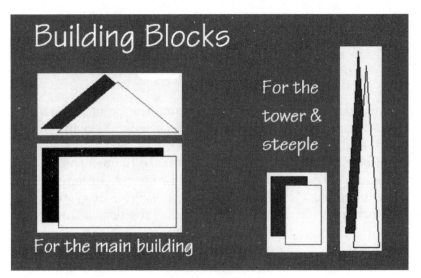

Figure 2.9　Here are the visual building blocks for the logo.

When these shapes are reduced in size, you need to zoom in to work with them so you can grab the handles and the object and move them into place.

The tower segments have windows in them. The two lower sections of the tower have rectangular windows; copy the basic black rectangle and scale it (using the handles) to fit one section, then copy that one and scale to fit the others. The top section of the tower has an oval window; copy the basic black circle, scale it down roughly to size, then drag the handle at either the top center or bottom center a bit to make the ellipse. Center each of the windows in the tower sections (use the Center command from the Align dialog), and group each section with its window.

Creating Transition Elements　Now life gets a bit more complex. The sections of this tower are connected with some architectural ornamentation. This cannot be omitted—in the first place, it is in the original logo; change such things at your peril. In the second place, without the ornaments, the tower doesn't look elegant.

These transition elements are familiar, and all are available except for a trapezoid shape. That is something easy enough to fix.

Actually, you have a few options at this point:

- You could make a copy of the black box, move it close to the tower sections, shrink it a lot, and then zoom in to work with the various tools.

- You might just zoom in at the start and set to work with the tools, creating items as needed—on the spot, so to speak.

- You could do a bit of both—zoom in, then duplicate and create as needed.

The last option is the procedure that appeals to me, but that is strictly a personal choice.

After zooming in, I grabbed a copy of the basic rectangle, shrinking it down a lot (more or less to size, in fact). Then I copied it again, filled it with white, and made the rectangular unit for the connector segment, grouping it at the end. Using the Straight Line tool, I created a trapezoidal solid, more or less the same way as in the Smallville seal's torch earlier in this chapter. I filled the trapezoid with black, moved it into place at the top of the rectangle, and adjusted the size. Both the trapezoid and the rectangle get grouped to make a single shape.

This trapezoidal shape is used to do two things. First, it gets copied to each of the transition points—the tower base to the first section of the tower, first section to second section, second section to third section, and, flipped upside down, as the transition to the steeple. It also serves as the means for setting the relative width of each section of the tower. The section above the trapezoid is adjusted to the width of the trapezoid's smaller side, and the wider side (and the rectangle to which it is connected) determines the width of the section below. See Figure 2.10.

Figure 2.11 shows how the tower looks with connecting segments added. The additional details are either black rectangles (at the top of the first and second sections) or wide lines drawn in with the straight-line tool.

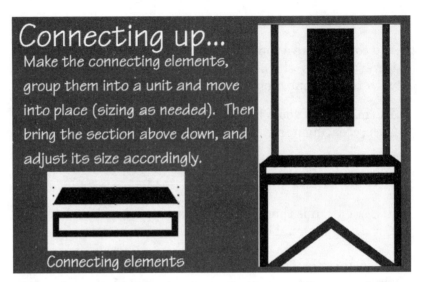

Connecting up...
Make the connecting elements, group them into a unit and move into place (sizing as needed). Then bring the section above down, and adjust its size accordingly.

Connecting elements

Figure 2.10   Here's how the connecting trapezoids are used. The two tower segments are "stacked" with the connector in between.

Creating the Tower Detailing   The rest of the architectural detailing on the tower consists of some more rectangles and some heavy black lines. Most of this work—all of it, really—is done while zoomed in on the tower sections. In effect, you work on a blown-up set of drawing elements. The zoom capability makes it much easier to work with details like this—another strong plus for doing things like this in the computer. Copy a black rectangle that is about the height of the base-to-section transition shape, and a bit wider than the first section of the tower. Locate it about a fifth of the way down from the top of that section. Make a copy of that rectangle; shrink it down a bit to fit side to side in the middle tower segment, a bit from the top. Make a copy of one of the composite rectangles (the ones with a black background rectangle and a white foreground rectangle, grouped together); make it a bit wider than the middle section, and insert it between the middle section and the transition shape connecting to the third section (the lantern). Use the Straight Line tool to fill in the pilaster details and the rick-rack at the top of the first tower section. I set the line width to 3 points in my drawing; the idea is to

Learn Desktop Graphics and Design on the PC

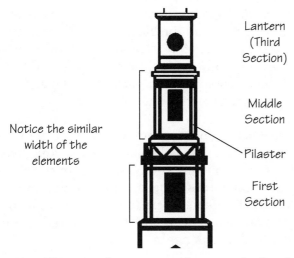

Figure 2.11　Here are the tower sections, stacked and connected.

set the line width to about the same as the vertical black edges of the tower sections.

Topping Off the Tower　Finish the tower by adding the cross on the steeple. Zoom out (use the ^2 hot key to zoom to the current page) and make a copy of the basic black circle, dragging it near the top of the steeple and shrinking it down to about a quarter inch. Then zoom back in so that you are looking at the small circle, the top of the steeple, and about an inch or so of free space above it.

The cross consists of a ball at the tip of the steeple, from which the cross itself rises. Make the ball by shrinking the black circle still further (mine is about an eighth of an inch across), then stretching it a bit at the top or bottom to make it elliptical. Drag a copy with the Copy tool, color it white, and shrink it a tad, then put it back on top of the black oval. Group this, and use the Copy tool to drag a copy over to the top of the steeple.

You draw the cross itself with the Straight Line tool. It is a simple vertical line passing up from the ball at the tip of the steeple, crossed by a diagonal line. The diagonal suggests that the cross is oriented on an angle different from the front

of the church building. Ungroup the original of the black-and-white ball, and shrink the black oval to make a finial for the vertical stroke. Copy that finial to a point alongside the cross arm. Use the Rotation tool to rotate the oval to match the angle of the crosspiece, then place it on the end of the crosspiece, and add a copy on the other end.

Remember to save your work regularly.

The tower with its steeple is completed. Before going on to the church and its porch, wisdom suggests saving your file. Convenience suggests using the Group tool to select all the tower elements from cross to base, and grouping them. A&L Draw will pop these elements up to the top layer as part of the grouping process; you can use the ^K hot-key command to move them to the back again.

Adding Details to the Main Building The architectural details of the church building consist of a porch and some windows. Begin by making a copy of the basic black circle and moving it to the center of a triangle, scaling as necessary. Make a copy of the basic black rectangle, and scale it down so it has the height and about three-quarters the width of the large composite rectangle.

The circle in the middle of the triangle is a window. Three more windows—arched ones—are needed for the gallery windows of the church building, as shown in Figure 2.12. They are composed of a black circle and a black rectangle, grouped together and copied as needed.

You can enhance the windows by suggesting the glint of light on the glass. Use the Curved Line tool to make a free-form shape, edit out unnecessary points, then make it long and skinny.

The ornamentation along the line formed at the junction of the triangular pediment and the main block of the church facade is made up of more rectangles. One black rectangle

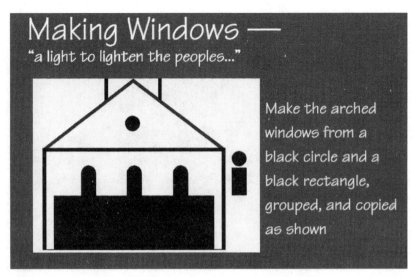

Making Windows —

"a light to lighten the peoples..."

Make the arched windows from a black circle and a black rectangle, grouped, and copied as shown

Figure 2.12   Here's how to make arched windows.

covers the junction, and it is a trifle wider than the building; the second black rectangle is the width of the building, and it is located below the first. Two wide, skinny white rectangles (make one, then copy it) serve to break the lower black rectangle at this junction into a series of lines suggesting the decorative molding at the base of the church's pediment. These rectangles are broken by small vertical blocks made up of a vertical black rectangle with a white rectangle in the middle, grouped together and copied into position. See Figure 2.13. Remember to save the original so you can copy it again and again in different places.

The porch details are essentially the same as the details at the junction of the main block of the building and the pediment. In fact, the easiest way to make that series of blocks — a sort of balustrade around the top of the porch's roof and some suggestion of the porch's roof molding — is to copy the blocks used in the pediment. Grab them all with the Group tool, use the Copy tool to bring them down, then switch to the regular Pointer tool, and scale them into place. Adjust sizes and the placement of things, and realign the posts in the balustrade so they project up, rather than down.

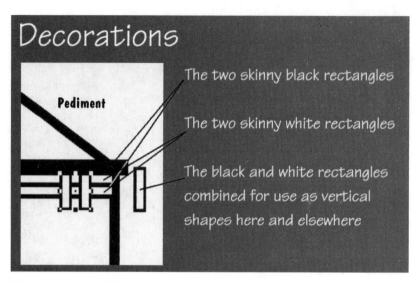

Figure 2.13   Adding decorative cornice elements.

The arch-filling
shape

To fill in the arches flanking the main entrance to the porch, the design calls for one more special shape—three sides of a rectangle, with the fourth (bottom) side a curve. Use the Straight Line tool to draw the top and two sides, then draw the curve with the Curved Line tool. Connect the lines into a single shape, and fill it with black. Then make a copy, fill it with white, mount it on the black shape, and group the two shapes. Put the first shape in place, and then copy it to the second arch.

Another milestone reached: The whole building is finished, and all that remains is the suggestion of the railing on either side. To lock things up and make sure the drawing doesn't get mucked up, zoom out to Current Page size with a ^2 hot-key command, then group all the church elements together as a single object.

This is also a good time to check that things look right. For example, when I zoomed out, I became convinced that the whole construction looked improbably top-heavy, and the tower looked too broad for the church building. So I slimmed the tower group down, then ungrouped it and made some minor adjustments to compensate for the squeeze. Finally, I grouped the whole construction—tower and church building.

Making the Railing Making the railing is the simplest thing so far. Make a skinny black rectangle, about three-quarters the height of the porch. Then copy it and make the copy shorter. Put the two next to each other, with a space about the width of the rectangles in between. Align them on the bottom, and group them. Then make five copies, one after the other. This time, align to the top, and group all six. Move it into place, then use the Copy tool to drag a copy over to the other side. Flip the whole thing horizontally with the Flip ⬦ command on the Arrange menu, and move that set of railings into place.

The railing on the left side of the design

Add these railings to the grouped church by selecting the church and each railing section, then pressing ^G.

Adding Text Finally, it's time to add text. Use the Typeface tool to get to the Type Attributes dialog box. If you are using the A&L Draw typefaces, choose Classic Medium; if you are using printer typefaces (that is, if you have chosen any printer device and can access Windows TrueType faces), select Times New Roman. There is a definite advantage to using the TrueType faces in this case: St. Mark's in the Bowery uses little round dots between words, and they aren't available in Draw's typefaces.

Input each line separately (that is, select Add at the end of *St. Mark's* and again after *in the Bowery*). The code for the single curly apostrophe is Alt+0146; the code for the little dot is Alt+0149. Next, stretch each line (use the corner boxes, so the scaling is correct) to fit. See Figure 2.14 for the finished project.

I think the point is made—perhaps "done to death" is more like it. With a couple exceptions, only three shapes were used in making this image. Nor is this as extreme a case as it

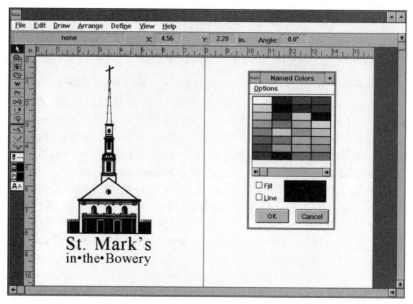

Figure 2.14   This is what the project should come out looking
like, more or less, allowing for all the usual variations that can
happen when different people do the same thing.

might seem. In fact, the basic plane or solid geometry of
things is the greatest boon to the design process there is.
Most people can learn the requisite skill of seeing the geometry in things fairly easily, and that keeps the whole business from becoming hopelessly arcane.

Achieving Client Satisfaction

So, a second logo is done. At this point, having made the design, I would normally send a copy to the client for a check,
to make sure we were still on the same wavelength. (If you
are doing graphics for yourself, you are your own client; be
self-critical.)

For a black-and-white image like this, I would very likely fax
it directly from my computer, using a fax modem.

> Fax modems are inexpensive these days. I've tried several, and I prefer the Hayes Accura as the easiest and most generally reliable.
>
> I use Delrina's WinFax Pro software. Again, I've tried several variants, and this is the one that has proven most reliable.

I prefer to send clients work via fax simply because it is fast and cheap. A local phone call costs less than a postage stamp (much less than a messenger service); a transcontinental fax is usually under a dollar. Effectively, faxing from the computer is just another way of printing—and that makes it a natural. The only problem: When I started doing this, I was on the competitive edge; now, everyone does it.

Developing a Logo for a Community Group

As I was writing this chapter, a new political club being formed in Manhattan's Chinatown asked me to design a logo. Consider this the live test of the theory discussed so far.

Logos tell a story if they are any good at all. To make this logo, it is necessary to understand something of the role of political clubs in New York and something about the history of politics in Chinatown.

New York City politics is largely dominated by factions of the Democratic party. The old regular Dems—the folks who brought you Tammany Hall—have been largely eclipsed by reformed and independent Dems.

The political club is the basic organizing structure in the system. It is the means by which local leaders deliver the only real coin of politics: votes! At the club's office, the local leader has a place to meet voters.

The largest real difference is that the latter groups weren't getting their share of the cookies until they supplanted the regulars.

Chinatown has lots of associations, but they are shy of political clubs. Effectively, this growing community in lower Manhattan has been shut out of New York politics. As a result, Chinatown citizens don't get their share of things.

CIVICS stands for Coalition of Informed Voters to Improve City Services. Its *raison d'être* is to create an effective vehicle for the legitimate aspirations of its members (and others in the community it addresses) for representation, as well as for the legitimate aspirations of its leadership for political office.

Now, how the dickens do I get all that into a logo?

The basic elements are clearly going to be textual: The acronym CIVICS is essential, and someplace it needs to be explained. This club is based in Chinatown, and its core membership consists of immigrant and American-born Chinese. The organization also has a Chinese name, and that needs to be in the design.

This is a political organization, and it is almost impossible to go wrong with a red, white, and blue color scheme. Since this is a New York organization, I immediately came up with a New York skyline.

As it happens, this all fits well with the uses to which the design will be put. First, the club wants a large sign to put in the window of its new offices. The office is on the third floor of a building in Chinatown with a window facing Mulberry Street; something bold and bright is in order. A smaller version of the sign will fit on the office door.

The club also wants a banner to carry to rallies. The simplest way to make that kind of banner is to use cut vinyl—which will dictate some design elements and colors.

Finally, the logo will find its way onto a membership card.

Notice that all these uses are rectangular spaces, wider than they are high. A fairly horizontal design appears to be in order. So far, all the design elements discussed fit well with that scheme.

Learn Desktop Graphics and Design on the PC

Creating a Skyline

The two elements that could prove troublesome are the Chinese name and the city skyline. Let's see if A&L Draw has clip art that can be used. Yes! See Figure 2.15.

Using the Library tool (second from the top in the toolbox), open the Clip Art Manager dialog. Select Props & Skylines in the left-hand panel, and select Skyline-City in the right-hand panel, then use the Add button to place this skyline in the work area.

The skyline is generic. It is clearly not the New York skyline, but that can be fixed. The colors are neutral, and that can be fixed, too. In short, the nasty part of the job is done, and all that's left is to make this a nice custom image.

Zoom in on the object, select it, then use the ^U hot key to ungroup it. Deselect the object by clicking outside it, then click on the object again, and drag it down. What comes down is one part of the skyline. Click on what is left behind,

Well, maybe you can see the three groups of buildings that compose the skyline.

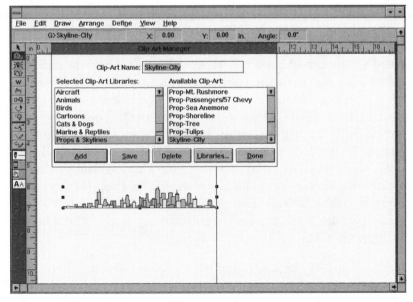

Figure 2.15   The A&L Draw Clip Art Manager contains a generic city skyline easily modified for the CIVICS logo.

and drag it up; another portion of the skyline is separated out. This group is made up of three parts, each of which has a different color.

To make this a New York skyline, I need to add four silhouettes: the twin towers of the World Trade Center, and the Empire State and Chrysler buildings. These are distinctive elements. The skyline itself is just sketchy, so I don't need details—just a suggestion, stuck in the right place.

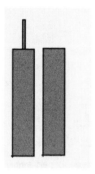

Drawing the World Trade Center The Straight Line tool does the job quickly. The twin towers are simple rectangles—a pair of tall and skinny ones, with another short and skinny one stuck on top of the left-hand tower to suggest the radio and TV broadcast tower.

Drawing the Empire State Building The Empire State Building and the Chrysler Building have a similar profile. The Empire State Building is about as tall as the World Trade Center without its broadcast mast, and the Chrysler Building is somewhat shorter.

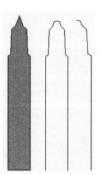

From right to left, the profile, the original and copy joined, and then the basic shape completed.

Make the Empire State Building shape first. Use the Straight Line tool to create a rough profile. The Empire State Building steps back toward the top, so add a couple jags inward at the top of the line. Make a copy of that line and flip it horizontally with the Flip ⬦ command on the Arrange menu. Select both lines and use the F7 hot key to make them into a single figure. Draw another line for the base, and select both pieces, again using the F7 hot key to close the shape. If the status line at the top of the work area still reports this shape as open, use the Line Editing tool to check for breaks, then repeat the last step. Make a copy of the radio mast from the World Trade Center, slim it down a bit, and stick it under the Empire State Building. Group the whole thing with a ^G.

Drawing the Chrysler Building To create the Chrysler Building, first copy the Empire State Building. Ungroup the copy and get rid of the broadcast mast. Use the Line Editing tool

Learn Desktop Graphics and Design on the PC

to select some of the jags in the upper part of the shape and delete them. Turn off the Line Editing tool and shrink the building down.

These new building shapes need to be incorporated into the larger skyline, and the whole thing needs color.

Coloring the Skyline Start by reassembling the clip art. Select them all; use the Align command (^N) to align the pieces on the bottom. But don't group the pieces quite yet.

First, wouldn't this make a nice red, white, and blue, patriotic part of the emblem? Sure enough. Open the Color dialog box with the Color tool; you may want to invoke the Stay option, since this dialog will be used a couple of times.

Color the big object—the main part of the skyline—white. Color the other, smaller pieces white. What about blue? Well, New York is a big city, and it seems to me we need some more buildings. Use the Copy tool to drag the big white piece just a bit to the left. Use the ^K hot key to push the new block to the back, and color it blue. Still not enough blue—so let's color the new buildings blue, too.

Adding the Buildings to the Skyline Put the new buildings in place. The twin towers need to be near the front (along the Hudson River), but with the low red buildings in front of them. The Empire State Building is in the middle, and the Chrysler Building is to the left of it and at the back. This takes some fiddling—moving the pieces around a little and shifting some forward and some back with ^K and ^F commands. When you get it to look just right, group the whole thing. See Figure 2.16.

Adding Text

Now for the text. The easy part of this is the label that reads *Coalition of Informed Voters to Improve City Services*. This is another job for the Wyeth typeface, in my judgment (you can use your own, of course). Use the Typeface tool to open the

Figure 2.16   Here are the steps in composing the skyline.

Type Attributes dialog, and select Wyeth (or whatever) and Centered (not vital, but you might as well). OK that selection.

Use the Text tool to add the text, and add it under the skyline. Use the Pointer tool to drag corner handles so the text is the same width as the base of the skyline, and snug the text block up underneath. Choose a color that you think is effective. I chose red, on the grounds that it would be flashier.

Designing the Acronym   The next piece of text is the acronym, which needs to be bold and striking. A&L Draw gives you some options, and you would do well to try a couple of them. In fact, you want to show the client a couple image options, and let those folks make the final choice—after all, it's their logo. See Figure 2.17.

In addition to the fancy stuff, you could use plain text—nice and bold, and colored nicely, with a strong outline. The A&L Draw Bach typeface (it looks to me to be a variant on Aachen Bold) has a school-spirit, rah-rah look, which seems to me appropriate in this case.

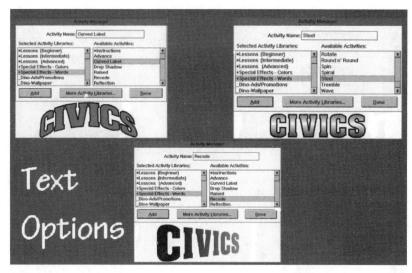

Figure 2.17 Here are some text options for the acronym.

Place the acronym in its varying forms behind and above the skyline and the long text label. Hmm—the receding lettering looks lousy that way, so pop it up front on top of the skyline, sort of reaching back.

At this point there are four variations on a basic theme, as shown in Figure 2.18. The colors are neat, and the visibility is pretty fair in each case.

But wait: Life is complex, and this is a political club in Chinatown, and you can (as they said in the 1960s) bet your bippy these folks want the name of the organization done in Chinese as well as in English. This poses some interesting problems.

Incorporating Chinese Characters The difficulty is that the Chinese writing system has so many characters. A modest subset numbers 5,000.

The standard coding system for characters used in most operating systems (including DOS and Windows) provides only

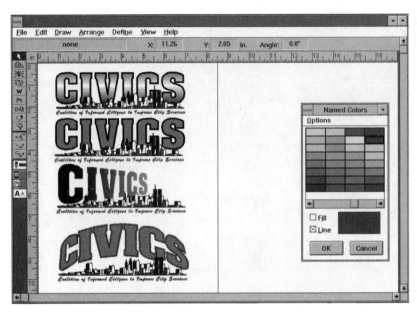

Figure 2.18   Here are four variations on the CIVICS logo.

256 slots for characters, including those you see and those
you don't.

There are several excellent ways to get around this, and the
Chinese themselves have developed the best of them. But
this scheme has not yet been applied in a consistent way for
desktop-computing operating-system software. What is
available is hard to get in the United States, anyway; for example, the Chinese-language version of Windows is marketed only casually in this country, and Microsoft does not
support it here.

Interestingly enough, the problem does not arise for other
languages whose character sets are alphabetic—Greek, Rus-
sian and other languages rendered in the Cyrillic alphabet,
Hebrew, and Arabic are all accommodated pretty easily by
standard computer operating systems and hardware.

Anyway, the vast size of the Chinese character set, coupled
with restrictions in operating-system software, make the so-

lution of simply adding a Chinese typeface unavailable in most cases.

I came up with three possibilities:

- Get a talented person to write the Chinese characters—with a brush, but using Western paper, so the edges will be sharp and there is little bleed).

- Get someone with Chinese-character software to print out the text on a laser printer. In these first two cases, you could scan the characters and import the result into A&L Draw. I have not discussed bitmaps and scanning yet, so these two options are not terribly helpful.

- Letter the characters by hand in the computer. This technique is entirely within the scope of the projects you have been doing and the tools available. For the purposes of this book, that is the approach I have taken.

Think of this as an optional, extra-credit part of the project, if you want. The letters to draw—should you accept this challenge—are shown in Figure 2.19.

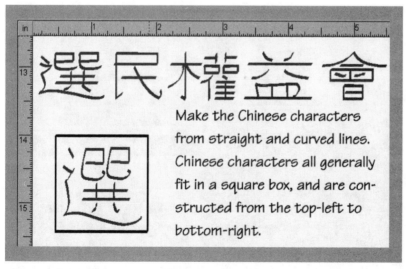

Figure 2.19   Here are the Chinese characters you draw.

Placing the characters is an interesting proposition. The placement is fairly obvious in the two designs where the lettering runs straight across. Put the Chinese characters (in red—a favored Chinese color) across the top. The other two designs involve some challenges.

The receding lettering style leaves a nice open space to the right of the word *CIVICS*. For the purposes of this exercise, I regrouped the characters and fitted them into that space. That is not the best solution, but a more elegant one would require some tools not available in A&L Draw.

Running the characters along the top of the curved lettering is not too difficult. Use the Curved Line tool to make a curved line along the top of the curved word *CIVICS*. Adjust it as needed to make it as smooth and even as possible.

Move the characters so they are evenly spaced along the line, centered over *CIVICS*. Then use the Rotation tool to adjust the angle of each character so its base is more or less on a tangent to the curve. When things are more or less the way you want them, take away the construction line. See Figure 2.20.

Figure 2.20   Here's how you add the characters to a curved baseline. Rotate each character slightly as it sits on the curve.

Learn Desktop Graphics and Design on the PC

Positioning elements on a curve is a powerful design element. It is important enough that the most advanced packages automate this function. Interestingly, the automation sometimes doesn't work. In that case, you can use this technique to solve the problem.

The Client Decides

I printed out the designs on the Fargo color wax thermal-transfer printer and took them over to the club. After the members bought me lunch (very good curry on noodles in a Vietnamese restaurant), they huddled together and chose the design with the curved lettering. Sigh.

Actually, I didn't like the curved version. I preferred the straight-across version with the steel shading. I liked the contrast, and I liked the suggestion of adamant insistence on good service from government. See Figure 2.21.

But it's the client who decides.

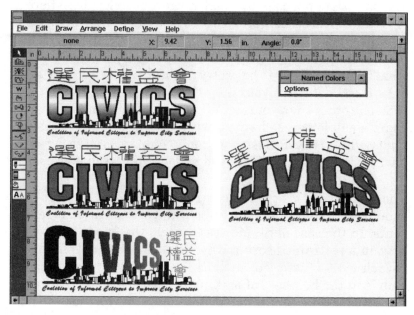

Figure 2.21   The club liked the version on the right (with some modifications not shown here). I preferred the one at the top left.

Good-bye to Logoland

You have made three different logos. Two of the exercises were based on real live clients.

Along the way, you've played with some interesting options A&L Draw offers for shaping text and other things to your design needs. Blended color, for example, figures in a couple of the designs, and Draw allows you to access this through its Magic Color Cubes—a quick and painless way to do it.

After a longish digression, the way in which things can be reduced to geometry (without the pain of returning to high school and Euclid—or Lobachevsky, if you did the new math) was demonstrated.

Along the way, you've heard something about what goes into creating a logo—or at least, what I think is involved. This is not science, it is art—and the number of opinions on the subject is legion.

The basics are not controversial, however. Generally, where a logo exists, you stick pretty close to it. In fact, there are excellent reasons to redraw it into the machine, rather than simply scanning it and pasting the scanned version down. But what is drawn needs to be pretty faithful, and it is important to let the client check your work (if you are designing for someone other than yourself, of course). Most companies are chary about letting folks mess with what is, after all, the sign under which they do business. Some companies go so far as to have a distinctive typeface designed for their exclusive use.

The other thing that is not controversial is that the logo should tell a consistent story about the organization it represents. In the case of St. Mark's Church, the image is a bit arty, in a restrained sort of way; St. Mark's is an Episcopal church with a history of support for the arts. The political club is in the business of making waves; a good deal of rah-rah infuses the designs submitted. They are intended to be

decidedly in your face. Neither of these designs would suit a
bank or a medical practice—where an institutional image
should be (at least) at the heart of the design. I mean, would
you want a rah-rah bank?

This was a rather involved project. The next one will be simpler—sort of restful, and oriented to reviewing things.

Project 3:
Biz Forms

In case you hadn't noticed, you've done quite a bit, if you've been following along and working through the projects.

If you haven't been following along in the book and doing the exercises, this is a good time to stop merely reading and get with the hands-on part of things. The thesis of this book is that you learn by doing.

But all practice and no theory makes for—well, it might make for some design problems.

Theories about Design

The problem with theories about design is that there are too many of them.

The problem with books about design theory is that they generally reflect the prejudices of the authors for a particular theory—often, the current fad. Then too, many try to be global in the application of such a theory.

Generally, it seems to me that books offering global theories are out of touch with the times. Global theories worked reasonably well in the relatively homogenized society of 19th-century Western European cultures. In such a society, a single canon of taste tended to predominate; a dogmatic approach, in which the canon was extended to every possible object of reference, could prevail without looking silly.

Other homogeneous societies, particularly China and Japan, had equally refined canons—quite different from those of Western Europe, and defended with as much vigor by their adherents.

A whole bunch of things have happened in the last century or so, and the result has been, in part, to render such uniformity impractical.

There is another problem with global theories: Design itself is not uniform. Different kinds of design demand attention to different details, if nothing else. For example, you can see similarities between the school of architectural and interior design known as the Bauhaus and a concurrent design movement in Switzerland resulting in a range of new graphic-design elements—notably, some particularly useful, spare typefaces. The connection is made easier by the fact that the Bauhaus is a good expression of a common German sentiment (I am tempted to say, spiritual malaise) of the time, and many Swiss share a common culture with their German cousins. Both these movements show a fascination with the orderliness of things technical, imbued with a sense of the democratic socialism that prevailed throughout European and North American society in the early part of the 20th century. Its literary expression—and the conflicts it engenders—might be found in Shaw's *Major Barbara*.

That is where most books on design theory, taken as a whole, leave things. It is too superficial an analysis, conflating movements in design inappropriately.

There are exceptions: Mrs. Jenner, who is much more knowledgeable in these matters than I am, likes a book written collaboratively by Richardson, Coleman, and Smith, late of Southern Illinois University at Edwardsville, called *Basic Design: Systems, Elements, Applications* (Prentice Hall, 1984). These authors have different points of view, and they have been willing to use all of them in presenting their notions of effective design. The book is historically informed and refuses to write off older canons, but it learns from them what is good and useful. This book fails only in its general limitation to Western European canons—but that keeps the book to a manageable size.

There is another approach: Some books are written with particular kinds of design in mind.

For example, Jan White's books on desktop publishing and the elements of design appropriate to that field won't tell you much about creating posters or advertising. But for designing a book or a newsletter, they are excellent.

The advantage of well-focused books is substantial. Generally, a single canon is set forth, that applies very well to a particular kind of design. This allows for a kind of design pluralism. A designer adopts the canon for the specific area of design in which he or she works in any given project and according to personal preference.

Most of these books—whether general or specific—are intended (as, for that matter, are most of the books on computer-graphics applications) for people already trained in design. For the most part, a certain common culture and education is assumed.

Things change; cultures change. The culture in which we are living is changing so quickly it is hard to say what's "in" and what's "out." The historical precedent that comes to mind is the fertile period of the 15th and 16th centuries in Western Europe. Many different canons contended, and each had merits. Tremendous things happened before things settled down.

Something of the same sort seems to be happening now. The old boundaries—especially, the old homogeneities—are disappearing. Corporations, for example, function transnationally; they have to accommodate all sorts of things—including designs for everything from products to business

forms—to still-diverse cultures. In the process, this global-
ization is beginning to found a new high culture. It's exciting;
it also makes life a bit more complex.

So let's say a design can be informed by a variety of idioms
transcending the local limits that have hitherto obtained. It
probably should be.

The Question of Taste

Another way to approach design is to turn to the question of
taste. In discussing taste, let's set aside for the moment a
particular canon's dictates and look at the mechanism at
work, from which canons emerge.

This is not a new approach. There is a substantial literature on the
theory of taste. One of the best discussions of the subject is Professor Ernst Vollrath's *Rekonstruktion der Politischen Urteilskraft* (Stutt-
gart: Clett Verlag, 1975). Notice that this is a book about politics?
Surprised? Don't be. Taste has always had political implications; it
has always pitted community values against artistic freedom, among
other things. (As it happens, I studied with Vollrath; what is more
interesting, I did it in the United States, after I came back from Ger-
many.)

What is the judgment of taste, exactly? Basically, it is a *claim*.
I, as designer, claim that the design I advance is the most
beautiful, most effective, most whatever way to tell the story
or portray the event, or whatever the intention of the design
may be.

Frankly, I think the heart of the matter is in *telling the story*.
That gets changed a bit—not a lot—when a product is being
designed. The story a chair tells, for example, is of comfortable seating, or some such. Have you noticed that a really
good chair almost invites you to sit down and rest?

Learn Desktop Graphics and Design on the PC

Or, to pick another example (from the *Basic Design* book cited earlier in this chapter): van Gogh wanted his paintings understood not only as great works of art, but also as nice decorative pieces. He shows them decorating the walls of his bedroom at Arles, in his painting of it. He was telling a story about art.

Use your imagination to add an echo-chamber effect.

The other important element is the claim that is made. A claim is not a universal truth existing somewhere out there, independent of the person advancing it. It is entirely personal; at the same time, its nature is to be universal.

Now, under what circumstances could such a claim be advanced? How could something be a personal opinion, yet claim to be universally true and obvious to any reasonable person?

Clearly, if the matter were merely personal opinion, any claim to universal truth would be plain silly. But suppose the claim were based on something observed in the object of the judgment that *this is beautiful* (or *effective,* or whatever). The object and its attributes are in common space; you see it much the same way I do. I stand in front of the painting; you can stand there, too. I can ask you to see what I see in looking at it. And I can ask that you let the same elements we both see affect you. Finally, I can say, if you see as I do, that you concur in the judgment of taste.

This kind of judgment arises not from the application of a canon, but from contemplation of the thing in its appearance(s). For the record, the precise technical term for the kind of contemplation that lets a thing's own appearance determine the story it tells is *critical judgment.*

I will restrain myself, and not list the multitude of scholarly citations that go with this discussion.

Design as an Expression of Critical Judgment

Good design begins with a critical assessment by the designer of the circumstances surrounding a design. Effective designers do this almost by instinct (actually, it's from training that has evolved into habit). What's the story to be told, and what's the best way to tell it?

Sometimes, something just demands a design—the designer gets intrigued. For example, designer Bruce Wasserman was intrigued by a rubberized neoprene material. He wanted to do something with it, and he ended up creating a line of business cases for The Smarter Image (which dropped the project when it stopped making its own products).

Another example: When Chrysler introduced the Plymouth, the then-new agency doing ads for DeSoto (J. Stirling Getchell, Inc.) was appalled by the stodgy ads created for the new car by a competing agency. The agency created a whole series of ads on spec. These ads turned out to be wildly successful, and the agency got only its expenses reimbursed. Of course, a while later, Chrysler moved the Plymouth account to Getchell.

In each case, something was present to the creator, and it dictated what was created.

Good design is also aware of the current fashion, because the current fashion dictates what will be accepted by a target population. In effect, a design is ratified by that population. A good way to get a sense of what works today is to look at the advertising in the upscale magazines.

Bernard Modern and COPPERPLATE variants seem popular now; Caslon Open Face has been eclipsed.

For example, a few years ago, an awful lot of advertising used a typeface called University Roman. You couldn't turn around without facing yet another application of that florid typeface. Recently, I have seen that typeface used only in clearly second-rate jobs (usually combined with other, rather bland typefaces in ways I thought were ineffective).

Ads are also good clues for other aspects of design. Take a look at older ads—you can see a lot of them in Watkins' *The 100 Greatest Advertisements* (Dover, 1959). These ads have lots of copy. Now look at recent ads for clothing or cars—they are almost entirely visual, with only a small amount of copy. The current wisdom seems to be that people react to pictures, rather than text—but it's by no means a hard and fast rule.

You need to strike a balance in all these (and other) elements. A product design balances form and function; sometimes form is more important (look at some clothing items), and sometimes function dictates form. The design for a brochure balances the need to provide information—usually, as text—with the need to have visual impact.

It's all a matter of judgment.

Designing Business Forms

Forms are a real design challenge.

First, a form has to structure data in a way that helps its conversion into information. It is amazing how often forms fail to do that. Most people have a handle on the data to be collected, but the structure of that data simply escapes them. Consequently, the forms most people end up using are miracles of confusion.

Second, forms need to be easy to use. In most cases, the person who creates the form does not use the form or have much to do with the interpretation of the data collected. But many forms are difficult to understand.

Third, at least three different kinds of forms are used in most operations. Paper forms are still with us (alas). Electronic data processing dictates on-screen forms—sometimes in a graphic style, and sometimes in text-only style. Then there are hybrid systems. Figure 3.1 shows some examples.

Of course, you could type up forms in a word-processing program. In fact, with mastery of such software, you could do a really bang-up job. It is also true that most forms-design systems use design tools much like the ones in A&L Draw.

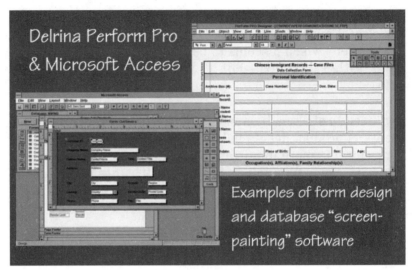

Figure 3.1   Here are two on-screen forms.

For the purposes of this book, it makes sense to use A&L Draw to demonstrate form design. The forms will be perfectly useful when printed on paper.

In the real world, it makes sense to use a forms-design program where possible. Programs such as Delrina's Perform Pro and Form-Flow (there are others, but these are used by a lot of government agencies) do nice forms and tie neatly into electronic information systems as a front-end. When you use a forms-design program, you can connect paper forms, desktop data entry, and departmental or company database systems in a single design procedure.

In some cases, the whole system is exclusively electronic. Most database-development software supports more than one kind of data-entry forms-design program (or *screen painter*).

Again, the obvious: All of these are simply special cases of the general-purpose drawing software (like Draw). The skills are directly transferable.

Creating a Better Admissions Form

Smallville Community College sends out an admissions form to any student who requests it (remember the flowchart in Project 1?). How could that form be made better?

Consider Ms. LeGrande's original admissions form, created on her venerable typewriter years ago, shown in Figure 3.2.

You could argue that this form does the job, and it costs nothing to use it. The counterargument is that it is not a very professional form—and the data-entry clerk argues that it doesn't fit the school's new database system used to process applications. Your job (should you choose to accept it; if Ms. LeGrande finds out and objects, the chief administrators will disavow your existence) is to create a new form.

In this case, the database system already exists, and you will have enough trouble with one new form; wisdom suggests leaving the data-entry screens alone. On the other hand, you want to make the new paper form fit with the data-entry screens. Your first job: Examine those screens.

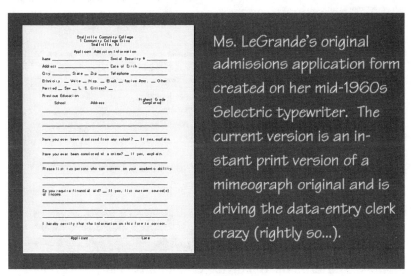

Ms. LeGrande's original admissions application form created on her mid-1960s Selectric typewriter. The current version is an instant print version of a mimeograph original and is driving the data-entry clerk crazy (rightly so...).

Figure 3.2   Here's the original admissions form.

On-screen Forms

This will change, perhaps fairly soon. Pen-computing is—interesting...— and voice capability is getting very good.

Data-entry screens are forms. They are filled out on the computer, rather than with a pen. This makes certain design choices preferable over others. See Figure 3.3.

First, most database systems distinguish several different kinds of data:

• *Alphanumeric* or character data covers most information.

• *Numeric* data consists of numbers used in calculations.

• *Dates* and other special kinds of information usually have special data types.

• Most database systems have one or more *logical* data types, including a standard true/false (1 or 0) option, which is used to represent the contents of check boxes.

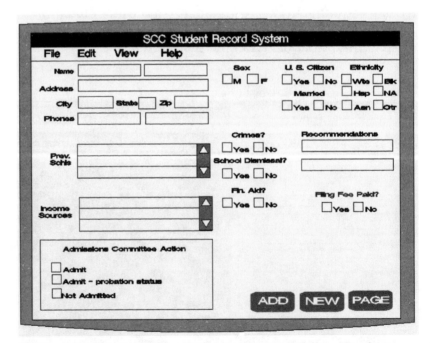

Figure 3.3   Here's the Smallville Community College Student Record System database data-entry screen, page 1.

A database designer (it is hard to call such people *programmers;* most database design is so automated these days that a person making one does little if any coding) uses different data types to speed up the data-entry process.

The flow is also controlled; the designer specifies the order in which fields (represented in the form by boxes) become active. As a field is filled, either the cursor jumps to the next field automatically, or the operator hits the Tab key to jump to the next field in sequence.

Any competent database designer paints the screens so that the flow seems logical. That is, related information appears in the same part of the screen, and the flow is fairly conventional. For the Smallville data-entry screen, the flow is from personal information to background data to admissions decision. The name-and-address block is filled out first, then the cursor jumps to the check boxes to the right. If the screen painter supports it, the designer might have added an instruction so that once one box in a group is checked, the cursor jumps to the next group.

Other kinds of data-entry control, mostly for validation purposes, might play a part, but not in this simple form. Good database design is a separate subject, but one that is increasingly important to designers working in business. Many companies now include people with graphic-design experience in project task forces who are charged with the design of mission-critical systems. Their design expertise plays a part in all aspects of the human/machine interface.

One vital datum is flagged in red (you can't see the red because the picture is black and white): the *Filing Fee Paid?* legend. No college would act on an application until the check for the application fee had cleared.

Actually, the form is flawed. Ms. Bookkeeper, the registrar, will almost certainly want two date fields added—one for the day the application is received (hitherto stamped on the paper form) and one for the day the Admissions Committee acts. She might also want a date field for the day an acceptance or rejection letter is sent.

Aha! An exercise! Set up your own Smallville Community College Student Record System screen.

If you have installed a database system running under Windows, you might want to make this an exercise with the screen painter in that system.

If you want to use this exercise to test Draw's capabilities as a prototyper, here are some hints: The whole screen is composed of rectangles and text, except for the buttons. Those are rounded-corner squares (from the Symbol tool), squished down and labeled.

Making the Matching Paper Form

To create the matching paper form using A&L Draw, set the Preferences dialog under the View menu to show rulers and grid; set the grid increment to a quarter inch, and check the Front radio button adjacent to the Grid check box. The Front setting means the grid appears on top of any solid objects you create, rather than behind them. From the File menu, use the Printer Setup command to set the printer to your black-and-white printer (and consequently, the page layout; make sure your printer is set to portrait—vertical—printing).

Entering the Logo Now go to the File menu and use the Open command. You are given the opportunity to save the new file; do so (give it a name of not more than eight characters, such as FORM, and save it). Then the Open dialog comes up. Open the file in which you saved the Smallville Community College logo.

Learn Desktop Graphics and Design on the PC

When I saved the file, I saved both black-and-white and color versions. Now, I can select the black-and-white version with the Group tool (the finger). Press the Control key and the insert key (^Ins), or select Copy from the Edit menu, to copy this version of the logo to the Windows clipboard.

Do another File Open, say no to the *Save Changes?* message, and reopen the new FORM file. When it is up on the screen, use the Paste command on the Edit menu (or the Shift-Ins hot key) to paste in the Smallville logo.

Shrink the logo (using one of the corner handles) to about 1 inch wide, and move it to the top of the screen—say, about 1 inch from the left side.

Adding the Title Next, add the form title:

Smallville Community College
Application for Admission

Probity suggests that a fairly standard, rather institutional typeface be used; it is better for this purpose to choose a printer typeface. So, use the Typeface tool to get the Type Attributes dialog box, click on the radio button by the selected printer's name, and from the list of printer fonts choose Times New Roman (that's one of the basic TrueType fonts that comes with Windows; you are sure to have it). Use the Styles button to make the text bold, and then OK out of Type Attributes. Use the Text tool to enter the form title, and place it adjacent to the logo. See Figure 3.4.

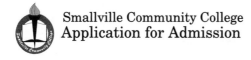

Figure 3.4   Here's the heading, with logo, for the SCC Application for Admission.

Creating the Applicant Information Block The first block of information collected on this form is basic data about the applicant. Since it is a fairly discrete group of items, why not make it clear that this is so? Use the Symbol tool to get a square. Place it in the work area, then use the Fill tool to turn off the fill altogether (select None from the Fill dialog radio buttons). This leaves a box with a border. Move this box so it is just below the header, and size it so it is about a third as high as the page.

The next step is to create a header for this first information block. Copy the box and size it. Use the Fill tool to change it back to solid fill. Then, using the Color tool, change the fill color to 20 percent gray and the line color to white.

> Alternatively, you can turn the line off by using the Pen tool, and select the None radio button. The idea is to create a gray box with no visible outline.

Shrink the box vertically to about three-eighths inch. This gray box gets placed at the tippy-top of the first box, so that it sits just inside the first box's black outline. See Figure 3.5.

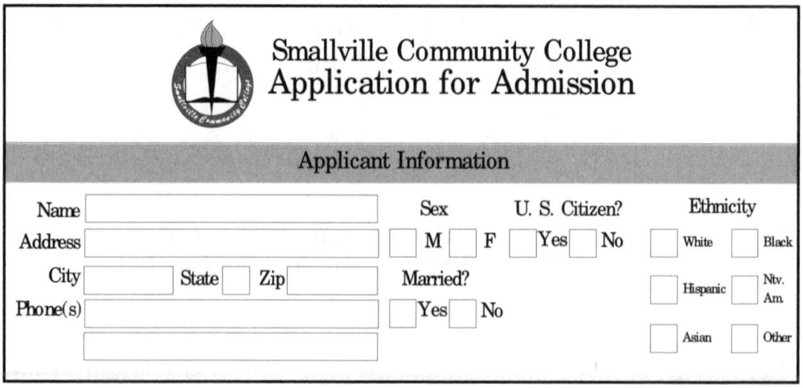

Figure 3.5 Here's the first information block.

Make a label for this information block—call it, say, *Applicant Information*. Place that label on the gray box, and selecting both, use the Align command to center these, then group the two together.

Use the Typeface tool to change the typeface to a 12-point font, and turn off the Bold option in the Styles dialog. Then use the Text tool to make labels for the various fields in the Applicant Information box—name, address, and so on, as shown in Figure 3.5. Also make the labels for the check boxes.

Finally, make the check box. Get another square symbol, and set its fill to none, leaving a clear box with a black border. Make that box about a quarter-inch high. Copy it, and make the copy a quarter-inch square.

The rest of the work on this box is a matter of laying things out. Make copies of the various boxes, set up the sizes, and use the Align command (^N) as you move the various elements into place, as shown in Figure 3.5.

Setting Up the Applicant Background Block Setting up the second information block on paper brings up a difference between paper forms and screen forms. The on-screen data-entry form has scrolling fields; you can't do that on paper. These are among the more trivial items that try people's souls.

Begin by making the block. Copy the block outline and gray header with its text from the first block. Select the text, and use the Text tool to replace the text with *Applicant Background*. See Figure 3.6.

The information contained in the scrollable fields is collected in the paper form in what is called (by Delrina, the popular form-making software vendor, at least) a *comb*. Make this comb by filling a box of the appropriate width with some lines (made with the Straight Line tool) to separate the related elements.

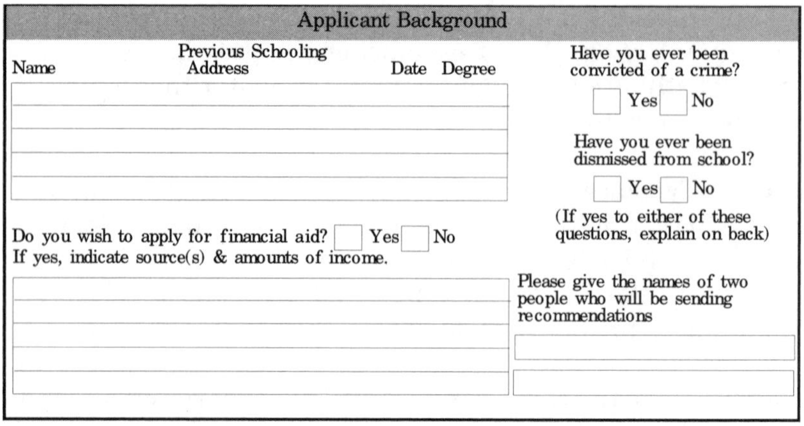

Applicant Background

Name	Previous Schooling Address	Date	Degree	Have you ever been convicted of a crime?

□ Yes □ No

Have you ever been dismissed from school?

□ Yes □ No

(If yes to either of these questions, explain on back)

Do you wish to apply for financial aid? □ Yes □ No
If yes, indicate source(s) & amounts of income.

Please give the names of two people who will be sending recommendations

Figure 3.6   Here's the second information block in the SCC application form.

Finishing the Admissions Form   The last two blocks of information are for the student's signature and the Admissions Committee's decision. They look like Figure 3.7.

Whistle While You Work

However quotidian form design may be, it is nevertheless an important business application of design. Neat, attractive forms make work go faster.

Applicant Signature

I certify that the information on this form is correct and hereby apply for admission to Smallville Community College.

(Return this form with the nonrefundable application fee in the supplied envelope.)

Signature   Date

Admissions Commitee Action

□ Admit   □ Admit – probation   □ Not admitted

For the committee

Figure 3.7   Here are the last two blocks of the admissions application.

Then too, this exercise illustrates something about judgment in design. The most obvious example of this is the choice of gray fields as the headers for each of the blocks. Many form designers choose black with white lettering (this is called *reverse* printing—white-on-black instead of black-on-white). In my judgment, that is harsh to look at and gains nothing. But this is entirely a matter of taste. The way I organized the information is also a matter of taste.

In the next projects, taste becomes all-important.

Project 4: Presentation Graphics

Presentation graphics covers all those nifty pictures that support speakers—making business presentations, mostly, but also such things as General Schwarzkopf's briefings a couple of wars ago. Almost certainly, most of the images generated on desktop computers have been presentation graphics; this was the first area, almost a decade ago, where desktop graphics played big.

Types of Presentation Graphics

Presentation graphics can take several forms.

Large printed charts on an easel have been around for a long time. Charts on an easel work well when the presenter has a staff person to change the charts. Charts are the best option when you don't know what the setup is in a new place. But charts are unwieldy, and they are not cheap to make (figure $12 to $15 per square foot).

Another traditional favorite is 35mm slides. Desktop computer systems are nearly ideal for creating slides. Slides are wonderfully colorful, they are transportable, and a standard carousel holds a lot of images—enough for a long presentation. Slide shows can be changed fairly easily, and you can mix standard sets with audience-specific sets. (See Project 5 for more on slides.)

A desktop film recorder, such as the Polaroid Digital Palette, can print a 2,000-line slide in less than 3 minutes, and a very crisp 4,000-line slide in 5 to 7 minutes. Service bureaus can produce still higher resolutions using top-performing film recorders such as Management Graphics Solitaire (also the darling of the special-effects studios) and the Agfa Forté. A 4,000-line slide projects well enough in a large room on a large screen that everyone can see it clearly. (See Appendix A for more on film recorders.)

The problem with slides is that the room generally has to be dim. Darkened rooms are soporific. Add a dull speaker, a dull topic, or dull slides—or a combination of all three (entirely possible)—and you are sure to hear snoring.

Until recently, overhead projection was the best choice for presentations to small and midsize groups. First, the equipment is readily available and sufficiently low-tech that maintaining it in running order was a simple matter. Second, overhead foils could be processed in all sorts of ways. Even UNIX users could do it (not elegantly, generally speaking—but even a UNIX jock can put a piece of copy-machine-compatible film in a laser printer). The room didn't need the lights dimmed—overhead projection works reasonably well in normal light. The images are generally readable. Finally, the cost is low, and the technology didn't require either an expensive film recorder or a service-bureau connection (also not cheap).

The new gimmick in presentation support involves the use of a small notebook computer as the projector. Plug in a converter (a VGA-to-NTSC box, which costs about $400 to $500), and most of these highly portable computers can drive a TV monitor. Plug in a special color LCD panel (not cheap—about $3,000 for a good one), and the images can be projected using a standard overhead projector.

All of these strategies have their place. All of them except the last can be executed using A&L Draw.

Doing a presentation from the computer generally requires the use of a program that can read the images and send them to the screen. A&L Draw doesn't include such a program. Other popular (but more costly) PC/Windows graphics programs—such as Micrografx Designer and Corel Draw—include such software. Another option is to secure a program that can accept images in a variety of formats and make a screen show from them—such as Brightbill-Roberts' venerable Show Partner.

However, if you are going to be doing lots of presentations, and you want to explore computer-based presenting, you are a candidate for one of the specialized presentation-graphics programs. There are many to choose from, and each has special features.

The main features that set presentation-graphics programs apart from general-purpose graphics software (other than the ability to generate PC screen shows) are the ability to make number-driven business charts, to automate the standard formats used in presentations (bulleted lists, tables, charts, and special illustrations), and to provide rudimentary leave-behinds and note sheets.

I confess that I use these specialized programs for some presentation sets. But I am just as likely to use a general-purpose program if I want complex graphics or if I want more sophisticated composition options.

Making a Good Presentation

Let's talk. Making a good presentation isn't a natural skill, and the rules do need to be discussed. The rules are simple enough, but you wouldn't know it from the number of awful presentations that are given. I have to sit through presentations; the following section is pure self-interest.

What's the Purpose?

When setting up a presentation, be clear what the purpose is. You have data to lay before the audience, but there is also an interpretation to which you believe that data leads (or at least, to which you wish your audience to believe it leads).

Visual Impact

If the presentation is live—that is, a real person is doing the talking, with the images as support material—it is essential that the graphics don't distract from the presenter's interpretive discourse.

This can be a problem: It is easy for a designer to make images that are visually stunning, so that an audience pays attention to design issues and ignores the message. That is a big-time no-no! That is a case where the medium becomes the message, as the saying goes.

On the other hand, one company that specializes in making presentation graphics for presenters has convincingly documented its claim that a presenter has about 8 seconds to make any given point. If the audience members aren't paying attention at that point, they start wondering if that's a gravy stain on your tie (or, are those pearls real?) and thinking about other things outside the subject of the presentation. That short initial-impact period means that substantial visual impact is important.

The Windows Notepad icon

Balancing between the need for impact, without the impact becoming a distraction from the overall goal of the presentation, is a matter of judgment consistent with the issues raised in Project 3.

Begin setting up a presentation by making some notes. The ideal tool for that purpose is Windows Notepad—one of the accessories that comes as part of the Windows package.

Whom Are You Talking To?

Be sensitive to the audience you are addressing. Different audiences respond to different kinds of presentation-support material.

Is your audience composed of technical experts in your field? They want hard facts, and they will not respond well to clever illustrations. Austerity tends to work better here.

A more general audience, including people not generally familiar with the technical aspects of your topic, may need more whimsical illustrations. These graphics can provide a change of pace, letting people take a breather so they can better absorb the hard data and interpretive material.

By all means, if you are planning a long presentation (over 20 minutes), build in a short break every 15 to 20 minutes or so. Use a contrasting image to tell people that a break has been declared.

Some audiences like what would normally be considered bad presentations. Amy Wohl, a well-known consultant and speaker on information technology, commented in a column that MIS pros wanted to be overwhelmed with material they didn't really understand. There is no substitute for figuring out what the audience thinks makes a good presentation; there is also no accounting for taste.

Just the Facts—But Don't Skimp on 'Em

The assumption is that a person making a presentation has command of the hard data on the subject. Most of the time, the assumption is justified.

The other assumption is that the presenter has sufficient judgment to assemble that data into facts.

Facts are composed of data and an interpretive judgment.

The trick is to get all the facts before the audience; you rarely have time to present all the data. There is a tendency to skip some kinds of factual information that could make the story being told come alive for the audience. Often, *those* facts would make the case.

Say you are making a presentation on sales. You chart the sales figures for the year. You compare them with figures for last year on a layered chart. One salesperson has been particularly effective, and you have learned she is *brilliant* at working the phones. So, add a picture of this star; combine it with text saying something like "Why is Ms. X a standout salesperson? She logs more customer calls."

Ms. X feels great—she's been recognized. The senior-management types get an important message about Ms. X, but also about the importance of phone use.

Plan Like Crazy!

Remember high-school writing drills? You learned to make outlines? If you never use them elsewhere, use an outline of some kind when making a presentation.

Specialized presentation-graphics software usually has a built-in outliner linked to the graphics part of the program. Make the outline, and the software automatically translates that into slides. Windows Notepad works as well in many cases.

Keep the notes simple; this makes it easier to translate them into slides. Generally, for any major item (a slide topic), you list only three or four subitems. If you have more subitems, it is time to break the larger topic down into components.

Different speakers use different formats for outlines. Some prefer greatly detailed outlines; others prefer a list of talking points.

Whichever you choose, you want this to be the foundation of a script. A simple script inserts a name or picture of the visual with the text or talking points that relate to it. This script is doubly important if someone else is managing the visuals; it becomes a list of cues when to change the picture.

Notice something important: What is on the slide is *not* the same as what the presenter says. Nothing is so deadly—and so common an error!—as to put the slide on the screen, then turn to look at it and read it off.

Do the note-taking first—*before* you make the images.

Making the Slides

With a good working plan in hand, it is time to set up the slides. The working plan guides you in two ways.

First, the working plan provides the material from which text slides are made. Most slides used in a presentation are bulleted lists—the main topics around which you organize the presentation.

Second, the working plan makes clear when it is important to put in a visual that is *not* merely text—a chart, a picture, a combination of things. It can also suggest when a digression might be important. If a presenter really has the pulse of the target group, it might even forewarn when embarrassing questions are likely to come up—for which you can be forearmed.

The working plan also suggests how to make more interesting visuals. For example, if you are making a set of 35mm slides or a computer-managed show, special effects and build sequences can be effective tools for keeping the audience awake and attentive.

By the way, build sequences and special effects are virtually impossible with overhead foils. But you can *write* on overhead foils.

Along the way, as images are made, you think through important design considerations: What will unify the presentation? How are different elements in the presentation set apart? How long is the presentation (talking time per slide is about three to five minutes)? How does the slide fit with the discussion to hold audience attention? What kind(s) of leave-behinds will extend the presentation?

Most business presentations rarely last longer than 30 minutes, with 20 minutes an average time. Most presentation topics take a couple hours to get across. The leave-behind material enables you to increase your access from 20 minutes to 2 hours.

The presentation proper sets the listener up; the leave-behind material should have a deal-closing capability.

Rehearse and Prepare

When the images are finished, a smart presenter does a dry run or two to check the way the whole thing flows—images and discussion taken together.

On the day of the presentation, the presenter arrives early enough to see that things are set up—that the presentation platform, for example, doesn't obscure the screen. Check lighting. Check to see a projector creates a screen-size image. Make sure audience seating is arranged so people can see. If written material is part of the presentation, seating means tables as well as chairs—and pencils! If the session is going to be a long one, water should be available—for the presenter, of course, but also for the audience. And so on.

The best-run operations—corporate or hotel—have a facilities manager whose job it is to see that things like this are taken care of. A really competent facilities manager can deliver an ideal setup for anything from a 20-minute meeting in the conference room down the hall, to a week-long conference. These people are the Perle Mestas of the corporate world, and they are gold! If you are fortunate, you have such a person available to help you, and you consult long and hard with this person—and the name and facility goes in your Rolodex, and you send flowers.

Presentation Checklist

❏ What's the purpose?
❏ Who's the audience?
❏ What are the facts?
❏ What is the plan?
❏ Create the images.
❏ REHEARSE!
❏ Check the site.
❏ Present!

Success!

If a presenter covers all these steps (and there are times when that simply isn't possible), there is a good chance that the presentation will influence the audience for whom it is intended.

That is the purpose of the exercise.

Making the Images

Of course, this is not a book about making presentations; the focus is on making the images that support presentations.

That begins with the creation of a background template. An effective background—with variant formats for different kinds of information—lends unity to the whole enterprise.

The background template also determines how much information can appear in a given image. A complex background will accommodate less information. The background elements take up more space, leaving less room for text, charts, or pictures.

A simple background provides more space for information, since there are fewer elements taking up space. That can be a liability: Don't be tempted to fill the screen with too much information.

The trick is to strike a balance.

The simplest background—some color with a title—was used to make the overhead foil for President Murray Hill, to support his presentation of the organization chart in Project 1. That was OK as a first effort, but frankly, it was far from brilliant.

But the academic world is conservative and would not appreciate too strong a presentation, anyway.

Background Templates

Hansel Grunder is the president of Acme Fardels, Inc. (fardels are bundles of twigs). The company is coming up on its IPO (initial public offering of stock), and Mr. Grunder is about to make the definitive presentation to a bunch of fardel-industry analysts. It is important to the success of the IPO that this presentation impress industry analysts with Acme's marketing savvy in a tough economy. It has to be clear that Acme has a brilliantly conceived fardel product line, priced attractively, that will sell well. It is also important that these analysts come away with the sense that Acme Fardels has a strong financial position and is an attractive investment opportunity.

Acme Fardels is known to the marketplace by the attractive Acme Fardels, Inc. logo—a deep, rich red background, with a bold, twinkling gold *ACME,* a fardel bound up with a red ribbon, and the words *Fardels, Inc.* in white. See Figure 4.1. This logo has achieved a degree of recognition, and Hansel is rather proud of it. His kid designed it, and it won a prize in the local high-school art contest. In fact, the kid used A&L Draw; it was saved in a separate file, then exported as a Windows Metafile. In this format, it can be used with almost any Windows application, including other A&L Draw designs.

Figure 4.1   This is the black-and-white version of Hansel Grunder's logo.

On the other hand, this is going to be a low-tech presentation. There just aren't that many fardel-industry analysts, so Hansel has invited them to a fairly nice luncheon to be catered in the boardroom in the Acme Building. The presentation will be done using overhead-projection foils as support material. Your job: To make the presentation materials.

The job could be done with predesigned laser-printable overhead foils. They are commonly available from desktop-publishing houses such as Paper Direct. The company can even supply coordinated paper for the leave-behinds.

The advantages are obvious; the disadvantages are legion. The most important objection is that the presentation will lack the special character of being an ACME Fardels presentation, because stock templates always look like stock items. The second objection is the lack of color control.

For this presentation, a Fargo color wax thermal-transfer printer is an excellent choice. It makes elegant overhead foils in full color. Rather than using the standard Fargo Windows driver, I'd choose the Zenographics SuperPrint driver. This gives you access to SuperQueue, and that means you can eventually print the foils as a single job, in the background, with greater facility than you could with the standard Windows print manager system.

Begin by using the Color tool to get the color chart on the screen, and set it so it will stay there with the Stay option from the pull-down menu. While you're at it, turn on the Show Names option as well, so you can see different colors by name.

This is a presentation for industry analysts. A very cautious choice would be a deep blue, but that might be *too* conservative. Acme Fardels is forging ahead into a new incarnation as a publicly held company. Some of that should come through as well. A blue shade, but not too blue, might be effective. Shade 100-050-025-012 is a good choice for this. Like the deeper saturated blues, it qualifies as a dark color, and therefore it is a good background color. It is vivid and not particularly tranquil in effect—it has something electric in it. At the same time, it is not startlingly energetic.

Use the Symbol tool to get a square, and fill it with this color and without an outline (set the line color to white or choose None from the Pen tool dialog box). Place the square on the page, and stretch it to fill the page completely.

Let's liven this up a bit more. Get another square, and fill it with a bright sea green—shade 100-000-025-000. Make this square into a broad stripe along the right side of the blue background, about three-quarters of an inch wide, running top to bottom.

Import the Acme logo Metafile (ACMELOGO.WMF is supplied on the disk). Place it in the lower right corner, on top of the sea-green stripe, and size it so it is about 2 inches wide and 1 inch deep. Move the sea-green stripe so it is centered behind the logo. See the left-hand pattern in Figure 4.2.

This is not bad, and it might do as is. Or, you might want to try a variation.

Move the vertical stripe to the left side. Slim it down to about a quarter inch or so. Copy it (or make a new square, filled with the same sea-green color), and make it a broad horizontal stripe. Place the logo at the lower right, on top of the horizontal stripe. See the right-hand pattern in Figure 4.2.

Each of these patterns has advantages. I like both of them. With the single-stripe version, you have to be a bit more attentive to how text and graphics are placed. The two-stripe version is a bit more conservative. I'd go for the two-stripe version—conservative looks good right now.

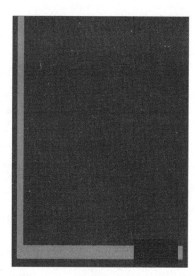

Figure 4.2 Here are two patterns for an overhead foil background template.

A couple comments on color: An old jingle starts, "Blue and green should ne'er be seen." The background template uses blue and green together; is this a mistake?

Not so, given the shade chosen. It is a cool green—somewhat out of the ordinary, refreshing, but not a startling color, with a goodly amount of blue in it. Notice the blue. It is rich, but it is not overly quieting. The cool sea green should have a slightly calming effect— toning the blue field down a bit, without diminishing the aggressive character of this shade of blue.

Still, the sea green contrasts nicely with the blue. It works well with the exciting, rather passionate red background of the Acme Fardels logo.

Color is very important in this kind of thing. You must play a kind of head game—psychology—with the audience. Learning to play that game is not simple, and risks are involved. Nor can this psychology of color be entirely quantified, so the risks remain fuzzy.

Look at some of the excellent books on the psychology of color. The Lüscher Color Test is commonly available; it's intended as a psychological test, but you can ignore the testing theory and simply think through the implications of Dr. Lüscher's observations about color. You're well advised to look at some of these books, and also such online guides as Pantone's ColorUp or MediaNet's Show-Starter (a complete adviser on presentation setup). However, nothing substitutes for judgment and taste.

Save the template in a file (call it TMPLT1.GED). Then, save the file again (use the Save As option on the File menu), and call that file something like ACME1.GED. This keeps the template design inviolate and opens a copy with the template ready to use.

If you view all pages (^3 hot key), Draw displays four pages. So you have a choice for developing the slide series: You can develop each slide in a single file, or you can put up to four 8½ by 11-inch slides in a file.

For overhead-projection foils, this is not a crucial choice. Generally, the sequence is not so tight that having four slides in a file is all that useful. In programs such as Micrografx Designer or (to a lesser extent, for speed considerations) Corel Draw, where the number of pages available is considerably greater, doing the whole show in one or two files is a real plus.

With 35mm slides, as you shall see, setting up four slides per file can make the design process a lot easier. For the time being, let's keep to a single image in a file for overhead foils.

The Agenda Slide

The game plan for the Acme presentation calls for invited industry analysts to be received in the outer office of the Acme Fardels executive suite by Hansel and his sister

(Gretl, CFO and also a major stockholder). After white wine and designer water with the *de rigueur* pigs-in-a-blanket *hors d'oeuvres* while waiting for everyone to arrive and get cozy, folks troop into the boardroom.

Personally, I *hate* to walk into a presentation and see a blank screen. I prefer that there be something decorative on the screen—sort of a backdrop—or some kind of agenda slide. The Acme folks have chosen the latter option.

Creating the Title An agenda slide is a list with a title. The best title is *Agenda;* everyone knows what that means, and the purpose is to get the information across while people settle into their first course, a fruit cup.

Set the lettering to one of the A&L outline typefaces. Of the typefaces supplied with A&L Draw, only two are suited to presentation graphics:

- Classic is all right, but for bold displays it looks wimpy.

- Modern comes in two varieties (useful), and it is strong, clean, readable, and all sorts of other good things.

Choose Modern Heavy for titles and Modern Medium for text, and you won't go far wrong. When you are using Modern Heavy use the Pen tool to set the line to None. This makes the text a bit less bold.

Set the color to a nice yellow. The background is dark, so the foreground—text, in this case—has to shout a bit. A primary yellow is a good, simple choice. Cyan is another option, but it loses effect because of the sea-green stripes. You might think red would work; it won't, because red is really a *dark* color and has sufficient contrast only on a very light background. Pastel shades sometimes present a problem; pastels tend to look muddy on some backgrounds. In the present case, a paler yellow might prove effective (try shade 000-000-050-000).

Another consideration: What will your printer do with these colors? The screen uses a different technique to display color than do most color printers.

Use the Text tool to enter the word *Agenda*. Place it at the top, perhaps somewhat to the left. Stretch it so it is about 72-point type (or, with the text selected, use the Typeface tool to change the font size in the Type Attributes dialog box). The label should be about 1 inch high and 4 inches wide.

When I was setting up the type for this label, the outline was turned off. That made the type a bit less bold, and the letters a bit clearer, in my judgment. Still, it would be nice to make that title stand out more. Titles are ideal places for *drop shadows*—which may or may not drop.

Use the Copy tool to make a copy of the *Agenda* label slightly up and to the left of the original label. Then use the Pointer tool to select the original. Change its color to black. The black shadow (which, depending on several factors, can be any appropriate color or shade of gray), offset behind the label, gives an illusion of depth. See Figure 4.3.

Creating the List of Topics Create the list of items for the agenda list. Set the typeface to Modern Medium at 48 points, using the Typeface tool. Turn the outline on for this lighter typeface (use the Pen tool to change None to a solid line). Then use the Text tool to enter a series of items, with a blank line between each. (This is the short way to do this; for other lists, you'll use a one-at-a-time approach.)

Figure 4.3   A drop shadow—in this case, offset to the right and down—gives the label a bit more oomph.

Place the text on the background. While it is still selected, pick a color for this text. The choice I made might surprise you—a very pale lavender shade (012-012-000-000). This background shade is light enough to stand out well, and not so vivid as the yellow I chose. Choosing this color scheme, I have made a statement about what is essential (the label *Agenda*) and what is subordinate (the list of events).

One last element: Bullets. Folks expect them, and they emphasize the list character of this kind of a slide. For the bullet, I chose a triangle on its side from the Symbol tool, with the point toward the text. It looks a little like an arrow, without being too arrowlike. The color is the same as for the list text. Shrink the bullet so that it is the same size or a tad smaller than the capital letters at the beginning of each line. Then move it to a position to the left of the text, and make copies with the Copy tool, one for each item on the list.

The completed agenda is shown in Figure 4.4.

Figure 4.4   Here's the completed agenda foil for the Acme Fardels IPO presentation.

Some other programs allow compensation for this kind of color change through a printer-calibration routine.

Save the file, and run a couple test prints—one on paper and another on an overhead-transparency foil. Notice that some of the colors change. In particular, using this printer and this driver, the colors rich in blue tend to be darker on the prints than they were on the screen. In particular, the sea-green stripe is substantially muted. As it happens, the results with this combination aren't too bad.

In a lighted room, using an overhead projector, this slide will project well, and it should have some real punch. The look goes beyond the standard, boring bright yellow on dark blue that is the sign of the novice. At the same time, it is not an aggressive design.

The Welcome Text Slide

At a meeting like the Acme Fardels IPO presentation, inevitably someone (almost always someone junior to the most important presenter) plays host and introduces the rest of the team. Acme is unconventional; Hansel himself will say the words of welcome and introduce presenters for the company overview (sister Gretl) and for the industry overview (Griselda LaStrega, president of Griselda's Goodies Confectionery Company—famous for gingerbread—and a member of the Acme Fardels board).

Making the slide for the introductions is simple. First, use the Save As command on the File menu to save the first slide under another name (save ACME1.GED as ACME2.GED).

The newly named version—ACME2.GED—becomes the version to work on. If for one reason or another things get messy, the fallback is to open the original template and start from scratch. Since colors for text elements have already been set in the first slide, it is easier to change text elements than to have to remember the particular shades you used.

Revising the Title So first thing, use the little-finger Group tool to grab all those text elements, then drag them over to the empty window to the right.

Select the *Agenda* shadow text (the black text). Use the Text tool to replace it with the word *Welcome*. Then select the *Agenda* foreground text (in yellow). Again, use the Text tool to replace it with *Welcome*. This way, the shadow and foreground text elements stay in the same relative positions, while the title is changed for the new slide.

Use the Pointer tool to select the whole label (shadow and foreground), and drag the whole thing back to its proper position at the top left of the new slide.

Revising the Body Text A simple way to handle the body text would be to take the list of items from the old slide and replace it with the new text. There is a better, more effective way.

Select the list of items. Use the Typeface tool to change the typeface to Modern Heavy, and set its alignment to Centered. (Things look better to me if I set the Pen tool dialog to None, turning off the type outlines.) The block changes to bolder type, centered. Use the Text tool to replace the text in this block with *Hansel Grunder*.

Copy this block twice. Then, replace one of the blocks with the name *Griselda LaStrega* and the other with *Gretl Grunder*.

Go back up to the Hansel Grunder text block. Copy that block using the Copy tool and dragging down to just below Hansel's name. Use the Typeface tool to change this block to Modern Medium, and, using the Styles button, change the style to italic. You can leave the text at 48 points, or you can change it to 36 points, as I did, to make sure there is enough space for things. See Figure 4.5.

Hansel Grunder
CEO, Acme Fardels, Inc.

Figure 4.5   This is more or less the way the introduction items set up in the Welcome slide.

Use the Copy tool to make copies of this smaller, lighter type-face element, placing one just above and one just below the name elements of Griselda and Gretl.

Replace the text in the box above Griselda's name with *Industry Overview;* replace the text in the box under her name with *CEO, Griselda's Goodies* and, on a second line, *Member, Acme Fardels board.*

Replace the text in the box above Gretl's name with *Company Overview;* replace the text in the box under her name with *CFO, Acme Fardels.*

As you go along, use the Group tool (the little finger) to select each of these name and title groups. Then align them verti-cally (^N) and group them (^G).

Finally, adjust the spacing and the alignment of the three groups so they fill the slide nicely, with decent amounts of space between them. See Figure 4.6. And of course, save the slide before printing to the color printer.

Figure 4.6   Here's the completed Welcome slide.

A Slide with a Chart

The lunch item on the agenda doesn't require slides. But Griselda's Industry Overview requires slides, and they have to contain charts.

Whoops! A&L Draw does not have a chart-making module. This could appear to be a problem. Not so; in fact, it may be a blessing. Some chart-making modules are more trouble than they are worth—and they make rather miserable charts, to boot.

First things first: Let's get the slide ready.

Actually, many outside presenters come with their own slides, in their own design. This can be good, or it can be a disaster. If the presenter is fairly good, the slides will be elegant and will represent a tasteful change of pace in the show.

More often, the presenter will have miserable slides, and they will prove more soporific than the ones you have prepared.

In this case, since Griselda is a good friend, Hansel has had her slides made to match the rest of the presentation. He is a wise man—especially since Griselda would have used her rather too-sweet logo in slides of her own making.

Revising the Title Take the ACME2.GED slide, rename it as ACME3.GED with the Save As command from the File menu, and delete the text. Use more or less the same procedure you used in the previous section to change the title—shadow and foreground—to *Industry Overview*. Since this text will be too large to fit on one line, make it a two-line title. See Figure 4.7.

Creating a Chart Fine, now for the chart. The assumption—and it is a good one—is that you have one of the Windows spreadsheet programs. For the purposes of this exercise, I am

Industry Overview

Figure 4.7　This is the two-line Industry Overview title.

using Microsoft Excel. I could equally well use Lotus 1-2-3 for Windows or another program. I could also use a stand-alone chartmaking program, such as Delta Graph. Since the chart is a fairly simple one, and Excel has a good charting module, it does just what I want, easily and quickly.

Open Excel (or whatever spreadsheet you choose). On the blank spreadsheet that comes up, create a data set. On the first line, starting with the second column, put in some dates (in the example, *1990* through *1994 to date*). On the second line, put the sales figures (in thousands) for Acme Fardels. On the third line, put the overall industry sales figures for the same periods. Then, use your spreadsheet's charting procedure to generate an area chart, as shown in Figure 4.8. Area charts are ideal for showing relative performance.

Clean up the chart a bit: Change the text, for example, to something better than the default MSSans, and deep-six the hot-key labels on the areas along with the legend. Then, with only the chart selected, use the Copy command in the Edit menu to put the chart on the Windows clipboard.

Use one of the standard Windows procedures (there are several—the most common is Alt-Tab) to flip through open applications until A&L Draw pops up on your screen.

Simply use the Paste command on the Edit menu in Draw to move the chart from the Windows clipboard into your ACME3.GED file. Save the enhanced version.

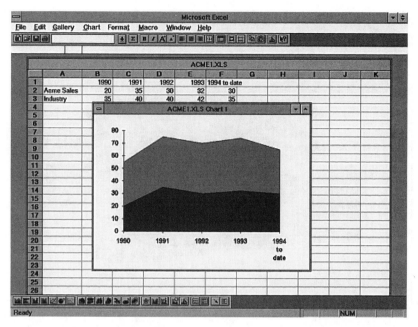

Figure 4.8   Creating a chart in Excel is simple. The data set is at the top, in the spreadsheet proper, and the chart has simply been dropped on top of the spreadsheet.

Are there limits to this procedure? Certainly. First, spreadsheets place severe limits on color choices. No elegant designer palette is available, and type choices are similarly limited.

Against these limitations, spreadsheet-chart makers are easy to use and remarkably able. All the major chart styles are quickly available. The chart stays tightly coupled to data. And so on. In Excel, this mostly involves pushing the buttons on the button bars—that's how I produced the 3-D version shown in Figure 4.9.

Whatever. It is still important not to rely entirely on the spreadsheet-chart maker for everything. Do some of the labeling in Draw, where you can more readily control type size and the like. In this case, it is a good idea to label the two

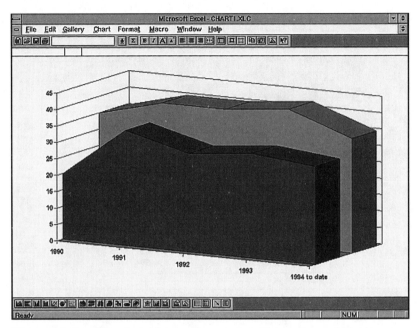

Figure 4.9   Here's a three-dimensional version of the Acme-to-industry comparison chart.

sections of the chart—the industry section and the Acme Fardels section—and to give the chart as a whole a title—say, Share of Market. Finally, add an interpretive remark: *Acme consistently provides more than half the fardels sold in the domestic market.* See Figure 4.10.

Not too shabby. Save this file, and print it.

Chart Slides and Table Slides

Gretl Grunder has a more complex job. She needs to present both nice charts and nice tables.

Tables are, sadly, hard to do in A&L Draw. There isn't a simple solution. My own procedure in this case involved collecting the information for the table in Excel, copying the appropriate lines to the clipboard, pasting them into the

Learn Desktop Graphics and Design on the PC

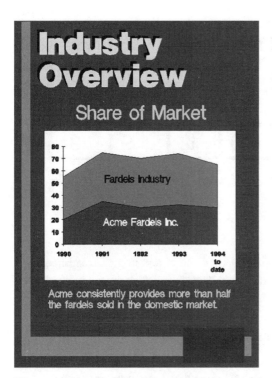

Figure 4.10   A chart from Excel fits nicely in an A&L Draw slide.

A&L Draw Text dialog box, and more or less manually adjusting spacing and type size on the fly.

Finally, after the data is in place, use the Symbol tool to add a square; turn the fill off by setting the Fill dialog to None. Add some straight lines to make a grid, and you have a table, as shown in Figure 4.11.

The matter is a bit more complex, because the Paste command from the Draw menu bar is not available. You can use the generic Windows Paste hot-key combination, ^Ins (that is, hold the Control key and press the Insert key to paste).

	1990	1991	1992	1993	1994
Assets	20	35	30	32	30
Cash	5	10	10	10	12
Liabilities	16	10	12	9	9

Figure 4.11   This is the table for the Acme Fardels financial presentation.

Thus, the procedure is to mark the line of text in the spreadsheet and copy it to the clipboard with Shift-Insert. Switch to A&L Draw and open the Text dialog with the Text tool. Paste the text with ^Ins. Then adjust the spacing between words or numbers, removing the tabs between items and substituting spaces. Add the text to the evolving chart, and then go back and adjust as need be.

This procedure is not elegant. Without the use of the spreadsheet, you could probably build the chart just as fast and with about the same amount of work. The only advantage to using the spreadsheet is that it collects all the information in one place.

To make the table more graphic, and if the data is in your spreadsheet, you might want to graph the data from the table and add the graph to the slide. With an overhead foil, there is plenty of space to do this. Choose a line chart (rather than bars or areas), and let your chart-making software generate a legend. Then paste it down, and size it to match the table. See Figure 4.12.

The result is appealing, and it makes the story clear. Gretl has a nice visual to support her presentation of the company finances. It is likely that, should the analysts get bored, they will spend some time looking at the pictures.

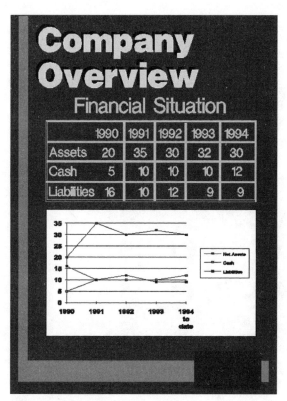

Figure 4.12   Here's the Acme Fardels financial picture.

Other Uses for Overhead Foils

I use foils like these in my own presentations when a computer is not available. For example, in many colleges where I have taught—even today—I cannot count on finding a connection for my notebook computer. Overhead foils are a solution that almost always works. They are also handy in presentations where you need to be able to add comments (such as during a Q&A session). You can write on the foil's jacket, or else put another clear foil on top and write on that.

I sometimes find I use black and white, much as I prefer color. For example, in my advertising classes, I need to show

Figure 4.13   These old-time ads are surprisingly durable teaching aids.

early print ads, which are inevitably in black and white. See Figure 4.13.

For these black-and-white images, I tend to use an inkjet printer rather than the Fargo wax thermal-transfer printer. For color overhead foils, it depends on how elaborate the image is. Also, a scanned image sometimes comes through better when it's printed using an inkjet printer.

No Color Printer?

So you don't have a color printer? You do have options.

First, you could get a color printer. Several models work fine for both day-to-day black-and-white printing and occasional color printing. They are also useful for testing designs intended for color-process printing, since they apply the same CMYK color model in creating their output.

Hewlett-Packard and Canon offer color inkjet models that are affordable and always coming down in price. Star Micronics has a color thermal-transfer printer that is modestly priced and does nice standard printing along with high-quality color printing. If you want to have your cake and eat it too, the Fargo color wax thermal-transfer printer is not expensive, and it is possibly the easiest color printer to use of any I have tried. A modestly priced option adds dye-sublimation printing—a knock-your-socks-off photorealistic printing option normally out of reach in desktop graphics setups.

Another option is to have your transparencies produced by a service bureau. Many shops offer excellent service, with one-day turnaround. Most can take your files and process them for you; in many cases, you can send the files over a telephone line, using a modem.

When you are dealing with a service bureau, make sure you have a conversation about the files the bureau likes to receive. Some want the basic file from your application; this is particularly true if the shop uses the same software you are using. Otherwise, the shop may want you to send a general-purpose file that can work with software it likes. Common formats to consider are encapsulated PostScript (.EPS) and Windows Metafile (.WMF).

A&L Draw supports both .EPS and .WMF formats for export. It also supports some others that are less useful these days. TIFF output is helpful only in desktop-publishing applications, and CGM is an artifact of older days. The only variant you might use is the CALS format, which some branches of the Federal government prefer.

When you are exporting from A&L Draw, be aware of some important limitations. The most important limitation has to do with included graphics, such as the charts imported from Excel. In a word, Draw won't export them. If your images include imported elements, and you must use a service bureau, find one that has A&L software (any one of the family will do). Or, get the bureau to buy a copy (preferably with this book); it's cheap enough. Or something. Then you can give the shop the original A&L .GED file.

Keep It Simple

Most presentations are genuinely simple affairs. Most do not require more than you have seen demonstrated in this chapter. In fact, you want to be extra careful before making things much more complex. It is very easy to make presentation-support images that distract from the presentation.

On the other hand, some advanced techniques can make a presentation stronger—nothing elaborate, mind you, and much better tuned to 35mm slides than overhead-projection foils.

Those techniques, and the special considerations involved in making slides from the computer, are the subject of the next project.

Project 5:
Slides and Scans

Once upon a time, the only practical way to graphically support a presentation to a group of more than, say, 20 people was to use 35mm slides. In those long-ago days (say, eight years ago), major PR (public-relations) firms had major profit-center sidelines, using special slide-making graphic-design systems that cost something like a quarter million dollars a seat. The slides were expensive—and really nice!

Desktop computer graphics changed all that rather quickly. Prices dropped. The technology changed somewhat. But 35mm slides remain a wonderful medium for several reasons.

The foremost reason is absolutely gorgeous color. Making slides (and photographic prints, for that matter) is a photographic process. Depending on the film chemistry, different color values prevail and different effects are possible. Inevitably, the colors that result are richer than those produced by all but the most expensive printing processes.

By definition, all photographic output is *true color*. This means that all the possible colors an eye can see—and probably more besides—can be captured on film. Moreover, because of the way in which the chemistry works—and the way the information is passed to the camera from the computer— smooth color gradations are possible in a way that is harder to achieve in other output processes.

A high-quality 35mm slide can be projected onto a larger screen, to be viewed by a larger audience. It will appear much sharper than an overhead-projection foil simply because it is produced at a much higher relative resolution than any commonly available printer can produce a color overhead foil.

In short, color slides (and photographic prints) are way cool.

How Computers Make Photographs

Computers make photographs by using a special printing device called a *film recorder*. Think of this as a camera attached to a mechanism that changes computer data into patterns of light.

Essentially, the driver software in the computer accepts image information and converts it to three sets of data: one set each for red, green, and blue colors in the picture. This data is passed to the film recorder. The film recorder then puts this information, one color at a time, on a sort of color TV tube, one scan line at a time. At the right time, the camera's shutter is opened and the picture is painted on the film, one color and one line at a time.

The machine to do all this is not simple to make, and it is therefore not cheap. The faster and more able it is, the less cheap it is.

Desktop models, such as Polaroid's Digital Palette CI-5000, start around $6,000; you get a mechanism in a box about the size of a large shoe box, a 35mm camera back, an instant-print back (the basic kit comes with the one, and the second instant-print back should fit into that price as well), and the Polaroid-made equipment to process and mount Polaroid instant-slide film. Other entry-level film recorders are priced in the high-four to low-five figures.

I made test prints for this project using a Polaroid Digital Palette; it's my favorite because of its size and price.

The top-of-the-line products are major capital investments, intended for heavy-duty production environments. These are usually installed in service bureaus.

If you make lots of presentations, and you need (or want) to use color slides, then a desktop film recorder is a wise investment. It gives you control over some important time factors, among other things. If you need perfect, quality-color images to impress a client, film output is a good answer, and if volume dictates, a film recorder is a good investment.

Otherwise, find a good local service bureau and work with it.

I recommend a *local* service bureau, if possible, over one of the cheaper mail-away operations. If a local shop makes a boo-boo, you can deal with it face-to-face; if the shop is half a continent away, this is hard to do.

If your area has no local service bureau offering slide-making services, stick to major players. Autographx, in Boston, offers national service; you can easily arrange to have your credit card billed. Jack Ward Color Service, in New York, is well respected in the graphic-arts community. Both of these companies can receive data files over the telephone via modem, and both can arrange 24-hour turn-around.

Setting Up for Slides in A&L Draw

Perhaps the trickiest part of making slides is getting the measurements right. Slides do not have the same relative dimensions of length to height as a sheet of 8½ by 11-inch paper. This relative measurement (technically, the *aspect ratio*) has to be set correctly. If not, you stand a good chance of cutting off part of the picture when it comes time to print it on film. The effect is not unlike cutting off Aunt Tilly's head in those snapshots from long-ago summers.

A&L Draw makes this procedure a bit more complex, because it sets page-size information from the designated output device's driver. If you have a film recorder, this is fine, since you will have set it for the correct device. Bingo—the virtual-page dimensions are right there on screen.

Your *virtual* page will be *lots* bigger than the actual slide. A 35mm slide has dimensions too tiny to allow for the computer to zoom and pan and all that stuff. So, you work on a much larger virtual page of the correct aspect ratio, which is then scaled down automatically to the correct size at print time.

If you don't have a film recorder, you must set this page size another way. And to do this, you need to know what it is.

Here is the magic number: 11 by 7.334 inches. Write this down. Better: Jot it on a PostIt and stick it on the edge of your monitor.

And how, you ask me, do you set the 7.334-inch dimension? After all, the rulers are set to show inches in quarter- and eighth- and sixteenth-inch increments. It ain't hard, folks; 7.334 inches is equivalent to a smidgin more than $7\frac{5}{16}$ inches.

So, to begin: Open A&L Draw. If you have a film recorder, use the Printer Setup command on the File menu to select it. Make sure you have set the film recorder for slides, and bingo, you will have correctly sized pages. Save the file, call it something like SLIDE.GED, and keep it handy as a preset template for film-recorder output.

If you don't have a film recorder, set your machine to any printer you like. Use the Symbol tool to get a rectangle, and make it 11 inches wide and $7\frac{5}{16}$ inches deep. Turn the symbol outline off using the Pen tool. Save the file (as SLIDE.GED), and let this serve as your template.

Learn Desktop Graphics and Design on the PC

The Advanced Presentation Slide Set

Hansel, having made his presentation (see Project 4), decides he needs to take it on the road. Not enough of the industry analysts he wanted to convince came to lunch. He has decided he wants slides this time around, and he wants a real whiz-bang look.

Hansel could simply rearrange his current images. He could open them in A&L Draw, move things around, and shoot them out the back to his local service bureau. He could, but he doesn't. He will recover some of those slides, but a slide show is not an overhead-projection show, and his presentation is being made in different circumstances (a hotel meeting room, rather than the Acme boardroom; over continental breakfast, rather than lunch). Hansel is no dummy; he thinks through these issues and comes up with a different look suited to the different presentation circumstances.

Color Selection

The first thing that has to change is the color scheme. You've heard this before: Use dark backgrounds in slide shows at your peril! A dark slide in a dark room is soporific (unless the presenter is very dramatic).

To make life a trifle easier, I have prepared a color chart of some favorite combinations. It is printed in the color section of the book. It is also available, as COLORS.GED, on the disk.

By no means should you regard this file as the last word. Dozens of other possible color combinations will work well. And by no means should you trust the printed version. Process printing uses a different color-making rule than does either a screen or a film recorder. Look at the colors on your screen. Ideally, print the colors to a slide, and project them or look at them in a magnifying slide viewer.

Note also that I have included some color sets that might be considered risky. In particular, conventional wisdom is nervous with a green background, and the coral-red background might prove too dark—and too spicy!—for many situations.

Hansel, being a cautious soul, opts for a light-blue background. In fact, the light-blue color set in the chart is OK by him, but he decides to lighten the blue background a bit more.

First, he opens the color chart, and he uses the Group tool to pick the color set he likes. He then copies this to the Windows clipboard with a Copy command from the Edit menu.

Then he opens the slide template; he doesn't have his own film recorder, so this is a $7\frac{5}{16}$ by 11-inch box. Off to the right of this, he pastes the color set he is choosing. Since he wants to lighten that blue a bit, he uses the color tool to choose color 100-025-000-000 (instead of the 100-033-000-000 used in the color set). He then saves the slide template as SLIDE1.GED, to keep it as a template for this show. He saves it again under another name that will indicate that it is the first slide of the show (SHOW1.GED).

Text and charts and so on can readily be pasted onto this background as is. But that does not make for a custom look. In the presentation for Project 4, a contrasting stripe was added, along with the ACME logo. You can do that again—but slides, because of their vivid color, let you apply other, more interesting design elements.

Among the most interesting of these elements is to give the background *texture* with a nicely embossed or engraved pattern. This is fairly easy to do.

Embossed and Engraved Patterns

Let's do a dry run first. Scroll the A&L Draw screen down to an empty page. Use the Symbol tool to add a square. Use the Color tool to change this to a 40 percent gray fill. Set the Color tool to named colors and to stay on screen; you will be using it a lot. Use the Pen tool to set the line attribute to None.

Make your life easier in this part of the exercise: Use the Zoom tool to zoom in on an area about twice the size of the gray square.

Set the Typeface tool to A&L Draw's own typefaces, and select Bach—the typeface used for the Acme logo.

Add the word *ACME* to the screen using the text tool. Don't place it on the gray square. The reason is simple: I want you to fill this text with 40 percent gray, too, and if you put an unoutlined, 40 percent gray word on a 40 percent gray background, you won't be able to see it.

So, fill this first ACME with 60 percent gray—two shades darker than the background. Use the Copy tool to drag off a copy of ACME down and to the right—just a little bit, so the two copies overlap by at least half. Fill this second ACME with 20 percent gray. Use the Copy tool again to drag off another ACME, and fill it with 40 percent gray. Drag it up so it fits sort of in the middle between the darker and lighter ACMEs. Note the stacking order: Darker gray, lighter gray (offset right and down) and in-between gray (centered between the two on the diagonal). See Figure 5.1.

Figure 5.1   Two sets of ACMEs: The top one shows the stacking order described for engraving, and the bottom one is stacked for embossing. Compare with Figure 5.2.

Now comes something a little tricky. Use the Group tool to select the whole set of three ACMEs, and use the Copy tool to drag off a copy of the whole thing.

Then, click on the rearmost (darker) ACME, and change it to 20 percent gray. Click on the middle ACME, and change it to 60 percent gray. Leave the topmost ACME 40 percent gray.

Hint: The Current Color box in the Color tool indicators—both in the large color palette box and the little swatch by the Color tool in the toolbox—will change to the color of the selected object. Use that to tell you when you have selected the correct ACME.

Group each of these sets of ACMEs—one set with the rearmost ACME dark, the other set with the rearmost ACME light. Then drag each set up so it sits on the 40 percent gray square. Zoom out. You should now see that one group looks as if it is slightly sunken, and the other should look slightly raised. See Figure 5.2.

Figure 5.2   The top ACME is engraved; the bottom ACME is embossed.

Learn Desktop Graphics and Design on the PC

It's all a matter of simulated lighting effects, and it's not perfect—but this venerable technique works like a charm with most fairly bold, solid-color objects and can be used to lend texture to a solid background. Now all you need do is apply the same technique to the background in your ACME slide. You have two options: You can have one large embossed or engraved ACME, or you can have a pattern—in which case embossed will almost certainly look better than engraved.

Drag one of the ACMEs from the dry run up to the window adjacent to the slide background; let's use that as a working copy. (You may as well delete the other elements from the dry run, so they don't clutter things up.)

Ungroup the working ACME set, and change the topmost ACME to the same color as the background—100-025-000-000. Change the rearmost ACME to 100-050-000-000 and the middle ACME to 100-003-000-000. These are the shades that correspond to the grays used in the dry run—the main slide color, two shades darker and two shades lighter. Group this set, and drag off a copy to the middle of the slide.

Now, for a single ACME set engraved or embossed, simply make the ACME big, and (with both background box and ACME group selected) use the Align command (^N) to center the two sets.

You will then need to ungroup the ACME set, and adjust the darker and lighter ACMEs, so that only a tiny edge of each is visible around the topmost ACME. Otherwise, the lighting effect will be betrayed, and the illusion of depth disturbed.

Test this for effect. Create some Modern Heavy text in the title color (yellow)—something like *ACME Fardels, Inc.* and maybe a slogan (*The World's Best-Loved Fardels*). Place it on top of the background, with big embossed ACME in the middle. See Figure 5.3.

Note that the distinction between embossed and engraved is less obvious at larger sizes.

Figure 5.3   The test slide shows a single engraved ACME as the background element.

Move the yellow text and the large ACME off to the side for a moment, leaving just the background. Select the working copy of the still-small ACME set; this time, make sure the color order is set up for embossed. Copy this set to the Windows clipboard by pressing ^Ins. Paste it on top of the slide background, toward the upper left corner. Drag off about four copies, evenly spaced down along the left side—five copies in all. Adjust the spacing between them so they are nice and even, and use the Align command (^N) to line them up neatly.

With the Group tool, select four of the five ACME sets. Drag off a copy and place it so it is offset vis-à-vis the first vertical group of five ACMEs. Group and copy both vertical sets to the right of the first two sets. Finally, make one more copy of the set of five, and place it along the right side of the slide. Adjust the alignment and position of each element, then group all the embossed ACMEs together, and center that group on the slide background using the Align command. Place the yellow text back on top of this to see how it looks. See Figure 5.4.

Figure 5.4   The slide background shows an embossed pattern of ACMEs.

Each of these options has merit. The slide with the entire background full of little ACMEs could stand by itself. The single large ACME probably needs more stuff to make it feel complete. The acid test, by the by, is a print from the film recorder; nothing will so accurately tell you what you have.

I ran test prints on the Polaroid Digital Palette using print film. As it happens, I find that the print film I use has color values similar to the 36-exposure rolls of Polaroid Presentation Chrome that are one of my films of choice for 35mm slides. (My other preferred film, Polaroid's Polachrome, is developed on the desk, but Presentation Chrome gets sent to the photo lab.) The test prints tell me that my blue will be a bit different in my final slides—not a surprise—and the overall embossed pattern will look a bit more interesting.

To polish this template up, I add a dark-blue border, using the same blue I used for the dark shadow in the embossing. I

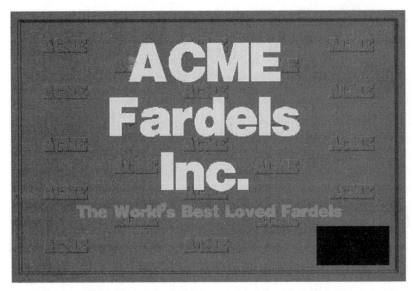

Figure 5.5   Here's the first slide, more or less finished.

place the ACME logo in the lower corner. The result is something very custom, very special—and it makes Hansel's presentation look that much more professional. See Figure 5.5.

Special Features of Slides

Many of the images for this show are the same as the ones used in the overhead-foil presentation. Things change a little for use in slides, of course.

The most important change is that slides tend to be horizontal (landscape mode) rather than vertical (portrait mode). There is no special reason why this should be so, but it is commonplace, and this is one of those conventions it is generally wiser to accept than fight.

Among other things, this means that titles tend to run across the wider image in a single line, rather than being on two lines. The title is filling a different space. For example, in the Industry Overview slide, the title and explanatory text are placed somewhat differently. See Figure 5.6.

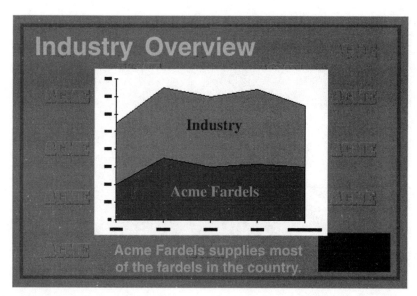

Figure 5.6   The Industry Overview slide contains an Excel graph.

But slides also allow for some other special effects that can pay off in a better presentation.

Build Sequences   One special effect is the *build sequence*—a bulleted list that is used several times in the show. As it is repeated, the completed items on the list are checked off in some way. An obvious application is in agenda slides. Another use of build sequences is to emphasize a series of closely linked points.

Build-sequence effects can be created in different ways. The simplest way is to change the bullet used. In the first build-sequence example—Hansel's agenda slide—as each major item is completed, the slide is flashed on the screen again, with the item checked off. See Figure 5.7.

A more sophisticated approach might use the checkmark—or just leave the old bullet—but change the color of the text and the bullet as the item is completed, as in Figure 5.8.

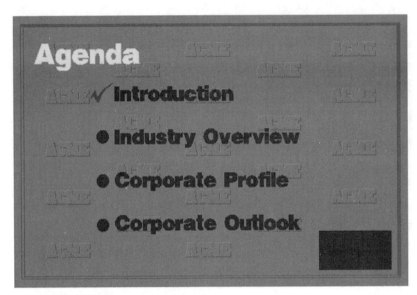

Figure 5.7   This is a simple check-off slide.

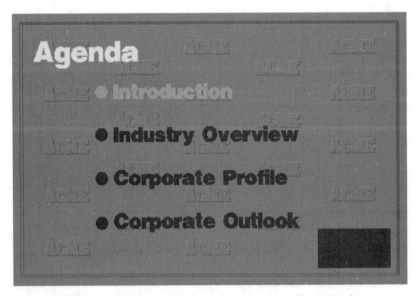

Figure 5.8   Here's the simple build sequence with grayed-out text instead of a checkmark.

Build sequences add polish. Use them sparingly. An agenda build sequence is very effective, especially if the presentation is quite long with several speakers in a morning-long session. Flipping to an agenda slide showing points covered is also useful after a break.

If restlessness is a problem, there is also merit in asking if the presentation as a whole should be re-thought.

> Use A&L Draw's multiple-page feature to make build sequences. A single Draw file usually accommodates six slide-size pages, and rarely do you want a slide with more than four one-line points in a build sequence, or a sequence of more than five slides.
>
> Group the background as a single unit. Set up the first slide (with all points active). Copy background and foreground text to each of the windows for the subsequent slides (one for each point to be ticked off). Then adjust the subsequent slides with checkmarks or darkened lettering, as you choose.

More Involved Pictures Slide shows are almost always used in more elaborate presentations, so they frequently include more involved pictures. For Hansel's road show, this means a more complex corporate overview. The audience at company headquarters could see the elegant new (and paid-for) factory and clearly superior (and nonunion) workforce Hansel had assembled to produce high-quality fardels, but those bankers in New York couldn't tell a fardel factory from a brewery. Hansel wisely decided to show a picture of the Acme Fardels factory—emphasizing that this spotless modern facility had already paid for itself in improved productivity and lower per-fardel cost.

Whoops! Change gears! All the images thus far have been *vector drawings*. The only pictures Hansel has of the Acme Fardels factory are photographs—which are not vector drawings and are not in the computer.

No problemo. Gretl was a smart shopper, and when Hansel started on this computer-graphics thing of his, she bought him this book, you see, and among the software included with the book was a program called Picture Publisher.

Bitmaps, Painting, and Scanning

Picture Publisher represents the other part of the larger computer-graphics picture. Rather than dealing with images defined in the computer as complexes of geometric data, Picture Publisher acquires, makes, and modifies bitmaps—patterns of colored dots. As computer users, we are familiar with bitmaps; what's on the screen is a *bitmap display*.

Some programs in this category are intended mostly for creating the images. Windows PaintBrush is a simple example. Fractal Painter is perhaps the best top-of-market example.

Other programs serve special purposes. Most software intended for animation, for example, is built on a paint-program foundation.

Finally, bitmap programs like Picture Publisher start with an image-acquisition and image-editing foundation. That is, in their earliest incarnation, these programs were intended to control scanners in the process of turning photos and the like into digital data, and then correct the acquired image.

Simple image editors are still around, and they have a place. But a full-featured program like Picture Publisher offers a whole range of image-editing features that a simple image editor doesn't have. Top-of-market products—Picture Publisher is an example—offer most of the image-creation capabilities of a top-notch paint program, as well as editing tools.

Using a Scanned Image

The sample slide in Figure 5.9 gives you the idea: The slide combines a scanned image with explanatory text in what I hope is an effective composition.

Figure 5.9   This is what you're aiming for.

Acquiring the Image

If you don't have a scanner, you have two options: Buy a scanner, or have a service bureau scan images for you. Both options are viable; buying a scanner may prove cheaper if you are going to be doing any amount of serious computer-based graphics.

Scanners come in three generally available varieties:

- Hand scanners are little boxes you roll over the material to be scanned. Cost: low hundreds.

- Flat-bed scanners look like the top part of an office copying machine—which is just about what they are. Cost: street prices begin at $800 to $900.

- Drum scanners are very expensive (five figures) and very accurate. Frankly, the best flat-bed scanners can rival drum scanners costing 10 times the amount.

A hybrid of the first two designs shows up every so often, in which a small box that lies on top of the image to be copied contains a mechanism like that of the flat-bed scanner, which does its own rolling. Don't even bother looking at a scanner that doesn't do color.

If you don't get a scanner, you still want image-editing software. Vast collections of royalty-free photographic images are available for trivial sums. Small collections are included with Picture Publisher. Larger collections, on Kodak Photo CDs, are available commercially.

TWAIN Scanning

If you have a scanner but no TWAIN driver, call your scanner maker and ask for it.

If you buy a scanner, or you have one already, make absolutely certain you have a TWAIN driver for it. TWAIN is a standard for scanner/computer interfacing developed by a technical committee headed by folks from Hewlett-Packard. It supplants older program-specific scanner interfaces; these are still available, but they are limiting. If you have a TWAIN driver for your scanner, almost any Windows program that can handle scanning can use this single scanner interface.

As it happens, Micrografx was an early adopter of the TWAIN standard, and Picture Publisher supports it along with a selection of proprietary drivers. The two different scanning capabilities are indicated in Picture Publisher's File menu, shown in Figure 5.10. The Scan option accesses proprietary scanner drivers. The Acquire is the standard option for using a TWAIN interface for scanning.

Scanning with a TWAIN interface varies to some extent from scanner to scanner; some TWAIN interfaces are more sophisticated than others. The basics are simple enough.

Setting Up to Scan Turn on your scanner and give it a moment or two to warm up. Choose Acquire from the Picture Publisher File menu. The TWAIN interface should appear.

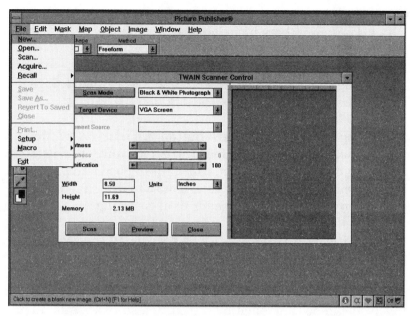

Figure 5.10   Picture Publisher's work area shows the File menu with Scan and Acquire options and a typical TWAIN interface.

In my experience, the most common reason for the TWAIN interface not to appear, but to produce an error message, is memory shortage; if you get that error, turn off Picture Publisher, turn off other Windows programs that may be hogging memory, then launch Picture Publisher again, and try File Acquire again. This usually clears up the problem.

Setting up to scan is fairly simple. For the scanner I use, I choose the type of image I am scanning: True Color Photograph for any color image and Black & White Photograph for any grayscale image seem to yield the best results.

Set the target device (or whatever that is called in your setup) for color. I usually scan for a VGA display at 150dpi (dots per inch); 150dpi or 300dpi seems to work for black and white. These numbers have generally worked well for me; you will want to play a little and talk to your printer, perhaps, before settling on the numbers that work best for you. Also, things change depending on how the scanned image is going to be used.

Previewing Notice the Preview button in Figure 5.11? Most flat-bed scanners have this feature. Effectively, previewing does a quick scan of what's on the scanning bed and pastes it into a preview window. Use your mouse to drag a marquee around any part of the image for final scanning.

Frankly, it is best to do as little as possible in the scanning phase. It is better to scan at a higher resolution and lose some in the editing process. It is better to scan in color, even if the end product is going to be black and white (the loss involved can be controlled by the editing software). To all of this, add "generally speaking" and "always experiment."

The whole purpose of the exercise is to get that image into the machine, where you can do all the neat things that can be done in digital editing.

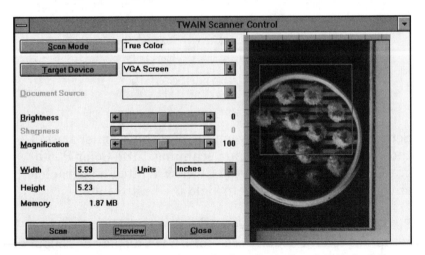

Figure 5.11 A preview in the right-hand window is marked for final scanning.

Digital Editing Adjusting for sharpness and contrast is perhaps the most common editing chore.

Figure 5.12 shows the kinds of things that can be done. This is a section of a picture of a lavish Chinese meal. The original is in glorious color, but this book is using black-and-white pictures.

Picture Publisher's conversion utility (from the Image menu) changes the original picture from color to gray-scale. That involves changing a palette of thousands of colors to 256 shades of gray. The loss is partly compensated by automatic optimizing.

The second of the three pictures in Figure 5.12 shows the same grayscale image after Picture Publisher's unsharp filter is applied from the Effects command in the Image menu. This is a digital application of a traditional photographic technique. Parts of the image are slightly blurred, others are sharpened, and the result is a brighter, sharper image to the viewer's eye. Hit it right, and the picture develops an almost three-dimensional realism—not unlike that obtained using a lens with a short focal length.

The third picture applies a standard sharpness filter to the grayscale image. This sharpness filter blackens lines and eliminates blurring. Again, the effect is to make things look

Figure 5.12 The color image at left is converted to grayscale, then passed through two different filters—a sharpness filter and an unsharp filter.

sharper to the viewer's eye. It is not so strong an effect as the unsharp filter effect.

Each of these effects can be applied in varying degrees. There is no substitute for experimentation, since different effects work differently in different applications.

In the three pictures in Figure 5.12, I would probably go for the rightmost one—the one with a standard sharpness filter—rather than the middle, unsharp-filtered picture, if I was looking to go to print. The startling white of the bowl in the middle of the picture is too white in the unsharp-filtered picture. Send this image to a typesetting machine, and that white will look burned-through, so to speak. In any event, I would certainly want to test-print this image with as fine a screen as possible (using a half-tone setting of 100 lines in the Print dialog box), on a high-resolution laser printer (600dpi minimum), if I had the option.

> Even under the best of circumstances, and with all kinds of test shots, eventually you go with *something*. For example, in one promotional piece for a public-radio play, I had thumbnails of the famous-name narrator, the two principal actors, and the play's author. No matter what I did, I could not get the bright white spot off the forehead of that famous-name narrator.

You can do other things with careful editing. Take the head-shot I use of myself (for anyone foolish enough to ask): I wear thick glasses. Take a picture of me, and the refraction of light in my lenses cuts a hole in the side of my face and in my eye. Using Picture Publisher and a lot of care, that kind of damage can be removed. See Figure 5.13.

Back to Hansel's Factory

Hansel would work from a photograph, probably in color. I didn't have a handy shot of a factory, so I scanned in an an-

Figure 5.13   All that flesh and eye on my right (your left) was put in by me—even the glare! About half that space was refraction, originally. I also added a little more hair.

tique photo (old enough to be out of copyright) showing a state-of-the-art factory circa 1875.

I applied an unsharp filter to the picture; I wanted maximum brightness. I adjusted for size and dots per inch. All these are effects on Picture Publisher's Image menu. Then I saved the file as a TIFF file—a bitmap file format originally intended for desktop publishing and readily imported into A&L Draw.

I might have chosen one other effect in this case. The photo came out of a book, which means it had already been rasterized or turned into dots for printing purposes. The scan shows an unpleasant moiré pattern. Under some circumstances—most especially, if I had done a high-resolution scan, where losing some resolution would not have been a problem—I could have used Picture Publisher's pattern-removal filter to smooth away that pattern.

To put this picture in place, all I needed to do was open my template and use the A&L Draw Import command on the

File menu, tell it the name, type, and location of the file, and click on the OK button. Place the picture, add a title and some explanatory text, and you have a nice picture of the Acme Fardels factory to show the bankers.

Scanning and editing bitmaps—from photos or other sources—involves a good deal more than is covered in this brief exercise. Then too, there's the whole business of painting—creating bitmaps from scratch. Also, you can do some things in a bitmap editor or a vector-drawing package; using the two kinds of programs together is an important creative approach.

That you have an incredible wealth of options using a bitmap program should be clear from the range of tools available in Picture Publisher. In the preceding exercise, I used only two facilities: acquiring an image and then making it better in a global way. Call it a taste of things to come.

Fiddling Around with Film

At this point, you should have a good sense of the basics: You have seen how color is used, and you've learned a professional trick or two to add a special something to a slide background. You understand the special aspect ratio (11 by 7.334 inches; keep muttering this number to yourself and people will think you are a designer, or something).

It is a large subject; there are books on this topic alone. Magazines aimed at the substantial niche market of presentation graphics carry how-to articles in abundance. All that is useful; practice in making presentations is even more useful.

In the next project, you'll get to practice some of the more sophisticated capabilities of Picture Publisher.

Project 6:
Painting

Sometimes life is complex, as I keep telling people. Before moving on to "real art," or whatever it is we'll be doing, some quality time with Picture Publisher is in order. Think of this as a break.

In the last project, you saw that Picture Publisher is an able tool for editing images, whether you scan them yourself or use images supplied in digital form.

Picture Publisher can do more than that. It is a powerful and flexible image-making and image-processing tool. It has a splendid pedigree (Micrografx, its maker, practically invented desktop graphics on PC-family machines); it is demonstrably easier to use and more able than comparable products from other vendors.

In short, Picture Publisher is a hot item.

> Increasingly, using prescanned images read off of a CD-ROM is a popular option. In addition to substantial libraries of professionally taken and processed photos available at relatively modest cost (which includes all royalties), Kodak offers Photo-CDs. Take your pictures to a dealer offering this service, and you get back a CD-ROM with your photos already in digital format, in three resolutions.

Picture Publisher's Work Area

Let's start with something fairly simple: a tour of the work area.

In addition to the menu commands—including the Image menu you used to access the effects for Project 5—Picture Publisher offers a fairly simple tool bar along the left side of the screen. See Figure 6.1. Click on most of those tools, and a bunch of related options fly out. Some of the tools are special-purpose applications of special effects available from the menu bar. Others are actual creative tools.

Right under the menu bar and above the work area is a space that changes depending on the tool selected. This is where Picture Publisher puts controls for specific tools such as brush-size and -shape controls when you are painting.

At the bottom of the screen is a status line. Micrografx may be the best software vendor when it comes to using status lines effectively; in all its software, the status-line messages are

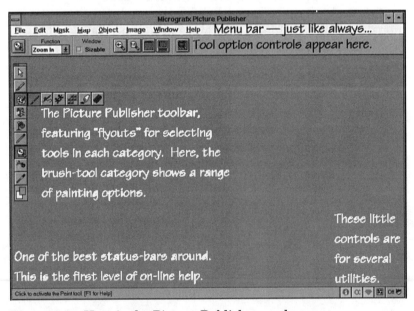

Figure 6.1   Here is the Picture Publisher workspace.

useful (and that is not always the case in other applications!). Among other things, the status line tells you what you are doing, what the program is doing, how to stop the program from doing it, or how to get help—depending on circumstances.

To the right of the status line at the bottom of the screen, Picture Publisher shows some special utility buttons. The "i" button pops up a little information box about the picture currently selected. The next two buttons control advanced options for editing and viewing image masks (sometimes called *friskets*). Next to that is a button for showing color palettes; it pops up the current palette in a dialog box, with options to open other palettes. The last button is the Color Shield tool. The Color Shield is a special masking tool that masks by color, rather than by area.

The best way to get comfortable with Picture Publisher as a creative tool is to use it.

Making a Photo in the Computer

Most of us have snapshots that are far from brilliant. Figure 6.2 shows one of my nieces as a child, taken in a Taipei park alongside yet another concrete copy of a baroque fountain. It was scanned into the computer in true (24-bit) color at a medium resolution (300dpi). I cropped to keep the interesting part (the kid), and (for the exercise at hand) converted the picture to grayscale.

> This file is in the Samples collection, called STATUE.TIF. To open this file, use the Open dialog in the File menu, set the file type to TIFF or All Images, and set the drive and directory to your sample-file location. You will either see the file name or the thumbnail of the picture; double-click on it.

The Masking tool fly-out shows various mask-making and editing tools.

The Crop tool is on the Masking tool fly-out, the last one in the row. Point to the beginning of the area you want to save (com-

Figure 6.2 My niece poses next to a baroque fountain in a Taipei park.

monly, an upper or lower corner), and click and drag to the end of the area. Let go of the button, and the picture is cropped. If you make a mistake (it happens), use the Undo option on the Edit menu immediately. Picture Publisher has only one level of undo, so correct now or forever hold your peace.

Convert the image using the Convert option on the Image menu. I have generally found it preferable to scan in as much color as I can (using my scanner's TWAIN driver true-color option); this gives Picture Publisher the maximum amount of information. Picture Publisher changes that into a good grayscale rendition—better, in my judgment, than a grayscale scan of the colored original. You'll learn how to fine-tune the tone balance.

My niece, on the other hand, may simply wish I would lose this photo altogether—on the assumption teenagers are rarely happy to be reminded of their childhood.

Charming as this lass may be, I can't say the setting does much for me. I think this picture would be infinitely more charming if the fountain and the kid were seen in the midst of a tremendous bank of flowers—as we are about to do.

Masking the Subject

Begin by getting rid of the useless parts of this picture. The easiest way, in this case, is to use the Paint on Mask tool to select what you want. Select the Paint on Mask tool from the masking fly-out (it's the button just to the left of the Magic Wand button). Look at the top of the work area, on the tool control bar, and make sure the plus-sign button is depressed—this means you are adding to the mask rather than subtracting from it. Now, simply move the circle indicating the active brush area in the picture, holding the left mouse button down, and paint on the masking needed. In this case, paint the mask onto the statue and the kid.

If you have a graphics tablet, rather than a mouse, this is where having a stylus will pay off handsomely. (See Appendix A.) It is much easier to do this with a stylus than a mouse, in my opinion.

My own preference for this tool's use is to work around the outline of the area to be masked first, then make the masking brush bigger and take out the stuff in the middle. It also makes sense to zoom in on the area being masked.

When you have masked all the various parts of the background—in fact, everything that is not kid and statue—use the Invert option on the Mask menu from the menu bar to change things around, so stuff in the undesired background is masked, as shown in Figure 6.3.

Make sure one of the little color swatches at the bottom of the screen is set to pure white.

If it's not pure white, click on the Color Palette tool at the bottom right of the work area, and click on the pure-white patch. The status line on the lower left should say *100, 100, 100% RGB*. One of the two swatches—the one on top—will then change to pure white.

Figure 6.3 Here's what the statue and kid look like after masking and cropping.

Then choose the Solid Fill tool (third over on the Paint Bucket fly-out). Click the Paint Bucket cursor on the masked background, and it will be painted over with white. Change the mask back to the statue and kid again, using the Invert command on the Mask menu.

You may want to be doubly sure by saving the cropped picture in a file, called TEMP.TIF. Use the Save As command on the File menu, set the file type to TIFF, and fill in the name.

Choosing a New Background

Now for the flower bed: Among the samples supplied with this book is a file called GARDEN.TIF. To open this file, use the Open command on the File menu, set the file type to TIFF or All Images, and set the drive and directory to your sample-file location. Then double-click on the name or thumbnail (depending on which is showing). Figure 6.4 shows the garden.

Now you have two images, each in its own window, in the work space; one of the kid and the statue, the other of the garden. The job is to make them into one nice photograph.

Figure 6.4   The garden is in the GARDEN.TIF file.

Click on the kid-and-statue window; the mask should be on, and it should be around the image. Use the Copy command on the Edit menu to put the masked portion on the clipboard. Then, click on the garden window to make it active, and use the Paste command on the Edit menu to drop the kid-and-statue image into the garden.

The image that has been added is much like an object in A&L Draw: It can be scaled, sized, and skewed, and—well, all kinds of neat things can be done to it. Feel free to play. I have scaled the picture to match the size of the garden.

When you are finished pasting the image and playing with the options, click on the selection arrow, and the inserted picture gets a special mask. See Figure 6.5. You can move or

Figure 6.5   The kid and statue are dropped into the garden.

otherwise alter this image when that special mask is showing the image as selected.

The kid and statue need to be incorporated into the background. The easy way to do this is to tuck them in behind some of the flowers, making it appear as if the fountain is in the midst of the garden, with the little girl standing by it.

Use the Paint on Mask tool as before, this time to select some flowers in the middle of the garden. Copy this section to the clipboard with the Edit menu's Copy command, then paste it back in to the developing picture. Remove the painted-on mask with the Remove Mask command from the Mask menu.

Notice the continuing analogy to the kind of things you are familiar with in the drawing environment: Each of these pasted images is an object; they are in layers; and they can be moved up and down relative to each other.

Now locate the kid and statue in the general area of the part of the garden you just copied. Then move the copied bit of garden back in place to cover the lower part of the kid and statue. Once the two pieces are in place, use the Combine command on the Object menu to merge these objects back into the developing picture. The whole thing becomes a masked part of the picture; you can remove the mask (using the Remove command from the Mask menu).

Making the Fit Seamless

This image needs some refinement. Most especially, the edges need to be softened a bit. Use the Smudge tool located on the Brush tool fly-out (the palette icon). The Smudge tool is represented by a finger smudging paint. In the tool-setting windows, set the brush size to four pixels, feathering to 10, and pressure to 25. Now, work along the hard edges to soften them just a bit.

Brush tools include (from left to right) Paintbrush, Airbrush, Cloner, Pattern Brush, Smudge tool and Eraser.

Another tool is useful: the Clone tool, number three on the Brush fly-out. This brush copies what is in one place to what is in another, and you can use it to smooth out discontinuities at the edges of merged images as well as correct unpleasant image elements. Notice the pointers on the selected picture: one with an x in the middle and the other a plain circle. The x area is being copied; the clear area is where you are actually painting—cloning the stuff where x marks the spot.

As you clone, adjust the source x to copy elements of the garden background along the edges of the merged sections.

You can change the relative position of the x. The button on the tool control bar (underneath the menu bar) showing the circled x and labeled Source controls the x-location. Click on this button, then use your pointer to move the circled x to the place where you want to copy. Release the button, then begin painting with the open circle where you want the copy to begin.

Take the completed image and run the Effects command from the Image menu. Then use the Unsharp filter with the radius set to about 30 and strength to about 60 to sharpen the photograph. The result is shown in Figure 6.6.

This is a real example of what digital photography can do, and it is the hottest aspect of computer graphics at the moment. This technique is used both for artistic and design effects, and also for sometimes scurrilous purposes.

Figure 6.6 Here's the cropped version of GARDEN with the kid and statue in place.

Creating New Works of Art

You can use Picture Publisher's tools for everything from re-covering old and damaged photos to creating entirely new works of art.

The artistic element is fun as well as useful. I recently saw a pretty picture of a famous model. The picture showed the model posing sort of as Venus rising from the sea.

I scanned the image and played. Using the Effects command on the Image menu, I reduced the number of colors in the scanned and cleaned-up image (I set the reduction to 16 colors, with an optimized palette). I then applied a second effect—the pop-art artistic rendering.

I painted on masks for the water, filling it with a cyan shade (setting the transparency option on the tool control bar to about 75 percent), and the little piece of sky that showed (same transparency setting, but a bluer blue fill).

In a separate window, I sketched a cockleshell, which I copied to the clipboard and then pasted about where the model's (missing) feet would be. I used the Clone tool to lap some water up around the base of the cockleshell. After touching up some spots, I printed the result on a Fargo color printer, and Mrs. Jenner, a more discriminating artist than I, approved of the result.

Here's the cockleshell for my version of Venus on the half-shell.

There is an issue in this kind of work: If this is art (and that is a much-debated topic), then I should be able to play at liberty and show my work. But the original picture, which is the foundation of my work, is someone else's work; that person also has rights. Figuring out whose rights are involved is not as simple as copyright owners and publishers—and attorneys and the courts, who have unclear ideas on the subject, to judge from published decisions—would have you think. That's why I described this image, but didn't display it. The idea is to suggest some things you might try as exercises.

Figure 6.7   I rejuvenated an old photo.

Recovering Old Photos

Take a picture of my father's relatives from the old country. It was in pretty bad shape after nearly a century in an old photo album. But once I got it in the computer, Picture Publisher quickly sharpened it and cleaned up the cracks in the surface. See Figure 6.7. In a couple of passes, I could give it a nice old-time sepia or silver-point finish.

Playing Around with Digital Painting

Picture Publisher is a very powerful program. This brief demonstration project shows only some of the capabilities of the program. You've used one brush; there are many more (the main Brush tool has a dozen different variations). You haven't even touched the various fill options, and only a few of the image-adjustment options were used. There are *books* on digital painting; this is a quick sampling. In any case, the best way to learn this program is to *play*.

As the projects get more involved with the artistic side of design (the part real artists—and some designers, interestingly enough—deny), you'll be coming back to play some more.

Project 7:
Posters

Making posters is fun! It is also useful. You can create grand, costly posters like the ones you see in shops, and you can create posters to promote whatever cause you favor. On a more modest scale, you can create little flyers to stick up on grocery-store bulletin boards to sell off your old furniture or promote a new service in the neighborhood.

Posters of one sort or another have been a staple form of advertising for thousands of years. Ancient Pompeii featured signs on the wall to promote local products. In the Middle Ages, a notice called a *siquis* (*si quis* means "if anybody") posted on walls served the same purpose as today's want ads. Those notices on grocery-store bulletin boards are a continuation of the custom. Ancient China had big-character posters—and modern China, for that matter, still has them.

In short, posters are a universal communications medium, and you have the best poster-making tools around.

Creating a Large Poster

Smallville Community College is the cultural center of Smallville. Some fairly competent professional artists have taken up residence in the town, and they have developed an artist-in-residence program with the college. Each year, they stage an art show, a feature of which is the collectible poster produced in limited numbers on the spot for a hefty contribution.

Setting Up the Poster

Posters tend to be vertically—portrait—oriented. It is a convention, not a fixed rule, but in this case it seems simpler to stick with the convention.

> For testing and printing purposes, I chose to use the HP PaintJet. On opening A&L Draw for this project, I used the Printer Setup dialog to select this printer and turned on the rulers and the grid from the Preferences dialog.

To make the background, use the Symbol tool to get a square, and place it in the work area. Size this square so it fills the entire panel by moving it to the upper left corner and stretching it to fill the area. This background is important; depending on the background color, the colors for the copy (the text on the poster) change. After the basics of the design are in place, you'll come back to this. The initial color choice is a deep rose for the background (000-068-050-000). Save the file.

Devising a Still Life for the Icon

This is also an icon—hopefully, of an artist.

> Icons have nothing to do with religious pictures; an εικων is a picture, pure and simple. It is also a kind of simile—that is, the picture suggests a likeness. The image for this poster has to have some kind of likeness to what artists do. The idea is to bring the concept of an art show to the fore. That is, it's a matter of "bringing things together"—also a Greek notion, συμβαλλειν. (All this Greek reflects the fact that a bunch of philosophers some two and a half millennia ago came to the conclusion that being is a matter of being seen, which is part of why graphics is important to this day.)

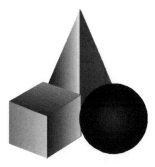

Figure 7.1 The pleasing assembly of three-dimensional shapes is my geometric still life.

The icon that works for me in this case is an easel with a painting on it. To keep the painting neutral, I choose to create a kind of geometric still life—some three-dimensional graphic shapes in what I hope is a pleasing composition. See Figure 7.1.

Making this assembly involves two problems. The first part—making the shapes—is not particularly difficult. The second part—suggesting shading—involves some careful thinking.

Effectively, you have to simulate the effects that can be automatically achieved only in high-end 3-D graphics software.

Creating the Basic Shapes Create the basic shapes first. These basic shapes are the side of the pylon and cube, the top of the cube, and the circle from which the sphere is going to be made. See Figure 7.2.

The circle, of course, is easy. It is simply the basic circle shape. Insert it with the Symbol tool.

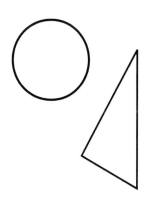

The other shapes are constructions. For example, the pylon is a construction made from two triangles. Use the Straight Line drawing tool to draw a vertical line, then continue to make the slanting base and close the triangle with a third leg from base to apex. If the status line at the top of the work area tells you this is still an open shape, force it closed with F7, the Close Shape command from the Draw menu.

The sides of the cube are parallelograms. The basic shape is drawn with the Straight Line tool. Two verticals are con-

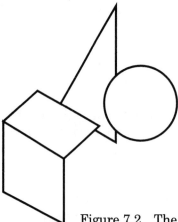

Figure 7.2   The basic shapes are simple.

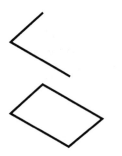

The first angle and the completed top of the cube are easy to draw.

nected by two diagonal lines. The F7 command forces closure if necessary.

The top of the cube is a bit more complex: Start with a diagonal line parallel to the top of the cube side, then angle it back in a second leg, more or less 30 degrees from the first line. Turn off the Line Editing tool, and use the Copy tool to drag off a copy of this angle. Flip it (using the Flip command on the Arrange menu) both horizontally and vertically. Move the flipped copy back so its ends are right by the ends of the first angle. Select both of these pieces, and use the F7 command to close the two into a single polygon.

Shading the Shapes   To give these shapes shaded color, use the Magic Color Cubes. Using the Activity tool, import the Magic Color Cubes into one of the work area panes, and move the basic shapes next to them. Ungroup the color swatch collection so it can be used.

The simplest item to color is the sphere; it is also the practical limiting factor. Select the sphere, click on the Fill tool, and select Shaded Round from the scrolling list of options. While you're at it, turn off the outline with the Pen tool; set it to None.

Learn Desktop Graphics and Design on the PC

The Shaded Round option is limiting because you cannot adjust the position of the highlight. You are stuck with the bright spot in the middle, and you are stuck with the black parts. What you can change is the "to" color. I chose to use red.

Color the triangle with one of the Magic Color Cubes. Having decided to make this pylon blue, I used Daylight/Vertical (second row, third column). Select the color cube and save it with a ^Q, then select the triangle and color it with the ^R Recall command. Change the alterable color to a darker shade of blue, using the color picker (I used 100-033-000-000). Again, turn off the outline by setting the Pen tool to None.

To convert this triangle into a fairly decent 3-D pylon, drag off a copy of the triangle and flip it vertically. Match the two vertical sides together (use the Align command to correct baselines). You may also want to change the alterable color of the second triangle.

I used a darker shade, 100-050-025-000. I also turned the outline on for this triangle, changing it to the same darker shade, to define the edge-on look.

Assemble the cube in stages. First, color it. I am making it green; I used the basic Seagreen/Vertical color cube (eighth row, third column), and I changed the alterable color to 075-012-075-000. I also turned off the outline. Next, copy, flip, and match sides, as in constructing the cube, and then change the alterable color for the second side to a darker green (I used 100-050-100-000). The last step is to turn on the outline on the copied side to define the front edge.

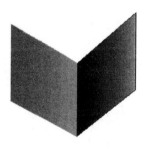

Notice the difference in the two sides.

Before you group the two sides into a single item, you want to adjust the second side for perspective. Use the Line Editing tool to access the points. Make the whole parallelogram angle up a bit more to match the angles of the cube top. Turn off the Line Editing tool and shorten the second side a bit.

The last part of the cube is the top. Move the basic shape into place, then use the Line Editing tool to adjust it to fit. Color it the same as the alterable color of the left cube side, 075-012-075-000.

Almost certainly, this cube will require some editing. You will need to adjust all three pieces with the Line Editing tool to make them look right. For example, it may be necessary to adjust the shape of the top and then adjust the sides to match. Look at the example in Figure 7.1 to see how the cube should appear. Also, note well: It is not easy to get this part of the illustration to work perfectly. The best way to get a sense of what a solid looks like in two dimensions is to take such a solid and look at it from different angles.

When the cube pieces all fit together and look right, group them.

Then select all three geometric solids and group them together. Insert a square using the Symbol tool, make it a bit longer than it is broad, and give it a neutral line and fill color—say, 007-030-040-000. Move this to the back (use ^K), and place the group of geometric shapes on it. Group the whole thing.

Making the Painting and the Easel

The background is in place, and the image for the painting is done. Now to make an easel with a canvas on it.

The Legs of the Easel Start with the legs. This tripod is made using the Straight Line drawing tool. Draw a line leaning about 20 degrees off the vertical. From the top, draw another

The tripod

Learn Desktop Graphics and Design on the PC

line down, leaning in the other direction—effectively the two legs of an *A*. Draw a third line, vertically bisecting the angle, and a little shorter than the legs of the *A*.

Select all these lines and make them fairly thick. Set the Line Thickness option to 5 points (Fat). Group the whole thing. Then draw a couple little lines to represent stretchers connecting the three legs. These should be fairly thin lines. Color all the lines a dark red.

Embellishing the Canvas The canvas is a square inserted using the Symbol tool, filled with white, with the outline set to Fat and colored the same red as the tripod. It is stretched vertically a smidgin, and it is placed on top of the tripod a little above the stretchers.

Make the decorative scroll for the top of the canvas with the Curved Line drawing tool. After drawing the basic loop, you need to edit the scroll. With the line selected and the Line Editing tool on, turn the control points on (^4) and remove any extra points (you should have only the endpoints plus one point in the belly of each curve. When you have it right, set the line to Fat and color it dark red to match the tripod (if it's not already set that way). Then drag off a copy, flip it horizontally, match it up with the original, and align it. Group the two pieces. Place them on top of the canvas.

The scroll

This partial scroll shows the control-point locations.

Constructing the Easel Assembly Select all the pieces of the easel and canvas and align them vertically. Put the finished image (geometric shapes and background) on top of the easel, group the whole thing, and then place it to the left of the poster background. Adjust things so the easel assembly fills that left side, pretty much, leaving some room for text above and below.

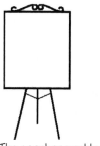

The easel assembly

Adding—and Coloring—the Lettering

The text for this poster is done using the A&L Draw native typeface, Classical Medium. This is not my favorite Roman typeface, but it has an advantage in this case: It scales beautifully as a graphic. And you want BIG letters to the right of the art.

In fact, that is the word: *art*. But the letters are positioned vertically. Use the Text tool, and type in *art* in lowercase letters (at least, *I* like lowercase letters for this purpose; it is a matter of taste), one letter to a line. Then place this text block. Scale it so it fills the left side of the developing poster.

On the deep-rose colored background, I find a rich light blue works well (100-025-000-000 works well to my eye). The contrast is effective, and blue is a color to which most people react positively (as, in fact, they do to pinks in the deep- or dusty-rose shades).

The art part of the poster is complete. All that remains is to add some text. At the top of the easel, I placed the text *Smallville Community College Artistes-in-Residence* using the A&L Wyeth typeface that has hitherto been used in other Smallville College work. Switching back to Classical Medium, I placed a centered block telling folks what the poster is for: the annual art show and sale. I colored both of these dark blue. This color contrasts well with the deep rose, without being quite so in-your-face as the lighter blue. The finished poster is shown in Figure 7.3.

There is some psychology in this poster.

> There are some ways to add drama to this poster. The easiest way is to change the color of the poster background and coordinate the lettering colors to match. In the lower panels of the sample-file work area, (ARTSHOW3.GED on the CD-ROM), I include some variations with shaded backgrounds made by applying the Magic Color Cubes and differently colored lettering.

Printing the Poster

A poster has to be postable, and it has to be printed. Smallville needs one poster, not a thousand. There are a couple of options for posters like this.

Learn Desktop Graphics and Design on the PC

Figure 7.3 The finished Art Show poster design.

First, many service bureaus have large-scale printers for something like this. Commonly, these service bureaus work with architectural firms. If they've been around awhile, they will have something like a Versatec electrostatic plotter. These mammoth printers use a roll of 40-inch-wide paper, and they are commonly driven by something like Freedom of Press, a program that processes PostScript page-description language into a form the Versatec plotter can deal with.

Other firms may use something like a Hewlett-Packard ink-jet plotter, or a variant form of the same thing from Laser-Master. Very high-end shops will also offer Iris prints—deluxe quality, but at a fairly substantial cost. All these devices make big prints from your design.

The trick is to get this poster design out into PostScript.

A&L Draw exports to Encapsulated PostScript—but with restrictions. Draw's PostScript filter (as these things are called) has problems (as is generally true of Computer Support Corporation filters) with elements not actually gener-

Renewed interest in large prints means new options and lower prices are coming.

Into every life a little rain must fall.

ated by Draw. Unfortunately, that means all the (non-CSC) lettering in the image will be lost.

Printing to File There is a better, more reliable way. You can print to file using a PostScript driver. The simple solution, in my experience, is Zenographics Zscript/SuperPrint. Install it for a color printer (SuperPrint supports several in its standard over-the-counter version, including the HP PaintJet and the Fargo Primera). Then print to that color device through the Zscript interpreter to a file. Be absolutely sure to use the Windows PostScript Driver's print-to-file settings! This driver is called by Zscript, and the two in combination have been rock-solid reliable in getting me PostScript files that can be used with service bureaus.

The (much better, and cheaper) alternative is to use a service bureau that has an A&L graphics product (there are several). Then the service bureau simply prints your file using the software it has on its machines.

By the by, if you do not have the latest Windows PostScript driver (v. 3.58 as this is written), download it for the price of a call to the Microsoft BBS (206/ 637-9009).

> For a job similar to this one, I used National Reprographics, an old, established service bureau here in New York. It printed the poster on the Versatec using Freedom of Press, and the PostScript file was produced in the manner described.
>
> The cost was about $15 per square foot, plus charges to encapsulate and laminate the poster to take the rigors of being outdoors in direct sun—about $75, all told.

Tiling the Output There was a reason I chose to print to the PaintJet. With this printer, in particular, it is easy to fill the entire page with color, and this suggests an option: Tile the output.

To *tile* means to print out the poster in sections, then mount them as a single picture. This sounds cumbersome, but it really isn't. Very large posters are frequently printed this way.

To set up for a tiled full-size print of the poster, use the View command to view all pages. Remove any bits and pieces you may have in other panels of the work area (such as the Magic Color Cubes). Select the whole design with the Select All command from the Edit menu. Then simply drag on the lower right handle to fill all (four, in this case) pages.

Print this expanded version using the Print All Pages option from the Print dialog. What comes out is four pages. Either wheat-paste them where you want the poster, or mount them on a single piece of Fome-Cor or bristol board. Be careful to match and trim, and the result will be perfectly acceptable.

Wheat paste is a cream-thick mixture of water and flour. It makes paper stick to walls very nicely.

Designing a Cut-Vinyl Poster

The second poster—for the Smallville theatrical troupe—was executed in cut vinyl. Vinyl is durable and colorful, and it makes a great poster. Vector-drawing programs like A&L Draw provide exactly the right kind of information to the machine that cuts the material.

You have seen cut vinyl used as paint on things like FedEx trucks.

Posters designed for cut vinyl are executed in solid colors. The material works best when the images are not too intricate (the word *too* is subject to interpretation). Essentially, the knife is mounted in a plotter, instead of a pen. Where a standard plotter draws lines, the vinyl cutter cuts lines. The lines it cuts best, of course, are the lines defining shapes. These shapes can then be picked and mounted on sheet plastic, bristol board, or what have you.

The St. Mark's logo from Project 2 can be executed in cut vinyl—and it is actually pretty intricate.

Creating the Art

The Little Theatre folks have decided on an ambitious project. They will produce all of Will Shakespeare's history plays over the course of the spring semester. These plays encompass the murderous end of *Richard II* through the equally murderous end (albeit different) of *Richard III*. (They are giving *Henry VIII* a miss, on the grounds that its authorship is suspect.) These plays cover the history of English dynastic wars known as the Wars of the Roses. This name comes from the house badges of the contesting parties, red and white roses. Stylized roses make an effective design element for this poster.

Old illustration books are excellent sources of do-it-yourself clip art.

As it happens, I have a few books on heraldry, and I quickly found a Tudor rose to scan into the computer using Picture Publisher (see Figure 7.4). I scanned at fairly low resolution, in black and white. I saved the result as a TIFF file, a bitmap graphics format A&L Draw understands. Use the same procedures discussed above, and set your TWAIN interface appropriately.

Making a Tudor Rose Open a new A&L Draw file. Since you will be sending this file to a service bureau, it is unnecessary to choose a printer, but you will surely want rulers and a grid.

This file has to be changed into a vector image; the vinyl cutter can't work with a bitmap such as a TIFF image. Many drawing programs support automatic tracing (the process for making a vector image version of a bitmap); Draw doesn't. But the Curved Line tool works pretty well for tracing images that are not overly complex.

Figure 7.4   A Tudor Rose.

Figure 7.5   The traced elements (on the left) get assembled into the final Tudor rose (on the right).

Use the Import command on the File menu to import the scanned raw rose. Select the Curved Line tool, and draw around the major elements of the rose. After you have traced the scan, almost certainly you will want to switch to the Line Editing tool and adjust things for smoothness. Assemble the elements, and group the result. See Figure 7.5.

To keep the hand-drawn look, I set the line to a fairly wide (9-point) calligraphic setting using the Pen tool. This means the outlines have thicks and thins, and they will vary depending on how the pieces are rotated. Notice, too, I drew only one each of the little T-shaped and pointy pieces, then copied them and placed them. The trick to placing them is to move the element so that the bottom point is where it should be, pretty much, then rotate the element into place after anchoring the bottom by moving the rotation center-point target. Finally, I didn't try to trace the little dots in the middle of the rose; I simply made a small circle and copied it several times.

Making Two Roses   I need two roses (one for York and one for Lancaster). It is no great trouble to drag off a copy of the first rose. The simple way to handle the color issue is to simply change the fill color globally (if the first rose is white, make the second red).

A limitation to cut vinyl: the color palette. Most service bureaus stock maybe two dozen colors, and you need to know what they have.

I chose something a bit more involved. In the sample file (PLAYS.GED), notice that the centers of the roses are pink. Making the center of the first rose pink is no special problem; changing the color of the copy means ungrouping the rose, selecting only the parts to be filled with red (leaving the pink part alone), and then regrouping everything. It takes a minute or two, but the result is a bit more interesting.

Developing the Copy

The copy for this poster is pretty simple. It needs to tell who is doing the plays and what the plays are, and it needs to capture some attention. See Figure 7.6.

Use the Text tool to add three separate lines of text:

Smallville Community College

Little Theatre Society

presents

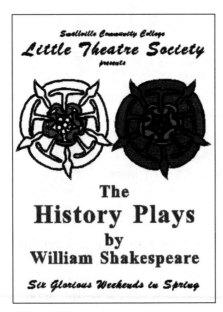

Figure 7.6   The finished History Plays poster design.

I chose the official college font, A&L Draw's Wyeth.

There is a reason for making these separate elements: I want to size each line separately. *Little Theatre Society* needs to be bigger than *Smallville Community College* and *presents*.

I chose to set the main copy, *The History Plays*, in red A&L Classical Medium type. Again, each line is created separately, so I can size the lines independently. Once they are the right size, I can align the lines of type and group them for convenience.

Take a look at the sample file (PLAYS.GED); notice the second version of the poster. The basic design is fine, but it would be useful to have a version of the poster that lets the theater manager put in a piece about the next play in the series, with dates, ticket prices, and so on. Properly managed, this means a single poster can announce the entire series. Simply change the show-specific part of the poster.

> Were this poster being printed, rather than being executed in vinyl, the same strategy would still be useful. Print the poster once—black with two spot colors—and let a local, less costly printer print a few of the run each time, with the show-specific data. A few more could be set up with particulars about the cast, and sold as souvenirs, or something.

"Printing" the Poster

Of course, this is not really going to be printed, in the usual sense. You might make a nice print on the Fargo printer (if you have the dye-sublimation kit for this printer, the results will be particularly spectacular). Show it to the client (I did; they were very appreciative). But the purpose of the exercise is to get this cut out and mounted, after all.

Have no doubt: Find a good person at a service bureau and cherish that person. This relationship is pure gold.

The service bureau I work with for cut vinyl, The Graphics Workshop in Plainfield, NJ, is a very good example of what to look for. Audrey Angrisani, my contact there, has plenty of experience, both as a designer and as a computer-graphics user, and she has all the major software packages. I simply send her the file over the modem or on disk. She checks the design and makes sure that all the elements are in correct form for her process. Then she goes to work. A few days later, I get the poster back by FedEx. This is a very complex piece of work for the cut-vinyl process; the price-tag is about $125. Most jobs will be less costly.

Flyers

Posters are special-event items. Flyers—the kind of thing that gets stuck up everywhere (even when there is a "Post No Bills" label around)—are bread-and-butter work. My heaviest client for flyers is my wife; she regularly uses color and grayscale flyers to promote her classes and other projects at the college where she teaches. I end up making so many of these, I keep a couple standard templates on hand, just to support her needs.

The basic design for the full-page "broadside" version incorporates scanned images based on porcelain designs from art that is now out of copyright (Figure 7.7). I place these in "windows" on a complementary color band. To make them stand out a bit, I put a black shadow behind the bitmaps.

Printing Out a Flyer

A low-cost color printer is ideal for printing flyers. Using Fargo's oversize paper (to provide full-size 8½ by 11-inch output) or standard inkjet fanfold on something like a PaintJet, you can run off a couple dozen at a cost of about 45 cents. The grayscale version is even cheaper per copy.

Figure 7.7   The poster template in the grayscale version (on the left) and with pictures and lettering in a final version. In the color version, the top band is a slightly bluish green, and the bottom band is blue.

If you have a color DeskJet printer, which offers higher-resolution printing than the PaintJet, I recommend having the color copies made at the local copy center using a color laser copier. The cost per print will be substantially higher, but the copies will be permanent. Color DeskJet ink is water-soluble, and that is not a good thing for posters.

If you choose a grayscale flyer—for very low cost, against the loss of a stunning effect—it is better to print it on your laser printer, rather than going to the copy center. The copying process results in loss of resolution and delicacy in shading. It'll work, but the result won't be as pretty.

Producing a Flyer with a Coupon

Sometimes it is useful to have a coupon on flyers. Interested readers tear off the coupon, which has a note about the subject and a phone number or something equally useful. Figure 7.8 shows a variation designed to promote Mrs. Jenner's Saturday courses in Chinese language.

Adding Tear-offs

Adding little tear-offs to a flyer like this is truly simple. Using the Typeface tool, set text alignment to centered and the type size to about 12 or 14 points. Type in a couple lines that capture the advertised service or product. Add it to the flyer. Use the Rotation tool to turn the text 90 degrees. Place it at the lower left of the page, then use the Copy tool to rubber-stamp the text across the bottom. Generally, expect to get about eight coupons at the boom of the page.

Creating a Background Graphic

Notice the faint picture in the background of this poster? It's a variation of the one in the upper right-hand corner of the flyer in Figure 7.7.

Figure 7.8   This flyer features tear-off coupons.

To make this picture into a subtle background, I brought it back into Picture Publisher. I selected the Fill tool (the paint bucket from the tool bar, then the third tool from the left for solid fill). Make sure to select white as the fill color (it should be the top color chip of the two at the bottom of the tool bar; it is isn't, switch on the palette at the bottom right, and select white that way). Set the transparency (top right of the tool settings) to about 80 percent. Then click anywhere on the bitmap and watch it get lighter. You may want to do this twice with that transparency setting. But do it a bit at a time, as Picture Publisher has only one level of undo. And be sure you save the faded version in a different file.

The Fill tool fly-out and its options

An alternative procedure is to darken the picture, with transparent layers of black or gray. This works well if the picture has a background that fills the entire area of the final design.

Use lightened images where the lettering is going to be large, dark, and bold, in fairly saturated, rich colors. Use darkened images when the lettering is light and can be set off from the background with white outlines and the like.

The aim, in either case, is to increase the contrast between the background image and the foreground lettering. Expect to run a check print or two in addition to checking things on the screen; in this case, the check print is more accurate.

For neatness' sake, score the paper just above the coupons by folding the group back and forth a couple times, then clip between each coupon.

Creating a Display Card

Flyers are cheap enough to make, and you stick them all over. Flyers with tear-off coupons are still better; the reader gets something to take away as a reminder. If you score the tops of the coupons, so the flyer still looks fairly neat as the coupons are removed, they are not a bad solution.

But polish requires more. How about a display card with text, pointing to a pocket at the bottom just the right size for business cards?

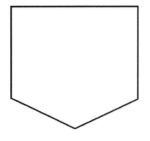

Set up A&L Draw for printing to your laser printer, with rulers and grid on. Set the grid to quarter-inch spacing and in front, so objects won't hide it.

Set the Pen tool to a nice fat line. Use the Straight Line tool to create a shape like the one in the margin. Make it nice and big—as wide as the page and about 7½ inches from top to bottom. Place it at the top of the page. This shape frames the message and acts as a pointer to the card pocket to be constructed at the bottom.

Not brilliant, but you get the idea.

OK, what are you going to sell? I have used this idea for all kinds of things, including my own business. How about something like Figure 7.9?

Selecting Card Stock

Print your display card on light card stock.

Figure 7.9   I've used text in a box; you could also put in a picture.

Printing on card stock is an option for some, but not all laser printers. LaserJet IIIs, and in general, all printers built on the Canon full-size printer engine, can handle card stock up to 60 lb. weight. Small-footprint printers—HP personal laser printers (the IIP and IIIP)—can't take the heavier paper. If your printer has a straight-through paper-path option, you can probably print light card stock. If the printer has a convoluted paper path—and sadly, that is becoming more common—then the card stock either will not feed in the first place, or it will jam.

Card stock comes in lots of varieties. I usually use index-card stock. It is flexible and has a smooth finish. In my HPIII/WinJet800 setup, that means the toner will adhere better (on less smoothly finished paper, the toner tends to rub off).

Card stock also comes in colors, and color is always good. But I prefer a different trick.

Using Metallic Foil

It is possible to buy special metallic foils for adding color to laser printed documents. This is commonly available from desktop-publishing supply houses (such as Paper Direct, which has an 800 number) and larger computer stores (such as Fry's, in the San Francisco Bay Area).

In the present design, after printing the basic design, I would pick a flashy color—an electric blue or a vivid magenta. Cut out a piece of the metallic foil big enough to cover the *CHEAP Graphics* portion of text, and stick it in place with the supplied little sticky dots. Then pass the card through the laser printer a second time (set things up to print a blank page). The heat fuses the color to the areas where there is black laser printing, and it ignores the areas where things are not printed.

This sounds more complex than it is; it takes a couple of minutes and it works pretty well.

Making the Card Pocket

Now I have a card with a printed message in a box. It is time to revert to elementary school, folks, and make the card pocket.

Look at Figure 7.10. I've indicated two areas to cut out on the right and left. What remains is an upside-down T-shaped extension. The cross at the button is about an inch and a half deep. At the top of this, I've indicated a score line; it means "fold here." Fold up at the second score line above it (about a quarter-inch to three-eighths inches up from the first score). Finally, do the folds on the cross (or wings, if you prefer). They fold to create the pocket in front, and the ends tuck behind the vertical part of the card. Staple the ends once or twice, and there is a nice pocket. Tuck in some business cards, and post *that* in your local grocery store.

Standard business cards are $3\frac{1}{2}$ inches wide and 2 inches deep. So, your pocket needs to be a smidgin wider (say, $3\frac{5}{8}$ inches or so) and shallower (say, an inch and a half). Otherwise, getting the cards in and out might be a problem.

Figure 7.10 To make a card pocket, follow the cutting (heavy, dashed) and folding (light, dotted) lines.

Learn Desktop Graphics and Design on the PC

There is no reason why you can't draw in the cutting and scoring lines as guides. But if you do, make sure your cuts don't leave any lines showing. Ideally, when you make the cuts, use sharp scissors, and make each cut a single sweep.

The Fruits of Your Labor

Lots of companies would be delighted to sell you fancy card holders of various sorts — at fancy prices, too. Sometimes it is prudent to substitute labor (your own) for capital (money out of your pocket). It makes sense to do it yourself. Here's why.

First, creating your own promotional materials can be a lot of fun, and it's a nice way to change pace and relieve stress. Second, simply because this is not a mass-produced product, it will stand out as different. Difference in advertising sometimes suggests difference in product, and product differentiation is a major issue in promotion.

If you need hundreds of displays, clearly this is not the procedure to follow. But most promotional materials have a limited lifetime, and only a few are needed.

Posters like the ones in this project may be one of a kind. The cost is low enough to make that practical. Flyers of the kinds demonstrated here are intended to be run off in dozens (the colored ones) or even hundreds (the grayscale ones). As to the display card — effectively, a fancy flyer — practically speaking, you can adopt this procedure for up to a dozen (more only if you have some friends, and perhaps some wine and cheese for a help-me-out party some Saturday afternoon).

Project 8: Promotional Goodies

Posters and their lesser cousins provide latitude for the artist. The results can be spectacular and truly satisfying. But design encompasses fun as well as art. So let's look at other types of promotional goodies, beginning with T-shirts.

Making T-Shirts

When Fargo started shipping the Primera, the company experienced a bit of a shock. Of all the different supplies it sold, the category hardest to keep in stock was the iron-on transfer paper. You can print your design backwards on this special paper and iron the result onto a T-shirt. Remember rainy-day activities, when you drew with crayons on a piece of old sheet, then put a piece of old paper bag on top and ironed the colors in? This is the same idea. It is, after all, wax thermal-transfer printing.

In general, if you can get it into the computer, you can print it, and if you can print it, you can put it on a shirt. Do you have a picture of your spouse or child? Use Picture Publisher to scan it, size it, and mirror it horizontally. If you don't want to do your own scanning, you can have your photos processed as Kodak Photo-CDs; use the low-res copy for this application.

Print out your scanned photo on iron-on transfer paper (Fargo sells it directly and through its dealer network). Iron it onto the T-shirt.

Fargo offers iron-on transfer paper; so does Star Micronics, for use with its J144 color thermal transfer printer. Both products work well; I found it a bit easier to feed the paper accurately in the Fargo.

In either case, the only weakness is that you can't wash the shirts in hot water. Use cold water and no bleach, and the shirts will stand up fairly well.

This same technique works well for sweatshirts, and on fine-knit lisle cotton sport shirts. This last option gave rise to an idea.

Developing the Company Look

The team look is fine; the team think is sometimes less interesting, of course.

I have long admired the team look that some companies present, commonly achieved by putting members of the team in a shirt with the company logo. I decided my team could look a bit more professional when we went to trade shows if we could have custom shirts with a logo. Naturally, it was a last-minute—and untested—idea, and I didn't want to spend any money having the shirts made up.

A trip to Sym's (a local discount clothier) provided some nice-looking cotton lisle sport shirts for about $12 apiece. That seemed a reasonable enough price.

Designing the Team Look

As you may have gathered, I like heraldry. The device I dreamed up consisted of a monogram of DJC (for Donald Jenner Consulting), surmounted by a crested helm—in full and glorious color, natch. The left-hand monogram in Figure 8.1 was made using the Printer Fonts setting, then adding the three letters (DJC) in a calligraphic face commonly called Vivaldi or Vivante. The letters were positioned to appear linked. A variation on the theme could be done using A&L Draw's Classic Medium typeface, by adjusting letter

Figure 8.1 Two variations on a monogram.

widths and heights, as shown on the right-hand monogram in Figure 8.1.

The rest of the team design consists of a helm, which is assembled from some simple geometric shapes. The slightly flattened globe for the headpiece is a circle inserted with the Symbol tool. The neck and shoulder pieces are freeform objects, drawn with the Curved Line and Straight Line tools. To make the shadowed bit for the shoulder piece, I duplicated the gray shoulder piece, changed it to black, and adjusted it for position. The grille for the face is a black rectangle (inserted with the Symbol tool and sized) and a set of gold-colored bars. You can draw one bar with the Curved Line tool, and duplicate and flip it as needed. See Figure 8.2.

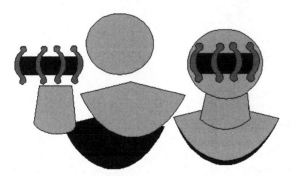

Figure 8.2 The helm and its elements consist of simple shapes.

Figure 8.3   Here are the crest elements and the assembled crest (notice the white feathers are outlined in black, so they show up).

The crest—the thing that sits on top of the helm—consists of a coronet with a tuft of feathers in bright colors. I am not a great draftsman, and anyway, highly stylized feathers are appropriate—thank heaven! All these elements are drawn using the line-drawing tools in combination. For example, the top parts of the feathers are made using the Curved Line tool, and the shafts are made with the Straight Line tool. Remember to end the shape by closing it (attaching the end of the line to the first node). The crest elements are shown in Figure 8.3.

Finishing the design is simply a matter of putting the elements together: Place the crest at the top of the helm, and the monogram overlapping its base. Group the whole thing. See Figure 8.4.

Figure 8.4   The finished monogram is at left, and its mirror image for making transfers is at the right.

Reversing the Image for Printing

To use the monogram for neat-looking company shirts, it needs to be reversed—use the Flip <> command to mirror the design. You may want to resize it; I think anything much bigger than 3 inches deep is going to look rather too boastful. I found that by making the image a bit smaller than that (about an inch and a quarter wide), I could put five copies across a page and make three rows. In short, I got 15 copies on a sheet of transfer paper, as shown in Figure 8.5. I printed this to Fargo, cut them out, and ironed them onto the upper left breast of the shirts. I had a couple left over, which went onto sweatshirts.

Tip: When you go to iron these on, you want a fairly hot iron, and you want to press hard. The idea is to get all the wax off the transfer and onto the shirt, and well into the material.

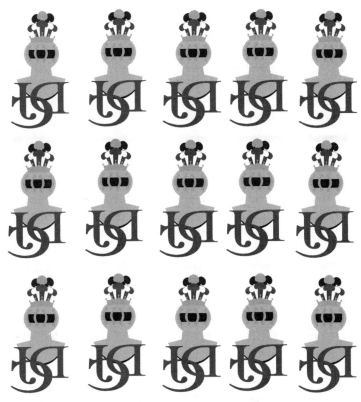

Figure 8.5   This figure represents the printable area on a Fargo transfer sheet, with a whole bunch of logos ready to clip and iron onto shirt fronts.

Promoting Products with Neon

Putting a logo on a shirt is a way of promoting—in this case, a business. Effectively, each of the associates wearing a company shirt is identified with the company, and by extension, its offering.

With ID this cheap, it makes sense to think about promoting a *product* as well. Our friends at Acme Fardels could do with this kind of promotion; fardels are in the buggy-whip category (not a lot of interest in buggy whips these days, you know). Although a spiffy shirt won't entirely renovate the fardel market, it might mean that what market there is, will be held by Acme. So, what might lend excitement to fardels?

First, you want some neon! I don't mean real neon, of course—but drawing a bright neon line around something is a look-at-me icon in modern societies. It's also kind of a neat trick.

Look at a neon tube. Notice that the color is not solid; it is more saturated toward the edges of the tube, and lighter—almost white—toward the center of the tube. That's the effect you need to create.

Creating a Neon Tube

In A&L Draw, open a new file. Use the Preferences command in the View menu to turn on the rulers—and most important, turn on the grid with a quarter-inch setting.

Hint: Hold the Shift key as you draw to constrain lines to perfectly vertical or horizontal directions.

Use the Straight Line tool to draw a wide, fairly shallow box; make sure it is a closed shape. Since this shape needs to be edited, you cannot simply use the Symbol tool to insert a square, then modify its width. You have to draw it. Fill this shape with a nice bright color (I chose blue). Use the Pen tool to set the outline type to None.

Click on the Fill tool (the little paint bucket). Look at the scrolling menu in the Fill Attributes dialog. Select Shaded Straight from this menu. The sample box will be shaded

Figure 8.6   This part of the neon box shows the editing process to get a precisely 45-degree corner.

from the selected color through to white. Click OK, and this shading will be applied to the box you made.

Now you need to edit the box. Click on the Line Editing tool. This box must be made into a trapezoid, with the ends slanting inward at precisely 45 degrees. That adjustment is easy; just look at the grid. For each grid mark down in the depth of the box, the two bottom corners must be moved inward one grid mark. See Figure 8.6.

This box is only half of the neon tube. Copy it, and use the Flip ∧ V (vertical) command to put the white part at the top. Edit the bottom box so its endpoints continue the trapezoid shape. Once everything matches pretty well, group the whole thing into a single section of neon tube. See Figure 8.7.

The next step is to copy this section of tube. To do so, drag off a copy a couple inches below the first section. Then use the vertical Flip command again. Drag off another copy, and use the Rotation tool to rotate this third section 90 degrees. Copy that one and flip it horizontally. Now, you must move them into position, corner to corner (adjusting a tad as you go) and fit them together to make a nice neon square, as shown in Figure 8.8. Actually, the tube is too thick for use (neon tubing

Figure 8.7   Your neon trapezoid should look like this.

Figure 8.8   The tube sections fitted together create a pretty effect with a little bit of a 3-D look.

is thinner) and the angles are too sharp (neon tubing is bent glass, after all)—but these are details.

Using Neon to Sell Fardels

Let's use this technique—and some others—to add spice to Acme fardels.

Find the file in which you stored the Acme logo. If it was stored in a separate file, life is easy; if you saved it only as part of another file, open that file. In either case, use the Group tool to select the entire logo, then put it on the clipboard with the Copy command from the Edit menu. Open a new file and paste the Acme logo into it. Turn the rulers and grid on.

Making the Frame   Use the technique described in the preceding section to make a neon square. Make the tubes about two-thirds to three-quarters of an inch wide and about

7½ inches long (that is, the initial rectangle you draw should be about 7½ inches wide and three-eighths of an inch deep). Again, I chose a fairly vibrant blue as the basic color. This is the frame for the picture.

Adding Clip Art This is a good place for some clip art, too. Computer Support Corporation makes lots of clip-art collections; one of them is a collection of dinosaurs (cleverly called the Jurassic Art collection).

CSC's Jurassic Art clip art is something new. The company's artists have created the images in such a way that they can be ungrouped, and parts can be treated as if articulated. This project uses that capability, as you can see from the sample file, NEON.GED.

If you don't have this clip-art library, you can copy the image from my design file on the disk; of course, this means you don't get to see the dancing Velociraptors.

Dinosaurs are still in favor, so I chose to include the Walking Tyrannosaurus from the collection. It is accessed using the Library tool (the icon is a shelf of books). The *T. rex* is placed in the work area in the usual way.

After placing my dino, I squeezed him a tad by sliding the bottom center handle of the selected image up just a little. This seems to improve the 3-D character of the image. The *T. rex* looks more like he's walking toward me.

Fetching Fardels Now it's time to get some parts of the Acme logo. Ungroup the logo and select the fardel (the bundle of twigs). Drag it up to the *T. rex*'s mouth, and shrink it so it is about the right size—like something our dino might carry in his mouth. Select the dino and ungroup him. Then, click on the upper part of the head (the piece with the eyes, nose, and upper jaw). Use the Bring to Front command on the Arrange

Figure 8.9   The T rex is carrying a likely fardel.

menu (or ^F) to put that part on top of the picture. You should now have the following stacking order: upper jaw, fardel, rest of the *T. rex.* The fardel should be in the dino's mouth, like a doggy fetching a stick. See Figure 8.9. Group the whole thing, and save the file!

Incorporating the Logo   Take the big gold ACME from the logo and place it behind the *T. rex,* toward the top of the neon square. Take the white Fardels, Inc., and change its color to black. Then use the Text tool to take out the *Inc.* Place *Fardels* at the bottom right of the ACME.

All you need now is a slogan. Something like *They're Dino-mite!* seems to fit. I used a special typeface (called, appropriately enough, Dinosauria) that is part of the Jurassic Art collection. I colored it red, put it at the bottom of the square, and stretched it to fit neatly. See Figure 8.10.

Select the whole finished image, group it, and save the file.

Figure 8.10   The finished product promotion image.

Setting Up for Transfer Printing To set up the dinosaur image
for printing on a shirt, drag off a copy and size it to about 3
inches square. Then flip it horizontally (use the Flip <> command) and copy it to make a sheet of transfers. Print them,
cut them out, and iron them on.

Customizing the Whole Presentation Drawings like the one in
Figure 8.10 scale nicely, almost without exception. Hansel
could easily scale this image up to poster size, either for
printing at a service bureau, or for tiled output to a local
color printer in Gretl's office.

Guidelines for Creating More Promotional Goodies

A whole category of service bureaus specializes in taking
your art and putting it on everything from key chains to coffee mugs. You want a watch with your image on it? Every

I like mugs, myself; I have
dozens of computer-
company promo mugs—
a regular collection!

airline magazine carries at least two ads for companies that sell them. Magazines specializing in computer graphics also carry ads for this kind of service.

Doing this is almost painless, but here are some wrinkles you may want to consider.

Make Sure the Service Bureau Uses Your Software

This is one case where it is essential that the service bureau use the same software you do to process your images. Most service bureaus should have at least A&L Draw, and really should have the premium version, A&L Editor. It is a common enough product.

The reason the service bureau should work with the same software is simple: Almost certainly, some adjustment to the image will be in order, and this lets the service bureau do it with no fuss, no muss, and no bother to you.

If you have to use a service bureau that does not have your software, in most cases it claims to be able to work from your print. Send a fairly large print—a couple times larger than the final image on your mug or whatever. When the service bureau reduces it, that should take care of any little imperfections in the picture.

Ask for a Sample

Generally, you must pay a small fee for a sample; do it. You need to see the way the service bureau handles your picture before you spend substantial dollars on a carton of something you decide you don't like.

Match Your Image to Your Application

The picture in Figure 8.10 is very colorful. It will look nice on a white shirt; a beige mug would be OK, too. But it would disappear on a dark background.

Some of the neatest—and most modestly priced—promotional goodies are in the nylon-bag category. At one trade show I attended recently, instead of the usual badge holder, the show sponsors provided exhibitors and favored attendees with a promotional novelty.

This neck pack consisted of a zippered pouch with a see-through pocket on the front just the right size for show ID and business cards and a pen—and all the other things you need to have at hand on a show floor—on a cord to hang around your neck. Each pouch carried the Laptop/Palmtop logo—naturally.

The company that designed this pouch is Dan Goods Manufacturing of San Jose, California. The company has a whole catalog of promotional items, on each of which it will print your design. Fanny packs, wine and picnic sacks, floppy-disk clocks, sunglasses—all kinds of neat business gifts at all kinds of prices. Every one of them can carry your design. But look at the item, and plan your design accordingly.

A Custom Printing Option: Silk Screen

For some kinds of design, it pays to use a specialist, rather than a general-purpose promotional-item supplier.

I live in New York. I have found a woman who is a silk-screen specialist who has done some really special work for me. The best part of this is that I can control the design with some precision.

Silk screen is a kind of painting. A cloth screen is produced photographically, leaving the patterned areas open. The screen is placed on top of the area to be printed, and special paint is squeegeed down on the surface. One screen is made for each color (which makes this a variation on spot-color printing).

One of the nice things about silk-screen printing is that the film positives from which the screens are made can be produced quite handily on a laser printer.

To make these originals, you need special overhead-projection foils designed for a laser printer or photocopier. *Don't try this with ordinary overhead foils! They will melt and ruin your printer.* Check your printer manual, or consult with a reputable supplier. My personal choice for this has been 3M's branded foils, which have worked well.

If your design is to be done in one color, simply do the work in black and print black on white (the white, of course, being clear). If your design is in color, you need to print each color separately. You also need to print registration marks so the person doing the silk screening can match things up precisely.

Practically, in a program such as A&L Draw, which does not have automatic separation capabilities, you need to restrict a silk screen to a couple colors. You have to manually determine the separation, and that is a great deal of work. The elements in the design should be simple; this is not a process that will reproduce complexity well.

A registration mark

To make the registration marks, add a circle symbol, and set the fill (with the Fill tool) to None. Set the line width for this symbol and in general to 0.5, using the Pen tool. Set line color to black.

Shrink the circle to about a quarter-inch, and draw two straight lines, intersecting at right angles in the center of the circle. Group the whole thing, and copy it so that there is one mark in each corner.

To print, select all the elements of one color—say, blue or red. Change those elements to black. Then, while holding the Shift key, also select the registration marks. All the elements of the chosen color plus all the registration marks should now be selected.

Put a piece of laser-printable overhead foil in the hopper of your laser printer and print the page, setting the Print dialog box to print Selected Objects Only. The film prints, with the elements you have selected.

Go back to the picture. Deselect the registration marks (hold the Shift key, and click on each mark in turn). Then reset the color of those items just printed. Do the same procedure for each color until you have a set of black-on-clear sheets, one for each color, with registration marks on each. Print a colored version, if you can, to guide your silk-screen artist. Hand over the films and the colored version, and you should be in business.

Useful Design

This project serves a couple purposes. The open agenda, obviously, has been to suggest some neat things you can do with the designs you are making. Folks, these are real-life items. I am wearing the DJC (monogram) sweatshirt as we speak—and thinking I'd better make another, since this one is getting a bit ratty.

The hidden agenda is the discussion of designing for production.

The purpose of the exercise (as my old headmaster used to say) is to create useful designs. Useful designs accomplish specific goals. A poster is a way of communicating. A logo is a statement. And so on.

If the design you create looks great on the monitor, but it doesn't translate into something handsome for a more public venue, then you have not accomplished the purpose.

Creating useful designs is fairly straightforward. First, know the story you are telling with your design—and stick to it. Second, keep that story simple—and the design, if anything, simpler still. Every scrap of the surface used does not need to be covered with lettering or pictures. Think about the Dino picture: Simple, clean, and it tells a story in the picture (the slogan is strictly reinforcement). Don't take my word for it; look at any glossy magazine, and notice which ads have the best effect. They won't be the ones with a lot of busy stuff in them—I'd lay odds on that, if I were a betting person.

Part of keeping it simple is thinking through where the design will appear. If you are going to print on beige paper or something of the sort, try putting a beige background behind your work. Do things look right? Fine. If not, change it now! Print a couple of variations to see what looks good. No matter how experienced you get, you will still need to test things.

A little work up front will give you real creative satisfaction when the final product comes out.

That creative satisfaction can be a problem: It can be so satisfying that you will feel guilty taking money for your work. Consequently, every organization to which you belong will feel free to hit you for a freebie. The horror is you'll do it, because this stuff is *fun!* A word to the wise: Ask the organization to at least foot the bill for materials.

Project 9: Computer Graphics and Desktop Publishing

Distinctions between computer-based design, computer graphics, and desktop publishing do not exist. Desktop publishing is nothing more than the application of a range of special and general-purpose computer-graphics tools to traditional printing technology and current alternatives.

Example of an alternative printing technology: the desktop copy machine.

Actually, almost all publishing these days is desktop publishing. The tools used are pretty much the same ones you can buy at the local cheap-software store. A lot of the traditional technology has entirely disappeared, simply because the computer-graphics tools (including the subset specifically tuned for publishing) are so good and so cheap. For example, the art of typesetting is pretty much a hobby these days.

That's not all good. *Printing* technology has not changed (it has expanded, but that is not the same thing, exactly). Things that make for good design—the use of white space—have certainly not changed. The fine points of good typography have not changed. But fewer people have learned these arts—and quite a few others of equally hoary age—by doing them.

Inevitably, you will use the computer-graphics tools and skills you are developing in some kind of desktop-publishing application. Sometimes, it will be to apply the finishing touches to work done in another program. Sometimes, the entire desktop publishing project is best done in a drawing or painting program. In either case, the test of skill comes in as you take the project from the computer through the final product.

Business Cards

Business cards are the most useful thing anyone can have. They are *identity*. They are cheap. Everyone should have several—one for each identity.

A standard business card is three and a half inches in one direction by two inches in the other direction. It can be vertical or (more conservatively) horizontal. You can design the card and print a copy for reproduction by the local instant-printing shop, or you can roll your own, like the hero-PI in "The Rockford Files."

The old president of Smallville Community College, Murray Hill, has retired. His successor is the eminent scholar (and superb fundraiser), Elizabeth Lee, Ph.D. She needs new business cards, and she needs them *now*.

Creating a Business Card

Open the Smallville logo file (LOGO1.GED), and save under a new name (say, BCARD1.GED). This file has a couple of versions of the Smallville logo in it: one in color and one in grayscale. You could do a color business card, but that is pushing the envelope a little far, and anyway, President Lee would not get her cards back soon enough. So select the entire color version and delete it. You will use the grayscale version only. Select the whole of the grayscale logo, and make sure it is grouped with a ^G command. Turn on the rulers and grid, and you're ready to roll.

Drag the logo off to the side (into the other window), out of the way. Use the Symbol tool to insert a square symbol in the main work area. Use the Fill tool to turn off interior fill (set the dialog box to None). Move the box to the top left corner of the work area. Stretch the box so it is 2 inches deep and 3½ inches wide—standard business-card size.

Select the logo and scale it down by grabbing a corner and sliding it inward. Drag the reduced version of the logo so that it fits neatly in the card-size box.

The college logo can be placed on the card in several different ways. The way it is placed will depend on (or determine) how text is placed. One alternative is not shown in the margin: You could fade out the logo, changing to paler grays, and place it square in the center of the card, with text over it. Taste plays no small part in the choice.

For the first try, I chose a design placing the logo on the left, filling more or less the entire left third of the card.

Time to add the text: Again, there are options. I prefer, generally, to put address and phone information at the bottom of a card, and to put company names at the top of a card. I center the name (and title) between the two.

So, I added *Smallville Community College,* using the same A&L Wyeth typeface that is part of the logo. For the rest of the text, I used the A&L Classic Medium typeface (I could just as well have switched to a printer typeface, of course). The result was the business card shown in Figure 9.1.

Frankly, this version looks too pedestrian and amateurish. It lacks zip. One of the glories of working with a computer

Figure 9.1   Here's the first try at the business card for Small-ville's new president.

graphics program is that nothing is graven in stone, only electrons, and you can try a different design.

Jazzing Up the Biz Card

The next version moves President Lee's name and title to the bottom of the logo and groups the college address information to the right of the logo. I put the college name in the same Roman-style typeface as the rest of the text, and I enlarged the word *Smallville* so that it is the same width as the words *Community College*. See Figure 9.2. The interesting thing about this second design, it seems to me, is the way the different text elements (college name and address; person's name and title) are anchored by the logo. Another interesting thing: I can use a larger logo, and larger type for the college name, and still have a nice sense of open space.

Figure 9.2   This design looks a bit better.

Logos (Project 2) serve a number of purposes and should be designed for flexibility. Logos need to be effective in both color and black and white, and may have to work in a variety of contexts—on a poster, on letterhead, even on T-shirts!

Four Variations on a Theme

Note: All images in this insert were output to Polaroid Digital Palette using Zenographics SuperPrint.

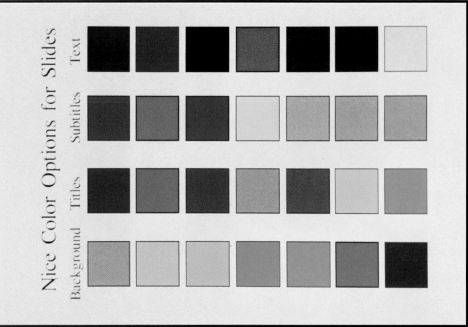

When designing slides (Project 5), think of each row on this chart as a set of best matches for presentation support images.

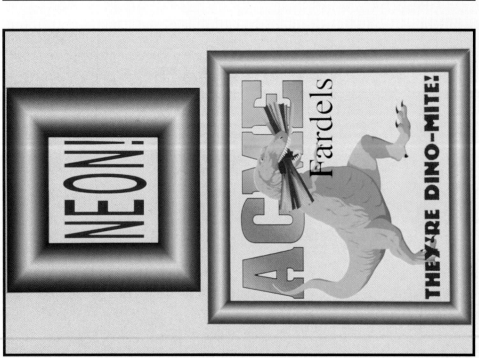

This is the T-shirt version of the Acme logo (from Project 8: Promotional Goodies)

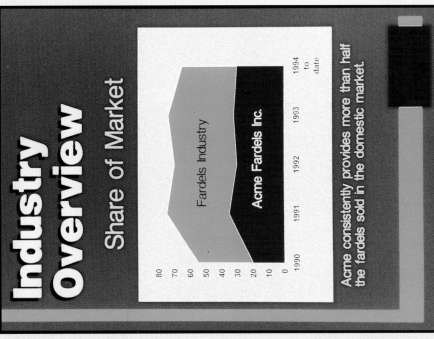

Overhead projection foils (from Project 5) seem to work best if used in vertical, or "portrait," format. Use colored backgrounds for wax thermal-transfer printing.

From Project 5, a simple slide and a more complex one with an added bitmap image. The common background makes for unity.

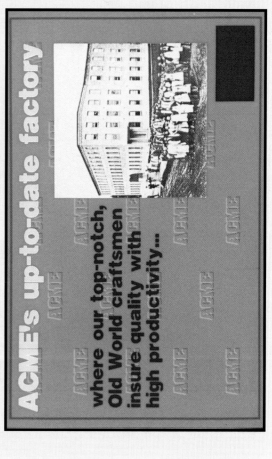

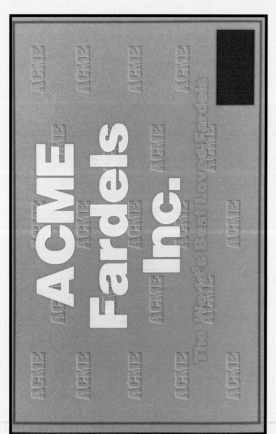

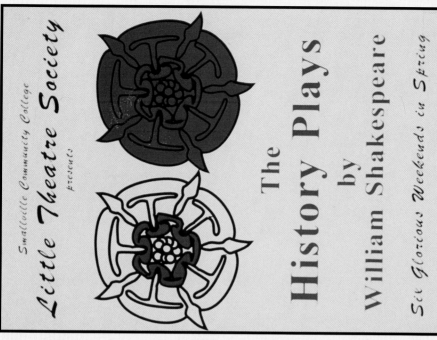

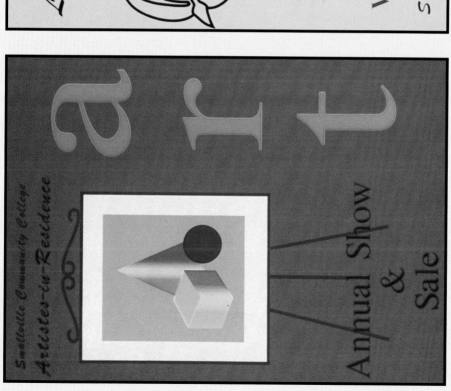

Two poster designs from Project 7—one intended for ordinary printing and the other for cut-vinyl

For simple technical drawings, fancy and expensive CAD software is overkill. In these examples from Project 11, Arts & Letters® DRAW gets the job done.

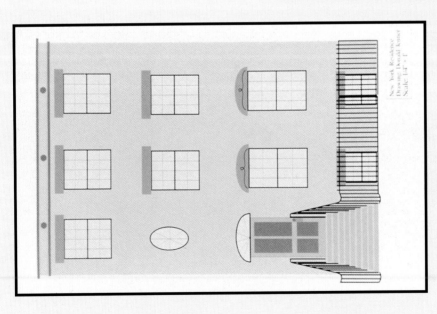

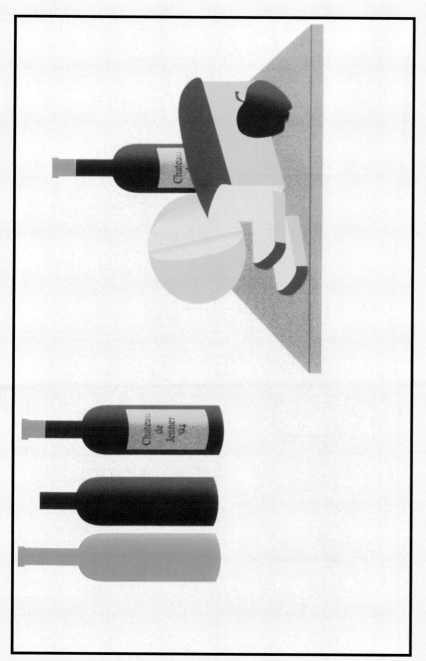

The wine bottle "steps," showing color shading.

The "drawing" section of the still life—less subtle than the painting, but not without use.

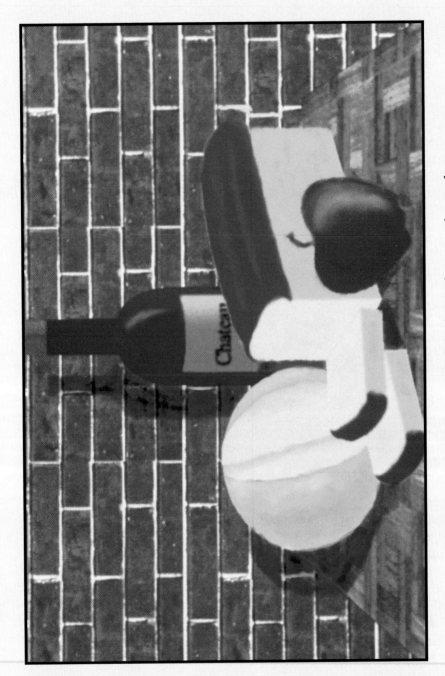

The still life from Project 12: While this might not make me famous, it ain't too bad as a demo of what can be done!

Elizabeth Lee, Ph. D.
President

Smallville
Community College
Smallville, AS 00000
444-555-5555

Figure 9.3   A vertical business-card layout uses the same text and logo.

Let's try one more possibility. Having some options is good, when you show work to a client—even when you are the client.

For a vertical design, select the box and stretch it so it is 2 inches wide and 3½ inches deep. It is easier to stretch the box than to rotate it. Since all the text has already been entered, you can simply copy it, rather than reentering it. See Figure 9.3.

Making Samples

At this point, with three designs, it makes sense to show President Lee what you've been doing. There are several possibilities, including that she will send you back to the (electronic) drawing board. One way to avoid that last unpleasant possibility is to not only present a single page with the different designs, but to walk in with some samples.

Redoing things is not fun.

To make the samples, select the designs in turn and line them up neatly. Use the grid to do this, perhaps, rather than the Align command (especially if you have not grouped everything). Then use the Group tool to temporarily group them, and drag off a copy to the adjacent window. Use the

Hint: Hold the Shift key down as you draw straight lines, and they will stay on the vertical or horizontal.

Straight Line tool to draw in some crop marks—little lines used to guide cutting. After the crop marks are drawn, select the boxes around the different card designs and delete them. See Figure 9.4. Print this page, as well as the page with the basic designs.

The next step is fairly obvious: Cut these samples out, using the crop marks and the fact that you know the final samples should be 2 inches by 3½ inches.

You can cut the samples with scissors—especially if you have very long scissors. It is easier with a paper cutter.

I find a 12-inch-square paper cutter—essentially, a large board, ruled with a half-inch grid and a big knife attached on one side—a useful tool in my studio. It is useful for sample making, and it is useful for a whole range of other small jobs you do yourself. Paper cutters are not terribly expensive, and they can be found at better stationery, art supply, and photography stores.

Figure 9.4   The samples, with crop marks, are ready for printing.

Now take the designs and samples to President Lee, and there is a real chance she will choose one of your designs as is.

Printing Business Cards

President Lee likes the design illustrated in Figure 9.2. She wants 1000 cards. This is simple to do. A fairly upscale copy shop can deliver the goods from your photo-ready output.

To set things up, select the card design with the Group tool, and drag off a copy to one of the unused page-size windows. Then drag off a second copy and set it immediately below, so the edges of the two card-size boxes form a single line. Draw in crop marks to indicate the corners and the dividing line. Zoom in on the two cards to make final adjustments and set the zoom lines as precisely as you can. This is called a 2-up layout, and it is what most instant-print shops find most convenient for business-card printing. See Figure 9.5. You should print this layout as close as possible to the center of the page.

Figure 9.5   Here's a two-up layout for business cards.

Instant-print shops come in several flavors. Some are limited to using a variety of copiers. Some have offset-printing capability, using either low-cost paper plates or (almost as low-cost) disposable metal plates. I have generally been happiest with the last variety. This is real printing, and the results, even from laser-set photo-ready originals, will often pass muster for professional work.

If you expect to be doing serious printing in quantity, get to know your local instant printers. Try a couple out, have conversations with them—maybe even take the person running the press a cup of coffee. Find the shop with which you are most comfortable, and that seems responsive. The result is a working relationship that can save time and trouble. Printers generally need to be watched, but the one you work with regularly will soon learn just how far you can be tested before you go ballistic, and will consequently require less watching.

The best of these small print shops are very good—as well as cheap.

Emergency Business Cards

"The right laser printer" means a laser printer that can handle light card stock.

All this is very nice, assuming you have a couple days. But a call comes in that President Lee has to dash out of town to visit some state legislators. She needs cards *now*. With some care—and the right laser printer—you can accommodate the good Dr. Lee.

Most current-model laser printers will print to within a quarter-inch of the paper's edge. That means the print area is 8 inches wide and 10½ inches deep. That will accommodate exactly 12 business cards.

Use A&L Draw's Printer Setup command to set your printer—and the page area—to landscape (that is, horizontal) orientation. All four working windows in your business-card design file should now be landscape oriented. Pick an unused page window. Put in two vertical lines, creating three vertical panels, each 3½ inches wide. Draw in three horizontal lines, spacing them to create four horizontal panels, each 2 inches deep. What results is a grid of 3½ inch by 2-inch boxes.

Select and group the elements of the business-card design President Lee has chosen—without the surrounding box used in the original design work, of course. Copy it to the upper left box in the grid you just made. Use A&L Draw's grid to help you center it as nearly as possible. Drag off three more copies, filling the first vertical panel with the four copies.

Group the entire column temporarily with the Group tool, and use the Align command (^N) to align these elements vertically. Then drag off a copy of the entire column to each of the adjacent vertical panels. When all the columns are full, use the Group tool to temporarily group each row, and use the Align command to adjust for horizontal alignment. Now you have a full page of business cards. Take out the grid lines you drew in at first (if you print them, they will just give you grief when it comes time to cut the cards up). Your 12-up page should look like Figure 9.6.

Figure 9.6   A full page of business cards is ready for emergency printing.

Print the resulting page of cards on the laser printer, using light card stock—the same kind of index-card stock discussed in Project 8 will do nicely, or you can experiment with other kinds of stock. You will almost certainly have to hand-feed the card stock; remember to open your printer's trap door for straight-through paper feeding.

When a couple of sheets are printed (in short, as many multiples of 12 as you need—allow for some waste, because you will lose some in the cutting process), take all the pages outside (or open the windows wide) and *lightly* spray each page with some kind of fixative—crystal-clear glossy Krylon is what I use. This has two effects: First, it eliminates the possibility that the laser toner has not fused properly to the heavy paper (that can be a problem). Once a page is sprayed, you have to work hard to rub the printing off. Second, the laser printing will get just a little glossy. The effect is somewhat like thermographed printing, often called raised printing by business-card print shops.

You absolutely must use a paper cutter (scissors won't do it).

To cut these sheets into business cards requires a little care. First, inspect the sheets and check with a ruler to see if the unprinted margins are more or less even. Sometimes—especially with hand-fed sheets—the laser printer doesn't quite feed correctly, and the margins will be a sixteenth-inch or an eighth-inch off. You can compensate when cutting.

Second, trim off the margins. Nominally, that means trimming a quarter-inch off each edge, adjusted for any misfeeding discovered in the previous step.

Third, cut the columns. Use the scale along the top of the paper cutter. Make the first cut at 7 inches (10.5 – 3.5=7); make the second cut at 3½.

Fourth, take each panel (of 4 cards), and cut every 2 inches (that is, at 6", 4", and 2").

Check the cards, discard any that are seriously off center or tilted, and the rest will do nicely as an emergency supply until the professionally printed version comes back.

Learn Desktop Graphics and Design on the PC

Printing your own business cards is nothing new. The latest gimmick in the desktop-printing specialty stores includes laser-perfed card stock for 10-up business cards. You can get plain stock or fancy papers, including some with colored backgrounds or decorations on them. These 10-up sheets assume portrait-mode printing, and the setup procedure is pretty much the same as described.

There is no doubt that these preperfed cards are less troublesome than the cut-them-yourself procedure. But the cuts are not as clean; the laser-perfed edges are just slightly ragged. Then too, if you choose one of the printed-background models, you guarantee your card will look like someone else's. I actually know a design professional who used these in an emergency—and got chuckles.

Doing It Yourself

The issues are *control* and *substitution of labor for capital*. If you run your own office, you understand. Sometimes doing it yourself means spending time you have instead of dollars you don't.

There is also a therapeutic value to doing it yourself. As it happens, I find making business cards very therapeutic; the same applies to a whole range of simple DTP chores. In a certain sense, a lot of this is low-level work; it is ideal for those times when you're ruminating on a problem in the back of your head, and you need to keep your hands busy and out of trouble.

Rule of thumb: Small jobs needed quickly are done in the studio. Bigger jobs, or jobs where time is less crucial or where a level of quality beyond desktop tools is required, get farmed out. The PC graphics world has evolved to support both options.

An obvious question: How do you learn this? Sure, you've got this book; it is a limited resource.

One of the best sources of neat applications has been *Aldus Magazine* (and if the Adobe-Aldus merger, announced when this book was being written, goes through, I sincerely hope the magazine survives). With a variable frequency, the magazine runs a cheap-tricks section.

What is a *cheap trick?* Here is the August 1991 definition from *Aldus Magazine:* "A great Cheap Trick saves money, but also has a certain æsthetic; it's a system-beater, it's a scavenger's delight, it's snake oil." In short, it is a creative solution.

Customized Post-Its

Take this idea, attributed to Lee Shiney. Everyone uses Post-Its—those little notes with a slightly sticky strip on the back. And every so often, a customized version is an effective tool for making a point. Custom-printing Post-Its is not cheap, but Shiney figured out how to do so on the desktop.

The technique is simple enough. First, make a template. Turn on A&L Draw, set it for your laser printer with Printer Setup, and turn on the rulers.

Making the Printing Template

To make the printing template, measure the Post-Its you are going to print. They come in a variety of sizes; my favorite size is 2 inches wide by 3 inches deep (they fit everywhere—in my wallet, on the edge of my monitor). Use the Symbol tool to insert a square, then size it according to the size of the Post-It you are going to print. Duplicate the boxes—for my favorite size, I easily get 9 to the page. (See Figure 9.7.) Print one or more of these sheets.

Now, here's the first tricky part of this: I am assuming that, once you've made a template, you'd like to reuse it. So, select all the boxes on the page, and drag off a copy with the Copy tool to the adjacent work-space page. You need to place these boxes so they sit on the second page exactly as they do on the first page. Use the grid, and zoom in as necessary.

When you think you have the location more or less right on target, create a message. This could be a logo variation, or a simple text message—you choose. I use *Do This Now!* colored with a 20 percent gray (both line and fill), so it is effectively a background for whatever I write on the Post-It.

Using the boxes on the second work-space page as guides, place the message (or logo or whatever) in each box. Print a sheet of this second page. Take this page and the first page (the empty boxes), put them together, and see if they match correctly. If they do, you're in business; if not, do some fine-tuning until they do.

When the template boxes and the message boxes match up, take the boxes off the page with the message. You now have the page with boxes, and the page with messages.

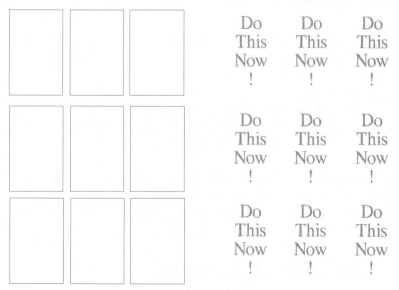

Figure 9.7   A custom-printed Post-It template and fill.

Printing the Post-Its

The following technique works with printers I have tested; it should work with any printer based on the older Canon engine (HP IIs and IIIs, older Apple LaserWriters) and in principle, any laser printer that can handle light card stock. If your printer is one of the compact models (HP IIP and IIIP, the Texas Instruments and Sharp printers), you may have problems with this.

If you are going to have problems, it will be with a Post-It coming off and getting stuck in the mechanism. Most likely, this will be at the first set of rollers the in-feeding sheet encounters. If that set of rollers is fairly accessible (generally the case for the HP personal laser printers; less obviously so for Sharp/Texas Instrument printers), you should be able to clean things out if they get stuck. But do this at your own risk—especially for printers without a straight-through paper path. The project has been tested successfully here in my studio.

Take the sheets with just boxes printed on them. Place one Post-It in each box. Place the first sheet of Post-Its in the manual-feed slot of your laser printer. Select one of the messages, then use the Print command's Current Page option from A&L Draw's File menu. You can set this option for as many pages as you need to print, hand-feeding each. If your printer has a straight-through tray, use it.

You can peel the Post-Its off the template pages as you need them, or you can peel them off and repad them—they won't quite line up, usually, but they will stick well enough to be convenient for use when you want them.

Mailing Labels and Name Tags

The techniques for multi-up desktop printing are enormously useful. It is surprising how many small jobs there are.

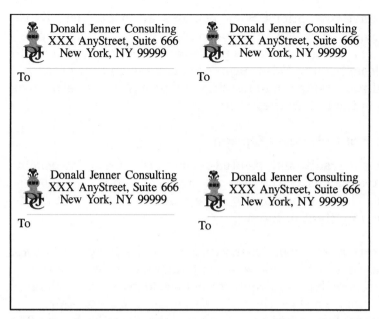

Figure 9.8   Four-up mailing labels are easily created.

Some examples: What is nicer than custom mailing labels? I mean, people pay *money* for that kind of thing! And the laser-printable label stock is available in 8½ by 11-inch sheets.

Set A&L Draw's Printer Setup dialog to landscape (horizontal) orientation. Divide the page in quarters. Then place logo and text as needed, and print the pages with 4-up (or 6-up) mailing labels, and whack them apart with the paper cutter (see Figure 9.8).

Use a smaller label—say, 4 inches wide by 3½ inches deep, with the printer set in portrait (vertical) printing mode—to produce custom name tags. You could print the name tags on label stock or light card stock (or even heavy paper), and put them in badge holders.

Stationery

Stationery is commonplace. I get lots of calls to design new business stationery for folks going into a new business. The relationship between this and biz-card design is pretty clear.

I have lots of entrepreneurial friends.

You have two options: Some people want printed letter-writing paper, or they want color in some way; this means producing a design, making a photo-ready version, and going to the local printer. Other people want a design that fits in a word-processing template; they will print their letterhead as part of the letters they write.

The Printed-Paper Option

Take the traditional, printed-paper option first. The design has two elements: the letterhead proper and the envelope head. The two should look more or less the same, but they have important differences.

Operations requiring an institutional look—lawyers, doctors, banks (in short, people who want other people to think they are responsible)—normally do not use logos on their business stationery. The look they wish to achieve requires a fairly staid typeface, centered at the top of the page. See Figure 9.9.

Placement Most businesses, however, like a logo. The question becomes one of placement. For example, one client, a

---

ARMAND TH. PETTIFOGGER
ATTORNEY AT LAW
123 FOURTH AVENUE, SUITE 321
ANYTOWN, AS 99999
(555) 555-5555
FAX: (555) 555-5556

Armand Th. Pettifogger, Esq.
123 Fourth Avenue, Suite 321
Anytown, AS 99999
(555) 555-5555
Fax: (555) 555-5556

Figure 9.9   This is a straightforward, institutional letterhead, set in Bold Engravers Roman and Bernhard Modern, respectively (the latter is rather more risqué, not for the faint of heart).

television production company, wanted a large logo, which for effect had to be placed almost a quarter of the way down the page. See Figure 9.10.

More often than not, I tend to put logos in the upper left corner of the paper, but sometimes it makes just as much sense to put the logo to the right of the text, as in Figure 9.11, or put the whole thing on the right side of the paper. The rule is to try different placements and sizes until you find one or two that seem to work well. Run off samples to see how they look on paper; the screen is not a perfect model of the final output.

The smallest type size you dare use for the envelope head is 8 points, as in the address line.

Since the letterhead is to be printed, you have some interesting options. Print at your highest possible resolution, to very

Figure 9.10   For a letterhead with a large logo, it makes sense to put the address data at the bottom of the page.

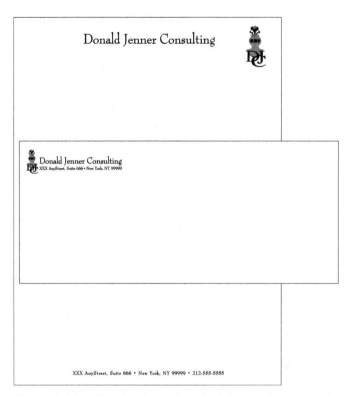

Figure 9.11 Here's a letterhead with matching envelope head.

white, slightly heavier paper (standard copier paper, 20 lb., is not as opaque as you want; 24 lb. is a minimum, and 32 lb. is usually ideal). Print one sheet with the letterhead, another with the envelope head. Then go shopping for paper.

The desktop-publishing paper stores offer a wide selection of papers with special borders and other printing. If you use these, you can take advantage of their designs to frame your logo or text. Coordinated envelopes and business cards make a set. The problem is that other people may have the same look.

Shopping for Paper Shopping for paper can be interesting. For example, I recently found a low-cost stationer selling Crane's Bond for $20 a ream (500 sheets). Although some nice letter papers come from other companies, Crane's 100 percent cotton is at the top of the heap. It is (quite literally) the Tiffany of papers. In fact, all that nice money you have in your wallet is printed on paper made by Crane for the Treasury (it also recycles the used bills, making them into a pretty paper called Old Money—lots of double entendre in that). The client for whom I bought this paper was very impressed when I handed her her new image—especially when I told her Crane's paper was provided for no extra charge.

Using One Color If the client will spring for it, and the design will accommodate it, in your opinion, consider printing in a single color. This is easy enough to do, and it adds less than $20 to an instant-print shop's charges for the average job. Colors to consider are deep reds and blues on ecru (cream-colored), white, or pale-gray paper. On white or ecru paper, a rich gray is also handsome.

Be fussy about the color. Ask your printer to show you the Pantone guide. This guide is a set of color swatches used to specify ink colors for printing. The guides fade a bit over time, so you need to see the one your printer uses and pick from that one, unless you are sure it is a new guide. Generally, deep, fairly saturated colors will work better than pale colors.

For Word-Processing Users

Things are easier if you or your client use a computer to generate letters. Modern Windows-based word-processing software is friendly to graphics, and it is easy to create a template with a letterhead or envelope head.

For example, I use Microsoft Word for Windows. I have several different templates that incorporate my letterhead—for memos, business proposals, and so on.

To create a letterhead, start by exporting the graphic in a standard format your word-processing software uses. Commonly, the easiest is the Windows Metafile (.WMF) format. In A&L Draw, select the items to be exported, then use the Export command on the File menu to access the dialog. If you have set up a library directory where you store templates, set the Export dialog to send the file there; set the Selected Objects and Windows Metafile option, and press OK.

In your word processor, set up a frame to include the graphic and whatever text is appropriate, and use the footer for such things as the address line. If your software supports different first-page and general headers, you might want to set up the general (but not first-page) header as a continuation-sheet header, and have the address information repeat on all continuation sheets.

The Bottom Line

PC-family hardware is the current machine of choice for business. Using graphics on these machines to handle common business-graphics needs makes sense, and it often saves a bundle. Custom-designed stationery can be costly—or you can do your own design work and get equally professional results at half the cost.

The best part of the whole thing is that when you get bored with the old design—or it is time for a new look—changing things is not a big deal.

Project 10: Advanced Design: Brochures and Pamphlets

You'd think that, in this electronic age, paper handouts would be a thing of the past. Uh-uh. Simple, effective brochures are alive and well; they are cheap, and they can be very effective.

Big, glossy pamphlets and brochures are neither simple nor cheap. They are the province of design specialists who earn their money not only in the design process, but in seeing the job through the printing process.

But a lot of the time, that is not the kind of brochure you need. Most of the time, a simpler statement will do nicely—something that tells the story quickly and effectively. Although serious desktop-publishing (DTP) tools can make the job easier, a graphics program will often do very nicely. Even if the specialized DTP software is available, you can still generate the graphics for a brochure in a program like A&L Draw.

The Basic Half-fold Brochure

Fold a sheet of 8½ by 11-inch paper in half, and it makes a nice program. Fold an 8½ by 14-inch sheet in half, and it is a
• striking program. Or leaflet. Or brochure.

Brochures have two sides, at least one of which—the outer side—is best done in a graphics package.

Real-World Example #1

Here's an example: Overdo Productions is a radio and television production (you saw a version of its letterhead in Project 9). A couple years ago, Rosemarie Reed (who *is* Overdo Productions) reinvented the radio drama. Based on a searing novella (I always wanted to say that) by Omar Rivabella, "Requiem for a Woman's Soul" turned out to be a popular offering for the nation's public-radio stations.

Rosemarie Reed's problem was simple: How could she and American Public Radio (the distributor) develop some excitement about this rejuvenated approach to radio programming?

The campaign had several dimensions, two of which involved effective graphics produced on the desktop.

The first graphic was simple. A short description of the project (this was the first in a series of radio dramas) and the novella itself were written up in a word processor. The page was set up to print two columns side by side on standard 8½ by 11 paper, oriented horizontally (landscape). The text was printed 2-up by copying it from the first column to the second column. I printed this copy on fairly heavy (32 lb.) smooth white paper and set it aside.

To produce the setup shown in Figure 10.1, set margins to a quarter- or half-inch, and set the space between columns to twice the size of the margins (in this case, 1 inch). When cut, this leaves a half-inch margin all around.

I scanned the cover art from the hard-cover copy of the book. I cleaned it up—mostly a matter of adjusting contrast and removing patterns. Using an earlier cousin of A&L Draw (this was a couple years ago; Draw was not available then), I

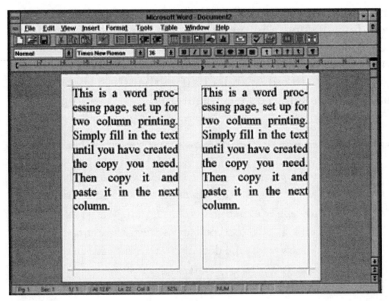

Figure 10.1   Two half-pages of text are created by using a word processor's multiple-column feature.

placed the bitmap cover image 2-up on a horizontal, 8½ by 11 working area, and added the series and drama titles. (I can't show you the design because I don't have a license from the picture's owner—though, of course, Overdo Productions does.)

I copied the cover-design file to a disk, and I took the disk and the printed pages (a hundred of them) to a local printing and photographic services shop sporting the then-new Canon Color Laser Printer. Henry Cimetta, the owner, popped the preprinted pages in the CLC and my disk in his brand-new super PC, opened the file in his copy of the graphics software, and printed it out in color to the obverse sides of the preprinted pages.

Pull the pages out of the CLC hopper, stick them on the big guillotine paper cutter, and whack them in half. *Voilà!* Two hundred little flyers, in color, with text.

Why bother with all this? Well, Rosemarie Reed needed the flyers fast so she could take them the next day to a conference of broadcasters. Using desktop tools, we produced this flyer (at a cost of 50 cents apiece—acceptable for a small-run item like this) in a day and a half, rather than the week it would have taken to do a conventional design-and-print job.

Comment on the picture: The picture was taken from a painting, which had been photographed, then printed on the book's jacket. When a photograph is printed, it is broken up into dots (rasterized). Scan that picture, and life gets complex *real* fast. The dot pattern in the picture doesn't match the dots of the scanning resolution (essentially, another rasterization). Patterns develop; these are called a moiré pattern.

Picture Publisher has a tool to resolve this. From the Effects dialog, choose Pattern Removal; usually, you need the Heavy pattern option. Apply the effect, and most—if not all—of the pattern goes away. After applying this effect, you may wish to apply smoothing, sharpening, or unsharp filtering to further adjust the picture.

Another option, which may prove more useful than one of the sharpening filters, is the Tone Balance command on the Map menu. Use this command to adjust shadow and highlight aspects of the image, which effectively modifies both apparent sharpness and color interactively.

As we say in New York: Oy!

Real-World Example #2

A more detailed promotional brochure, giving details of cast and cost, was the campaign's second graphics element. Again, time was a critical issue; this time, the brochures needed to be mailed at the beginning of January—which meant producing the job in late December, a period when printers like to be home with their families, celebrating Chanukah or Christmas and the New Year.

This was a bigger job—the run was long enough and complex enough that we needed a regular print shop to do the job. On the other hand, all the design was well within the limits of desktop design tools.

Again, the text for the inside was set up in two columns of an 8½ by 11 sheet. As it happens, I used a page-composition program, but I could as easily have used a high-end word processor. The only significant difference was the need to produce thumbnailed head shots of the narrator, the two actors, and the author. See Figure 10.2.

Once the text pages with the head shot looked right and tested more or less correctly on the laser printer, I set the printer driver to generate a PostScript file of the page and copied that to disk.

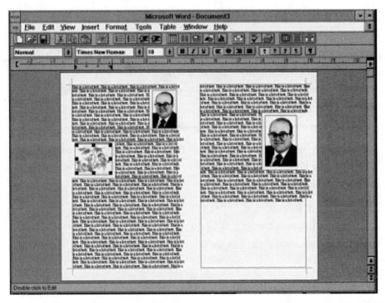

Figure 10.2   Most advanced word processors permit the insertion of *frames*—placeable and adjustable containers for pictures and text. (The ragged-right margins in this example are an artifact of the screen display and would not print that way.)

Then you just take your PostScript file to your print shop and get the final version.

Getting what you expect to get when you take your PostScript file to a print shop is simple, but you need to watch for some things.

First, to make it work, you must work with PostScript on your proofing device (in this case, the laser printer). Phototypesetters, used by print shops to process the files you make, use PostScript. If you use it, too, you will get something sufficiently close in most cases that the proof will be an accurate test of the final version.

Second, you need to be sure your print shop uses the same typefaces you do. Most print shops do not use TrueType yet; they use Adobe Type 1 PostScript typefaces preinstalled in their typesetters. You have two choices: Either use a typeface your print shop has, or set the PostScript driver to include a copy of the typeface description in your PostScript file. The former will be much less likely to pose problems and will produce smaller PostScript files.

Third, your laser printer will normally not produce as many shades of gray as a high-resolution typesetter does. Generally, the higher the resolution of the device, the more gray shades are available; 300dpi printers produce not more than 10 or 12 shades, whereas the typesetter can produce four times that many. This means you will need to check bluelines if the page to be printed contains photos. You are looking for hot spots, and your print shop is an indispensable helper.

There is no substitute for experience. But the good news is that after a couple times through the process, getting what you want will no longer be a major challenge.

Setting up the outside of the brochure was a graphics job. For the title of the play, I chose to use a typeface called Umbra. This is a shadowy type, and that seemed appropriate to the gruesome character of the play. It is aggressively modern and powerful—again, appropriate.

Then there was the luck element: This novella had been produced as a stage play in the Netherlands. The poster announcing the play used a clever idea: The designer used dribbles of "blood" to suggest the gruesomeness of the story. Why not pick up on that design element? The client loved it; in fact, she was in the brainstorming session that came up with the idea.

Here's how this would play in A&L Draw.

First, open a new file, setting the printer for landscape mode, with rulers and a quarter-inch grid. Since a wider margin is in order, draw in some lines to indicate the margin. Normally, A&L Draw picks up a quarter-inch margin all around the page edge; you need to add a quarter inch to the right side of the page and set the inside (middle) edge for the cover at 5¾ inches. Use the Straight Line tool to draw in the lines, then use the Pen tool to make them dashed lines so you will remember that these are construction lines to be taken out before you print.

Umbra is a printer typeface; I didn't have an equivalent A&L typeface, so I set the Type Attributes dialog to Printer Fonts and the size to 72 points. Then I added the word *REOUIEM*. (Whoops! You say I misspelled REQUIEM? Nope. Watch and see.)

Set the Type Attributes dialog for about 32-point type, in the same typeface, and add *FOR A WOMAN'S SOUL*. Place these words right under *REOUIEM,* and adjust the type so the second line is the same length as the first line. Use the Vertical alignment to make sure everything is nice and neat.

Now for the blood. Pick the Curved Line tool. Start drawing about where the little crossing line would be, if the *O* used in REOUIEM had been a *Q* the way it should have been. Draw way down, then swing around to make the blob at the bottom of the drip, drawing up the other side and closing back at the top. Make sure it is a closed shape. Effectively, the drip of blood makes the *O* into a *Q*. See Figure 10.3.

REQUIEM
FOR A WOMAN'S SOUL

A Radio Drama in
Four Twenty-nine Minute Segments
Adapted by Rosemarie Reed and Richard Broadhurst
from the original novel by Omar Rivabella

Figure 10.3   The cover design for the second REQUIEM brochure shows the construction lines, which will be removed for the final printing.

Fill this shape with a deep, rich red. I used 024-100-100-000. Ultimately, I need to match this color to a Pantone number (which the printer will use to get the right shade at print time), but I can do that later.

The rest of the job was really simple. Using another printer font (Avant Garde—clean, modern lettering), I added the descriptive material.

This cover went to the printer on disk as a PostScript file. After the usual alarums and excursions (some files had to be redone and sent by modem), the bluelines came back and looked great. A week and a half later, with a holiday in the middle, we got back 2,000 brochures, which were sent overnight to American Public Radio in Minneapolis for mailing. Total time, including holidays and printing: two weeks. This would have been impossible without desktop graphics capabilities.

The only real difficulty in doing this project in A&L Draw has to do with color. The dribble of blood that makes this design is red; everything else is black. That means doing a spot-color printing job. One plate is generated for the black printing, and another is generated for the red printing. Effectively, some technique is needed to print a file for each of the two plates.

A&L Draw is not set up to do this kind of separation. If this entire job were graphics, you could simulate the separation up to a point. But in this case, although you could print one page with the black lettering and another page with the red dribble, at some point in the Q there would be an overlap, and the colors would be messy.

There are two answers: If you are dedicated to doing it yourself, you can look at more powerful software packages that have built-in separation capability. That is not a bad solution.

On the other hand, if most of the time you are using your desktop hardware (printers and so on), and only occasionally using printing requiring the extra step of separations, why not let the printer do the job? It is not terribly involved, and it will not add greatly to the cost of the job. More to the point, you avoid the extra and somewhat more perilous step of making separations yourself. So either you can ask the printer to work with your PostScript output, or you can (perhaps, if the printer has more advanced software) let the shop process the .GED file.

Producing Programs for Events

Programs—the kind of thing folks get at plays and the like—are another good application for graphics software. See Figure 10.4.

For example, every year the college where Mrs. Jenner teaches has its Asian Heritage Month. A program is in order for the opening day. Another brochure is needed to list the month's events, for general distribution to the college and

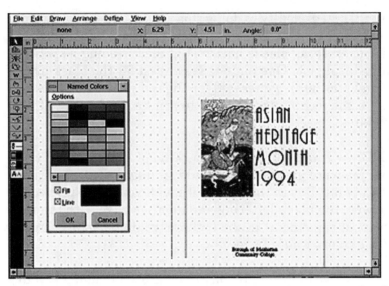

Figure 10.4   This layout for a program cover shows a couple of construction lines, which are removed before printing.

the larger community it serves. I particularly like the way the opening-day cover developed.

In previous years, I have used Chinese elements in the design; this year, I chose to focus on South Asia. The illustration is from a Persian-style painting made in the 16th century Mughal court of Akbar. The original was colored. I converted the selected portion to grayscale, and then substantially adjusted the tonal balance to change the contrast.

Adjusting the contrast is important. The college's reproduction office is not what you'd call sophisticated. We're talking pretty basic photocopying, folks—a printing method that leaves much to be desired, especially if the machines are on the tired and cranky side. Try for subtle grayscale images, and you'll be disappointed. But a nice contrasty image usually comes out looking more or less the way you planned. This works well enough on art work, generally; it is less successful with photographs, for obvious reasons.

Again, because I have a wide range of typefaces installed for general use—what A&L Draw calls printer fonts—I elected to use Plaza, an Art Deco font that seems to work well with arty designs. The inside of the program was set in plain old Times New Roman, using a word processor in the way demonstrated in the first section of this chapter.

Three-Panel Brochures

Folding a piece of standard-size paper in half is simple enough. Setting up a brochure with two folds and three panels is only a bit more difficult, and the results are more useful. Three-panel brochures fit in #10 envelopes (standard business size), and they can easily be self-mailers.

A couple issues come into play. Some of them are mechanical: Dividing a piece of paper into three sections is not as easy as dividing it into two sections. Some of them are design issues: Three panels of 10-point or 12-point type can be a bit overwhelming in an age that likes pictures.

The mechanical issue arises because A&L Draw doesn't automatically know how to divide a page into three panels. A word processor does; a page-composition program does. As it happens, the number is not a nice even number, expressible in eighths or sixteenths of an inch. But you can get close.

Setting Up the Template

Turn on A&L Draw. Set the printer, and specify landscape orientation. Assuming a laser printer, A&L Draw will give you a page-size work area of 10½ inches, allowing the usual quarter-inch unprintable area all around. Turn on the rulers and a quarter-inch grid.

Place a construction line (use the Straight Line tool; constrain it by holding the shift key as you draw) at 3 $\frac{7}{16}$ inches. Place another construction line at 7 $\frac{1}{16}$ inches. This is very close (within tolerable limits) to where the folds are for a three-panel brochure. Add construction lines at four-sixteenths (one-quarter) inch on either side of the fold lines.

Once again, the DTP-oriented paper stores have addressed the market. You can purchase stock for three-panel brochures already made up, with scored lines for folding in the right places and so on. Some are preprinted with designs (you just add your own copy); others are plain (add your own designs as well as copy). You still have to figure out where to put things on the page. If you use a graphics program to add art, that means doing the calculations and construction lines.

Suggestion: Make a template with these construction lines already in place, and then reuse it as need be. Simply open the template file, and save it under a new name for each brochure project.

The Basic Layout

The basic layout for three-panel brochures does not change. The outside always has a panel that is the cover (the right panel). The left panel is the panel people see as they open the brochure; it should carry the main message. The middle panel is either the back of the brochure, or it is the panel that carries the return address. See Figure 10.5.

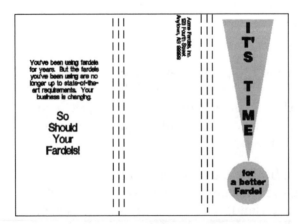

Figure 10.5   This is the basic layout for the outside of a three-panel brochure (naturally, the construction lines are removed before printing).

Learn Desktop Graphics and Design on the PC

Using Grayscale

In the case of Acme Fardels, Hansel's daughter, Gretchen (she just got her MBA in marketing), has decided the company needs to add some excitement to its concept of a 21st-century fardel. Her first interest is in building acceptance for the new line among existing customers and getting the attention of other fardel-using firms, now patronizing other fardel-makers. (It was Gretchen who pushed the idea for the T-shirts described in Project 8.)

Gretchen has decided on a complex campaign, starting with a direct-mail piece. The cover design is simple enough to make, as shown in Figure 10.5. In the cover panel, she inserts a triangle symbol, turns off the outline, fills it with 20 percent gray, and stretches it. She adds a 20 percent gray circle (also without outline). Now she has an exclamation point—an icon for Look at Me! She uses bold text fitting the outline of the screamer (an old-fashioned term to describe an exclamation point) to tell the basic story.

Gretchen carries over the same screamer motif on the inside panels. On another landscape-page work area, she copies the original set of construction lines and lines them up. Then she copies the screamer to the left and middle panels of the new page. The Acme logo, rendered in grayscale (this is a low-budget brochure, at least in its original incarnation), can be placed on the third panel. See Figure 10.6.

Printing up a small batch of these brochures for testing is simple enough. Use a fairly heavy paper—you are printing two sides, and this avoids print-through; you eliminate seeing ink from the other side of the paper. Print the first side, then put the printed brochures back in the printer and print the second side.

Set up the word processor for three-column printing, and write the text for the brochure. Print the text over the inside of the "preprinted" brochure. In effect, you've created a background element (the screamer) for the text pages.

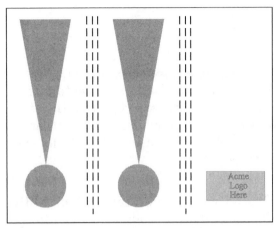

Figure 10.6   On the inside page of the brochure, text starts at the left panel.

Customizing the Brochures

Find one of the static-removing guns used for old records, use it on the pages to get rid of printer static between runs.

With grayscale, this brochure doesn't look too shabby. But Gretchen is an ambitious person. She tries it in grayscale, but she also makes a two-page set (outside and inside) and takes it to the local copy shop. She has the two pages printed back to back in one color (say, deep red or deep blue) on a nice-looking paper (ecru or something more exciting—try a deep red on a pale-peach paper, maybe with a slight texture to it). She could also have the graphics paper (from A&L Draw) printed in one color, then have the text (from the word processor) printed on the inside, in black or some dark color.

The result is a completely custom look. Gretchen can mail these brochures all over. Simply seal them with a round self-sticking label (every stationer sells them)—coordinated to the paper color, perhaps. For preferred customers, she might include a personal letter and her business card with the brochure.

Creating a Counter Display

Gretchen might even want to create a counter display for this brochure—a holder for a dozen or so, which Acme Fardel dealers might put on their counter for customers to use. A holder like this can be bought from DTP supply stores, or Gretchen might get her younger brother to help out (time the kid took a serious interest in the family business and stopped playing computer games).

In the demonstration file 3-PANEL.GED, I have included Junior's template. Copy it to the clipboard and paste it into a new file, with the printer set to portrait mode. Ungroup the image and get rid of the large rectangle (it is there to suggest a page boundary). Center the rest of the thing on the page, and print it out on light card stock. Cut the thing out, using the heavy dashed lines, then fold on the dotted lines and paste the tabs to the back. This will easily hold a dozen brochures. You could customize it further by printing on the reverse side of the card (where it will fold up and be visible after assembly) something like a company logo, or a TAKE ONE message.

The Big-Time Variant

Switching to legal size (8½ by 14-inch) paper gives you two options: You get three larger panels or four panels of the same size. For mostly aesthetic reasons, I prefer to stick to three panels (I like the order in which they present information). Use this larger format for some kinds of programs.

The Reply-Card Variation

Three-panel brochures—every size—make interesting tools when you want to secure a response.

Print on light card stock. Ask your printer for reply-card stock, and you'll get the right thing. Use the left panel of the outside for the information you want the respondent to fill in—name, address, and phone number, certainly—and any other information that might be needed. The copy might be something like *Yes, I want to know more about Acme Fardels.*

Please have a sales representative call me. Or it might have a series of check boxes with appropriate options. On the other side—the inside page's right panel—put the return address in the middle and either a place for a postage stamp or the usual copy for prepaid return mail (consult the Postal Service for details). Print a dashed line on the inside page at the right fold (you can just leave the construction line), and perhaps a little scissors dingbat. Now your customers can detach the card and send it back.

The Brochure Deluxe

The brochure deluxe is a small folder, just the right size to put in a #10 envelope. You can insert a set of small cards (actually, I use heavy paper rather than card stock) with informative copy; the folder accommodates six or eight of them, stepped so that the headline for each card is visible. I print a panel for the folder cover—in color, for real zip—and then paste it in position.

Most people on whom I have tested the result have been impressed.

You can buy brochure covers—and if you are doing a long run, you probably will have to. For a short run—under 100—these covers are too costly, at 80 to 90 cents apiece. They are easy enough to make.

For medium-size runs (more than 100 and less than 1000), making brochure covers is an excuse for a party, perhaps. Get some folks together, lay on some wine and cheese (serve it *after* most of the work is done), and set folks to work. It's fairly mindless exercise, except for the placement of the colored cover panel.

Making the Brochure Folder

Start with a lightweight card stock, in 8½ by 11 cut sheets. Pick something interesting—a nice colored stock, or something with a pattern. For example, I have used linen-finished ecru card stock, parchment-finished card stock, and card stock in deep blues and reds. One combination that I have seen and admired, but not tried, combined an earth-tone green card stock with a pale tan panel for the cover text—truly handsome, and the recycled paper was definitely PC.

Working with Your Card Stock Place a fairly sturdy ruler—plastic or wood; metal is too hard and will damage the paper in the next step—exactly and evenly, 2½ inches from the bottom of the sheet of card stock. Using the edge as a guide, fold the bottom flap up. Finish the fold by running the edge of the ruler along the fold to make it lie very flat.

Fold this whole thing in half along the vertical axis, and again, flatten it well by running the ruler along the fold.

Now you see the cover taking shape. The next step is to trim the folder. The process of folding causes the edges of the flap to stick out from the sides—it is simply a matter of displacement, and the fix is simple. Use a paper cutter to trim the open side of the folder so that the final width of the folder is 3¾ inches wide.

The last step is optional: If you think you might want to put a business card in the folder, consider making two small diagonal cuts on one of the flaps with a craft knife. These imitation die cuts let you tuck the card in where it is visible, and it is easily removed by the recipient. Be careful when you do this. You want to cut through only the pocket flap, not the outer cover, and you want the cuts to be small. Use a ruler as a guide, perhaps. See Figure 10.7.

Making the Cover Design To make the cover design for this folder, set up A&L Draw for your printer—color or black-and-white, your choice. Insert a square symbol, set its fill to None, then size it so it is 3¼ inches wide by 5 inches to 8 inches long.

I prefer to make the cover panels shorter, rather than longer, to emphasize the fact they are panels.

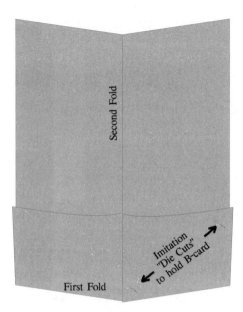

Figure 10.7   Here's the general layout for a brochure cover.

Put appropriate text and pictures on the panel, and then group the design (omitting the box). Figure out how many panels you can print on a page. For example, on the Fargo Primera color printer, I can get four panels if I am careful about size. On the laser printer, setting the paper for landscape, I can get six panels (three across, two down). Set up some guide lines, and duplicate the panel design accordingly (more or less the same way you did for business cards and mailing labels in Project 9). Figure 10.8 shows some sample panels.

Pasting the Cover Panels Cut out the panels and paste them carefully. Center them from side to side, evenly mounted—either toward the top or the bottom or in the middle of the cover, depending on what you think looks right. Make your life easy: Use a good-quality glue stick, or a slightly thinned rubber cement. Neither of these sticky substances is permanent, but they should stick long enough for the purposes of a short-term promotional piece.

Figure 10.8   Here are a couple of Acme Fardels panels for the brochure cover.

Making the Innards

Here's how you make the innards for the brochure cover.

Set up your word processor for three columns, 3¼ inches wide. Make the side margins a tad wider than the minimum quarter-inch (say, 0.35 inches) and leave a good half-inch gutter between the columns. Write the text for the longest of your cards in the sets, making it not more than 8 inches long. The second card should be designed to sit on top of the first, so that the headline of the first is visible above it, and so on. Needless to say, you can put in pictures as well as text. You can fit up to four cards in a pocket. See Figure 10.9.

Ideally, you will set up pages with three panels—one of each size on a page. This lets you print 3-up, and then trim to final size for each set of cards—3¼ inches wide by 8 inches, 7⅝ inches, and 7⅛ inches respectively, say). Then, print the cards on different colors of paper, coordinating with the brochure cover and the other cards.

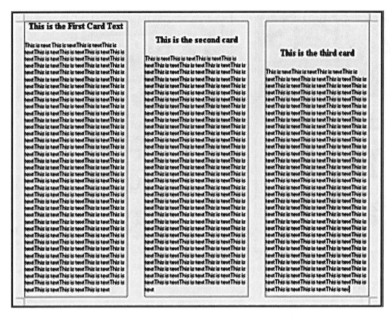

Figure 10.9   The insert cards used in the brochure, created in Microsoft Word for Windows, step down in size.

When choosing the paper for the insert cards, think about the effect different colors have. Pale blues work differently than pale pinks, and vivid colors have stronger effects. You have to play with the color choices a bit until you find the best combination of colors and (for that matter) textures to make the most pleasing and effective set of inserts for your brochure.

Brochures and Pamphlets Are Neat

You should get the feeling that I like brochures. I think they offer tremendous scope for developing designs that work for promotional purposes. Many of these design concepts work in other places.

For example, you could use the brochure deluxe design for a press kit. But most press kits are executed with full-size covers (able to accommodate 8 ½ by 11-inch paper). These covers are relatively cheap—about 40 cents apiece—and there is no reason not to use premade covers. But sticking a panel on them works nicely in this kind of setup. For a small run of covers—say, up to a couple hundred—this is much more practical than having custom-printed covers, and it takes considerably less time. The look is just as custom.

As you get further into design, you will undoubtedly want to try your hand at booklets and pamphlets. Again, the tools you work with in this book will stand you in good stead for managing the illustration aspects of such items, even after you move to more elaborate page-composition software for the final production.

And anyway, making these things is fun.

Project 11:
Advanced Graphics:
Technical Drawing

Technical drawings include such things as floor plans, architectural renderings, and engineering drawings. Normally, drawings like this are done in CAD (computer-aided design) programs. On the one hand, CAD programs have special features that make drawing to scale particularly easy. On the other hand, CAD programs are usually not terribly convenient for sketching, and they are not cheap.

A simple drawing package like A&L Draw has many of the features needed for technical drawings. If you are doing the occasional floor plan—for example, trying to get ideas for moving furniture around—or sketching an idea, it makes sense to use A&L Draw for the job.

A Simple Floor Plan

One of my clients (not design; this was one of the management systems clients), in days gone by, was a large New York City private social-services agency. The division with which I worked, a community mental health clinic, developed computer-assisted training programs as part of its larger education effort. Though rather diffuse in its operation, the computer lab was enormously successful with many clients, and it eventually needed bigger quarters. The agency shifted it to bigger quarters, and the next job was to renovate the space. I was asked for advice.

This job did not require a detailed, perfectly scaled drawing. It *did* need a good enough drawing, with enough notes on it, that the carpenter and the guy doing the built-in furniture could deliver the goods.

Setting the Scale

As it happens, I no longer own a plotter (space is limited in the studio). Windows can drive the plotters, and the larger format many plotters can deliver would have been nice, but you cannot have everything.

On the other hand, color is terribly useful in a drawing like this, and the HP PaintJet delivers a good color drawing for this purpose. Setting A&L Draw for the PaintJet in landscape mode, I have a working area 11 inches wide and 8 inches deep.

The space to be organized is 36 feet by 24 feet. There are two columns and a small office with cinder-block walls that can't be changed, along with windows, doors, and the need to accommodate a schoolroom in the space. My drawing had to show these areas and how they related to the rest of the space.

The Basic Layout

To do the layout, turn on the rulers and the grid, setting the grid for quarter inches. The first thing to add is a scale statement—more for convenience than anything else. Set the scale so one-quarter inch equals 1 foot.

Begin by inserting a square, then sizing it to the correct dimensions—in this case, 9 inches (times 4, represents 36 feet) by 6 inches (times 4, represents 24 feet). Make the square solid black. Drag off a copy of this square, make it solid white, and shrink it a bit in each direction, then center the two squares, white on top of black, so a fairly heavy black border shows. Group the whole thing, and think of this as the room.

Add the columns next. Insert another square, and fill it with solid black. The columns in this room are 2 feet square, so size these black squares to cover four quarter-inch squares (that is, one-half inch per column side). Drag the first column into position by dragging on the center point of the square so that the markers on the ruler line up at the third inch from the left and the third inch down. Drag off a copy of this column, and place it at the sixth inch from the left, 3 inches down.

The permanent office wall of cinder blocks encloses the space at the upper left of the room. Use the Straight Line tool to connect the dots, starting at the 3¼-inch mark on the left wall, and finishing at the 3¼-inch mark at the top wall. When the line is drawn, use the Pen tool dialog to set it as a 5-point Fat line.

To make the windows, insert another square. Set its line width to Hairline, and set its fill to Vector. When you select vector fills, a little scroll box in the Fill dialog is no longer grayed out; use it to select the kind of fill you want—in this case, a diagonal-line file such as 17. In this building, windows are 4 feet wide, so make the hatched square 1 inch wide. Then squeeze it down so that it is just about the thickness of the black border representing the walls of the room. Place three of these windows about 2 inches apart on the top wall, and two on the right wall.

To create doors, first make a copy of the window and set it to solid white fill. Position it in the upper wall of the enclosed area, right by the column. Then turn off the outline with the Pen tool dialog. Do the same for other door areas.

Doors are indicated with a curved line showing the direction and character of the door's swing, as shown in Figure 11.1.

Finally, add some labels. This area has several functions, so add labels indicating function, as shown in Figure 11.1.

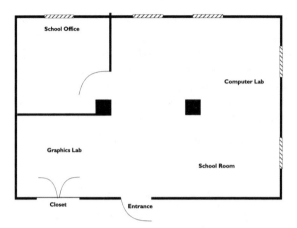

Figure 11.1   The first layer of the Computer Lab floor plan looks like this.

Group everything except the scale statement, and save the file.

Adding the Details

Change the line color (in the Color dialog, make sure to select Line and deselect Fill) to cyan. Set the Line dialog to Fat, and draw in the partitions for the school room.

This is the simple way to do things. I eventually went back, as the plan developed, and changed this plan to indicate the more elaborate partition, with Plexiglas inserts, using the same wall with windows as for the outer walls. But for this exercise, the simple indication is adequate.

Now the space you actually need to design is clear. It's time to put in the furniture. I chose to use green to indicate the Formica-covered built-in desk areas that this space will have. These desk areas run around the walls of the computer lab and the graphics lab; another free-standing desk is centrally spotted in the computer lab. Use the Straight Line tool to make the irregular shapes, and pull in a square and size it to make the free-standing desk. See Figure 11.2.

What dimensions, you ask? Computer desks need to be 3 feet deep. They need to be 27 inches high (machine height) for most people. Here's the rationale:

A 3-foot deep desk allows the computer monitor to sit well back from the operator—a good 18 to 20 inches is a minimum desirable distance.

Twenty-seven-inch high desks sit at just the right height for most people sitting in a normal chair, so they can have feet flat on the floor and a proper angle for the arms and hands at the keyboard.

So the desk space I drew in is three-quarters inch wide (represents 3 feet) and is labeled as 27 inches high.

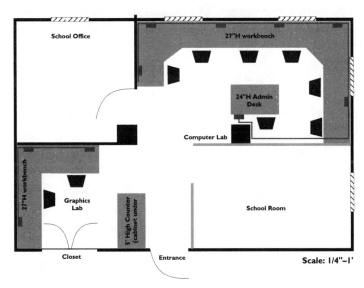

Figure 11.2 The completed floor plan, with scale, is missing only the explanatory notes.

To indicate the workstation locations, let's put in chairs. To keep things colorful, I made them blue. Make the desks as simple trapezoids, about 2 feet by 1½ feet (one-half inch by three-eighths inch), and space them out about where you expect a monitor, keyboard, and mouse setup.

Finally, in red, draw in the basics of the cabling. The main lab is to be networked; specify the conduit for the power and the networking connections in one step (this is a very simple sketch; in fact, the two would normally be in separate conduits), with little red boxes along the line to indicate where you want power and network connections.

The only thing this drawing needs is some notes to make clear what is going on.

Printing the Drawing

You have options, even without the advantages of a larger-format printer or plotter.

You can print the floor plan as is directly to the PaintJet. This gives you a nice 11-inch-wide drawing. Or, you can scale the whole drawing up, and print it on several pages as a tiled drawing.

The scaling is easy: Select the entire drawing, but exclude any notes and the scale. Drag on a corner until the drawing is twice as wide. Change the scale to read ½"=1'. Print the whole drawing and assemble it.

A Dynamic Floor Plan

The first floor plan was static. This next one is not; it is for those folks who like to move furniture around. New Yorkers know a lot about that problem. We're constantly trying to figure out what placement of furniture provides the maximum amount of living space in our (typically small, New York) apartments.

Take, for example, a typical New York bedroom—which (as is commonly the case in New York) does double duty as a study.

(This room belongs to a friend and colleague at the university where I teach.) The overall room dimensions are 18 feet by 12 feet, 6 inches.

Set A&L Draw for the laser printer (black and white is just fine for this job), and your grid to one-eighth inch. Use a scale of one-half inch equals 1 foot, so one-eighth inch is 3 inches. That is a reasonably close tolerance, and it has the advantage of matching measurements on a ruler.

The Basic Room

Begin, as before, with a white rectangle superimposed on a black rectangle to indicate the basic box of the room. The room is further defined by two boxes that accommodate structural members, plumbing and wiring, and so on (the building is 40 stories high, and you have to put this stuff somewhere). The wall for a closet with accordion doors, adjacent to the bedroom door, makes the entrance into the bedroom a sort of minihallway. There is one 6-foot-wide window, on the wall opposite the closet. In short, there's nothing that you haven't seen already in the previous floor plan. See Figure 11.3.

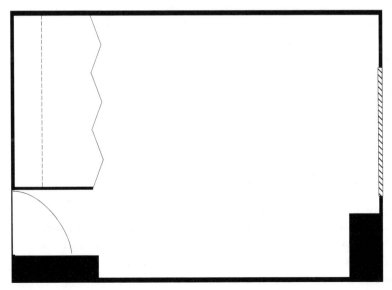

Figure 11.3 Here's the basic bedroom floor plan.

Making Furniture

Move over to the second page of the work area, and make the rectangles representing furniture there. You may want to color them, or (since you're set up for black and white) fill them with a black raster fill.

Most furniture is fairly rectangular stuff. So, the simple way to do this is to have one basic rectangle from which you drag off copies to be sized as needed. You want to label each piece as you make it. Make one basic solid-black lettering label, and keep it safe, making copies as necessary by selecting the original label, using the Text tool to change the wording, then adding it (*not* replacing). Use the Center command on the Align menu to line up the furniture representation and the label, then group the whole thing.

By the by: American-made furniture is commonly made to old-fashioned feet-and-inches measurements; European and less-costly stuff is made to metric measurements. This will make your measurements a bit more . . . interesting? You could work on a metric scale, of course (A&L Draw supports metric scaling). It's your choice.

As you draw the pieces of furniture, you place them in the room. See Figure 11.4. Essentially, the computer becomes the equivalent of a piece of graph paper and cut-out bits of paper. The advantage, of course, is that you can easily make copies—both electronic and hard copy—so you can compare the results. You do the drawing once, and then you play forever (or for at least as long as the lease runs).

Orthographic drawing is the kind of thing that junior-high-school lads learned in shop classes when I was a boy. Fortunately, my parents corrected the bias—they taught me how to cook and clean house.

Architectural Renderings: The New York Townhouse

Floor plans are about the inside of the building; architectural renderings show the outside. They can be fancy, even photorealistic; generally, they are not. The idea, in most cases, is to accurately show one or more faces orthographically.

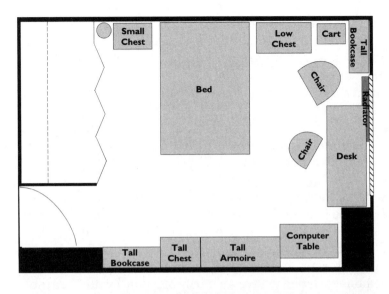

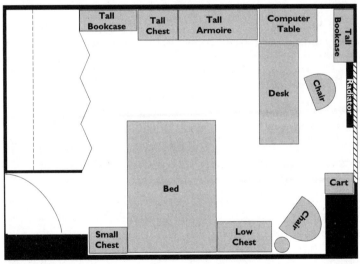

Figure 11.4   Just shove the furniture around; use different work areas to compare different layouts on the screen.

A program like A&L Draw is nearly ideal for simple architectural renderings like this. A traditional CAD program is almost always overkill.

New York is littered with elegant townhouses built from the early 19th century through the first decade or so of the 20th century. Some of them are very grand; most were originally middle-class houses, and they have only become grand as housing costs have risen. These houses commonly have 4 or 5 floors (including the basement—which commonly contained the kitchen in days gone by, as well as a family dining room). The main floor was the parlor floor; today, it usually has a small living room and dining room and perhaps a small kitchen. The upper floors had a water closet and bedrooms; these days, they are frequently a separate apartment. The whole house is linked by narrow stairs, either along one side of the house or (in a favorite example) in a stairwell in the middle, lighted with a skylight. Windows are generous (candles and later gas lighting were not entirely satisfactory). These houses usually have a charming, small walled garden.

A friend (a very successful lawyer—he could afford to buy the house!) asked for a drawing of his townhouse. It is a good example of the genre.

What Is a House?

Essentially, a house is a box, with details. Nowhere is this more true than in New York townhouses. So, after opening A&L Draw, setting the printer (for the example, a laser printer in portrait mode) and turning on rulers and grid (quarter-inch, with the scale being one quarter-inch equals 1 foot), the first drawing element is a square. Put it off to one side, and copy it as needed.

Drag off a copy to the main work area, and size it. The townhouse you are drawing rises 32 feet above sidewalk level. The drawing shows the main floor, two upper floors, and one floor (the basement—commonly, there would be a cellar beneath that) that is only half above the sidewalk level. The two upper floors have 8-foot ceilings; the parlor floor has a 12-foot ceiling. Things like roof and beams to carry the floors are between levels, and about 4 feet of the basement level shows. The house is 24 feet wide. Make this first box (the house) 6 inches wide and 8 inches deep.

Color it a light gray. This house is a modest one; it is made of brick, not the pink to reddish-brown sandstone of far more posh brownstones. The brick is currently painted a pale blue.

Window Treatments

The first detail to create is a window. This house will have four kinds of windows, three kinds of which will be very similar. The upper-story windows are 5 feet tall and 4 feet wide. They are crowned with a simple lintel—a block of stone set into the brick to carry the wall across the window embrasure. The windows are double-hung, and they have six panes in each section.

Drag off another copy of the basic square. Set its fill to solid white, and set the thickness of its outline to a 2-point (Wide) line. Use the grid to make the shape 1 inch wide and 1¼ inches deep. Draw a 2-point line across the rectangle in the middle, and draw standard-width lines to divide each section in half horizontally. Then divide the window vertically in thirds with two standard-width lines. Make the lintel from another copy of the square, squeezed down to a quarter-inch deep and an inch and a half wide. Color it gray—a shade darker than the gray used for the house proper. Center it just at the top of the window. Use the Group tool to temporarily group the whole thing, and drag off a copy. Make the whole copy a permanent group while it is still selected, with a ^G command. Your window should look like the middle one in Figure 11.5.

Go back to the first window. Use the Group tool to select just the window, and shrink it vertically about three-eighths of an inch. Group the whole thing, including the lintel, and drag off a copy, which should also be grouped permanently, while still selected. Then shrink the whole thing horizontally about a quarter-inch.

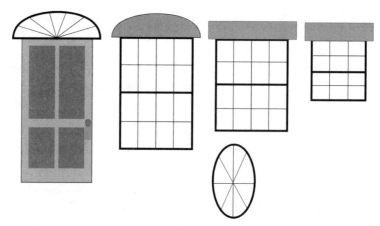

Figure 11.5 Here are the window and door details for the New York townhouse.

Go back to the original working window. Get rid of the lintel, group what's left (temporarily, with the group tool) and stretch it vertically to 1½ inches. Make a new lintel with a straight line for the bottom and a shallow curve along the top. It should be a quarter-inch wider than the window and centered vertically over it. Temporarily group the whole thing, and drag off a copy. Now use the Group tool to select the whole original working window in its modified form, and make that a permanent group with the ^G command.

To make the door with its fan light, first get rid of the grid indicating the window sections and panes. Change the lintel color to solid white, and draw in lines radiating from the center point of the demicircle's base line to make the lunette. Drag the (former) window frame so it is about 1⅞ inches long. Set the outline for standard width, and fill with a pale gray (say, one shade lighter than the house).

Drag off a copy of the original square, fill it with gray, and make the panels for the door—two long ones on top, and two shorter ones on the bottom. A much-reduced little rectangle with a darker gray circle mounted on it becomes the door-knob and lock plate.

One more little window is needed. Insert a circle, shrink it to about three-quarters of an inch, and squeeze it so it is an oval. Draw a cross and an X through it, as shown in Figure 11.5. This oval window lights the stairs at the first landing.

Placing the Details

The house has three of the middle-size windows across the top story. Two are fairly evenly spaced, toward the right of the house as you look at it—3½ feet from the right wall, then 3½ feet from the left edge of the first window. The third window is eccentric—it is about 1½ feet from the left of the house (it's the water closet, and that room doesn't need to be quite so big).

The second row of windows starts three-quarters of an inch from the bottom of the top row. Two middle-size windows sit below the top-floor windows, but underneath the eccentric window on the top level, the little oval window indicates a stair landing.

The ground level (the parlor-floor level) has two longer windows and the door. It starts a full inch from the bottom of the middle-level windows. The door is centered below the oval window, and the two long windows are below the right and middle windows of the middle level.

Two small windows are centered vertically beneath each of the long windows, with their bottoms even with the baseline of the house.

Notice that the doorway is well up above sidewalk level. Like all self-respecting New York houses, this house has a stoop, reached by a stairway. Under the stairway, adjacent to the lowest-level (kitchen) windows, is the doorway to the basement level. The whole house is about 5 feet back from the front of the property.

Expect to work on the rise of the steps a bit; you have to fill the area with the right number—in this case, nine.

Make a staircase. The riser is the basic box, colored gray and shrunk, with another, even thinner one on top of it for the tread. See Figure 11.6. Group the whole thing, and copy it to just beneath the door. Drag a copy off that one, and put it at the baseline of the house, dragging it wider on each side, so that it is even with the left of the house and commensurably wider on the right side. Make copies of the step (I prefer to start from the bottom), making each one narrower than the one below.

Tell your friends to buy copies of this book; I want to buy a house like this.

The next detail is the railing that climbs on either side of the stoop, and then extends along the open area in front of the house, with a gate at the right side. Use the Straight Line and Curved Line tools to draw 2-point lines. Refer to Figure 11.6.

Finally, there is a sort of corbel at the roof line. This is a purely decorative element, not a true structural corbel. It consists of two skinny, wide rectangles and two lines and three circles, colored one shade darker than the house color itself, as shown in Figure 11.7.

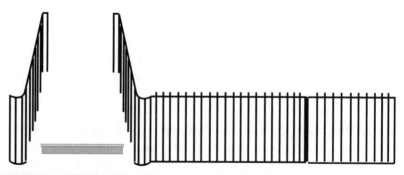

Figure 11.6   Details of the stair and railing for the New York townhouse are shown.

New York Residence
Drawing: Donald Jenner
Scale: 1/4" = 1'

Figure 11.7 Here's the completed front elevation of the New York
townhouse.

A lot of this exercise should be familiar. Think back to the design of
the St. Mark's logo in Project 2. That is a simplified elevation, and
the principles for producing both are the same. Here, the difference
is that you want the result to represent the original with as much
accuracy as possible. In the St. Mark's logo, there was no such concern; in fact, the image of St. Mark's is clearly not to scale, for design
reasons. For example, the tower on St. Mark's is made taller and
thinner, for effect.

Technical Sketches

Drawing programs are ideal tools for sketching ideas. A&L Draw is a bit lacking for technical sketching (it was not intended for it); more able software, with a bit more CAD heritage, would be helpful. But for *occasional* sketching, Draw does just fine.

Consider the simple fastener. A pin, threaded at each end, takes an hexagonal nut. Drawing an outline is good; adding gray shading to suggest lighting and dimension will make it better, as shown in Figure 11.8.

To begin, use the Straight Line tool to create a polygon with cut-off corners. Bolts have a beveled edge, so a sharp-edged square won't do. Fill this shape with 10 percent gray. Drag off a copy and flip it horizontally; color this shape 30 percent gray. Finally, insert a square, and make it a bit wider than the polygon, and the same height, more or less, as the two polygons. Put it in between the polygons, and color it 20 percent gray. Turn off the outlines on all these shapes and align them horizontally, if necessary.

Create the shape of the bevel from a curved line and some straight-line segments. Fill it with a straight-shaded fill, and set the color to 10 percent gray. Turn off the outline. Copy the object and flip it vertically. Position one at the top of each bolt facet and one at the bottom. Group the nut.

Make the shaft of the bolt from an inserted square, filled with a straight fill and set to 30 percent gray, then rotated 90 degrees. Set to the correct width (depending on scale) and length. Position it against the bolt, and move it to the rear of the drawing.

Copy the nut from the top and place it at the bottom. The result is not too bad for a quick and dirty sketch.

The Virtues of Sketching

The whole purpose of Project 11 has been to look at what you can do with computerized sketching. Drawing programs are

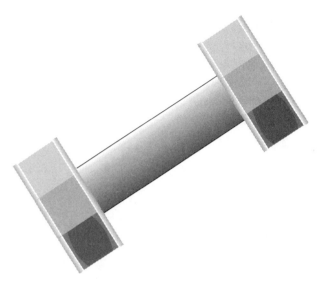

Figure 11.8   The bolt is capped with nuts at each end.

good for sketches where scale is an issue; drawing programs have scaling tools such as grids and rulers. Since objects on the screen are defined as mathematical relationships by the computer, changing scale is fairly easy. And sketches are great ways to try things out; that is why manufacturers have spent serious money computerizing design departments.

Another kind of sketching—call it art sketching—is done best in a bitmap or paint program. It is the ultimate in free-hand sketching, since things can be changed very easily (your image is graven in electrons, not stone).

As a design tool, sketching becomes a way of testing options. Sometimes the test drawing can be frozen and used as is— think of that as a time-saver. Sometimes the sketched element gets developed into something more involved, in a more complex drawing. You have still saved time, since the work you did in the sketching process can be recycled—you need not go back to do it again from scratch.

Project 12: Advanced Graphics: Illustration

You've seen it happen: Computer-generated images are increasingly replacing photographic images in product presentation (and lots of other places, for that matter). Sometimes the effect is so well done that it is quite impossible, without careful examination, to tell the difference.

Some of these illustrations, and the animations built from them, are generated using elegant—and expensive—software on equally elegant (but now rather less costly) workstation computers. More and more, though, standard PC-family hardware driving off-the-shelf software does the job.

Practically, a well-equipped PC and a graphics-specialized workstation deploy much the same computing power these days.

A Jug of Wine, a Loaf of Bread

To give you an idea of what you can do, let's try a nice still life—nothing too fancy, but enough to get the sense of shading and other effects that go into illustration.

Open a new file in A&L Draw. Turn on the rulers and the quarter-inch grid. Use the Activity tool (the light bulb) to import Draw's Magic Color Cubes; this is Draw's way of providing blended colors, as you recall from previous projects. Ungroup the color cubes so you can select them as necessary.

The Wine

Begin with a wine bottle. Draw it with the Straight Line and Curved Line tools. The neck of the bottle is a series of straight-line segments. The hip of the bottle and its base are curved lines. Begin by creating one side of the bottle. Use the Straight Line and Curved Line drawing tools to make a profile. Pay particular attention, as you edit the shape, to the "hip" where the bottle neck joins the bottle proper, and the curve of the base. Drag off a copy of the profile, and flip it horizontally. Line the two pieces of carefully, end-point to end-point, and use the Close shape command (F7) twice. The first time connects the lines; the second use actually closes the shape (it will fill with the default color).

Select the vertical sea shading cube (eighth row, third column over), and make it active with a Save (^Q) command. Apply it to the bottle by selecting the bottle and recalling the shading (^R). Change the dominant color from the too-greenish green to something with a bit more blue in it (I chose 100-037-037-000 from the named-color palette).

Make a copy of the bottle. Select the Line Editing tool, and select and delete the points at the top of the neck on this copy. Then, with the Line Editing tool still selected, use the Group tool to select both of the points at the top of the bottle's neck. Drag them down an inch or so. Turn off the Line Editing tool by clicking on it.

Color this shortened bottle with the vertical sunset color cube (fourth row, third column) by saving it (^Q) and applying it to the selected shape with ^R. Change the base color to a deep red (I used 050-100-100-000).

I like claret; if you prefer burgundy, change the bottle shape and use a less-deep red.

Move the reddened shape to the blue-green shape, and use the Align dialog to line things up, base to base and vertically. Group the result, and there you have a nice enough bottle of claret.

This bottle needs a label. Use the Zoom tool (with the magnifying-glass icon) to zoom in on the completed bottle. Draw

Figure 12.1 Here's the wine bottle—not a jug, I don't like jug wine.

the label with the line-drawing tools—straight lines for the sides, and curved lines for the top and bottom, as shown in Figure 12.1. Color it with the vertical earth color cube, and change the dominant color to a more tannish shade. Add appropriate lettering or other drawing. Group the whole thing, and save the file.

This is not too bad for a simple wine bottle; it could be better. For example, if I were being an absolute perfectionist, I would input the lettering letter by letter, then arrange them on curves to match the curve of the label. Perfection would also dictate some rather careful work on the lighting, to put in highlights to match the various curves in the bottle. In fact, I would need a range of vastly more sophisticated tools than A&L Draw offers (perhaps even true 3-D rendering) and a good deal more time. The details would add still more photorealism to the resulting illustration.

Art takes a while, and life is short, to paraphrase. Or, there are levels of exactitude in illustration.

The Bread

The first question here: What kind of bread do you want? (Aside from the kind that is green and made by the Treasury Department, that is.) *Baguette* would be nice, but I think I will stick to the standard loaf, the kind the Germans call a *Wasserkasten*—the kind Mom used to make!

This is essentially a rectangle, with a nice pillowy top. The top is a deep brown, the sides (where it has been in the loaf pan) are a warm tan, and the crumb is a slightly yellowish white (it is a *rich* loaf of bread).

Start with the side. It is a kind of parallelogram, with vertical sides and slanting top and bottom. Draw it with the Straight Line tool, and fill it with tan (try 000-025-050-000). Turn the outline off.

The crumb—that is, the interior of the loaf, the visible face when a slice has been cut off—has three straight sides. The top, where the loaf has risen above the edge of the loaf pan, is curved. It is not just a curve; it spreads out from the edges of the loaf like a pillow. Draw it and use the control points (^4) to adjust the curve so it is pleasing. If the shape does not close of its own accord, use F7 (the close shape command) to do the job. Fill the shape with a lighter, yellower tan (000-012-025-000).

Finally, make the top of the loaf. Use the Curved Line tool to draw a line from one top of the cut end, back along the loaf, then an arc (to suggest the roundness of the top), and back along the edge of the base of the loaf, ending in another curve along the top of the cut end. See Figure 12.2. If this shape does not close of itself, force it to close with an F7 command. Turn off the outline and fill with a deep brown (037-075-100-000). Use the Line Editing tool to adjust this shape (and the others, as necessary) to make all the edges match properly. You will probably want to keep the outline on the cut edge of the loaf, and color it to match the base of the loaf (that is, with a slightly deeper, tanner shade).

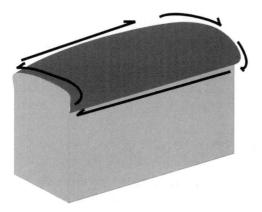

Figure 12.2 The black arrows show the process of drawing the top of the loaf.

This loaf of bread will look still more appealing with some of the cut slices lying in front of it. The cut slices consist of an edge made with the Straight Line tool, a crumb made with the Curved Line and Straight Line tools, and a crust made with the Curved Line tool. The outline, which is left on the crumb only, is colored to match the edge.

When you have made one slice, drag off a copy and rotate it. Position the two slices in front of the cut loaf so as to suggest they have just been cut from the loaf and are lying vaguely stacked. See Figure 12.3.

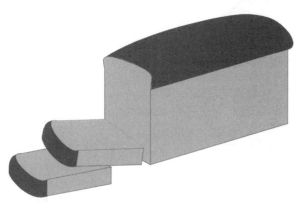

Figure 12.3 The completed loaf of bread with slices looks more appealing than an uncut loaf.

The Cheese

I know the poem doesn't call for it, but I like a bit of cheese
with my bread and wine. A nice round, golden Hollander
cheese would be particularly appealing.

This cheese is made from a circle, filled with the vertical
dawn color cube, the dominant color of which has been
changed from pale blue to 000-012-100-000 (a rich yellow
shade). To suggest that some cheese has been cut already,
draw a semicircle with the Curved Line tool, and close it
with a straight line. Set a somewhat darker outline on the
slice, then duplicate it and make it fatter. Then place these
cuts on the round shape, and adjust them to bow outward a
bit at the corners. See Figure 12.4.

The Fruit

Somehow, a still life needs a piece of fruit. So draw in an apple, using pretty much the same shading, a bit redder in base
color, as in the wine. Add in a brown stem, group the whole
thing, and perhaps rotate it as you place it. See Figure 12.5.

Thus far, you have a fairly interesting still life developing.
Wine and bread, cheese and apples—with this, you could
pretend to be hippies.

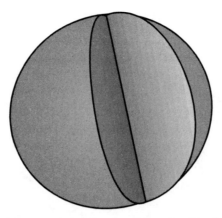

Figure 12.4   On the cheese notice the shading and the way the
outline is bowed out a bit. I also squeezed the whole image to take
it out of round, and then rotated it a bit.

Figure 12.5 This apple is tempting enough for Eve.

Painting the Still Life

There are two options at this point. You can add in some kind of a background, as shown in Figure 12.6. That is not too bad if a simple illustration with a sort of modern abstract feel is fine.

Figure 12.6 The still life is assembled on a nice tabletop.

Much of this could also be done—with greater effort—in a high-end drawing package.

The other option is to use Picture Publisher, with its painterly capabilities, to add additional realism and dimension to the image. Picture Publisher comes with some elegant backgrounds and some brilliant effects-generators, which can lend real polish to your picture.

A&L Draw's stuff is in vector format. Picture Publisher needs bitmap format, so a conversion is in order. Again, either you can export the whole still life, or you can export the individual objects and compose them in Picture Publisher. I prefer the latter option, as I want to fine-tune each element as I add it to the developing illustration.

Export the elements by selecting them one at a time, then using the Export command on the File menu to save each one as a TIFF (.TIF extension) file (for example, WINE.TIF).

Setting Up the Background

After starting Picture Publisher, first open each of the still-life elements—bread, wine, cheese, and apple—in the Picture Publisher work area. Then minimize them; this keeps them available for use, but it gives you an uncluttered screen.

Open a new picture in Picture Publisher. To do so, set the dialog to 7 inches wide and 5 inches deep, and for CMYK full color.

I associate this kind of a still-life with a brick-walled room. Picture Publisher comes with some nice textured fills, including several brick-wall fills. Choose the Textured Fill tool (the second option on the Paint Bucket tool fly-out), and from the texture name drop-down list, choose BRICK 1. Then fill the new picture with that brick wall.

New Wine, Same Old Bottle

The first element to add to this space is the bottle of wine. Double-click on the minimized iconic representation of the wine bottle. Then use the Magic Wand masking tool to mask the white area, followed by an Invert command on the Mask menu to select only the wine bottle. Copy that element.

Click on the new background to select it, then paste in the wine bottle. Now, let's see what can be done to make that bottle more real.

First, go to the Image menu, choose the Effects dialog, and use the Smooth option to soften edges and—most especially—the banding that is an artifact of the way drawing programs do blended fills.

Select a soft gray from the palette, and use the Pen tool to draw in the shadow at the lip of the bottle. Smooth that with the Smudge tool (next to last in the Brush tool fly-out) so it is a gentle shadow.

Use the Magic Wand and Paint On Mask tools to mask that clear bit in the neck of the bottle. Then use the next-to-last tool on the tool bar, the Sampling tool, to sample the brick wall. Pick the Solid Fill tool from the Paint Bucket fly-out, set the transparency to 80 percent, then fill the bottle neck with a little of that deep brick red—just enough to suggest transparency.

Use the same Masking tools to mask the label area on the bottle, and then invert the two masks so that the wine-colored area is selected. Pick a deep reddish-purple from the palette, and use the Solid Fill option to deepen the color of the wine.

Finally, add some highlights to the bottle. First, pick white from the palette. Then use the Airbrush tool, set to Scatter mode, to add a bit of white in a curve along the hip of the bottle and also at the bottom. Use the Smudge tool (also set to Scatter, and with fairly heavy pressure) to soften that highlight substantially. See Figure 12.7.

Figure 12.7 The edited wine bottle is placed against a brick wall.

Now to Get Cheesy

To get the cheese into the picture, do more or less the same thing. Bring up the cheese as exported from A&L Draw; mask the white areas, and invert the mask so the cheese is selected; copy the cheese, and paste it into the developing still life.

This cheese needs some serious work: shadows and highlights. Holland cheeses like this are not highly reflective, but soft shadows and highlights are in order.

The bottom icon of the tool bar has both active swatches; you double-click on the one that you want to edit.

Use the Sampling tool to pick up the color of the cheese rind. Double-click on the Color Swatch (the other swatch should be set to white). In the Color Editing dialog, in the K box, increase the value to 25 to increase the amount of black in that color.

Select the Paintbrush tool, set to 75 percent transparency, and Scatter mode. Paint in some shadow along the lower left quadrant of the cheese. Paint in a little white along the edges of the cut. Then use the Smudge tool to smooth things out, so that the shading proceeds evenly from light in the upper right areas to dark at the lower left. Work out the coloring in the cut area so that the light matches and looks right. Soften the edges of things all around. Save the file (I assume you have been doing frequent saves all along).

Picture Publisher also lets you adjust the shape and angle of the cheese. It can be positioned just to the left of the wine, and just in front of it. See Figure 12.8.

You may want to save interim versions of this developing picture in native .PP4 format, saving the mask layer along with the picture.

Figure 12.8   Wine and cheese. Paaarrty!

Bread!

Add the loaf of bread and its slices the same way you did the wine and cheese: Open the picture; mask the white areas; invert the mask; copy and paste into the developing picture.

This loaf needs lots of work. The top crust needs softening and rounding. The crumb needs texture. The sides need texture. And so on.

First suggestion: Apply the smoothing filter from the Effects dialog. This will soften the entire loaf.

Work along the edges and sides of the top crust with the Smudge tool to soften the edges and make them pillow out a bit along the main loaf and the slices.

Use the Sampling tool to collect a sample of the crust color, and then paint it on transparently along the sides, with the Brush tool in Scatter mode. Use the Smudge tool to soften and add a bit of texture on the sides of the loaf.

Use the Sampling tool again to grab the color of the crumb. Double-click on the swatch and increase the K and M values by about 10. Paint this color on in swirling strokes (loaves of bread are rolled up before they are put in the baking pan; good bread preserves that texture). Use the Smudge tool to blend and soften the texture. The result is shown in Figure 12.9.

Finishing the Still Life

The last item to be inserted is the apple. The process should be pretty clear by now. One thing: The shading is wrong; the quick fix is to rotate the apple to the left, so the highlight is in the upper right.

Strengthen that highlight by painting in some white (again, use the Paintbrush tool set to 75 percent transparency and Scatter mode), and smudging it so it is a gentle blush. Then apply the smoothing filter to the apple. See Figure 12.10.

Figure 12.9   The loaf of bread has been edited to add highlights.

Figure 12.10   The apple now has a blush.

All this stuff is still floating in midair. Since the laws of gravity have not been repealed, a tabletop is in order.

Open a new file in Picture Publisher. Make it about 5 inches by 4 inches, again, in CMYK full color.

Use the Pattern Fill tool from the Paint Bucket fly-out to fill this frame with a wood-texture fill (I used Parquet). Copy the whole image, and paste it into the evolving still life.

Editing this part of the picture is a matter of adjusting with the Rotation, Skew, and Perspective tools. Begin with the Perspective tool, selected from the Transformation drop-down menu. Pick the upper left (or upper right) corner handle and move it inward; the rectangle becomes a trapezoid.

Notice the little circles under *Rotation* in the tool controls next to the Transformation drop-down? They control the choice of rotation axis. The circle in the middle controls the z-axis rotation; click on it and move the rotation handle onto the tabletop so that it rotates to a flat surface.

Adjust the width of this surface from the sides, and adjust the skew so that the tabletop takes on the correct shape, reaching out from the wall toward you. Then move this tabletop to the bottom layer (use either the Order command on the Object menu or the Layers arrows from the tool control bar).

Last big adjustment: Make the table deep enough, and move the other objects so they appear to sit properly on the table. Use the Crop tool to get rid of unneeded bits.

When all the pieces are exactly the way you want them—and not before!—use the Combine command on the Object menu to merge all the image elements. Combining is irreversible. To preserve an editable version, first save the picture in Picture Publisher's native .PP4 format (select the File Types pull-down from the Save dialog box). Picture Publisher pops up a format dialog, with an option to save the mask channel—select that option. After the editable version is saved, go ahead and combine the elements and save the picture under another name in any format you choose. You can return to *status quo ante* by calling up the version with the mask channel intact.

This picture still needs some more work. First, notice all the added elements are now combined in a single masked area. From the Mask menu, select the Feather option and set the feathering to two or three pixels, with a centered orientation. This will smooth things out between the background and the foreground objects. Then, remove the mask.

Next item: Check all the objects. Are there things you wanted to do, but that the object boundaries prevented? Now's the time to fix them. (I worked a bit more on the loaf of bread—the least satisfying of the objects I made.)

Most important, since there are lighting effects, you need to add the shadows. Set the Paintbrush transparency to 80 percent, and the color to black. Then paint in shadows for the bottle and the cheese on the wall. The cheese also casts a shadow on the table. Shadows also appear under the bread slices, behind the loaf on the little bit of bottle than can be seen, and under the apple where it is against the loaf of bread. Save the whole thing—and save it again in TIFF format for use with other programs. The final version is shown in Figure 12.11.

Figure 12.11   This is the completed still life.

Of course, practice makes perfect.

Generic Painting

The point is simple: With the tools you have, and that you are learning to use in this book, if you can conceive it in your mind, you can make a picture of it on your computer.

There is another point: Although a more advanced vector-drawing program might allow you to create some of these effects without resort to a paint program, that extra facility is not necessary. Designers have effectively combined vector-drawing and painting software—and the techniques appropriate to them—for some time. The combination is sanctioned by tradition, if you wish, and it works well.

Your Turn

You have had a complete overview of computer-graphics tools commonly available for PC-family machines. You have hands-on experience making them do things that are practical.

Along the way, I have provided my views on the subject of effective design; there are other views on the matter, and finally, you will need to form your own opinions on the subject. If you are like most people, the more design work you do, the more people you meet with common interests, and the more examples you see through the lens of your own experience, the more your taste will evolve.

I think you'll like the result.

Appendix A: Almost All You Need to Know about Hardware

> This appendix is somewhat technical. You do not need to master its contents to do the projects or deal with the software included with the book. On the other hand, understanding most of this material can make you a more adroit user and a cannier shopper.

Setting up your computer-graphics studio involves two categories of equipment. *Hardware* is the category of physical machinery you operate under *software* control.

The Utterly Basic Comment

Hardware includes the computer proper, tightly integrated components that work with it, and other, more optional items, such as printers and pointing devices.

PC-family computers are particularly flexible in the mix-and-match aspect of things. That flexibility means you can have pretty much anything you want (and can afford) in a PC; it also means complexity (you have to make some choices).

If you know all this, skip ahead. If you are pretty new to all of this computer stuff, these first paragraphs are for you.

Complexity entails a degree of fragility; you need to have some idea about what will work together and what won't. That's OK. After all, familiarity with the machines you use means you are less often at the mercy of high-priced repair engineers. And never ever forget the basic concept: These are *personal* computers. They are intended to be used by ordinary folks like you and me.

Let me put that another way: My wife, who is a professor of Chinese Language and Asian Studies—and not at all a technician—is quite capable of opening her computer and making adjustments, including changing a chip or two. She has done it. You don't need to be a rocket scientist; you do need to have common sense and a willingness to read the instructions.

In short, the most complex parts of dealing with your machinery are things you really can do. The most important job, then, is getting the right bits and pieces. This makes the complexity more manageable.

The Basic Graphics-Capable PC

The basic hardware outfit consists of a system unit (in Figure A.1, that's the upright rectangular box on the left), a monitor, a keyboard, and a mouse.

The system unit is the most basic and least changeable of the components. Some are desktop units; some are intended to fit beside a desk or in the kneehole.

Generally, the latter kind, housed in what are commonly called tower cases, are preferable, if you have the choice. If you don't have the choice, consider buying a cradle so you can put the desktop box off the desk. The reason is simple: It's one less thing on your desk.

Full-size tower cases also provide ample room inside for an assortment of peripheral units—floppy-disk drives, generous hard disks, CD-ROM drives, and a full assortment of peripheral cards.

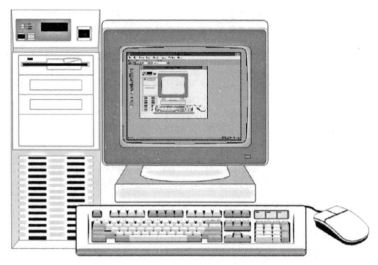

Figure A.1   This is a fairly standard PC-family computer, with basic graphics capability.

A better reason: The new generations of CPU (central processing unit) chips—the actual computer—tend to run hot. A bigger box means more room for air to circulate and more room for an extra fan. Keeping the CPU and other chips cooler contributes to their life span.

My biggest machine has three fans in it.

The CPU—The Machine and Its Ghost

Most PC-family machines are based on a 486 CPU chip from Intel. If your system is somewhat older, you may have an Intel 386 CPU. Or you may have one of several Intel-like chips—Cyrix's 486SLC (something of a hybrid of 386 and 486 designs) or AMD's interpretation of the 386 or 486 design. If you have just bought your system, and you have really gone all out, you may have an Intel Pentium— the latest generation in the family, with some marked improvements and capabilities.

CPU and CPU speed are two factors in performance.

The graphics software used in this book works well with any of these processors. The snappier the processor, the better it will work, generally speaking.

This CPU chip is normally located on a large circuit board with a range of other chips. For graphics, the most important are the BIOS chips and the memory chips.

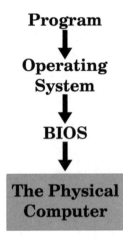

Program

↓

Operating System

↓

BIOS

↓

The Physical Computer

Think of the BIOS (basic input/output system) as glue. It is a small program built into the basic design of your system that works with the software to route information through the system. In fact, this is part of the operating-system software; the company making your computer uses the BIOS to match its design to the more generalized parts of the operating system (MS- or PC-DOS and Windows). If the BIOS is not right, compatibility problems occur.

Computer makers upgrade BIOS designs more often than they do the design of a computer motherboard. It is often useful to ask the technical-support staff of your computer maker if a BIOS update is available; if it is, you can quite easily change the BIOS chips (or sometimes, just run a software program) to update your system.

Real Memory (RAM)

Memory is a simpler matter: More is better. There are several reasons for this, but the main reason is speed. DOS needs memory; Windows needs memory; the graphics application you are using needs memory; the picture itself needs memory.

Actually, Windows can work around limitations in memory. It can swap some kinds of information back and forth between real memory and a section of the hard disk that it treats as virtual memory. But this takes time; the more often it is needed, the more things slow down. Put more real memory in the system, and things speed up.

Windows-ready, graphics-capable computers commonly come with at least 4 megabytes (commonly abbreviated Mb). You want at least 8Mb RAM (random access—real—memory). This gives the software some elbow room. In general, I have found a slightly slower CPU chip, running with more memory, will run faster overall than a faster chip addressing less memory.

There is a catch. Some computer vendors claim their systems will accommodate tremendous amounts of memory; actually, there are important limitations on how much memory you can put in the system. The general rule is that 386-based systems easily accommodate 4Mb to 8Mb, 486 systems based on an ISA (industry standard architecture) design accommodate 16Mb, and 486 (or better) systems based on EISA (extended industry standard architecture) or MCA (IBM's proprietary MicroChannel architecture) buses will accommodate as much as 64Mb of real memory. The newest designs are set up to handle 128Mb—but that is overkill.

The short rule: Start with 8Mb of RAM, but try to plan for more.

If this seems overly technical, well, it is. The issue is important, though. One large company had serious speed problems with its design systems; a simple memory upgrade eliminated the problem.

Other Things in the Box

Your system may also have external connections for a mouse, a printer, and a serial device (such as a modem) built into the motherboard. Alternatively, these are supplied as add-in cards, plugged into *slots* on the motherboard. Your dealer may refer to these as *ports*.

Generally, you want two printer ports and two serial ports. If your system has a mouse port, you want to be able to turn it off in favor of a serial port down the road. The reason is simple: When you start with graphics, you will surely use a standard black-and-white printer—that is what most of us have. But as you go further, you will want to add a color printer, so you need another printer connection. Similarly, you may

Adding a card with a second serial and printer connection is a low-cost option—commonly between $25 and $50.

start with a mouse, but you may want to move to a graphics tablet, which doesn't work on a mouse port, by and large. If you have only one serial connection, you will be caught making invidious choices between a modem and a tablet.

The Hard Disk—Your Computer's File Cabinet

One more item here: The hard disk. Generally, you want as big a hard disk as you can get. If possible, you want a SCSI (pronounced "scuzzy") hard disk. If you have a hard disk of less than 300Mb, you will certainly want to stack the hard disk, using one of several disk-compression products on the market. Graphics files are big!

SCSI is important; it adds all kinds of flexibility to your system. In addition to hard disks, you can hook CD-ROM drives, tape drives, scanners, printers, and film recorders to your system through SCSI.

The Display System

Most PC-family computers these days come with at least SuperVGA display capability. This means the picture you see can include up to 236 colors (plus 20 colors reserved by Windows for its own purposes). That picture can be up to 1024 dots (*pixels* or picture elements) across, and 768 dots up and down. This is not too shabby, and it is perfectly adequate for most graphics needs. This picture is controlled either by a graphics capability built into the system motherboard, or by a card inserted in a motherboard slot.

The monitor used is commonly called a SuperVGA monitor, and it matches the capabilities of the display-adapter hardware in the computer-system unit.

Use the little utility Win-Tach, included on the CD-ROM, to test your system's graphics performance. Look especially at the paint and chart numbers.

Older systems have VGA or a subset of SuperVGA. The VGA specification is for 16 colors at 640 × 480 pixel resolution; the common subset of SuperVGA is 800 × 600 pixel resolution, with 256 colors. Both of these specifications are acceptable, but they are better suited for office-automation systems than graphics systems.

The growth path for graphics users—and increasingly, for everyone else—combines a minimum resolution of 1024 × 768 with the capability to display lots more colors. Innovations in graphics-adapter design, combined with market demand, are reducing the prices for such capabilities by a factor of 5.

Display Adapters

High-color systems (capable of displaying 32,000 or 64,000 colors) and true-color systems (capable of displaying up to 16.7 million colors) add memory and on-board processor power to the display system. Not only do you see a more realistic picture, but you see it faster—commonly, 20 to 40 times faster.

You can also enhance graphics-display speeds by using *local-bus* technology. The graphics adapter plugs into a local-bus slot, and the central processing unit can squirt display data to it directly. This can dramatically enhance speeds. In fact, the fastest graphics board I have used (STB's Pegasus VL true color board) uses this strategy to deliver stunning performance.

The other really fast board in tests I have conducted, with good overall performance for design graphics, is ATI's Graphics Ultra Pro. This high-color card, in an EISA-bus machine, delivered performance similar to that of local-bus display cards. The EISA design provides a fast, wide-system access to the processor, obviating some of the local bus's benefits. Like most high-color cards, this one costs well under $400 (street price).

Here's a strategy to consider: If your system has display hardware built in, live with it—but make sure you can turn it off or replace the card as things change. Top-of-the-line display adapters now cost $750 (street price). Since the display adapter is one of the speed bottlenecks, sometimes changing display adapters can add a couple of years to your basic PC investment.

Monitors

Life would be simple if you could treat monitors and display adapters as a unit. But life is not simple.

Ideally, you will test the monitors your vendor offers, and choose one based on your comfort.

The short story on monitors is to buy the best you can afford. You will spend time looking at those pictures on the screen, and a good monitor will go a long way toward making that a less tiring proposition.

Most people have bought a system that includes a monitor matched to the display adapter the computer vendor has supplied. The vendor's interests are served by supplying the least costly monitor for the job. For office-automation needs, that monitor is perfectly good. For graphics applications, something else may be in order.

First, you want as fine a dot pitch as you can get. Dot pitch is expressed in millimeters (mm), and smaller numbers are better. Look for a number not larger than 0.28mm.

Second, you almost certainly will do better to use a multiple-scan-rate monitor. Unlike VGA or SuperVGA monitors, these multisynch monitors can adjust to the different scan rates required by higher-resolution display systems. The current crop easily supports noninterlaced scanning, which means that an annoying flicker is eliminated.

> The multisynch monitor was first popularized by NEC, and this company has tended to be at the front of the pack in new developments. Lots of companies make good monitors, but NEC monitors are remarkably good performers and have a good lifespan. My original NEC MultiSynch monitor is still in use after 7 years; later models are connected to my heavy-duty test-bench machines in the studio.

Monitors come in different sizes. Commonly, they are described as 15-inch, 17-inch, and 20-inch models. The 20-inch models are very expensive and very heavy, and they take up a lot of desktop real estate. Most people don't benefit from the added costs.

The same does not hold true for 15-inch and 17-inch monitors. The real-estate issue is not vastly different from one to the other. There is a price difference, but it is not as great. The bigger picture may be worth it.

Some (not all) 17-inch monitors comfortably support higher resolutions (requiring a different scan rate) than do 15-inch monitors. For example, I usually set my 15-inch NEC monitor for noninterlaced 1024×768 display; that gives me excellent performance with no flicker. If I want to use the higher resolution of my ATI Graphics Ultra Pro (1280×1024 — about 60 percent more information on the screen, with a sacrifice in colors available), I have to live with interlacing and a certain amount of flicker. I can push the monitor this way. But in addition to the flicker, I get really bitsy letters in the Windows menus—I am reading fine print all the time. I can't texturize my Windows desktop, either; the flicker is exacerbated.

If you go for the larger monitor, look for the specification to include 1280×1024 or better display, noninterlaced.

The 17-inch monitor two steps up in the series will support that same higher resolution in noninterlaced mode. The lettering will be bigger. And so on.

The in-between 17-inch model will give me the larger text, but it supports the higher resolution only in interlaced mode.

In fact, for most needs—including most design work—a best-of-breed multisynch 15-inch monitor, with a diagonal display area just shy of 14 inches, is perfectly adequate. If you have some extra bucks, 17-inch models supporting higher scan rates are a nice way to spend the money.

A few words on ergonomics: There has been a lot of concern about monitor radiation and other matters. The concerns are justified, and the monitor makers have addressed them. The toughest standards, supposedly, are those established by the Swedish government, so the monitor you use should claim to meet those specs. It should also support noninterlaced display at the highest level you will use.

The other step you can take to make things easier on your eyes is to keep a good distance from your monitor. That means, normally, you want a distance of around 1½ to 2 feet between you and the screen for normal work.

Pointing Devices

Mice

Mice are ubiquitous, most people like them, and they are usually included in the price of the computer these days. Some mice are very good; some are abysmal. If your mouse is in the latter category, buy a new one.

When you are using a mouse, the pivot point is the heel of your hand, about where the arrow points in Figure A.2. The

Figure A.2   The mouse is the standard pointing device.

mouse's tracking points are along a curve defined by the radius, heel to point. A good mouse for drawing has the track point (usually a little rubber ball) up under the switches for finer control with less fatigue.

For many moons, my own mouse preference was Microsoft's third-generation 400ppi (points per inch—the way accuracy is measured in pointing devices; more is better) shield-shaped mouse. I liked the way it worked for drawing.

Microsoft abandoned that design in mid-1993. The new Microsoft mouse is very good in many ways, but it seems to me a bit less ideal for graphics. Also, I have seen only right-handed models of the new design; southpaws may find this a problem.

What earthly good is a mouse like this?

On the other hand, I have been impressed with Logitech's new cordless-mouse designs. Cordless is good; cords get in the way. This mouse also has a particularly nice feel under the hand. The mouse body is a sort of rounded triangle, and it allows for good control when you are drawing lines.

Still another variant in mouse design is Appoint's Gulliver mouse. This mouse is tiny (vaguely triangular, about 2 inches across). It tracks very tightly for excellent control. Drawing with it is something like drawing with a fat stick of carpenter's chalk. I use this mouse a lot, especially with my notebook computer.

Use the Gulliver mouse with a cloth-surfaced mouse pad for the best tracking.

There are lots of mice out there. By all means, try before you buy. You'll be using this thing all the time, and you had best have one that feels good to you.

Trackballs

Think of a trackball as a mouse turned upside down. Instead of moving the box around on the desk, you twiddle the ball with your fingers. It is a good strategy, especially if your desk is crowded.

The key issue is the size of the trackball. The pea-size and marble-size balls used in some trackballs are useless for graphics. A good-size ball, about the size of a billiard ball, with some heft to it, will deliver good control.

Mrs. Jenner—a dedicated trackball user—likes to tuck hers in her lap when she works. You can't do that with a mouse.

The two popular players in the marketplace are Kensington and Microspeed. Kensington houses its trackball in a roughly square-shaped box; Microspeed's box is rectangular and sloped to provide a hand rest. Both companies wrap the buttons more or less around the trackball, where you can easily tap them with thumb and ring finger.

Digitizing Tablets

Tablets were first designed for CAD programs. They were expensive, and they demanded a lot of desktop real estate. Those problems have gone away, to some extent. You want a digitizing tablet if you find your design work takes you toward painting and bitmap editing in a serious way.

The reason is simple: Mice and trackballs are *relative* pointing devices. That is, the position of the mouse on your desk has nothing to do with the position of the pointer on your screen. Tablets can function this way too, but normally, they are set to absolute mode. In this case, the tablet's active surface is a one-to-one map of the screen; move the pointer with your hand, and the on-screen pointer moves to the same position. Tablets also offer finer control than mice and trackballs. Commonly, tablets have 2½ times the resolution of a mouse.

Learn Desktop Graphics and Design on the PC

What you probably don't want is the kind of tablet an engineer or draftsman uses. Such tablets—about 15 inches square, with a 12 by 12-inch active area—are too cumbersome, and the size doesn't buy you any advantage.

Look for a smaller tablet (up to 6 by 9 inches), and look for one that includes a penlike stylus, as well as the mouselike puck.

And anyway, the smaller-format tablets can tuck in your lap for a sketching session.

The bargain in this category, from AceCAD, is called the Ace-CAT. It is small (the active surface is a 5-inch square). It is very inexpensive (at around $125, it costs the same as a quality mouse). It comes with a stylus. You can buy a puck (around $75), or you can install the tablet driver so you can use the tablet alongside a standard mouse. It would be perfect if the stylus were cordless—but at this price, perhaps I should not complain.

Appoint's new Gliffic Plus tablet, shown in Figure A.3, is possibly the most innovative tablet on the market. This tablet

You want both a stylus and a puck or mouse. The stylus is great for drawing, but a pain for other computer chores. A mouse is better for everything else, but only so-so for drawing.

Figure A.3 Appoint's Gliffic Plus small-format tablet comes with both puck (mouse) and stylus—both cordless.

desk set comes with a small-format tablet, a cordless stylus, a cordless puck (using the same comfortable housing as the Gulliver mouse mentioned earlier), and—for portable-computer users—the ability to use a 9-volt battery instead of the standard (and included) AC power pack. In my tests, this tablet performed remarkably well. That it all comes in one box, at one price (around $300 list; look to spend less) makes it a simple buy. I use this Gliffic tablet with one of the desktop design systems here in the studio; its small size and natural feel have made it a favorite.

Wacom's pressure-sensitive tablet is the graphics-industry standard for design work. The company gets competition from Kurta and CalComp. All of these are high-end products, and the pressure sensitivity is used in high-end graphic-design environments. You can use pressure sensitivity to control things such as line thickness and paint density—or you could, if the tablet makers and the software developers would get together and agree on how it should all work. Wacom, CalComp, and Kurta tablets come with WinTab drivers supporting pressure sensitivity when used with a stylus, in Windows applications supporting this and other pen-oriented features. WinTab is apparently going to be yet another industry standard, and if you purchase a tablet, you should insist that it have a Windows driver that meets the WinTab specification.

A 12-inch square CAD-oriented tablet that deserves special mention. Numonics produces the GridMaster. This tablet is actually a mat that lies flat on the desktop, with a little box into which the corded stylus or puck is plugged. Unlike other full-size tablets, this one's demand for real estate is mitigated by the fact that you can pile papers (not floppy disks!) on the unused area of the tablet.

One last thing: If you are using a tablet, you will need that extra serial connection I mentioned previously. Tablets simply do not work with mouse ports, in my experience. They should, but they don't.

That's the basics. You need a system unit with as much speed and as much memory as you can get, a big hard disk, a good display that you can sit in front of for several hours, and a comfortable pointing device. Now for the neat stuff!

Printers

Printers are the most important peripheral for graphics users. A good printer is always a proof press; the best of them are final output devices as well.

Monochrome: Black-and-White Output

Laser printers are cheap enough; treat yourself. They come in many varieties and at many price points. There is one within your budget limits.

The only real issues in buying a laser printer are whose do you buy, and is it PostScript?

I confess to having prejudices on this topic as well. I like Hewlett-Packard LaserJets and IBM printers from Lexmark (formerly IBM's typewriter division). I like HP LaserJets because they are a standard against which other printers are measured, and because they can be readily modified to serve special needs. I like IBM laser printers because they may well be the best-built printers on the market today.

If anything tips the balance, it is the ways in which the HP printers can be modified. Despite numerous assaults, Adobe's PostScript page-description language (PDL) remains the standard for graphics printing. But PostScript printers are *slow!* If you have an HP LaserJet, you have options that deliver fast PostScript.

Both options move the PostScript processing chores to your *host* computer—the machine on your desktop or beside your desk. Using spare computing capacity, a product such as Zenographics Zscript can process your design into PostScript language, translate that page description into printer commands, and squirt it out to the printer as fast as the printer can take it. A standard PostScript job that might take half an hour or more to start printing can now be finished in a few minutes.

Zenographics is a company that knows a lot about graphics software; the company has played successfully in the graphics marketplace since the mid-1980s. Zscript is currently marketed as part of SuperPrint, which is probably one of the neatest printer-control systems available—highly recommended. Use Zscript to drive SuperPrint device drivers, and you have the fastest printing available. I use this combination in the studio to create a degree of uniformity in controlling printers as diverse as the LaserJet, the DeskJet monochrome inkjet, my color printers, and my film recorder. It even manages network printing.

LaserMaster offers a variation on the theme. Like Zenographics Zscript, it processes PostScript on the host computer. Then it uses special hardware to drive the result out the back, directly to the LaserJet's video port. The result is higher resolution (about 800 dots per inch on my 300dpi LJIII; the LJIV version delivers around 1200dpi). This is nearly typesetter performance. Grayscale images—photographs and such—come out without annoying hot spots. So this setup is useful for testing photoediting, among other things.

Notice, in both these cases, I lose none of the standard HP functionality; I add capabilities. The cost is modest, and the background processing in each case means no lost time.

If the budget really won't stretch to a laser printer, consider one of the better inkjet printers around. Again, Hewlett-Packard's DeskJet is a player; the competition is Canon's

BubbleJet. Each is a superior product, and each delivers good results for proofing. But don't get the original printout wet; inkjet printer inks are usually water-soluble.

Color Printers

Printing in color used to be outrageously overpriced. Now, color printers are both good and affordable. You may not buy one right off the bat, but as you work with design, you will want to see your work in color.

More important, if you are checking your work before sending it out to a print shop, you will want to test your design. Happily, the standard desktop color printers use a color system not unlike that used in professional printing. You can get a good idea of what your final job will look like from a modestly priced color printer.

Color laser printers (sort of small cousins of color laser copiers) are available. They are very costly. Top-of-the-line color wax thermal-transfer printers—like the Textronix Phaser products—are also wonderful; they are also expensive, unless you are involved with graphics in a very big way with a corresponding budget. Now let's proceed to the real world.

Color printers you can afford come in two varieties: inkjet and wax thermal-transfer. Some of the color inkjet printers do very nicely as all-around printers; that is, they do black-and-white printing as well as color printing.

Wax Thermal-Transfer Printers Wax thermal-transfer printing is the old standby. A thin film ribbon is coated with bands of process-colored (cyan/magenta/yellow and sometimes black—respectively CMY and CMYK) wax. Special paper makes three or four passes through the printer, as patterns of process-color dots are laid down, in a manner not unlike that used in process-color printing.

Wax thermal-transfer remains popular in part because the shiny wax looks pretty. The colors are vivid and rich.

It used to be that all such printers were expensive. They needed a special connection to the computer—also costly.

That changed with the introduction of two new printers in 1993.

Fargo Electronics broke the price barrier with its Primera. It costs a third (or less) of what older wax thermal-transfer printers cost (about $750 on the street). The price per print is about 42 cents. It prints to paper and transparency film, and the results are good enough for proof and client approval, generally.

The Primera has a special feature. Change the ribbon cartridge and paper, and this printer does a variation on dye-sublimation printing. This optional, extra-cost feature adds $250 to the price of the printer. The result is color that is nearly photorealistic—that is, as good as it gets.

Look for new Primera products in larger formats and higher resolution. These products should appear about the same time as this book.

The graphics community has taken to the Primera. The price is modest, the results are good, and the dye-sublimation output is remarkable (especially since the nearest competing printer costs something like $25,000!). That the printer needs only a small amount of desk or credenza space is no small factor in a crowded studio.

Not to be outdone, veteran PC-printer maker Star Micronics launched its J144 color thermal-transfer printer. The J144 substitutes a resin-based pigment for the traditional wax, and it can use plain 24 lb. copier bond instead of special paper. Star has housed this printer in a small-footprint lunchbox—a vertical, instead of horizontal, cabinet. It can print at an eye-pleasing 360dpi (that's better than laser printing, and in color, it counts as high resolution). And the company put a $500 price tag on it.

The cost of consumables—color ribbon cartridges—is not cheap: three for $35. Each color ribbon for the J144 makes only eight color prints, at a cost of about $1.50 a print. Because the printer makes passes back and forth like a standard dot-matrix printer, banding is an issue. But much of this is offset by the utility this printer offers as a dual-mode printer; its black-and-white ribbons last longer, and the print is as perfect as a laser printer's.

Although the J144's consumables are costly, the lower printer cost translates this into a comparable price with the Primera. But the colors are not as vibrant as traditional wax thermal-transfer prints, to my eye. I found the colors dull and the banding very displeasing. In eyeball tests, however, the color output of standard color charts was close enough to regular printed versions that the J144 could be used for testing colors.

Color Inkjet Printers Desktop color inkjet printers come in a couple varieties. Most are more suited to business applications, such as Hewlett-Packard's DeskJet 550C and the color versions of Canon's BubbleJet. They print on plain paper, and they use a CMY cartridge to add color along with the standard black printing cartridge of noncolor inkjet models.

Hewlett-Packard offers a special paper with a water-soluble coating that makes its color DeskJets produce extraordinary color graphics. This special medium is not cheap (adding ink costs, each print costs about $1.75 to $2.00). But the combination of a fine 300dpi printing capability coupled with the bleed in the coating of the paper makes for a particularly rich color value, and the final output looks as clear as a photograph. Just don't get the print wet!

Strictly for graphics users, Hewlett-Packard offers its Paint-Jet printers. The company seems intent on killing the product, but users still want it, so the company still sells it.

The lower-priced PaintJet, a desktop model, takes special clay-coated paper—continuous-form (pin-feed) or cut-sheet—and overhead-transparency foils. It uses two cartridges: one for colors and one for black. It is not a high-resolution printer, at a mere 180dpi. But it is a workhorse!

Color is not as vivid as the wax thermal-transfer color of a Primera, but it is remarkably faithful to process-color printing output. This means you can check designs before they go to the print shop. Cost per copy is around 75 cents; that makes this printer acceptable for small runs of color flyers. And the printer is fast enough that you can do a short run in a short time.

Here's another place where Zenographics Zscript and SuperPrint pays off. Both the Primera and the PaintJet (and the Polaroid Digital Palette, discussed in the next section) are supported not only by their own makers' drivers, but also by Zeno SuperDrivers. Turn these low-cost color printers into PostScript devices by using Zscript to process your design, and SuperPrint to manage the printing process. Color printing takes time, but the Zenographics printer tools are particularly well-tuned for graphics output (the company's forte, after all), and you will find you get use of your computer back sooner, while SuperPrint takes care of time-consuming printer chores in the background.

Film Recorders

By and large, film recorders—essentially, a camera back attached to a box that translates computer-design information into light signals—are service-bureau tools. Even many computer-design studios blanch at the cost of a film recorder.

There is an exception, from Polaroid, called the Digital Palette (PDP). If your computer-graphics chores take you into a lot of presentation support—and that includes making slides—a Polaroid Digital Palette may be cost effective. It can also play if you are creating designs for clients. The PDP can also make snapshotlike prints that really impress. And, unlike all the other color printers in this appendix, the PDP is not just a good imitation of photorealism; it's the real thing. A Polaroid Digital Palette with both print and 35mm slide backs costs about $6,000. It is small enough to fit on a shelf, and it can connect to either a parallel printer port or a SCSI port.

Other Peripherals You May Want to Consider

Your graphics-capable computer and a good printer are the basics; a couple other things may merit attention down the road.

UPS

The most important of these, technically, is a line conditioner or uninterruptible power supply (UPS). A surge-protector—even a good one (and most people don't use good ones)—is not enough! Power companies think interruptions in power to your studio are just fine; your computer will not agree. If you are lucky, you will only find your computer suddenly rebooting—right in the middle of your probably unsaved several hours' worth of work. If you are not lucky, you will find your nifty new computer is now a very expensive paperweight. Buy a line conditioner or UPS, in short.

Scanner

The most important "other thing" in terms of graphics work is a scanner. Scanners come in a variety of sizes and capabilities suited to desktop-graphics studios.

You will be offered grayscale scanners, and handscanners. If you are buying a scanner for use in graphics, don't bother with these—they are intended for optical character recognition (OCR) applications and are almost useless for serious graphics work.

A good scanner for desktop graphics work looks something like (and actually is) the top part of a copier machine. It has a lift-up cover, a clear glass surface on which the object to be copied is laid. Inside, a moving head makes one pass for monochrome and three passes for color (one each for red, green, and blue shades) at different speeds, depending on the dots per inch (resolution) selected—usually under software control.

This box connects to the computer through a SCSI connection, or occasionally through a bidirectional parallel port.

Most bitmap editors and paint programs can control the scanning process; most often, this is through a TWAIN driver supplied by the scanner maker. You want to be sure there is a TWAIN driver (it is the current standard, much better than the older, strictly proprietary drivers of days gone by). Check with the vendor every so often, to see if there has been an upgrade (frequently provided for free).

Many pros spend a lot of money on a high-end flatbed scanner. The best of the breed (for example, UMAX's top models) rival $25,000 drum scanners in the quality of the scans produced. But most of the time, a 300dpi scanner will do just as well, at a price of $750 to $850.

Scanners serve a range of purposes. In addition to grabbing images for editing and incorporation into your designs, they can scan documents for faxing through your computer.

When you scan images for use in your designs, you are up against some important copyright restrictions. The common rule is that if what you use comprises less than a quarter of the entire image content, and if it has been so edited as to make it clearly different from the original image on which it is based, you have done something that varies sufficiently as to be considered a new image. But this is an area of very muddy waters.

Removable Drives

If you find yourself working with a service bureau, and you need to transport large graphics files (especially, large bit-maps and PostScript files), consider a removable disk system, a tape drive, or both.

Most service bureaus use 5¼-inch Syquest disk systems, which became popular when Macintoshes ruled the graphics roost. Syquest also offers 3½-inch removable disks with a larger capacity. Iomega's Bernoulli removable disks—more common in office-PC environments—are slowly gaining acceptance in service bureaus with lots of PC-using clients. Each technology has its advantages; buy according to what your service bureau will accept. These devices plug into a SCSI port. The added advantage: You can use tape drives for additional online storage for big files.

Tape drives are also a good investment—not so much for moving files as for backups. Hard disks are more reliable than in days gone by, but a copy in a safe place is a good security measure. You want a drive that can plug into your SCSI port, ideally (faster and neater), and able to handle at least 250Mb. Tape drives add a couple hundred dollars to the cost of the system.

One variant on the tape drive, from MicroSolutions, has proven a particularly good tool in my studio. This drive connects through a printer port and daisy-chains between the laser printer and the computer. It is fast enough and has good backup software. Because it plugs into the printer port, it can be moved to other computers in the studio, as well as doing backups across the network.

Appendix B: What Computer Graphics Is

A Short History of Computer Graphics

Since computers have existed—or for at least the last 25 or 30 years—the idea of having them generate pictures of one kind or another has been of paramount interest.

Some of this was strictly business. Governments wanted computers to use raw data to create photographically realistic images for benign or other reasons. Scientists wanted to take similar data and see in understandable terms what the data meant.

Some of it was strictly fun. Computer wonks in their glass rooms were bored. The data they dealt with was crafted in the imaginations of their hearts.

The problems were formidable. The computers available were set up mostly to move numbers around. The output devices—printers—really could not deal with much beyond the letters of the alphabet and the numbers 0 through 9.

The result was for computer graphics only a mother could love—and even she would not be likely to stick the result on the refrigerator door!

The first graphics printers were really plotters—machines that could move a pen along a straightedge in time-honored fashion. That was fine, because lines can be represented mathematically, and computers could be programmed to do the math, then move the pen and paper accordingly. It took time to do it, but it worked. Add additional computing capability, and the plotter could even change the pens for different colors.

The nerd—er, computer enthusiast—as artist

Another approach to the printing problem involved using letters, numbers, and punctuation in patterns. Cleverly arranged, these symbols could have the same effect as dithering and represent shading, up to a point. Print out the pattern on continuous-form computer paper, view it from a suitable distance, and the picture was—well, it was there, and there was something like craft, if not art, involved.

Things remained complex for quite a while. Serious graphics computing—lifelike pictures, even animation—slowly became possible, but at tremendous cost. First you built a computer. Then you wrote an operating system and graphics software. The cost was not small for all this, and after 5 years (if you were lucky) you had a proprietary system a few talented people (combining substantial expertise in computer systems with artistic ability) could use. The result was written with light on photographic film.

The first-generation computer graphics were quite amazing. An early application of this technology was used to make the Disney film *Tron*. At least one of the graphics programmers turned his contribution into a Ph.D. in computer science.

Microchips to the Rescue

A whole bunch of events, more or less taking off in 1980, conspired to change things.

First, several people figured out what bits and pieces could be assembled in what way to make a practical—and nearly affordable—personal computer.

Second, printer manufacturers developed modestly priced dot-matrix printers—that is, printers that created letters by banging a series of dot patterns along a line, rather than striking fully formed letters like a typewriter. These printers could, in principle, be programmed to produce any pattern on a page—including true dither patterns.

Most important, affordable computers with potentially graphical printers brought the hackers out of the woodwork. They started solving problems—for business, to be sure, but also for fun. Once they figured out how to share their expertise over the telephone (the origin of the BBS network), the result was a flowering of tools and toys, and waxing expertise.

This flourishing of BBS networks has been enormously important. This openness of information exchange simply doesn't exist elsewhere to the same degree, and it's one reason the United States stays about 5 or 6 years ahead of the rest of the world in the use of this technology. The enthusiasm is spreading; U.S. networking propensities are catching on and becoming an international thing. But it is still very much a U.S. phenomenon, and the results are impressive.

Desktop Computer Graphics—The Early Years

Once microcomputers were around, computer graphics came along speedily. On business-oriented machines, charting became a clear favorite. In those early days, Apple II computers had an advantage because of the way they painted the screen. Other computers simply generated characters, but Apples painted screens a dot at a time, and the location of each dot could be positioned under software control. Apple capitalized on this early design decision in later machines, including the Macintosh.

By 1985, IBM's PC/AT was coming on the market, along with Color Graphics Adapters and Enhanced Graphics Adapters—ways to make non-Apple mainstream machines display pictures. The other hardware advance was the advent of desktop laser printers.

Software vendors saw an opportunity. A whole raft of graphics applications "for the rest of us" (to steal a slogan from Apple) came to market. Desktop-publishing software, advanced charting software, and simple illustration software could be had for a few hundred dollars.

At the upper end of the market, the open architecture of the PC/AT and its clones made this machine the platform of choice for value adders. A whole raft of machines, using the PC/AT as a foundation, added sophisticated graphics support and powerful drawing and painting tools for professional applications. At $20,000 and up, these machines rivaled custom machines costing twice that much. They were workhorses.

The Promise Fulfilled

A current PC-family graphics workstation.

Once Intel started delivering the 386, and more recently, the 486, a competitively priced, fully graphical workstation could be built for as little as $2,000. Indeed, it didn't pay to eschew this opportunity. Soon, the PC-compatible marketplace was loaded with these powerful, affordable machines (about 70 percent of the computing world is PC-family machines; most of the PCs sold since 1990 are graphics-capable machines).

Along the way, the builders of all the bits and pieces that work with the computer to make a system function had not been slow to notice this jump in the market. Current laser printers deliver near-typesetter quality (and they can be made to do better). Color printers of several sorts—once a big-ticket, service-bureau-only item—now cost well under $1,000.

The software vendors have been even faster to take advantage of the current and predicted capabilities of PC-family machines. The trickle of well-crafted products that started in the late 1980s has become a veritable flood; few categories of graphics tools are unavailable for PC-family machines—charting and printing, video, you name it.

Even vendors who wrote for the Macintosh and prefer that machine have realized that playing with 70 percent of the market is more interesting than playing with the 15 percent of the computing marketplace owned by Apple. Mac applications are increasingly being offered in versions for the PC—not infrequently, in a more powerful version.

The Outcome of All This History

Since the machines are cheap, the software is cheap (and powerful), and using the software on the machines is easy, design professionals have slowly been brought to use this technology. It's something many of them don't like, and sometimes their objections have merit. But it is simply faster and cheaper to do a job on the computer, when possible; that translates directly into lower direct labor costs and better profits.

Computer Graphics Defined

Professional designers who use computers tend to mix and match a variety of software tools in the execution of a project. Vendors are not slow to pick up on this; they tend to bundle several tools in one box. The pros still tend to buy more than one product, looking for an optimal mix for the kinds of work they do. After all, *design* embraces a whole range of image-oriented chores.

Desktop Publishing

Using microcomputers as a convenient publishing tool is the second oldest graphics application for the technology. It has

The oldest use of computer graphics is something we will not discuss.

proven so successful that it has virtually eliminated a whole job category—that of typesetter.

The term *desktop publishing* refers to what can be done with page-composition software (products such as Aldus Page-Maker, Corel Ventura Publisher, and QuarkXPress) and advanced word-processing software (products such as Microsoft Word for Windows—or for Macintosh—and Lotus Ami Pro).

The two software categories overlap substantially today. Page-composition software, such as PageMaker, has added most of the features of a top-flight word processor. See Figure B.1. The *story editor* in such a program commonly offers spelling correction and other features, so that you can put together a whole publication. But the special strength of a page-composition program is that it provides visual page layout in sophisticated ways. Effectively, it translates the paste-up table of days gone by to the computer screen, adding powerful typesetting tools into the mix.

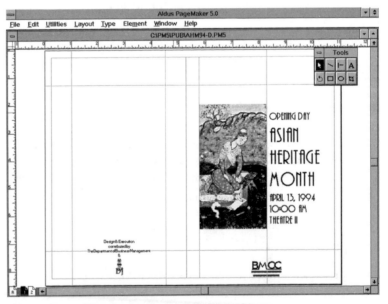

Figure B.1   Here's the PageMaker work space.

Different page-composition programs are focused on different kinds of publishing. For example, the common wisdom is that Ventura Publisher is strongest for some kinds of books and directories and is the most readily programmable of the major offerings. This makes it fairly easy to add links to databases, among other things.

You pays your money and you takes your choices (or chances). Each program serves different needs.

QuarkXPress is a Mac application moved to the PC/Windows environment. It offers industrial-strength magazine-design features, and it is particularly favored by designers working in shops with both Mac and PC platforms.

Aldus PageMaker, which created the business, was originally available only for the Mac. Aldus was the first company to produce a powerful, entirely equivalent PC/Windows version of its software. It may be the most generally useful of the major players. Among other things, the current version of PageMaker includes powerful add-in capabilities (my favorite is page imposition—the ability to correctly order pages on forms, which is a nasty chore if you have to do it yourself).

Advanced word-processing software, in a fully graphical environment such as Windows, has many of the same capabilities for design.

For long documents, a powerful word-processing program is better than a page-composition program.

Ami Pro, which Lotus acquired through its purchase of Samna (a company with a long history in the word-processing field), actually feels like a page-composition program. It offers sophisticated graphics placement capability, and it relies heavily on style-sheet setup, much like Ventura Publisher. At the same time, it offers all the powerful wordsmith capabilities a writer wants. Lotus has done a splendid job of integrating Ami Pro with its other products, so that this word-processing software is one of the most powerful business-document design tools around.

Microsoft's Word for Windows (now Word 6.0, and uniform on both Mac and PC/Windows platforms, according to the company) is more like a word processor than a desktop-publishing program—until you switch into page-layout mode. In that mode, image placement and layout are almost as flexible as in Ami Pro—and certainly adequate for most book or business-document design needs. In fact, many if not all of Microsoft's manuals have been produced using Word for Windows.

> Just to make things more complex, Corel Corporation—currently the purveyor of the leading drawing software (but that could change in a volatile market)—has added significant desktop-publishing features to its drawing software. Among other things, multiple pages (a common drawing-package feature) are now set up to accept text that flows from page to page and column to column.

Desktop-publishing tools—especially page-composition software—are important to the design process if your product is a printed piece.

Presentation Graphics

Business users have been making presentations forever. Not surprisingly, support for presentation graphics was one of the first things to be developed for personal computers.

Modern presentation-graphics software adds sophisticated charting capabilities to graphic design and rounds out the product with presentation management and viewing support. The metaphor that drives this category of graphic-design software is the slide show. The idea is to support a speaker both in the process of making a presentation, and in extending that presentation through effective leave-behinds.

Are software buyers fickle, or what?

At the moment, the leading package in this category is probably Microsoft's PowerPoint. It comes bundled with Microsoft Office—a convenient bonus for corporate information-resources managers. This represents a major shift. A few years ago, these same managers were in love with Harvard

Graphics. As it happens, the basics for this category are sufficiently well understood by now that the competitive difference aspects of the different vendors' offerings are slight.

Presentation-graphics software is intended for users whose understanding of the design process is limited. To guarantee a look that is at least minimally effective, these programs all come with templates. Pick a set of templates—all properly color-coordinated and tuned with cute display elements. Then plug in text (most presentations use lots of bulleted lists) and charts. Next, generate a set of speaker notes and a set of audience notes. *Voilà!* Instant presentation. See Figure B.2.

The problem, of course, is that everybody uses the same templates—even the same designer templates. It is awfully easy to screw things up. My favorite example of this is the slide set that combines a dark background, elegantly slim letter-

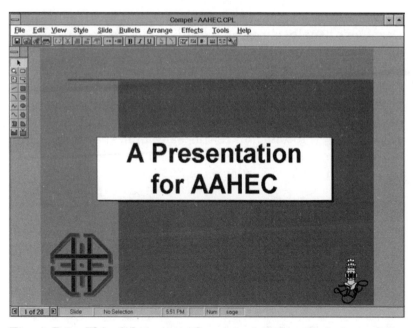

Figure B.2   This slide is part of a presentation made in Asymetrix Compel. The logo in the lower left is one of several linked graphics in this multimedia presentation.

ing, and large blocks of text on the same slide as a chart. A slide with these characteristics is invisible.

Fortunately, all the major presentation-graphics software packages support sufficient design capability that all these problems can be solved with ease. In fact, they all work more or less the same way. You pick the one that works best for you. That may be PowerPoint, or it may be Lotus Freelance (both are powerful and easy to use).

A new entry—and one I like for its flexibility—comes from Asymetrix, a company founded by Bill Gates's former partner. Called Compel, this presentation-graphics product does slides and overhead-projection foils, but it is particularly well-tuned for the next wave in presentation-graphics evolution: the multimedia presentation. Create the presentation at your desk, copy the files to your notebook computer, and play it back (plugged into a large screen or projection monitor) before your audience. Slick!

Designers usually choose a specialized presentation-graphics program when the job calls for it, but the designers I know usually escape to a more powerful graphics program for special elements—logos, and maybe even charts. The ability of Microsoft Windows software to integrate diverse tools in several ways (through the clipboard and two different linking protocols) makes this easy, almost natural. Certainly, it is more like the flexibility of a traditional studio than the software of earlier days.

Again, Corel Corporation has done something clever. The company includes a fairly able chart-making program, a slide-show program, and a nifty, easy-to-use animation program in the Corel Draw retail package. In a presentation I created using Compel I used a couple little animations to signal changes in the flow of the presentation. I created the animations in Corel Move, exported them to the Windows audiovisual format, and then played them back in Compel.

Similar capabilities are available in other advanced design software, such as Micrografx Designer 4.0. Designer comes with a slide sorter built in and an effective slide-show program. Like Compel, it can link to images created in other programs—as well as sending its true three-dimensional images to other software.

Bitmap Editors and Paint Programs

Painting and bitmap editing may be the hottest area in computer graphics for the next several years.

Paintbrush is ancient—at least 5 years old.

Computers can draw lines and geometric solids, or they can paint pixel by pixel. If you have Windows, you have a rudimentary paint program: Windows Paintbrush. This is a slightly modified, and rather primitive, version of Publisher's Paintbrush from Zsoft. Things have gotten vastly better since this program was developed.

The current crop of bitmap-oriented programs falls rather handily into two groups. One group is best used for painting. Software in this group can import images from other sources, and it can control a scanner. But it sings as a creative tool. It is very much geared to the artist (some programs more than others).

The other group is better tuned for editing an existing bitmap—a photograph or still-video image. It is less artsy in the way it works.

Programs in each of these categories have their place in the computer-graphics studio.

The more painterly programs are characterized by a wide assortment of brush styles. Commonly, different artistic media—colored chalk, charcoal, oils, and watercolor—are simulated so effectively that the work on the screen looks much as if it had been created using traditional artistic tools.

What can't be simulated, of course, is the way in which those tools work. A paintbrush loaded with oil paints and applied to a stretched canvas surface feels a certain way as the artist paints. A stylus drawing on a digitizing tablet (refer to Appendix A) does not provide that feeling. The compensation for this loss is the ability to mix and match simulated artistic media in new and creative ways.

Painterly programs such as Fractal Painter and CA-Cricket Paint are spectacular creative tools and adequate to excellent photo-editing tools. See Figure B.3. The richness of effects they offer dictates a fairly steep learning curve. Programs like these work best in the hands of people who know the artistic media being simulated.

Programs that are more tuned to editing scanned images— Adobe's PhotoShop, Micrografx Picture Publisher, and Al-

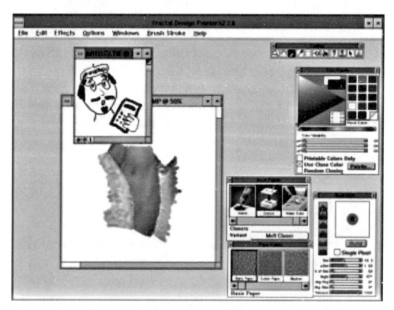

Figure B.3   Fractal Painter is one of the most powerful painting programs available for the PC/Windows environment. It offers a painterly feel—not surprising in a program written by people with fine-arts degrees.

dus PhotoStyler are the top-of-the-market products—are intended for photo touch-up, image editing, and bitmap composition. Although they offer painterly effects, most are more global in application. Brush options are commonly more limited. These programs are more like a photographer's darkroom, with image-enhancement capabilities. See Figure B.4.

Programs for editing scanned images are more easily learned and more likely to be of immediate use.

Different users do things in different ways. Some folks think bitmap editors and paint programs are the most convenient way to make pictures using a computer. My own view is that such programs are usually an accessory—but without any question the most important accessory in the designer's computer studio. In my own work, I am more likely to use a program such as Picture Publisher than I am to use the more painterly Fractal Painter. Most of what I want to do involves tuning up scanned images or modifying preexisting bitmaps,

Figure B.4   This picture is a much-edited image processed in Micrografx Picture Publisher.

and a program such as Picture Publisher does this a bit faster and with less confusion. On the other hand, enough overlap exists between the two kinds of bitmap programs that one will do for all purposes.

In addition to the top-drawer bitmap editors, simpler products are available. Some offer subsets of a full-featured program—Micrografx and Fractal both offer such scaled-down products. Some are rich in features but don't offer the processing speed or flexibility of the top-drawer products—Corel's PhotoPaint, included with Corel Draw, is in this group.

Others represent a first product offering for the PC—Ofoto PC/Windows is a subset of the product offered on the Mac, as is the bitmap-editing capability built into Deneba Canvas. Later releases of Canvas will probably compete for tier-1 honors (in a growing market segment).

Finally, CA-Cricket Image and HSC's ImagePrep are intended to scan and globally adjust images for contrast, brightness, and tonal values. These programs are great for people who just want to add a picture to a desktop-publishing project, but they offer little scope for design.

Illustration Graphics Software

Illustration-graphics software is for drawing (as opposed to painting). Lines and other geometric objects, defined mathematically, are stored as vectors in the computer. The computer sends the math to the display system, and the display system renders it as a design (or something like that). Drawing files tend to be a great deal smaller than bitmap images, because the information defining the picture in terms the computer understands is not as complex as a map of picture elements and appropriate colors.

Illustration-graphics software comes in different flavors, based largely on what the software is best tuned to do. For example, Micrografx's drawing programs, including its flagship software, Designer, reflect its heritage: technical-drawing programs. This orientation was more marked in the earlier incarnations of the program, and it is still a particularly nice tool for precision drawings. Some engineers and architects are on record as preferring it for sketching.

Other illustration-graphics software is more perfectly tuned for the kinds of illustrations used in posters, flyers, advertising, and so on. The various Arts & Letters programs are in this category, as is Corel Draw (currently the top seller in the category for PC/Windows machines).

More specialized versions of the software in this category are tuned for chart-making. Corel Chart (included with Corel Draw) and Micrografx Charisma (effectively, Designer with charting extensions) are good examples.

The current trend in graphics-software marketing is to build an entire system of picture-making and design tools around a basic, full-featured drawing program. Corel Corporation started this trend in its 3.0 release, including a chart maker, a bitmap editor, and a slide-show program in the box. Just for good measure, it put in an enhanced tracing program (scan an image, then convert the bitmap to a vector drawing) and an image-management program (store drawings in compressed archives). The company has enhanced these tools, and other companies have followed its lead. For example, Micrografx now includes its lower-end bitmap editor with Designer, and it builds image management into its programs.

The all-in-one-box marketing ploy usually combines a sterling drawing program with adequate graphics accessories. Most designers prefer more powerful tools, relying on Windows to provide integration.

Deneba's Canvas is especially noteworthy in the move to put all the tools you need in one box. Canvas is essentially a drawing program with bitmap editing built into it. This means that one product can do what in some instances might require two.

For most purposes, the illustration-graphics program is where design begins; not infrequently, it ends here, too. Even if substantial elements of a design project are bitmaps and charts, the drawing program is where images are composed, text added, and the final result sent to an output device.

This might change as bitmap editors improve. That might not be so swift, though. The bitmap-inclined designers have developed some tricks that are rather unattractive. For example, you've probably seen a magazine cover or advertising spread with a spectacular photo, but stuck in a corner or smack dab in the middle is a translucent patch of white, carrying a block of text. This shortcut is possible when working in a bitmap editor. A designer putting together similar elements in a drawing program has to compose the spread more elegantly.

The New Wave in Graphics: New Utilities

The computer-graphics marketplace is in the midst of a surge. More powerful platforms at bargain prices mean that software vendors can now move high-end tools to the PC/ Windows environment.

Morphing The most dramatic tool is *morphing*. This is the effect that lets that oil company show a fast car changing into a tiger. Several companies—notably, HSC and Gryphon—are now offering morphing software for PC/Windows systems. See Figure B.5.

The obvious use of morphing software is in multimedia projects; effectively, this is a species of animation. But the individual frames can be grabbed as bitmaps for use in still images. HSC's morphing software also features advanced warping capabilities. You can use it to fit a bitmap to a three-dimensional topography. Morphing software is not complex, and the learning curve is not steep. Applying this technique to design needs is a matter of creative thinking.

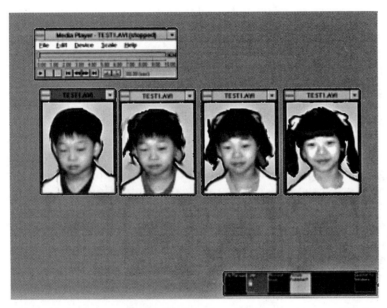

Figure B.5   A series of stills from a morph sequence created in Gryphon Morph. My nephew shifts to my niece, and back. The program outputs to standard Windows .AVI video format.

True Animation   True animation is available at several levels. Corel Corporation's Corel Move is one of the neater simple animation programs around, and it comes in the box with Corel Draw. Corel Move includes a rudimentary bitmap editor of its own, but serious animation uses Corel's bitmap program (PhotoPaint) and its flagship Draw program to create frames for fairly complex cell animations. Output is to Windows .AVI video format.

At the other end—the top end—of the spectrum, AutoDesk offers 3D Studio. This is professional-quality animation software. It delivers polished, fully rendered animations that easily exceeds corporate-video needs. Used by a talented animator, the results can be broadcast quality. It is pricey stuff, and it is not for the casual user.

The most obvious application for animations, as well as morph sequences, is in computer-driven presentations. Windows presentation-graphics software usually supports this through OLE (object linking and embedding, pronounced "olé"). The whole presentation, including stills and animations, can be packaged onto a disk for distribution.

Animations and morphing represent one direction advanced use of computer graphics can take. You don't start with these, but after you've worked through this book—as your comfort level with design and computer graphics rises—you might find it productive to add these options to your repertory. These are ways to expand design potential.

Drawing Made Easier Another class of graphics accessory can best be characterized as drawing software for people who don't want to draw. Examples are Shapeware's Visio, Aldus's Intellidraw, and Micrografx's ABC Flowcharter.

Shapeware, quite literally, rethought the foundation concepts for drawing software in designing Visio. Aldus's Consumer Software Division (formerly Mac-only Silicon Beach) has created some new design tools that can make things a great deal easier. ABC Flowcharter, as the name suggests, was intended initially for people interested in studying systems (not just programmers), but it has expanded to cover a range of diagramming needs.

When Corel Corporation decided Visio's drag-and-drop symbols were a crowd pleaser, it quickly added the feature to Corel Draw.

In most cases, full-fledged drawing programs do the same thing as these specialty programs. In most cases, the supposed ease of use and shorter learning curve claimed by the vendors seem greatly exaggerated. In most cases, the most attractive user features of these programs are being incorporated into mainstream software.

Clip-art Libraries One more class of graphics accessory is not itself a creation program, but an inestimable aid: Clip-art libraries make life simple.

Most drawing programs include hundreds, if not thousands, of predrawn images. You can use these images as is, or you can modify them to make other drawing elements. Other libraries, in different formats, are not hard to find. Both drawing and bitmap clip art are available. Drawing clip art is usually best if it is in the native format of the drawing program you use. Bitmap clip art works best if it is in one of four standard formats:

- TIFF is a standard for grayscale images, and it is increasingly used for color, as well.

- BMP format is the native Windows bitmap format; it can be either grayscale or color.

- GIF is a video-type color bitmap format.

- TGA is the Targa true-color format.

You choose the format(s) that work with your software, or you use a bitmap editor to convert from one format to the other. See Figure B.6.

Figure B.6 This is particularly interesting clip art from Computer Support Corp. Each dinosaur is completely articulated and can be posed. The clip-art collection included with A&L Draw has some samples of this dinosaur set.

CAD: Computer-Aided Design

CAD is where it all started. The computer became the drafting tool of choice, replacing the drafting table and T-square. It is still around, and on rare occasions it is a useful tool for designers.

Drafix Windows CAD from Foresight Resources does provide Windows support.

CAD software comes in lots of flavors. Most are really pre-Windows applications. If there is a Windows interface, it is more an afterthought than a main element in the program's conception. Most of these drafting programs are also intended for the speedy creation of mechanical drawings by draftsmen. That is, you can draw in them, but things work best if a bunch of locations and dimensions are typed in; the program then executes the drawing. This is not intuitive. Finally, most CAD software is expensive.

So why bother? Quite simply, because some CAD software is available with true three-dimensional rendering. Mechanical engineers want to see what a part will look like in place. Architects—and their clients—want to see what a building or space will look like. Top-flight CAD software either includes or can add three-dimensional rendering capability. Lighting and shading can be adjusted; the best packages can add multiple lighting sources and textures to a rendered design.

These features are also being added to more conventional software. For example, Micrografx's flagship program, Designer, now offers true three-dimensional rendering capabilities. In addition to geometric-solid primitives, any object can be created in three dimensions. Draw the profile, tell the software to sweep it around an axis, and *voilà!*—a true three-dimensional whatever. This object can be rotated on three axes. It can be lighted and shaded. The image can be moved to other programs in several different ways. See Figure B.7.

Other drawing programs provide more limited capabilities through *extrusion*. Both Corel Draw and A&L Editor (top-of-the-line programs) can extrude design elements, creating a limited three-dimensional image. Rotation is still limited to two axes, and shading and lighting are not automatic. But

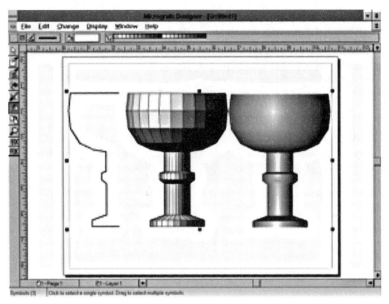

Figure B.7   You can draw a profile, sweep it, then render it in true 3-D using Micrografx Designer. You could then rotate this object in any direction.

for most purposes, this two-dimensional simulation of three dimensions is adequate. In the hands of even a practiced amateur, the results are largely indistinguishable.

Similarly, textures and *wrapping*—which fits a two-dimensional image on a curved three-dimensional object—are now appearing in standard drawing programs.

In short, CAD started it all, but the features that were useful in CAD are now quickly being incorporated into software that is more amenable to the designer's needs in other ways.

Extrusion is not truly three-dimensional. The X dimension is represented in two-dimensional space. Visually, you can't tell the difference.

The Final Word

OK, so you are not quite ready to make the final drawing of your company's product, indistinguishable at a casual glance from a photograph. That's not what this book is about.

The message you should take from all this is fairly simple.

First, on fairly inexpensive, commonly available business computers—the kind you probably have—you can do amazing things. A lot of these special effects are already available even in the simplest graphics software.

Second, being a trained artist or designer is not essential. That special training is nice to have, but a lot of the special skills are built into the software. What is *not* in the software is the conceptual capability of the designer, which can be learned (and that is the subject of this book).

Index

Nursing Management
for Patient Care

Nursing Management for Patient Care

Second Edition

Marjorie Beyers, R.N., Ph.D.
Director, Evanston Hospital School of Nursing
Evanston, Illinois

Carole Phillips, R.N., M.S.
Formerly Instructor, Evanston Hospital School of Nursing
Evanston, Illinois

Little, Brown and Company   Boston

Preface

The nursing profession has become complex and differentiated in the numerous types of specialties and levels of practice it encompasses. Nurses are becoming increasingly important in the health-care industry and can be found in various positions in every type of health-care agency. For the most part, nurses are employed by health-care agencies and consequently provide their services within the context of an organization. That organizational identity as well as the differentiation among the levels of nurses employed by a given health-care agency requires that nurses become managers. The differences in levels of nursing knowledge and practice are concomitant with the different levels of management roles that nurses fulfill. Some nurses manage patient care for a discrete number of patients, others manage both nurses and patient care, and yet others manage entire nursing or nursing-related departments in agencies within the health-care industry.

This book has been written expressly for the nurse who is making the transition from learning about individualized patient care to becoming a manager of that care within an organization. The newly graduated nurse often perceives a dichotomy between the role behaviors expected of a student and those expected of an employee in a health-care agency. The differences perceived are related to the emphasis on patient care. In most basic nursing education programs emphasis is placed on the nurse-patient relationship and related behaviors of the nurse in giving individualized patient care. As an employee, the nurse finds that the emphasis shifts to include managing other levels of nursing personnel and working with medical personnel in an organizational structure. The nurse who is beginning a first position in nursing must continue to develop role behaviors related to giving individualized patient care while also adjusting to the new role behaviors of a manager, which may or may not have been included in the basic nursing education program. It is our belief that the nurse who adjusts successfully to becoming a manager can better apply the knowledge and expertise in giving patient care that are gained in the basic nursing program.

This book has been developed on the premise that student nurses learn a great deal about human behavior in a basic nursing education program and that such knowledge can be used as the foundation for

learning management theories and principles. The beginning student of management can extend the knowledge of human behavior from the dimension of the nurse-patient relationship along a continuum that eventually can incorporate managing a large component of a health-care agency. Nurses can apply their knowledge and understanding of human behaviors in the nurse-patient relationship to the behaviors of people in organizations. Just as a person has a distinct personality, an organization also has a distinct personality that can be studied through the aegis of management.

The study of management in basic nursing education programs often focuses on leadership rather than on generalized management theories. We believe that nurses must be both leaders and managers and that knowledge of management theories and principles is necessary in order to give nursing care effectively within a health-care agency. Nurses who work in organizations should know how those organizations are structured, how they function, and how one can use the components of an organization to support active involvement in the dynamic processes of giving nursing care.

Management theories are important not only for maintaining effective nursing care but also for developing improvements in the nursing-care delivery system. Nursing care takes place within the health-care delivery system, and the total health-care industry is changing rapidly. As part of this rapidly changing industry, nurses should assume a prominent role in continually improving not only nursing care but also the health-care delivery system.

The basic premise of this book is that all nurses are managers. The text has been written as an introduction to management for use by those who are studying management theories and principles in basic nursing education programs and as a reference for the nurse who is learning to become a manager in the work situation. The theories and principles of management discussed provide a basis for understanding how organizations are structured and how people behave in organizations. The content of the book will enable the reader to study and analyze nursing management practices. In addition, the theories presented can be used as tools for working with others in the management of nursing care in a health-care agency. When working in an organization the nurse must learn to give expert, individualized patient care within the context of the organization and to use management theories in order to be effective within the organization.

Nursing Management for Patient Care is divided into three parts. Part I deals with general management theories on organizations and organizational practices. Content in the first part is designed to

provide the reader with a frame of reference about organizations that gives substance to the content presented in the second part. More specific information about management techniques in use on a day-to-day basis is included in Part II. Behaviors of managers who are functioning in patient-care units in hospitals are emphasized here, although the content is not exclusive to hospital management. Each chapter in the first and second parts of the book can be studied independently of the other chapters. Part III includes case studies designed to help the reader develop skills in solving management problems. That part gives the reader an opportunity to synthesize the content included in the first two parts by analyzing problems commonly found in nursing management. The cases provide a practical vehicle for the study of management as applied to the work situation.

The health-care industry is a complex business comprising many different types of health-care agencies. Some of those agencies are representative of new developments in the health-care delivery system and others are an admixture of traditional and progressive organizations. Most hospitals, for example, use a variety of traditional and progressive organizational strategies that are appropriate for a given setting. All the different agencies within the health-care industry require managers who deal with the problems that exist in every organization. Some problems are related to how people work together, others to the specific needs of an organization, and yet others to change processes ongoing in the health-care industry. The nurse-manager must have a flexible mind to analyze and solve those problems successfully. This book should serve to broaden the nurse's perspective of management and organizations and should increase the reader's ability to identify and resolve management problems.

We are grateful to the many people who assisted in the revision of this manuscript, particularly June Werner whose advice was invaluable, Barbara Blatecky who provided library resources, and all the persons mentioned in the previous edition who contributed to the initial writing. Many of the fine illustrations by Lou Pearson have been retained in this edition. We also express appreciation to the students who gave us helpful and challenging reviews of the manuscript and to our families who provided support and encouragement during the progress of this work.

M. B.
C. P.

Contents

I. A Framework of Management

1. Health-Care Organizations

You have selected a career in nursing. This career places you in the mainstream of the health-care industry, which exists for the purpose of providing services to individuals. As a nurse, you are primarily concerned with giving care based on your nursing knowledge and expertise. In becoming a nurse, you have learned how a person functions, psychologically and physiologically, and you have learned about the types of problems a person may encounter throughout the life cycle. You have learned that the essence of nursing care is helping people achieve or maintain a maximum state of "wellness" or health. In studying the process of nursing care, you have learned concepts and methods that can be applied in patient-care situations to help individuals achieve a maximum state of health. In order to achieve your maximum potential as a professional nurse, you must function within a health-care system that shares your goals in giving patient care. Functioning within this health-care system places you in an organization that supports you and that provides you with the environment and resources you need to administer nursing care.

While the functions of nursing care are carried out within the context of the nurse-patient relationship, the environment in which this takes place greatly influences the nature of that relationship. The environment in which you give patient care is usually a health-service agency, such as a hospital, a clinic, or some other type of organization that exists to provide care for patients. When working within such organizations, you rely on and cooperate with other health professionals. You also work with people who provide the supporting services that the care-givers require to carry out their specialized functions. In so doing, you share a common goal with others who have different academic preparation and specialized expertise; these others include physicians, physical therapists, occupational therapists, speech therapists, administrators, accountants, systems analysts, and housekeeping specialists, to name a few. You may relate directly to some of these persons, or you may use the services they provide without having direct personal contact with them. As a nurse, your primary function remains that of giving patient care, and you tend to know about the functions of other professionals through your day-by-day interactions with them in the patient-care setting. You relate only indirectly to those who work "behind the scenes," even though the environment in which you work is influenced by their functions.

Most nurses are employed by health-care agencies, and when a nurse accepts employment in a health-care agency, that nurse becomes a member of an organization. The organization employs the nurse because it requires the services that the nurse can provide for patients. The nurse seeks employment in the organization because that organization provides the medium in which nursing care can be given. Thus, there is an interdependence between the nurse and the employing organization. In order to implement the work necessary for patient care, the organization generally employs a number of other types of health professionals with different kinds of patient-care expertise. Each of these professionals also requires the supporting services of the organization to administer specialized care. In this respect, the organization provides for the interaction of a number of different professionals who cooperate in giving care and who are dependent on one another to provide the full spectrum of services that any given patient requires. There is, then, a mutual interdependence of all of the members of the organization on each other and on the organization. The professionals have expectations of the organization and of each other in this mutual relationship. Likewise, the organization has expectations of all of its members.

People employed by organizations expect the organization to provide a safe, efficient workplace and the mechanisms necessary to perform specialized functions. They also expect that the employing organization will provide them with a sense of identity and with the necessities of livelihood, such as salary and fringe benefits. The institution provides this medium for practice and expects that its members will contribute to the growth and maintenance of the organization in a complementary and productive manner. The organization, for example, expects that employed nurses will be competent in giving patient care and that they will use the health-care agency's material and human resources effectively and efficiently in administering this care. As members of organizations, nurses should know how organizations are formed, how they are maintained, and how people work together within them.

Organizations

Organizations are formed to meet the needs of society. Some organizations provide public services required by society. Others provide people with goods and products, such as automobiles and clothing. All organizations have certain things in common. To survive, they

must have a purpose and well-defined objectives, and they must produce something that is useful to society. To produce, organizations require a number of resources, including manpower, physical resources such as buildings and equipment, expendable resources such as materials and supplies, and capital. All organizations have some form of structure that designates how employees work together. The structure or design influences the way that people behave in managing the use of resources to achieve organizational purposes.

There are many different types of organizations, and these differ in purpose and in the amount or kind of resources needed to achieve this purpose. Organizations that use tools and machines predominantly in pursuing their objectives are technologically oriented. Those that use people as their predominant resource are called labor-intensive. Examples of labor-intensive organizations are schools and hospitals. Both schools and hospitals are public-service organizations that exist to meet a public need; schools meet the need for education, and hospitals meet the need for health care. Another difference in types of organizations is whether they are intended to produce a profit. An organization that produces automobiles intends to produce a profit. Public-service institutions, such as schools and hospitals, are usually nonprofit organizations.

A given organization, although it may be independent, can be part of a larger industry. An automobile plant, for example, is part of the larger auto industry. Hospitals are part of the health-care industry. Organizations are affected by other components of their industry in many ways. They may be in competition with one another for acquiring both resources and customers. These organizations can be publicly or privately owned and can vary in size, strength, structure, philosophy, and specific goals. New developments in one organization may affect other organizations in the industry and external factors such as state or federal legislation may affect all of the organizations within the industry. In such matters as state and federal legislation, the public tends to think of the industry as a whole because it is the industry, rather than a particular agency, that meets the needs of the public.

Use of the term *health-care industry* is of recent origin. There are many types of health-care agencies and organizations within this industry. Traditionally health-care agencies have been classified as either official agencies or voluntary agencies. The official or public agencies are tax-supported, and the voluntary agencies are supported

primarily by private funds. Most voluntary agencies are nonprofit and tax-free organizations, but there are private health-care agencies that are profit-making. Examples of public or official agencies are the Public Health Service hospitals, the Veterans Administration hospital system, the armed forces hospitals, and the Indian Health Service. The community hospital is the most commonly found example of the voluntary, nonprofit health-care agency. In general, the hospital is the central core of the health-care service industry, but new types of health-care agencies are emerging.

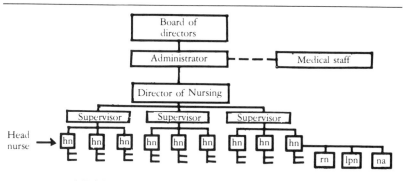

TRADITIONAL ORGANIZATIONAL CHART

The particular purposes of an organization stem from the reasons why the organization was originally founded and evolve from that point according to the needs of the community served by the organization. Community hospitals, for example, usually have originated from a realization of need by citizens in the community. In many instances, the citizens participated in planning, in raising funds, or in developing projects that led to the founding of the hospital. The authority for founding the hospital organization is granted by the state in the form of a charter. This charter includes a statement of the purposes and functions of the hospital, which must be fulfilled in the public interest through the administration of the hospital.

Public involvement in a community hospital continues after the hospital is established. The hospital's board of directors or trustees is usually made up of community members who are responsible for the administration of the hospital. Hospitals also involve community members in their functions through established volunteer services. The auxiliary or volunteer group enables people from the community to make an important contribution to patient care through various types of volunteer services. The people who use the hospi-

tal's services are members of the community, and as a result their expectations of health care and services greatly influence the hospital organization. Because of this continuous community involvement in hospital services, the values of the people in the community influence the philosophy and the values adopted by the hospital organization.

Not all hospitals are community-based hospitals. The armed services hospitals, for example, are federally operated. It could be said, however, that every hospital does have a defined community of users. The Veterans Administration hospitals are used by veterans, and the armed services hospitals are used by personnel in the armed forces. In this sense, the hospital organization functions to meet its community's expectations. These hospital functions are carried out by the people who are employed by the organization. It is the function, then, of health-care professionals who are employed by the hospital to conduct the operation of the hospital in accordance with the values of the community it serves.

Professionals who are employed by hospitals have the responsibility of using the resources available in the organization to meet the unique health-care needs of the community to be served. Some of the factors that determine the unique care needs include the geographic location of the hospital, the nature of the population served, the funds available, and the number and types of other health-care agencies present in the hospital's service area. Particular patient-care needs of a population are related to the type of environmental health problems found in the location, the hazards that accompany the types of recreation and employment available in the community, and the cultural diversity and age groups within the population. Health-care needs in an urban industrial center can be quite different from those found in a rural community.

Health-care delivery system is a term used to discuss the routes through which people receive health care. While hospitals are the central core of this system, other types of health-care organizations are being developed within the health-care industry. Two types of health-care agencies of recent origin are the Neighborhood Health Centers and the Health Maintenance Organization. Public Law 89-749, which is the Public Health Service Act (section 314) passed in 1966, provided for development of federally supported health centers. These Neighborhood Health Centers are developed to meet the health-care needs of the disadvantaged and the urban poor and to provide comprehensive health services within neighborhoods. The

Health Maintenance Organization is a public, nonprofit organization designed to be self-sustaining. The Health Maintenance Act of 1973 provided for development of HMOs particularly in areas of the country where the population is medically underserved.

These types of health-care agencies are like hospitals in that they employ professionals to provide health care. They also exemplify the efforts being made to evaluate and adapt health-care agencies to the current needs of society [3]. The delivery of health-care services is a national issue, and federal legislation has been instrumental in changing health-care organizations [1]. One change is that the differentiation between private and public health-care organizations is becoming less clear. This has resulted from the use of federal and state funds by private hospitals.

Medicare and Medicaid are examples of federal and state payment for hospital services. Medicare was first legislated in amendments to the Social Security Act, Title 18, and Medicaid was legislated in amendments to the Social Security Act, Title 19, in 1965. Other examples of legislation affecting professional health-care services are Public Law 89-239, Regional Medical Programs, and Public Law 89-749, Comprehensive Health Planning, which focused on the evaluation of health-care delivery in specified regions of the country. Current legislation also includes Public Law 92-603, Professional Standards Review Organization, passed in 1972, and Public Law 93-641, the National Health Planning and Resources Development Act, both of which are concerned with health-care services. All of these legislative acts have influenced the health-care delivery system in some respects, and new legislation will continue to influence how professionals function within health-care organizations [2]. Because of this influence, professionals in the health-care field must understand how to work in and how to exert influence through their professional organizations' activity in legislation. Professionals must also exert their influence within health-care organizations.

The Role of the Professional

The professional leadership of persons in key positions in the health-care agency provides direction and interpretation of the public's expectations for service. These people "professionalize" the organization: They set the attitudes and the emotional tone for all the employees. The values of these professionals expand the values of the community in terms of the organization's philosophy. Deter-

mining priorities for patient services and establishing the working order in the organization are the responsibilities of the professionals employed by the health-care agency.

Professionals, then, determine the behaviors of employees in the organization. The implications of professionalism are important in examining how professionals determine these behaviors. Professionalism embodies making independent decisions based on specific knowledge about a defined realm of practice. Through the processes of professional education and through continued participation as members in professional organizations, professionals are ideally indoctrinated with standards and goals for practice and with a concept of ethical conduct in practice. A strong identification with a profession encourages each professional to assume a personal responsibility for fulfilling the expectations of his or her role. The professional meets these expectations through professional competence applied with integrity and pride. An organization enhances professionalism when its environment allows for the freedom to be professional and when it adheres to standards of professional behavior.

The professionals in a health-care organization represent different areas of health-care services. These persons share responsibilities for identifying common concepts and goals of patient care and for working in a cooperative manner. The organizational structure places these professionals in proximity so that they can work together. They are separated only by specialized knowledge and by specialized function. If the ideologies and personalities of professionals are compatible, the common core of knowledge about patient care can serve as the basis for intertwining of effort. If they are not compatible, there may be contention among the various professionals. The care patients receive is enhanced or hindered in accordance with the working relationships among the professionals.

In addition to the responsibilities of professionals for coordinating their work with that of other personnel who give specialized care to patients, the professionals are often expected to function with a number of subprofessionals who perform segments of their work. When professionals are assisted by others with less educational preparation to carry out a portion of their functions, they must be competent in the practice of their profession as well as in supervision of subprofessionals.

Professional nurses in hospitals, for example, are expected to be competent in giving nursing care and in directing the work of licensed practical nurses and nurse's aides. The professional nurses

are the key personnel on the patient-care unit. They professionalize the organizational structure of the unit by providing a quality of patient care that is compatible with the philosophy of the hospital and with the services provided by all medical personnel. Professional nurses are assisted by persons with varying amounts of training and technical competence in patient care whose work must be supervised. The professional nurses are responsible for nursing care. What does this responsibility encompass in the total hospital organization?

It is possible for a nurse to work effectively on a patient-care unit without understanding the broad role of the nurse as part of the total hospital organization. A patient-care unit often seems complete within itself because the nurse is provided with supplies and equipment necessary for giving care and with methods of communicating with persons in other departments who are involved in a patient's care. The nurse relates most directly to the patients, to other nursing personnel, to doctors, and to all others who give direct patient care on the unit.

For this reason, nurses often perceive the hospital organization in terms of the organization of their own patient-care unit. Have you heard a nurse say, "I have never worked in a more organized hospital," because of that nurse's experiences in giving care on an organized unit in that hospital? Have you ever compared patient-care units with your friends, identifying the head nurse, the doctors, the geographic location of a unit, or the types of patient needs as causes of differences among units in a hospital? Nurses tend to evaluate the hospital through their reactions to experiences in their specific realm of practice. The patient-care unit is actually a "mini-organization" with the total hospital organization, and each of these "mini-organizations" can have its own personality and behaviors.

The personality and behaviors of the mini-organizations which make up the larger organization are a function of the behaviors of the individuals who make up the mini-organizations. Each person in the organization must be able to contribute to it in a meaningful way in order to maintain the integrity of the organization or structure. Because basic human needs are reflected through each person's individuality, his or her values and behavior determine how that individual contributes to an organizational structure.

Let us suppose that several chemicals are placed together. It is possible that the chemicals will not react. If they do, the type and degree of reaction will depend on the conditions surrounding the chemicals and the inherent characteristics of the chemicals. This is

similar to placing people into an organization where continuous interaction is expected. Among typical chemical reactions (and their related people reactions) are dissociation of the chemical (conflict or confusion in people), formation of an emulsion (temporary merging of individual goals), or formation of a new product. In the new product each chemical is still identifiable through chemical analysis. However, the characteristics of the new product are different from the characteristics of the individual chemicals. In a similar way a group of people who are united to achieve a common purpose has characteristics different from those of individuals within the group.

An organization is composed of a group of people whose identities are merged into the formation of a separate entity. An analogy can be drawn between the growth and development of an organization and that of an individual. Just as each person has innate qualities and learned abilities, an organization usually grows and develops within the traditions of a community which determine what the organization is and how it ought to act in providing service. The individual's personality colors how that individual functions in society. The person has certain powers to control what he will do, where he will go, and what he will achieve. An organization has this potential for control, being different in that a group of people must activate its personality.

The relationships between the structure of the organization with its own personality and with the individual employee are crucial to the success of an organization. First of all, it is important to note that people need organizations. Human beings have a propensity for order in their relationships, which the formal organization satisfies by arranging people in a structure. People in the organizational structure are given titles and job descriptions which define the expectations of their roles. Organizational behavior evolves around these roles and expectations. Each person interprets that role in an individual manner. The differences in the way the role of a given position is interpreted reflect each person's capabilities and aptitudes. People work with others in different ways, and relationships among people are variable.

Behavior of personnel enlivens the organizational structure and is a determinant of the organization's capacity for accomplishing its purpose. The structure supports cooperation among personnel. When the personnel behave according to their defined roles, there is usually harmony within the organization. This harmony exists when employees are well matched to the expectations of their positions,

when the arrangement of personnel is practical for accomplishing the work, and when pathways for communication are adequate and open.

On the other hand, discord within the structure implies that employees are not capable of meeting the expectations of their positions, that the expectations of the positions are not realistic, or that the organizational structure is not suitable for accomplishing the work. In this event the behavior of people in the organization may provide for change implementation through reevaluation of the structure and formation of a more workable order for the organization.

The behavior of all personnel is greatly influenced by the organization's philosophy. In a hospital this philosophy is basic in determining what constitutes quality patient care. Once this philosophy is defined it must be implemented by the employees in a way that best utilizes time, supplies, equipment, and human effort. To be successful in giving patient care as a group, all employees must share the same philosophy of care and common organizational objectives so that they can coordinate their efforts to achieve a common purpose.

Professionals have a major responsibility for the hospital organization's effectiveness. Because patients often perceive the hospital organization through their experiences on a patient-care unit, professional nurses are key persons among medical professionals. The continuous care provided by nurses is, for the patient, the hub of all activity in the hospital. The processes of management are used by nurses to promote their effectiveness as participants in giving health care. Nurses must be concerned about the functions of the total health-care organization and must relate in a constructive way to other medical professionals through the mechanisms of organized health services. All the work that nurses accomplish in the nursing-practice department, and more specifically on a patient-care unit, must complement that accomplished in the entire hospital. Nurses must accept the professional commitment of becoming effective managers of health care, and they must contribute to the evolution of health care through application of their professional standards and expertise.

Organizational Structure

An organizational structure is similar to the structure of the body and, as such, provides a rational design for the complexities of its function. The nurse contributes to and uses the resources of the organization and also functions within the context of the organiza-

tion. In this section some concepts about organizational structures of health-care agencies are discussed to give you a perspective about how you, as a nurse, relate to an organization.

There are many similarities that can be drawn between an individual nurse and a given health-care organization. A nurse, for example, has a value system and a philosophy. An organization forms an entity that also has a value system and a philosophy. Both the individual nurse and the organization have legitimate authority to provide patient care. The nurse has a license to practice issued by the state, and the organization is a corporation with a charter outlining its purposes and functions that is granted by the state. In a sense, an organization is an aggregate of components that make up the entity just as a person is an aggregate of body systems. Both have a "personality" and function through interaction of all components. The total result of this interactive function is greater than the function of the sum of all components, a phenomenon referred to as synergy.

The organizational structure of a health-care agency reflects its value system, its philosophy, and its particular needs to function. Nursing activities are coordinated with those of other employees through the structural design of the organization. These employees can be classified as (1) those who manage the overall organization to ensure that it carries out its mission, (2) those who carry out the processes of the function of the organization, (3) those who provide the necessities for the environment in which the processes take place, and (4) those who carry out the activities necessary to maintain the organization as an entity in the community. These classifications are not clear-cut since there is overlapping among the roles of personnel in all groups. The classification is useful, however, in examining the complexities of an organization.

The people who "manage" the organization are the administrators, the department heads, and the people who are concerned with the broad and general mission of the health-care agency in its community. Those who carry out the processes of the organization's function are the health-care providers: the nurses, doctors, dietitians, and all who relate directly to the patients. People who provide the environmental requisites are those concerned with personnel functions, those who maintain the physical plant, such as engineers and housekeepers, and those who take care of the financial aspects of the agency, such as accountants and computer specialists. The organization is maintained as an entity by those people whose activities are centered on planning, development, marketing, public relations, and

other such functions. These people ensure that the organization continues to have a source of clients, funds, and community support. Often these "maintenance" functions are carried out by the administrators in smaller organizations.

You can understand how complex an organization can be from the descriptions of the varied types of personnel who are employed in it. There are many different ways to organize people into an organizational structure. A hospital, for example may use a combination of structural designs to achieve its purposes. The interaction in a hospital is complex, and it is necessary to develop a rational order of relationships to ensure that the efforts of the people are efficient in carrying out the hospital's functions. Since the functions of employees are unique to their specific departments, the type of organizational structure that is appropriate for one department may not be suitable for another. The concept that form, or structure, should follow function is applied when planning the organizational structure for different departments.

There are several different models of organizational structures that have evolved from theories about how people can best be organized. The traditional model is called a bureaucratic model. Many of the theories concerning the bureaucratic model stem from the work of Max Weber [4], who perceived that an organizational structure should stabilize and clarify relationships among people in an orderly way. Among his principles of organizing are that there should be division of labor with specialization of function; that there should be a hierarchy in the arrangement of positions to provide for a flow of authority and control; that rules should be systematized to provide for uniformity and continuity and to ensure stability and coordination of effort; that relationships among people should be impersonal; and that technical competence should be provided for in the organization.

The bureaucratic plan for arranging people according to their responsibilities for doing the work of the organization can be illustrated by an organizational chart of a hospital.

TRADITIONAL ORGANIZATION—CHAIN OF RESPONSIBILITY

This chart (see p. 6) represents a traditional organization in which the chain of authority and responsibility is passed down from the board of directors to the hospital administrator and from the administrator to department heads. In classic management theories the lines formed by the diagram are referred to as the "scalar chain," illustrat-

ing the divisions of responsibility from the broad total responsibility of the administrator to the specific responsibility of personnel in a given department. As one traces the chain downward, the responsibilities of personnel become increasingly more specific. The functions of those at the top of the chain are broad functions that relate to the total organization, and the functions of those downward become increasingly delineated to a specific part of the total organization.

In traditional organizational theory, the concept of responsibility is closely aligned with three other concepts: authority, delegation, and accountability. Authority is vested in the board of directors, who in turn delegate authority to the chief executive officer, who delegates authority to the administrative staff, and so on down the line of the scalar chain. Responsibility must be accepted by the person who fills each position along the line of the scalar chain according to the functions delineated in the description of that position. Since a person cannot fulfill a given area of responsibility without authority to do so, it is necessary that authority be delegated along with the responsibilities of the position.

Authority and responsibility flow downward along the scalar chain while accountability flows upward. Accountability is a concomitant of authority which means that a person is accountable only for those functions for which he or she has the authority. When a person accepts the authority and responsibility for a position as delegated, that person is accountable for fulfilling the responsibility to those who delegate it. This statement implies that the person is not only accountable for accomplishing the work that has been delegated in such a way that the organization's goals are met, but is also responsible for the means used to achieve those goals or outcomes. A person becomes responsible for the position functions delineated by the organization when he or she accepts the position. Job descriptions that outline these functions are developed within organizations to communicate the expectation to the person who accepts the position. Job descriptions are formal statements of the functions of a given position in the organization.

Even when there are formal written job descriptions, however, the responsibilities of personnel in an organization are not always clearly defined. In some instances the formal and written descriptions lack specificity either because the position is not described well or because it is evolutionary and cannot be described with specificity. In other instances the interpretation of job descriptions changes over time as professional practices change. Professional judgment is es-

sential in functioning in an organization because human interaction and the complexities of organizational interaction defy explicit statements of function for every aspect of position responsibilities. Knowledge and common sense are two components of professional judgment that are learned in the processes of becoming professional during one's educational experiences as well as in one's work experiences.

The scalar chain serves then to establish working relationships among personnel, while position descriptions delineate functions more specifically. An example of how a scalar chain works can be drawn from any type of organization. A department head, for example, cannot possibly fill all of the functions for the entire department. The department head delegates functions to others who accept the responsibility for performing the functions. The person who accepts the responsibility has concomitant authority and is accountable to the person who has delegated the functions.

Persons at the top of the scalar chain are responsible and accountable for functions that take place in the entire organization; the department head is responsible and accountable for functions of the department; staff members are responsible and accountable for specific functions of their positions, such as nursing care, laboratory analysis, or supply delivery. Because functions are delineated with increasing specificity downward along the chain, the phrase, "That's not my responsibility" is commonly used. You may have used this phrase yourself, and when you used it you were saying, "I do not have the authority to make that decision or to perform that function."

In addition to outlining the scalar chain, the organizational chart also serves as a guide for understanding the plan for formal communication among personnel in an organization. Channels of communication usually follow the lines of responsibility. For example, the staff nurse goes through vertical channels when communicating with the head nurse. Communication is a vital link among persons who are involved in the work to coordinate the efforts of personnel. The lines of communication in an organization are clarified by job descriptions that outline the area of responsibility and authority for each position as well as lines of communication and accountability. When all the job descriptions for employees in an organization are viewed together, it is possible to realize how each person contributes to the total organization to accomplish the work.

Although organizational structures vary among health-care agencies, each one contains provision for authority, responsibility, and

accountability. A pertinent question at this point is, How does a given health-care agency arrive at its particular organizational structure? The major components that influence choice of structure include the work to be accomplished, the supplies and equipment required, the physical plant in which the work is done, the competencies of the people who do the work, and the geographic location of the physical facilities. All these components must be organized in a health-care agency so that patients receive effective, efficient, and economical care.

In a traditional hospital organization (see p. 6) the work is usually divided according to function. Departments are formed for provision of services, such as the laboratory department, the x-ray department, the surgical department, and the outpatient department. Personnel responsible for carrying out similar specialized functions are placed in a single department. In this way the physical facility can be planned to augment the work of the department, equipment and supplies can be centrally located, and communication among personnel with similar functions is facilitated. The chain of authority, responsibility, and accountability extends from the administrator down to the personnel of each specialized department through department heads.

One of the concerns in designing organizational structures is delegation of authority and responsibility. In general, authority and responsibility are delegated to the level in the organization where decisions most influence the people at that level. Decisions that are limited in their effect to a given department, for example, are made in that department, while decisions that affect the entire health-care agency are made at the administrative level. An organization can be centralized or decentralized. A centralized organization is a "tall" organizational design in which the locus of decision-making is placed centrally at the top of the organization. A decentralized organization is a "flat" design in which the locus for decision-making is disseminated to various departments or units.

In a decentralized organization, more decision-making authority and responsibility, and thus more control, is delegated throughout the structure. To be effective, a decentralized organization requires that decision-makers be competent since important organizational decisions are made at various divisions in the organization. The advantage is that people in the various decentralized units of the organization can adapt to changes more readily because they make decisions at a local level. A centralized organization provides for stability and uniformity throughout the entire organization since the

locus of decision-making and control is found at the level of the organizational hierarchy. In a centralized structure, decisions are made more slowly because more time is required for communication to pass to and from the decision-makers. A typical bureaucratic structure is a tall, centralized organization.

SYSTEMS AND MATRIX ORGANIZATIONAL STRUCTURES

The *systems approach* is another type of organizational design. In this design, communication flows horizontally and laterally, and there is more flexibility in decision-making than in a centralized, traditional organizational structure. Some theorists believe that most health-care agency organizations are actually open systems because there is a continuous flow of input from patients, families, professional groups, community groups, public policy, and state and federal legislation.

Theoretically, a system is composed of feedback loops including input into the system, transformation processes that take place within the system, output from the system, and feedback that influences the input into the system. One basic concept of systems is that of equifinality, which means that goals or values can be attained through a number of different paths or means. The system remains in equilibrium until some factor of input or of the transformation processes, called throughput, changes. The system adapts to changes and can be responsive to them because of the greater flexibility in decision-making.

In a systems approach, the patient, with individual needs and capabilities, is a source of input that becomes part of the system. The patient goes through the system according to his or her individual needs, using only those components or subsets of the system required for care. A physician or a nurse-practitioner routes the patient through the system, determining the pathway the patient should take according to the assessment of the patient's needs and the patient's wishes to participate in the diagnosis, care, or treatment processes. The subsets of the system are different specialized services such as x-ray, surgery, or diet therapy, and all of these subsets are integrated in the system to provide patient care. The cycle of events in the care of any given patient is individualized, and the patient is the focus of all of the services provided.

Yet another type of organizational structure is the *matrix organization*. The matrix organization is a group of mini-organizations within a larger organizational structure. There may be a skeleton of a traditional hierarchical structure, but there is no well-defined scalar

chain with its unity of command and clear delegation of authority and responsibility. Instead, people are arranged according to specialized processes or functions, and are responsible and accountable for managing these functions more autonomously than in a traditional bureaucratic structure. Communication flows in all directions: upward, downward, horizontally, and laterally. People communicate with others in the organization according to their needs for the use of resources or the functions of others. This direct communication among employees emphasizes the interaction processes among people rather than the structural design for communication designated by the scalar chain in traditional organizations.

For the matrix organization to be effective, the people in the organization must be secure enough and competent enough to assert themselves and to negotiate for integration of function in the organization. This type of organizational structure works well when there is a desire or need to modify the present working relationships and products or when innovation is desired. The interaction of individuals across organizational lines provides for checks and balances. People tend to relate to one another according to their areas of specialization rather than through superior-subordinate relationships that are formed in the traditional organizational structure. Because there is no strong hierarchical structure to provide for stability, authority and responsibility are distributed throughout the organization. Checks and balances occur as people representing their mini-organizations negotiate for resources, for input from other mini-organizations, and for development of mechanisms that provide for integration of function. There is potential for conflict within matrix organizations because the behavior of employees is emphasized, rather than strong unity of command and central control. The matrix organizational structure promotes independent thinking, creativity, and collaborative relationships.

Both the systems and the matrix organizational structures are more flexible than the traditional structure, and they are appropriately used in situations where there is continual growth and change. Both provide for meeting contingencies since decision-making authority and responsibility are located at the level of "processes" in the organization.

The systems approach is excellent for focusing on the work to be accomplished, especially when many different types of activities are required for patient care. An example of the systems approach in patient care is an agency in which the patient is routed to different

specialty areas. Nurses, dietitians, laboratory technicians, x-ray technicians, and social service caseworkers are subsets of the system that are integrated in giving care. Patient care is given in a composite of interrelated activities. The various medical personnel all cooperate in planning care.

Most organizations include variations of traditional and innovative structures. The nature of the work of hospitals defies a singular approach to organization of all departments. For example, the systems theories are easiest to apply when all the information about the requirements of patient care, the specifications for giving care, and the supplies and equipment necessary are well defined. All this information can be computed to determine a sequence of activities which most effectively and efficiently accomplishes the work.

However, the activities involved in giving patient care cannot be specifically described and analyzed for the inherent requirements of every patient because of the unknown element of differences in patient needs. Each patient presents an individual set of problems which cannot always be anticipated. Even though general and common needs of patients can be defined and planned for, the plans must be flexible to accommodate the individual. The matrix organization is suited to development of a flexible and responsive structure.

A matrix organization is effective in health-care agencies that are experimenting with innovations in patient-care service delivery. Mini-organizations are formed to provide specialized patient care such as crisis intervention, oncology, or cardiovascular-respiratory patient-care units. The personnel in the mini-organization form a specialized team or group to carry out the function of the unit. These personnel communicate directly with personnel in other departments, such as the laboratory department, the planning department, or the social service department. Through this direct communication they negotiate for provision of the support or resources they require to develop and maintain the mini-organization's specialized function. Each mini-organization depends on the supporting services of the total organization or macro-organization for administrative and management functions. The mini-units are different in that the services developed are unique to the types of care requisites presented by the group of patients who use the particular services.

The arrangement of people in an organization is affected by the type of work they do, by the placement of facilities in the agency, and by the patient's needs. All types of organizational structures deal with the provision of service to patients in which service is the focal point.

Organizational structures place people in a working order and depend on people to accomplish the work. Once the organizational structure is defined, the continuity of patient services depends on the behavior of the people who fill the structure.

Study Questions

1. What contribution do you, as a professional nurse, make to a health-care organization?
2. Describe the sources of legal authority that legitimize the function of the organization to provide patient care.
3. Describe how an organizational structure supports a board member's fulfillment of accountability for services provided by the health-care agency.
4. Speculate about what would happen if a department head did not accept the responsibility for patient services in the department.
5. How does an organizational structure design influence decision-making in an organization?
6. In what types of situations should a centralized organizational structure be used? A decentralized organizational structure?
7. Analyze the relationships you develop with other people in a hospital organization as a staff nurse by (a) listing the specialized functions of those that you have communicated with person-to-person, by phone only, and by requisition only; and (b) explaining how the functions of the people you have listed contribute to your patient's care.
8. Describe your expectations of a hospital organization as (a) an employee, and (b) a user of hospital services.
9. Describe how a health-care agency relates to its community. Using an agency you are familiar with as an example, explain how that agency cooperates with other organizations in the community in providing health care.

References

1. Ball, R. M. Background of Regulation in Health Care. In Institute of Medicine, *Controls in Health Care.* Washington, D.C.: National Academy of Sciences, 1975. Pp. 3–22.
2. Duval, M. K. The Provider, the Government, and the Consumer. In J. H. Knowles (ed.), *Doing Better and Feeling Worse: Health Care in the United States.* New York: W. W. Norton, 1977. Pp. 185–192.
3. Gosfield, A. *PSROs: The Law and the Health Consumer.* Cambridge: Ballinger, 1975. Pp. 1–19.
4. Henderson, A. M., and Parsons, T. (Trans. and eds.) *Max Weber: The Theory of Social and Economic Organization.* New York: The Free Press, 1947 (Copyright the Oxford University Press, New York). Pp. 329–331.

Suggested Reading

Aden, G. D.   Hospitals must lead the way in meeting public's demands. *Hospitals* 51:58–61, Nov. 16, 1977.

Aspen Systems Corp.   *Problems in Hospital Law* (2nd ed.). Rockville, Md.: Aspen, 1974.

Austin, C. J.   Redefining professionalism in health administration. *Hosp. Prog.* 58:70–73, 97, May 1977.

Bice, T. W., and Salkever, D. S.   Certificate-of-need programs: Cure or cause of inflated costs? *Hosp. Prog.* 58:65–67, 100, July 1977.

Buchele, R. B.   *The Management of Business and Public Organizations.* New York: McGraw-Hill, 1977.

Colner, A. N.   The impact of state government rate setting on hospital management. *Health Care Manage. Rev.* 2:37–49, Winter 1977.

Danielson, J. M.   Health consortium responds to total health care needs. *Hospitals* 51:69–73, March 1, 1977.

Dessler, G.   *Organization and Management: A Contingency Approach.* Englewood Cliffs, N.J.: Prentice-Hall, 1976.

Forward Plan for Health FY 1977–81, June 1975. USDHEW, PHS, DHEW Publication No. (OS) 76-50024. Washington, D.C.: U.S. Govt. Printing Office, 1975.

French, R.   *The Dynamics of Health Care.* (2nd ed.). New York: McGraw-Hill, 1974.

Friedman, E.   Medicaid: The primrose path. *Hospitals* 51:51–56, Aug. 16, 1977.

Friedman, E.   Medicaid: A crop of nettles. *Hospitals* 51:73–80, Sept. 16, 1977.

Friedman, E.   Medicaid: One seed for the crow. *Hospitals* 51:61–66, Oct. 1, 1977.

Friedman, E., and Wandorf, C.   Medicaid: A garden sown with dragon's teeth. *Hospitals* 51:59–64, Sept. 1, 1977.

Greenberg, W.   HMO's stimulate competition, FTC concludes. *Hosp. Prog.* 58:10–11, Oct. 1977.

Hall, V. C.   *Statutory Regulation of the Scope of Nursing Practice—A Critical Survey.* Chicago: National Joint Practice Commission, 1975.

Harlow, D. N., and Hanke, J.   *Behavior in Organizations.* Boston: Little, Brown, 1975.

Health Policy Making in Action: The Passage and Implementation of the National Health Planning and Resources Development Act of 1974 (Publication #41-1600). New York: National League for Nursing, 1975.

Kelly, L. Y.   Credentialing of health care personnel. *Nurs. Outlook* 25:562–569, Sept. 1977.

Kirlane, M., and Grimes, P.   Improving a hospital organization chart. *Hosp. Prog.* 58:85–89, Sept. 1977.

Leonard, A., and Rogers, I.   Prescription for survival. *Superv. Nurse* 8:22–24, Nov. 1977.

Luthans, F.   *Organizational Behavior* (2nd ed.). New York: McGraw-Hill, 1977.

Marriner, A. Adaptive organizational models. *Superv. Nurse* 8:44–50, Aug. 1977.

McLaughlin, C. P. Productivity and human services. *Health Care Manage. Rev.* 1:47–60, Fall 1976.

Monaco, R. J., and Smith, T. T. How supervisors can put systems to work in day to day management. *Hosp. Top.* 55:34, 36–41, Sept./Oct. 1977.

Prybil, L. O. Hospital boards face increasing demands. *Hospitals* 51:103–106, April 1, 1977.

Rosen, H. M., Metsch, J. M., and Levey, S. *The Consumer and the Health Care System: Social and Managerial Perspectives.* New York: Spectrum Publications, 1977.

Rosser, J. M., and Mossberg, H. E. *An Analysis of Health Care Delivery.* New York: Wiley, 1977.

Salkever, D. S., and Bice, T. W. *Impact of State Certificate-of-Need Laws on Health Care Costs and Utilization.* USDHEW PHS NCHSR Research Digest Series (HRA) 77-3163.

Schulz, R., and Johnson, A. C. *Management of Hospitals.* New York: McGraw-Hill, 1976.

Skerry, W. PL 93-641: Beyond planning toward control. *Hosp. Prog.* 57:10, 30, March 1976.

Somers, A. R., and Somers, H. M. *Health and Health Care: Policies in Perspective.* Germantown, Md.: Aspen, 1977.

Stagl, J. M. A look ahead at the forces of change. *Hospitals* 51:74–78, March 16, 1977.

Swanburg, R. C. *Management of Patient Care Services.* St. Louis: Mosby, 1976.

2. The Role of the Manager

What does a manager do? In order to answer this question, one must first answer some other basic questions. What is management? Are managers necessary? How do managers function in an organization? In the previous chapter we considered organizations, the general role of a professional in an organization, and organizational structures. This chapter is concerned with the role of the manager and with management processes. As you study these general management processes, consider your own concept of management.

The Concept and Processes of Management

During your life, you have had many experiences with management. You have belonged to organizations: a school, a church, or a youth club. Your experiences in these organizations have influenced your present concept of management. In addition to your experiences in organized groups, you have probably been a manager in many situations, since management is an integral part of human life. Have you ever managed something? Have you ever been managed? How did this management take place? In answering these questions, you will find that you already have a frame of reference about management. As you expand this frame of reference in the study of nursing management, you will find that your past experiences and your common sense are valuable assets in assuming a management role in nursing.

ELEMENTS OF MANAGEMENT

Chester Bernard [1] has written that organizations are social systems. Using this theory as a basis for management, you can view the role of the manager as working effectively within a social system to accomplish goals. Management processes such as organizing, activating, controlling, and evaluating are used to accomplish organizational goals. Underlying each of these processes are two major requisites in all management processes, communication and decision-making. The quality of the communication and of the decision-making is further undergirded by the manager's knowledge and conceptual ability.

Management is a composite of many interrelated components. The manager's personal attributes and capabilities affect how management processes are used. The management processes are techniques

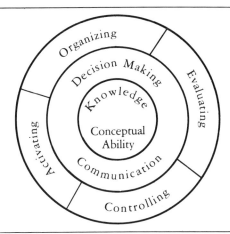

to be used in the perspective of the environment, the organizational goals, and the specific nature of the goals and objectives in the manager's realm of function, which in nursing management is patient care. Management techniques provide ways of dealing with the variable factors involved in achieving purposes, such as people's ideas and efforts, clients' needs, equipment, supplies, and the workplace itself. The manager's personal interpretation of situations and events and the manager's personal characteristics affect the way that the manager will use these management processes in bringing a sense of order to the integration of the variable factors inherent in accomplishing the work.

Management is an evolving field of study, and theories of management are being developed continually through observation and research. Just as nursing has a body of knowledge with specific terminology, management has its own body of knowledge and related terminology. Because management can mean different things to different people, the meanings of words and the interpretations of concepts can be confusing to one who is just beginning to study management. To develop a sense of management concepts and to facilitate communication about management, it is useful to develop a framework of thought about management processes. This framework can provide you with a mechanism for studying about management and for analyzing your own concept of management.

MAJOR MANAGEMENT PROCESSES
For our purposes in developing such a framework, let us consider that management includes four major processes: organizing, activat-

ing, controlling, and evaluating. These processes are interrelated and sometimes overlap. They are also continuous processes that extend throughout all management functions. The purposes of an organization are accomplished through management processes that bring people, supplies, equipment, and other resources together in an orderly way to perform a service or to create a product. In performing the desired service or creating the designated product, changes take place through the behavior of people as they use their ideas, knowledge, equipment, supplies, and facilities. The manager's role is to ensure that all of the necessary elements for performing the service or for producing the product are available, usable, appropriate, and maintained and that the efforts or behaviors of people are effective in the performance of the work roles that bring about the changes necessary to provide the service or to create the product.

Organizing. Organizing is an initial management process that takes place before the work is begun. It is also a continuous process that takes place as the work is being accomplished because portions of any activity are continuously organized in view of new information or new developments in any given situation. When organizing, the manager determines a plan that outlines the work to be accomplished, who should do the work, how they should accomplish the work, when the work should be carried out, and what materials or resources are required. The plan is based on an overall determination of a goal or of expected outcomes.

Organizing, then, is determining how the pieces of an activity can be arranged into interlocking sections. The manager's philosophy about the work, conceptual ability, and decision-making ability influence how people, places, and things are placed together as interlocking sections to achieve the determined goals. The manager forms a concept of the activities to be accomplished, sets standards for methods to be used according to his or her philosophy and knowledge of the prerequisites of the activities, and uses decision-making processes in determining how to arrange all of the components in an order that will both satisfy the standards for performance and achieve the desired outcomes.

Activating. Activating is the process of giving life to the plans made in organizing; it is a dynamic process of "making things happen." When plans are implemented in the work situation, people are performing the "processes" inherent in their functions. Activating emphasizes

the human relations aspect of management, particularly in health-care agencies, which are labor-intensive organizations. Some of the components of activating are making sure that people understand the expectations set forth in the plans, gaining the workers' acceptance of authority and responsibility, fostering their motivation to perform and to perform well, guiding people in personal growth through work experiences, directing the work, supporting the workers as they deal with the challenges and problems of their work, and supervising and coordinating all of the elements or inputs as necessary to accomplish the work.

The process of activating requires continual decision-making about people, places, and things to enable the manager to adapt to situations that occur and to accommodate the plans to the realistic working situation. Plans made in the organizing phase provide a frame of reference for these decisions. They also specify the general direction that the manager pursues in making decisions, so that consistency can be maintained. This consistency is a factor in establishing effective working relationships in the processes of carrying out the work and also in maintaining a perspective about the desired end results.

Controlling. Controlling includes aspects of both organizing and activating. The plans made in organizing are the basis for control, and the way that the plans are implemented in the activating phase affects the outcomes achieved. Control can be interpreted as providing stability and maintaining the work environment. Controlling is closely associated with activating since it comprises such activities as supervising, measuring performance, assessing situations, making decisions about changes that should be made in plans, and ensuring that people have the requisites necessary for their work. Controlling must take into account unforeseen problems or events, such as lack of planned resources, illness of an employee, or changes in external events, that have an impact on the activity being managed.

The essence of the process of controlling is manipulating the environment to create a desirable work situation and making sure that the workers meet the prescribed standards. This involves providing people with an environment conducive to work—one in which they may realize their potential by accomplishing the work in an appropriate manner that is satisfying to them. Controlling involves providing adequate time and sufficient supplies, equipment, and resources to do the work. Controlling also means providing sufficient structure so that the behavior of the workers is focused on the work

to be accomplished. Controlling is complex in that the processes of controlling are integral to every organizational activity. The manager who wishes to develop employees through work relationships can foster growth and participation by controlling the environment, the modes of interaction, the assignment of functions, and the information the employees receive about their work. That type of control frees the employees to develop and to grow in their work. When the organizational structure facilitates positive working relationships by formalizing job descriptions, for example, the job descriptions serve to "control" human activities.

Often the word control is associated with limit-setting and disciplinary action. Both are aspects of control that must be used by the manager. When the manager exerts control in the form of discipline, the manager is limiting the employee's behaviors to those acceptable to the organization. Such disciplinary action is most successful if other aspects of the organization are controlled in the positive sense by clearly defining functions, roles, and responsibilities that must be met by employees, and by providing the necessary requisites for effectively carrying out the work. The way one "activates" work in the organization is an integral part of the control process. Leadership and group interaction, both of which are discussed in a later chapter, are management behaviors applied in the activating of organizational work and both impact on a given manager's use of control processes.

Evaluating. Evaluating is also generally applicable to each management process; evaluating is planned for in the organizing process, is a component of the activating process, and both provide input and uses feedback from the controlling process. Standards determined in the organizing process are the criteria for evaluating. These standards include those that apply to the process of the work and those that apply to the outcomes. They are compared not only to what actually happens while the work is being performed, but also to the end results. The results of these comparisons are called feedback, and this feedback is used to determine new and better ways to organize the work.

Decision-making is an integral part of the evaluation process. The manager determines standards through decision-making and also makes decisions about what to measure and about how to measure performance. Decisions are also made about the types of tools that are developed to measure the qualitative and quantitative aspects of any activity. The feedback made available to the manager through

evaluation processes must be interpreted. For example, when desired results are not achieved, the manager must decide whether the initial goals are realistic, whether the number or type of employees is appropriate to accomplish the work, whether different or new materials should be used, or whether new procedures or performance standards should be developed. The manager has to achieve a balance in developing controls that are sufficient to provide for stability, but that are not limiting or restrictive of performance, and this balance is determined through evaluation. The manager also has to develop continually evaluation tools that are valid and reliable in providing feedback.

Relationship of Managers to the Organization

The management processes are implemented by managers to ensure that customers receive the desired services or products. In so doing, the management processes also focus on ensuring that workers receive guidance, support, and a sense of satisfaction from their work. In a health-care agency it is imperative that patients receive the best quality of care possible for the money spent. The employees are essential to the quality of patient care, and it is necessary that these employees experience a sense of satisfaction in their work because productivity is a corollary of job satisfaction.

Management of groups of people for achieving a purpose within an organization is a social process. Managers must provide for a state of equilibrium in which the workers' needs are satisfied while the organization achieves its purposes. This requires that incentives provided for the workers be as great as the contributions they are expected to make to the organization. The manager is also an employee of the organization and meets personal needs through work. In an organization, the manager functions within a structure and is supported by the structure. The manager contributes his or her own talents and resources to the organization and in return receives benefits from the organization. The relationship between the manager and the organization can be complementary.

ROLE CONFLICTS IN THE ORGANIZATION

A complementary relationship between a manager and an organization is the product of many factors. One basic factor is the similarity between the manager's expectation of his role and the organization's expectation of the manager's role. Getzels and Guba [2] have defined

a theoretical formula of different types of role conflicts that may occur. In addition to the potential for role conflict between the manager and the organization, there is also the potential for conflict between the role expectations of employment and the person's individual needs (role-personality conflict). While there are other sources of role conflict, these two have been selected for discussion in this chapter because they are commonly experienced by beginning managers.

Not all organizations are alike in behaviors. Some organizations are highly structured and tend to be closed, whereas others are more flexible and tend to be open. When a manager works in an organization, the scope and depth of his or her use of management processes is determined to some extent by the latitude allowed by the organization and to some extent by the manager's capabilities of expressing his or her personality. The effectiveness of a manager in any organization is relative to the relationship developed by the manager with the organization. When the manager's expectations are well matched to the organization's expectations of the managerial role, the manager will probably be effective. When there is dissonance between the manager's expectations and those of the organization, conflict can result and the manager may not be effective.

The other source of role conflict mentioned is the role-personality conflict. The manager accepts authority and responsibility for the managerial role and implements management processes to achieve work. When the manager's needs conflict with these role expectations, the manager may not be effective. This person may have difficulty working within the organizational structure and may have problems in communicating and in decision-making because of the conflict between personal needs and organizational goals.

A third source of potential conflict that exists between managers and organizations is professional role conflict. The professional brings an identity to the role of management that is distinct from the organization's structure and functions. Professionals are generally expected to initiate and follow through with implementation of management processes that are designed to meet professional standards. These professional standards are "cosmopolitan," that is, they are universally shared by the profession on a state or national basis. The professional may find that a given organization has local standards that conflict with the cosmopolitan standards. The potential for this type of conflict is great in hospitals since they tend to be stable organizational structures that change slowly. The profession of nurs-

ing is changing continually, and role expectations of the professionals have the potential for changing more rapidly than the organization's role expectations for those professionals. The nurse-manager should be aware of the values and attitudes held by the organization about nursing functions and roles. Because the professionals are accountable for maintaining a standard of practice, they are responsible for interpreting these standards to others in the organization.

Managerial Characteristics

The manager uses the processes of management to accomplish work and to ensure that this work meets professional standards. Through effective use of these processes of management, it is possible to demonstrate how these professional standards benefit the organization. The nurse-manager's capability for interpreting nursing to the organization and for prudently implementing management processes that "actualize" nursing in the organization is a major factor in producing effective management in a particular organization. The manager greatly influences the organization, as is demonstrated by variations in the way that different head nurses in a given health-care agency manage their patient-care units. The manager can be viewed as a liaison person who sets the tone for the nature of work relationships among personnel and the organization. Therefore, the manager's personal contribution is a very important aspect of organizational behavior.

What types of people make the best managers? This question is difficult to answer since different situations require different types of managers. In general, one could speculate that a self-actualized person will be a good manager. Shostrom's theory of self-actualization [3] is applicable to an examination of positive managerial characteristics. Shostrom has based much of his work on Maslow's theories of human needs (Chap. 6) and explains self-actualization as congruence between a person's inner core and his or her facade. The inner core is said to be the person's essential nature, and the facade is the person's public behavior. Some of the characteristics important in the communication functions of a manager are also characteristics of a self-actualized person.

Shostrom describes the self-actualized person as one who is capable of trust, is flexible, and has the ability to be responsive and open. He says that this person has a "permeable skin" that enables him or her to absorb new ideas and points of view. The self-actualized person is also expressive, being able to communicate inner feelings

and perceptions effectively, whether they be positive or negative. In describing the less actualized person, Shostrom uses the words "less trusting, more rigid, more controlling, more manipulative, and more concerned with impressing others than with expressing core feelings and perceptions." The less actualized person tends to be defensive and resistant. Shostrom views self-actualization as a lifelong process in which the person strives continually to reach a state of congruence between individual core feelings and perceptions and the external facade of behavior. The effective manager is also growth-oriented in the continual effort to develop realistic perceptions of role, function, and organizational goals and to deal openly and rationally with problems and conflicts that arise in implementing management processes.

The Manager's Relationship to the Organization

The nurse is primarily involved in managing patient care, and, nursing functions require support of many different types of personnel employed by a health-care agency. This means that in addition to relating to the nursing staff and to patients, the nurse must relate to numbers of other personnel. Some of these relationships are based on the dependence of nurses on departments which provide supplies, equipment, and services. Others are based on the need to coordinate patient care with services provided by specialized departments such as dietary, social service, and occupational therapy.

The complexity of integrating the activities of all these personnel is illustrated by the following comments from a patient:

I hadn't been feeling well for quite some time so my doctor finally talked me into going to the hospital for some tests. This is the first time I've been in a hospital as a patient. I didn't realize how confusing it could be! It is difficult to get to know what people are supposed to do for you. Why, I've been here for just twenty-four hours and just listen to my account of the number of people I've met already.

First there was the admissions clerk, then the orderly who brought me to this room. After I was shown about by the nurse's aide, who also took my temperature, I was interviewed by the charge nurse—I think it was the head nurse. Then my doctor came in, and after he left I was examined by a resident and two interns—separately and in rapid succession. Finally it was time for dinner and another man brought in the tray. After dinner someone came in and asked me if I wanted a newspaper. That was the ward clerk. Two nurses came in to prepare me for sleep—one made the bed and the other gave me some pills. That was after someone gave me an enema or two.

The next morning I woke up and watched the housekeeping man clean the hall outside my room. There wasn't any breakfast. Instead I talked with the laboratory technician who took some blood, and then I was taken to the

x-ray department by a fellow who said he was from the transfer department. In x-ray I met two technicians and a doctor who was in charge of my x-rays. Since I've been back in my room, I've seen another man with a breakfast tray, I've talked with the volunteer who checked my menu for tomorrow, to someone from accounting about my insurance number, and to the man who came in to fix the window shade. Now you are making my bed. I just wonder who keeps all these people straight? How do you know what is going on?

Integration by Organizational Control

This patient perceives an organization as a complex intermingling of people. The nurse perceives the total organization through the perspective of direct patient care. As one becomes increasingly involved in management, the interrelatedness of various departments becomes more obvious. The organization provides for integration of the many departments through organizational plans that assure employees stability, support, and routes and methods for communication.

STABILITY

Stability for employees means that the working environment is orderly and efficient. For nurses it means that linen is delivered to the patient-care unit, that special diets are prepared and delivered to patients, that someone is available to repair broken beds and other equipment, and that medications are available when patients need them. It also means that employees know where to obtain information, how to request supplies and services, and how to procure equipment.

For the nurse, efficient care depends on these services. Consider how your efficiency would be affected if you had to spend an hour to procure linen for a patient's bed or if you had to wait two days to get a bed repaired. What do you do if the patient wants his hair cut, a book to read, or a comb? Where do you get information about the insurance plan that your patient is so worried about?

SUPPORT

Supporting services provide stability by freeing the nurse to make alterations and adaptations when providing patient care. Patient care is dynamic; patient needs are constantly changing. Nurses are better able to cope with changes if their environment is orderly.

In addition to supporting employees through services, the organization supports them through policies and procedures which guide

decision-making. If the hospital policy states that all patients must have a CBC, a chest x-ray, a urinalysis, and a physical examination before a surgical operation, the nurse can make the decision that a patient be retained in his room until these tests have been performed. The policy gives the nurse security because it applies equally to the actions of the doctor, the x-ray technician, the laboratory technician, and the operating room personnel. All employees must comply with this policy unless there is good reason for an exception.

COMMUNICATION

Communication serves to integrate the work of employees by facilitating both the sharing and developing of ideas and the exchange of information and requests. The scope of communication ranges from automatic and specific communication to complex discussion. Specific communications include orders for supplies, requests for services, and reports that provide information. Requisitions for laboratory work and forms for daily reports are examples of automatic methods for communication. Meetings, conferences, and channels of communication are often made routine so that employees whose activities are interrelated communicate regularly. Just as a group of staff nurses requires communication, the groups of employees representative of all departments must communicate for coordination of efforts.

In order to provide stability for coordinated function, organizations have designed plans to integrate behaviors of employees. These plans are often referred to as standard operating policies, procedures, and rules. Organizations also require developmental planning, which is necessary for the perpetuation of the organization in a changing society. An organization must project its goals to the future to ensure that it will be able to accommodate readily to changing needs of clients and to maintain its level of goal achievement.

Standard or integrating plans provide for consistent interaction among employees. Developmental plans, in contrast, provide for change implementation. The integrating plans are geared to day-by-day operations and are often the result of developmental planning which brings about changes in these day-by-day operations. Developmental plans are either short-range or long-range. Short-range plans may meet the needs of the organization for periods of months while long-range plans may encompass periods of three to five years or more. Developmental plans are visionary in nature and are future oriented.

Both integrating and developmental plans are necessary for or-

ganizing, activating, controlling, and evaluating the work of an organization over time. You may be more familiar with standard integrating plans because of your short-term experiences with organizations. When you work in an organization for a short period of time, you learn how to work within that organization by following the integrating plans in carrying out your functions. When you assume a long-term position in an organization you can better perceive the differences between the integrating plans that guide your function and the developmental plans that are focused on change implementation.

When you assume a management position, you continually evaluate the effectiveness of the integrating plans in the day-by-day operations. As organizational functions change through new developments in technology, new definition of roles, or better delineation of patient-care measures, the integrating plans must be changed to accommodate new requirements for coordinating work. Some integrating plans become obsolete with the introduction of new technology or new methods of giving care. Developments in patient care, such as checking patient's blood pressure at every clinic visit as a part of risk management, may change the integrating plans. In some instances, new integrating plans are developed to ensure the successful application of changes in function.

The purpose of developmental planning is to devise better ways of providing services or to determine how the organizational functions can be changed to meet new needs. Legislation that creates new regulations, cost containment activities, and other types of external influences may create the need for developmental planning to determine how the functions of staff can be changed so that the regulations or constraints can be met while also accomplishing the organization's mission. The purposes, goals, and objectives of any activity, the types of materials and supplies needed, and the mechanisms for interaction among personnel for carrying out newly defined functions are accomplished by developmental planning. Integrating plans emerge from developmental plans as requisites established for stability in use of organizational resources.

Integrative Plans

Organizations have established integrative plans which guide personnel in working together. These include written and unwritten statements of policy, procedures, and rules. However, each organi-

zation differs in how it expects employees to work together. Norms of organizational behavior are established according to each situation. Integrative plans serve to stabilize the environment, to support personnel, and to provide for communication. Managers from all departments are involved in using these integrative plans; the nurse-manager is no exception.

COMPONENTS OF INTEGRATIVE PLANS

Integrative plans may be said to have three components: a concept, a procedure, and specific criteria that are crucial to successful results. These components are inherent requisites of all policies, procedures, and rules. A brief definition of each will clarify their purposes in the organization.

A *concept* is a broad general statement that is derived from the health-care agency's philosophy. *Policies* are most representative of statements of concepts. These serve to influence decisions made by personnel in all departments so that their work is focused continually on the agency's goals. Concepts serve as a guide for definition of procedures and rules.

A *procedure* is a guide to performance of an activity. Procedures may be very general or specific, depending on the complexity of the activity being performed and the capabilities of the personnel who use the procedure. Procedures are written in sufficient detail to provide the information required by all persons who are involved in the activity. Task structure, through specific and detailed procedural guides for performance of activities, is needed by personnel with less experience and education. Procedures include a statement of purpose, designation of who is to perform the activity, listing of supplies and equipment required, recommendation for methods or routes of communication, and criteria for performance.

Specific criteria that are crucial to successful results are usually stated as *rules*. These rules are single-purpose statements that define what must be done or what should not be done. Consider the rule: Personnel must wear masks in the surgical suite. This is an important rule that deals with only one of a composite of activities related to maintaining asepsis in the surgical suite. Rules are clear-cut and are designed to help personnel form habits which are conducive to good practice. Policies, procedures, and rules may be written for activities that involve every department or for activities that are specific to a given department. Generally they form a continuum of general to specific guides to action, the policy being the most general. Policies

that affect every department may be interpreted in procedures that are different according to a given department's responsibilities for performing an activity. In this case each department's procedures relate to the overall policy in such a way that everyone involved is working toward accomplishment of the same general purpose.

Policies, procedures, and rules may be unwritten in an organization. In this situation they are often passed along among employees by word of mouth. Unwritten policies, procedures, and rules are learned through an acculturation process when a new employee begins to work in an organization. Such bits of advice as "Always have a stethoscope when you work on 5 West because Mrs. Hill, the head nurse, does not like to see nurses without them," reflect an unwritten rule. Unwritten plans usually develop from personal preferences of managers or from accepted ways of doing things that have proved to be successful for employees. Sometimes they embellish the written policies, procedures, and rules and sometimes they contradict them. Unless the written plans are consistently enforced, the unwritten plans take precedence.

The interrelatedness of departmental functions is demonstrated by a hospital policy concerning admission of patients. The policy states that hospital beds must be kept available for admission of patients with emergency illnesses. This policy is interpreted by the admissions department and the emergency room. A procedure might be written to define the priority needs of patients that make them eligible for admission to reserved emergency beds. The procedure might be developed from guidelines established in the admissions department or the emergency room through practice. These guidelines may formalize previously unwritten procedures for those departments.

The nursing department may also have a procedure relating to this policy that might specify which personnel and which units are assigned to care for patients with emergency conditions. Another department that might be affected by the same policy is the housekeeping department. This department's related procedure may specify that three beds must always be available in the event that a patient must be temporarily placed in a lounge or a hallway when all regular hospital beds are full.

MANUALS OF POLICY AND PROCEDURE

How does a nurse find out about the written organizational policies, procedures, or rules? There are various methods that can be used to inform personnel of organizational expectations. Most hospitals, for

example, have a manual of operating policies, procedures, or both. This manual includes information about many aspects of patient care, such as admission and discharge of patients. Requirements of the hospital concerning medical records, transfer of patients, consulting services, and special care units can often be found in the operating policy manual. Some statements written for manuals are broad and serve to guide decision-making by personnel. Others specify the procedure to be followed in performing a sequence of related activities.

Specific and Nonspecific Policies. Consider two statements concerning admission of patients to a convalescent care unit. The first states: Patients who require extended care services for rehabilitation through occupational and physical therapy will be admitted to the extended care unit. The second states: Transfer of patients to the extended care unit must first be approved by the committee for continuity of care. The committee consists of a physiatrist as chairman, two medical doctors, two nurses, an occupational therapist, a physical therapist, and a social caseworker. Requests for approval must be submitted to this committee on form #276. All questions concerning prognosis, care requirements, and plans for future care must be answered in their entirety by the physician or head nurse.

The first statement is a broad policy that can be interpreted in different ways by different people. Rehabilitation has many meanings, and thus the rationale for admitting patients to the extended care unit may include a variety of factors. Referring personnel need only justify the patient's need for rehabilitation by indicating that the patient requires physical and occupational therapy. The second statement, however, is outlined in more detail. Interpretation of the procedure is limited to members of the specified committee. Both statements provide information about the operation of the hospital and influence decisions that are made by persons related to the patient's care.

Departmental Policy Manuals. In addition to the general policy manual, which specifies concepts and procedures of care for all employees, various departments in the organization may have their own policy or procedure manuals. Among these are the x-ray, laboratory, personnel, and nursing departments.

Departmental policy and procedure manuals serve many functions. They can be used to inform personnel of procedures that

should be observed, as a review of activities involved in performance of certain tasks or techniques, for orientation of new personnel, for teaching subprofessional employees, and for communication among personnel from different departments who perform related functions. For example, the nurse can determine how to prepare a patient for a laboratory test by reading about the test in the laboratory department's procedure manual.

Regulations and the Nurse-Manager

How does the nurse-manager become involved in policies, procedures, and rules? First of all, the nurse should understand the purpose of all these plans. Policies, procedures, and rules are organizing plans that direct and coordinate activities of all employees. When managers in each department observe these plans, they are supporting the hospital's goals to provide efficient, orderly, and safe performance.

Secondly, the nurse-manager should be well-informed about the policies, procedures, and rules, because the manager is expected to set an example by observing them. The manager's role also includes interpreting and clarifying policies, procedures, and rules and consistently enforcing them. Information, interpretation, and clarification are basic to effective enforcement. Cooperation of staff members is augmented if they understand the relationships of procedures and rules to the concepts from which they are derived.

Next, the manager is expected to evaluate the effectiveness of the policies, procedures, and rules with respect to their purposes. This is particularly true for procedures and rules. Because following procedures and rules falls into the realm of habitual activity, personnel sometimes become so accustomed to a rule that they cease to evaluate its usefulness in achieving the intended purpose. This may result in perpetuation of an activity long after the need for it has diminished because of changes in the related concept.

Nurses are primarily concerned with integrative behaviors directly related to provision of patient care, and this requires using procedures such as standard order forms, inventory methods, and record forms that facilitate organizational coordination. The nurse-manager's major responsibility in carrying out these plans is to ensure that they are used correctly and are effective so that staff members have adequate and appropriate materials and use them economically.

Finally, managers are expected to consider existing policies, procedures, and rules when devising new ones specific to the patient-care unit. The fact that all activities that take place in a health-care agency are related to achieving organizational goals cannot be over-emphasized. Because of the interrelatedness of departments, the planning of one usually affects the functions of another. Managerial planning is continuous and is most effective if it is shared with all who are involved in activities being planned.

Nursing Staff Participation in Developmental Planning

Human potential for planning is often not exploited to its fullest in nursing because the nurse tends to concentrate on the individual patient. The attention of the nurse focuses on the nurse-patient relationship; the combination of all the patient's needs at any given time determines the day-to-day goals for management. The pressures of meeting patients' needs on a day-to-day basis often takes precedence in the manager's attention. Continuous problems encountered in giving care or spontaneous thoughts about ways to improve services are often put aside by busy managers. It is necessary to spend some time meditating or reflecting on the services being given on a day-to-day basis to improve the way that services are provided, or to improve the services. Developmental planning is the term used to describe the manager's role in change implementation which begins with thoughtful evaluation of day-to-day activities.

Developmental plans can be short-range or long-range plans that encompass many different aspects of care for all patients served by the health-care agency. In a sense, developmental planning is necessary for adaptation of the organization's functions to the ever-changing needs of patients in a society that is evolving continually. Long-range planning is not only a necessary component of organizational management, but it is also a necessary component of professionalism in nursing. The profession evolves and changes through the activities of nurses who are visionary and who spend time in future planning.

IMMEDIATE VERSUS LONG-RANGE PLANNING

Have you worked on a unit on Tuesday, thinking that everything seemed organized, only to return on Wednesday to find that things were hectic? The expediency of patient care can be identified as a major cause for fluctuating goals for management on the patient-care unit. Patient care is expedient because patient needs cannot be

predicted in advance. A hospitalized patient may suddenly develop complications, and a newly admitted patient may have any number or variety of symptoms and needs that must be assessed immediately.

An immediate patient need requires an immediate solution if care is to be beneficial for the patient. Therefore, nurses focus their attention on patient care, which places demands on both their physical and emotional energies. Because of the expediency of care, the present seems more important than future planning.

Managers in nursing are therefore faced with what often seems to be a conflict—planning for the future while meeting the demands of the present. How does one overcome this conflict?

Planning for the future depends on a state of mind, one of thinking in the future while functioning in the present. Two things help the manager to achieve this state of mind. The first is a vision of activities and processes that would improve patient care—a mental picture of what future patient care ought to be. The second is a perspective of the health-care agency's functions, goals, and plans for the future.

The manager should develop a perspective of events that are taking place in the organization. Most organizations have long-range plans for improvement of patient services, such as building construction, expansion of services, or development of new services. Understanding the direction of these plans helps the nurse appreciate the need for planning nursing care in accordance with future plans for the total organization.

The perspective of organizational planning is enhanced if one is aware of the complexity of activities performed within the organization. The following analogy gives a clearer view of the nature of organizational planning.

Imagine that you are in a plane, flying at an altitude of 10,000 feet. The day is clear, and you can see the terrain below. You can see a winding river that forms semicircles that double back on one another. The surrounding earth appears irregular, with crevices, randomly placed trees, and numerous colors breaking the smoothness of its surface. As you continue to watch, a narrow ribbon of pavement draws your attention to a city you are approaching.

In contrast to the random placement of the water, trees, and earth you have just seen, the city appears precise and orderly. Houses are neatly arranged in rows bordered by streets. Water is contained in geometrically shaped pools. You can see tiny automobiles moving evenly along a pattern of streets. It is evident that the city structure has been planned. People have changed the rambling countryside

into a configuration that accommodates human activity. The change was brought about because the people were able to think, to make decisions, and to perform activities outlined in their plans to create the city.

The aerial view of the configuration of the city can be compared to the organizational chart pictured in the first chapter. The streets are routes of transportation and provide access to buildings, while the lines of the chart are access lines for authority and for communication. Both configurations represent structural plans that channel human activity, and both facilitate definition of how people formally relate to one another and to their environment. Both the city and the organization have policies, procedures, and rules that govern and direct human activity. However, one has to live in the city or work in the organization to know what actually takes place. One has to be personally involved to fully understand the behavior of people. A cursory view of a city's structure and governing plans only gives an indication of behavior. Similarly, behavior in an organization is only partially determined by the structure and the governing plans.

DRAWBACKS OF SHORT-RANGE PLANNING

Although the city may seem very orderly from the airplane, the configuration may actually be a product of random development over a long period of time. The residents of some cities bemoan the lack of planning and control of the city's growth. Other cities may have benefited from the vision of people who developed plans for the city's growth so that the construction completed in each era would complement that of the others.

Nursing management focusing on the patient's immediate needs is similar to the haphazardly planned city. A decision that meets one patient's needs today may hinder another patient's progress in the future. However, when nursing management is focused on the future, more consideration is given to the implications the decision has for many patients. When this occurs, nursing management is more like that used for developing the planned city.

PLANNING WITHIN LARGER STRUCTURE

Planning in an organization is complex because of the diverse activities that take place in segments of the organization. Consider the diverse activities taking place in the city: The city council is planning for improvement of streets and highways, the school board is planning for transportation of children to and from school, and a church

group is debating about where to build the new church. A storekeeper is taking inventory in preparation for a sale, and a family is deciding where to buy shoes for the children.

Organizational activities are also diverse, and this results in separate planning by each department toward accomplishing its own purposes. However, all activities are influenced by the structure and by the governing plans. The family must observe traffic signals when driving to the store to buy shoes. The storekeeper will only open his shop during hours approved by the city council. The school board will have to work within the limits of money available to it.

In the health-care agency people in each department must observe the general rules. Budgets and signals in the organization define boundaries for performance of activities. The nurse who develops a perspective of the total hospital organization realizes how activities of the departments are interrelated. This perspective is the framework in which the nurse operates to apply the management process to achievement of long-range goals that complement those of the total organization.

PROJECTION INTO THE FUTURE

In order to maintain the effectiveness of nursing practice, managers must develop goals which extend beyond the present. These goals may extend over a period of months or years if the management process is to be effectively goal-oriented. This requires projecting into the future.

Through making predictions about changes or trends in giving patient care, managers who are future-oriented identify where they are and then define where they would like to be. The question "How do you think care ought to be given in the future?" will help managers decide what the long-range goals should be.

PROGRESSIVE PLANNING

A manager may find that long-range goals are vague and overwhelming. To overcome these feelings, the manager can institute a method of progressive planning. This method involves analyzing the long-range goal to determine a sequence of subgoals that lead to its achievement. All the subgoals then become short-range goals. By reducing long-range goals to a sequence of realistic and attainable short-range goals, the manager can progress with more assurance of success.

Short-range goals can be used to channel the staff toward effort

beyond routine performance of daily work and eventually to achievement of long-range goals they would have considered vague, visionary, and unrealistic. Consistent accomplishment of goals also provides for motivation for staff members to continue the effort to achieve.

An example of a long-range goal you are familiar with is the goal to become a nurse. The sequential development of courses in the school's curriculum gave you realistic short-range goals to accomplish. You achieved a goal each time you passed one of the courses. Your short-range planning was limited to the requirements of each course. Yet, all the while, the broad goal, to become a nurse, gave you direction in your study.

Staff members are similar to students in the way they view goals. Although freshmen student nurses know they want to become graduate nurses, graduation is often a distant, somewhat vague goal. Junior students usually feel more confident than freshmen or sophomores about goal achievement because of their demonstrated ability to accomplish goals. Seniors find that the goal that seemed to be a vision during the freshman year is real and quite near. The curriculum in a school of nursing is planned progressively. The progression of plans provides for consistent and steady direction. It also provides for necessary feelings of accomplishment realized only when goals have been achieved.

FACTORS IN PATIENT CARE

The concept of developmental planning in progressive stages can be applied in nursing management. Planning for long-term goals in nursing begins with determination of measurable factors that remain constant in patient-care situations. These constant factors are those that affect most patients' care. Factors present in almost every patient-care situation can be identified as the patients' common needs, the nursing staff, the patient-care unit, the method for delivering care on the unit, and the health services available in the agency and community. All of these factors are necessary to patient care and all are within the management realm of the nurse.

It is useful to analyze the dimensions of each of these factors separately even though events in one affect the other within the organization. The analysis of events that take place in relation to each factor can be initiated with a brainstorming session. You might ask the question, "How do you think care ought to be given in the future?" Record your answers to this question and then consider

what changes would have to be made in each factor or category that is present in most patient-care situations. This is a beginning step in determining the type of data needed to analyze rationally the direction that your change implementation should take. Let us now consider some attributes of each of the factors mentioned to explicate the process of analysis.

Patient Needs. Analysis of patient needs on a given patient-care unit forms the basis for developing long-range plans that will improve care. These plans should be general enough to meet the needs of a number of patients, but specific enough to be applicable to individual patients. General needs can be identified by determining what needs patients tend to have in common. For example, if patients are grouped according to classification of illness on a particular unit, the common needs of patients will in turn be specific to this classification. The nurse is able to develop plans to meet common needs with much greater specificity in a unit largely populated by patients with respiratory diseases than in a unit where patients have a wide range of diseases.

Long-range plans focusing on better methods to meet patient needs include devising more effective ways of caring for the patient's physical and emotional needs, initiating programs that facilitate the patient's rehabilitation, and developing projects for improved patient teaching. The planner asks, "What needs are not being met effectively, and what can be done to improve service to patients?"

The Nursing Staff. Changes for improving the competencies of nursing staff members are based on analysis of each person's ability to give patient care (referred to as a needs assessment). Long-range planning can include development of educational programs to increase nursing knowledge and skill or programs that involve staff members in the development of plans. Staff members who are involved in goal-oriented activities for improving care often learn to improve their personal competency in giving patient care. Analysis of the competencies of staff members enables the planner to identify priorities. Development of staff competencies, for example, should precede their involvement in projects that require advanced knowledge and skill.

The Patient-Care Unit. The process of giving patient care includes performing routine operations that are influenced by both the physical environment of the unit and the organizational policies, proce-

dures, and rules of the total organization. Changes that might improve care can include improved arrangement of equipment and supplies, use of utility rooms, or other alterations in the physical environment that will increase efficiency and effectiveness. Changes can also be made in the organizational structure, policies, procedures, and rules of the unit, in the methods of supplying the unit with the resources it needs to give patient care, and in the methods of communication and cooperation among departments. Analysis of the use of resources and the effectiveness of communication and cooperation is the basis for planning for improvement.

The organization of the patient-care unit and the manager's pattern of leadership influence how long-range plans are developed. In a hospital, for example, the head nurse may be the person who guides all planning for managers on a given patient-care unit. The planner communicates with the head nurse throughout every phase of planning to ensure that efforts to change policy, procedure, or structure will be appropriate for the unit. It is essential that planning by a group of staff members on the unit complements the head nurse's plans for the total unit. Communication between the planner and other medical personnel in relation to plans should be discussed with the head nurse. Sometimes the head nurse gives approval for contacts; at other times the head nurse will represent the staff in contacting other personnel. It is the head nurse's prerogative to set limits for activities conducted on the patient-care unit. The head nurse provides support and guidance in planning and assistance in developing a realistic perspective of the hospital's goals and plans as they relate to the unit.

The Method for Delivering Care. Delivery of health care encompasses methods for providing patient services by the nursing staff as well as that given by personnel in other departments. Patient care can be improved by making changes that are either internal or external to the patient-care unit.

The method used to organize nursing staff is internal and can be analyzed to determine its effectiveness. Does it actually establish effective working relationships among staff members? Does the method support staff members and guide them in giving care? Is the method realistic for staff members' abilities?

Factors external to the patient-care unit include delivery of services by other medical personnel; therefore, analysis of the effectiveness of cooperation among all personnel is a concern for planning. Nurses who work in a hospital, for example, care for patients before and after

they receive health care in other departments. The nurse is the one health professional who is in constant contact with the hospitalized patient. Analysis of the effectiveness of interdepartmental cooperation may include questions about the adequacy of patient-care information, expectations of other departments, effectiveness of communication among health professionals for follow-up care, and efficiency in transporting patients to and from departments. The nurse-manager should play a prominent role in planning efforts which involve the policies, procedures, and rules established by all medical personnel.

Resources in the Hospital and the Community. The broad spectrum of patient needs requires that the nurse in the hospital be concerned with health services provided both for hospitalized patients and for people in the community. Patients return to the community when they are discharged from the hospital. Therefore, the focus of analysis of utilization should be, Do the patients receive "inclusive" care?

There are great variances in services available in communities. Do members of the nursing staff know about and use health services available for individual patient care? Is there communication between each service and the hospital? Are there adequate referral systems for patient utilization of services? Is there sharing of information about patients for continuity of care? These are but a few of the questions that can be asked in efforts to plan for improved patient care through utilization of available resources.

It is important that priorities for achieving long-range goals be established in a realistic way so that the staff members can accept their participation in the activities. A sequence of short-range goals should gradually lead staff members to finishing projects while also increasing their ability to participate in achieving long-range goals. The long-range goal should continually provide direction and motivation but should not become overwhelming or frustrating for staff members.

Progressive planning is a stimulus to accomplishment and is a necessary counterpart of change. The nurse who integrates a futuristic vision of nursing care with a perspective of the organization's goals into sound plans for changing the constant dimensions of the patient-care situation is able to direct the present situation toward the futuristic vision of patient care. This progressive planning is developmental and supports the long-term growth and stability of the organization.

Summary

A manager is a key person in an organization. Management is a function of life known to every individual: People organize, activate, control, and evaluate the activities of their lives. Sometimes people carry out these "management processes" without giving thought to the nature of the processes they are using. People who are managers, however, must consciously think about how they use management processes. One can learn to be increasingly efficient and productive as a manager by studying and practicing skills and techniques designed to improve management abilities.

The type of organization, the characteristics of the manager, and the relationship between the manager and the organization all influence how a manager conducts the processes of management. Integration of functions of managers throughout the organization takes place through existing integrating plans such as policies, procedures, and rules. These integrating plans serve also to coordinate the work of the personnel in the entire organization.

Developmental planning is a necessary function of managers and serves to ensure that the integrating plans are evaluated continually and changed in accordance with internal and external changes taking place. Developmental planning is a professional approach to influencing continually the nature of nursing functions and the way that nurses work within organizations. This developmental planning takes place in the social system of the organization and involves all aspects of the organization.

Study Questions

1. Every plan can be divided into three components: a concept of what is to be accomplished, procedures for carrying out the plan, and critical tasks that must be carried out at specific points during activity. Select a plan used for providing care in a health-care agency you are familiar with. Describe this plan according to the three components outlined above.
2. Choose one patient you have cared for and identify the policies, procedures, and rules you used when caring for the patient.
   a. Which of these policies, procedures, and rules are specific to nursing?
   b. Which of the policies, procedures, and rules are general to the total organization?
   c. What methods are used to communicate these policies, procedures, and rules in the health-care agency?
   d. Do the nurses participate in formulating policies, procedures, and rules?

Study Projects

Mary is a group leader on a surgical patient-care unit with a bed capacity of 68. Mary is responsible for the care of 35 patients. Her group comprises three registered nurses and two licensed practical nurses. Her first impression of the unit is that the staff does not communicate well, especially in teaching patients.

Mary realizes that as manager she must integrate her knowledge about the hospital organization, the nursing service organization, the management process, and her vision of staff-patient relationships into a composite of group activities that will improve patient care.

She believes that the primary force for controlling the quality of patient care will be the motivation of each staff member to perform well. Mary's philosophy is that staff members must reach a state of equilibrium in which their motivation is equal to the demands of the work. In keeping with this philosophy Mary makes an initial decision: Improved patient care should be achieved through group process.

Mary then decides to analyze the long-range goals she has for the staff members and for improving patient care. A summary of her analysis reveals the following:

1. The Patients
    a. The majority of patients present problems and needs associated with cardiac diseases.
    b. Patients receive excellent physical care but receive little or no information about the nature of and care required by their condition.
2. The Nursing Staff
    a. RN #1 rotates between days and evenings, relieving the evening nurse two days a week. She has exceptional qualities for assessing patient needs and formulates good care plans that usually are not actualized. She often states that rotating shifts decreases her ability to follow through with the plans. Her ideas are sound and she has a gift for logical thinking, but she must be prodded to share her ideas in a group.
    b. RN #2 has been employed as a part-time nurse for seven years and began full-time employment just three months ago. She is perceptive, efficient, and concentrates on immediate patient needs. She states that her long-term employment as a part-time nurse has caused her to form habits of coming to work, getting the work done, and then going home, forgetting the problems of the day. She then starts the new day free of yesterday's concerns.
    c. RN #3 loves to talk and is well versed in a variety of subjects. She is lively and energetic and is known for her ability to cheer patients. Her favorite subject is cooking so that almost every conference about the patients includes her description of their diets at home.
    d. LPN #1 is a resourceful person who does extra things for patients. She prides herself on her compassion and understanding of patients' reactions to their hospitalization. When care plans are discussed,

she emphasizes emotional aspects of care and never asks a patient to do anything he does not want to do.

e. LPN #2 is working to make enough money to enroll in a collegiate nursing program. She is curious about pathology and frequently asks about modes of treatment and medications. In conferences she often relates theories from a genetics course she is taking in evening school.

3. Method of Delivering Care
   a. Although the nursing staff is organized in a pattern of group care, the pattern is not totally accepted. It was initiated by the nursing supervisor, who felt that the staff reacted negatively to team method.
   b. The head nurse is well organized and tends to be somewhat authoritarian. She functions well with the unit administrator so that staff needs for materials are adequately met. Usually the head nurse prefers to communicate with staff members individually. She likes to keep records and has copious amounts of data about average length of patient hospitalization, about the most commonly used medications, and about the types and descriptions of emergency situations that occur on the unit.

4. The Patient-Care Unit
   a. Patients' rooms are two-bed rooms with the exception of four private rooms.
   b. The unit administrator is efficient and keeps supplies and communication flowing smoothly among departments. She handles patient needs for administrative services very well.

5. Resources in the Hospital
   a. There is a seven-bed coronary care unit in the hospital. Patients are usually transferred to various patient-care units by the coronary care staff once their condition has stabilized.
   b. The outpatient department has weekly cardiac clinics and material from the Heart Association that is available to patients free of cost.
   c. The laboratory has developed a system for participation in emergency cardiac care and also has several staff members who participate in research.
   d. The hospital has a social service department and qualified dietitians, occupational therapists, and physical therapists.

6. Resources in the Community
   a. There is a well-established Visiting Nurse Association. The nurses care for many chronically ill patients in the community, conduct classes for prenatal care and for bowel and bladder training, and participate in workshops for care of patients with cancer or with special disabling diseases such as multiple sclerosis and cerebral vascular accidents.
   b. A branch office for the American Heart Association is located in the community.
   c. A special civic committee has been formed voluntarily to determine the need for new community services for special groups. Its focus is on the aged, on children with learning disabilities, and on the adolescent.

Mary decides to centralize all the problems in her given situation in the formation of a single long-range goal: *to institute a program for patient teaching*. She has determined the following goals:

1. For the Staff
   a. To unite staff members through use of group process.
   b. To increase each staff member's ability to assess the total needs of patients.
   c. To increase staff members' nursing knowledge about care of patients with cardiac diseases.
2. For the Patient
   a. To minimize the negative effects of the patient's transition from the coronary care unit to the patient-care unit.
   b. To organize a system for providing patients with information and explanations they need about their diseases on a continuous basis, for hospitalization and for after discharge.
   c. To initiate cooperation among all medical personnel who participate in the cardiac patient's care.
   d. To develop a method for evaluating the effectiveness of patient teaching.

Before beginning to work with the staff Mary has determined that:

1. The long-range goal is within the staff's realm of responsibility and ability and that it is approved by the head nurse.
2. The goal is important for improving care and it provides direction for planning.
3. The goal is realistic for the patient-care unit and compatible with the goals of the entire hospital.

Study Questions
1. Evaluate the procedure that Mary has followed to determine her long-range goals. Do you agree with her analysis of the problem?
2. Define short-range goals that will lead to achieving the long-range goal you have determined for this situation.
3. If you were Mary, how would you proceed to incorporate the long-range plans in the performance of management processes?
4. Define the expected functions for Mary as leader of the group and for the staff members as group participants in relation to short-range goals you would plan for:
   a. The organizing phase
   b. The activating phase
   c. The controlling phase
   d. The evaluating phase
5. What impediments do you foresee in achieving the long-range goal Mary has identified?

6. What materials or resources would be helpful to Mary in working with the group?
7. Determine how Mary should communicate the results of the group's activities to others in the organization. What information must be communicated? Who needs the information? What channels and what format should be followed in communicating the information?

References

1. Bernard, C. *The Functions of the Executive* (30th Anniversary ed.). Cambridge: Harvard University Press, 1968.
2. Getzels, J. W., and Guba, E. G. Role, role conflict and effectiveness: An empirical study. *Am. Sociol. Rev.* 19:164, 1954.
3. Shostrom, E. L., and Knapp, L. *Actualizing Therapy: Foundations for a Scientific Ethic.* San Diego: EDITS, 1976.

Suggested Reading

Armstrong, D. M. Nursing administrator's expectations of OR leader. *A.O.R.N.* 25:859–864, April 1977.

Damos, V. R. Management skill: Objectivity. *A.O.R.N.* 25:195–196, Feb. 1977.

Donnelly, J. F. Participative management at work. *Harvard Bus. Rev.* 55:117–127, Jan./Feb. 1977.

Frazier, L. M. Preventive management for supervisors. *Hosp. Top.* 54:21–29, Nov./Dec. 1976.

Godfrey, M. A., and *Nursing '75.* Working conditions. How do yours compare with other nurses? *Nursing '75* 5:85, May 1975.

Hefferin, E. A., and Hunter, R. E. How we turned an idea into a program. Reality orientation. *Nursing '77* 7:88-91, May 1977.

Letellier, M. You can change nursing practice. *Nursing '77* 7:65–66, March 1977.

Lindeman, C. A., and Krueger, J. C. Increasing the quality, quantity, and use of nursing research. *Nurs. Outlook* 25:450–454, July 1977.

Longest, B. B. *Management Practices for the Health Professional.* Reston, Va.: Prentice-Hall, 1976.

McCool, B., and Brown, M. *The Management Response: Conceptual, Technical, and Human Skills of Health Administration.* Philadelphia: Saunders, 1977.

McKain, R. J. *Realize Your Potential.* New York: American Management Association, 1975.

Robinson, V. M. How to initiate change in practice. *A.O.R.N.* 26:54–61, July 1977.

Springate, D. D., and McNeil, M. C. Managemet policies in investor owned hospitals. *Health Care Man. Rev.* 2:57–67, Summer 1977.

3. The Organization of Nursing for Management of Patient Care

There are many variations in the ways that nursing departments are structured. In this chapter we will discuss the types of plans used to organize nursing departments in hospitals and the concomitant management roles of nurses. Some of the major differences among nursing department organizations will be discussed. These include the organization of a patient-care unit, the number of management levels in the nursing department, the placement of the department in the total hospital structure, and finally the patterns of care used to organize nursing staff.

The patient-care unit is the locus of nursing process in the hospital or health-care agency. Since the nursing department exists to support and facilitate the functions of the patient-care units we will first discuss some characteristics of the patient-care unit.

A patient-care unit may be autonomous in its function, its philosophy, and its objectives, but it is also an integral part of the total hospital organization. Personnel from many other departments who provide direct patient-care services and indirect supporting services, such as housekeeping, enter and leave the patient-care unit. These services are important for patient care and therefore must be considered when organizing the structure for patient care on any given unit. The staff nurse who is a manager of care on a patient-care unit needs to be familiar with the organizational plan for the patient-care unit and its relationship to the rest of the hospital. The nurse should also know about the types of medical and supporting services provided by the hospital. Knowledge of the contributions of other professionals helps the nurse plan for efficient and complete patient care. In addition, the nurse should be familiar with the types of services available to patients from the community. The nurse must understand how patients and their families obtain these services in order to provide for continuity of care.

The nurse-manager is concerned with the implications that patients' past and future care have for their current hospitalization. This is particularly important today when hospitals are becoming centers of health-care services. As patients increasingly understand health care, nurses are increasingly involved in helping patients learn about and use health-care services for a wide variety of care measures.

These can include regular physical examinations, particularly if the patient has a chronic health problem, nutritious food, rest, relaxation, immunizations, and care for minor and major acute health problems. The focus of the nurse-manager's functions is patient care, and this focus takes into account the ways the patient learns to use the services of health care.

The Patient-Care Unit

Each patient-care unit has a philosophy and objectives that articulate the scope of the nurse-manager's function. The philosophy and objectives should be written and need periodic review and revision. A philosophy is a broad statement of purpose, while objectives are statements of behaviors to be accomplished by the nursing staff to "activate" the philosophy. The objectives serve as the basis for application of the management processes discussed in Chapter 2: organizing, activating, controlling, and evaluating.

PATIENT-CARE UNIT PHILOSOPHY

You might ask, "Why spend time writing a vague philosophy that no one ever reads again?" It is true that a philosophy may seem general, vague, or more implicit than explicit. It is also true that in articulating a philosophy a group of people must brainstorm. They must explore their ideas in broad perspective, and they must make basic decisions about a definition of nursing care that will serve as a unifying device. When writing a philosophy, members of a group define what they mean by terms such as patient care or rehabilitation. Clarification of ideas, opinions, meanings of terms, and purposes is a necessary part of organizing. A carefully articulated philosophy serves as a common base or focal point for all the ensuing elements of the management process.

The a priori consideration for developing a patient-care unit's philosophy is the patient. Current emphasis on health care as a rapidly growing business has created a recipient of health services who is a consumer rather than an object of health care. Informed consumers ask relevant questions about the services they receive. Managers also should ask themselves questions such as: What is nursing care? Why do patients choose to come to this particular hospital? What do patients expect from the nursing staff? What is the patient's concept of nursing care? What constitutes a successful hospitalization for a patient?

The philosophy should include the nursing staff's description of beliefs about nursing care. Once written, the philosophy should be referred to in subsequent staff activities on the patient-care unit as a reminder of the focus of the staff's efforts. It is interesting to note that because a philosophy is a broad general definition about beliefs of nursing care, it usually remains valid even though the meanings of the words change as nursing-care knowledge evolves. The philosophy must be reviewed frequently, however, to ensure that current interpretation is relevant to current practice.

Unit Objectives. Definition of methods to be used to achieve the purposes stated in the philosophy is the process of formulating specific objectives for patient care. Objectives are clearly stated ways for activating the beliefs in the general statement of philosophy. If the philosophy states that "complete nursing care consists of provision of comfort, teaching patients about care and cure processes, giving support to the patient and family, and planning for the patient's future care needs," the objectives should specifically delineate the behavioral standards expected of the staff for making patients comfortable, for teaching, for giving support, and for health-care planning.

The form used to write objectives is of lesser consequence than is the nursing staff's understanding and acceptance of the objectives. Objectives should be perceived as reasonable and attainable goals by staff. Defining objectives that can be understood and accepted by the entire nursing staff serves to unify the staff members, who then share a common concept of their expectations for giving patient care. An individual nurse, after reading the objectives, should be secure in knowing what is expected, since objectives delineate behaviors required in the care of patients. As you write these behavioral objectives you are actually making decisions about what must be done to achieve the goals stated in the philosophy. Behavioral objectives help the staff know what they are supposed to accomplish. Applying behavioral objectives in giving patient care involves consideration of the physical environment of the unit, the competencies of the staff, and the work to be accomplished. In order to apply objectives more easily it is helpful to categorize them according to similar activities. Objectives so categorized will make it apparent that some activities can be performed in a sequence and some activities are prerequisites for others. Most nursing activities require judgment by the nursing staff to assess the individual patient's needs in terms of

the objective. Objectives help the staff organize patient care in a way that facilitates productivity.

The physical environment of the patient-care unit influences how work is organized. For example, an open ward of 20 patients facilitates direct contact of a nurse with several patients at a time; this is not possible when patients are in private rooms. Operational requisites for obtaining supplies and equipment and for activities such as preparing medications, charting, and conferring must be practical for the staff assignments. The physical facility affects how people work together because it influences the way people organize their work and the amount of time it takes to perform an activity. As a manager you must plan to use its good points and devise means to overcome its bad points.

Competencies of the nursing staff will determine how the work ought to be assigned to best meet the objectives. In addition to the staff's competencies, the manager must be aware of hospital and unit policies, job descriptions of staff members, and the unwritten but important relationships that exist among the staff members. With this information the manager can devise objectives that include methods and standards for the work so that the staff members are challenged to use their potential for professional growth in their positions. Writing a philosophy and objectives is part of the organizing process.

Actualizing Objectives. In the activating phase—the time in which staff members perform the work according to the prescribed plan—the manager guides and supports staff functions. Knowledge of how you can best assist staff members in their work is increased if you think of your own experiences as a staff member. What kinds of problems do you have when giving patient care? What type of information was necessary for you? How could you have been helped to provide better care? Information about the staff's collective competencies and about the problems that arise as work is being performed is essential to the manager's participation in the activating element.

Controlling Performance. The objectives of the unit are basic to controlling performance. In order to control the quality of care being given, the manager must control the work and the environment. For example, you may need to assist staff members by obtaining additional supplies, such as linen, so that they may complete the work. You may need to support a staff member who is having difficulty

relating to a patient. Another staff member may need assistance to learn how to turn a patient correctly. You may need to confer with a physical therapist about how to coordinate care so that a staff member can organize work better. In control, the manager must reward positive behavior and correct negative behavior. Controlling involves a myriad of activities, all with the purpose of ensuring that care is given in the proper manner and that the work situation provides for smooth functioning of all staff members.

Evaluating Performance. During the time in which the manager is involved in activating and controlling processes, he or she is also involved in evaluating. Because the methods used to give patient care often determine the results, each phase of all activities must be evaluated. Prescribed standards and tools for evaluation are the basis for comparison of what ought to happen with what really happens. Functions of the evaluator include observation, interpreting, record-ing, and a keen awareness of the interrelationships among events. Continual evaluation is essential for improving patient care and for assisting the staff toward professional growth. Data gathered from evaluation is used to revise or rewrite the unit objectives so that they are updated continually.

All of the care processes and operations of the patient-care unit are supported and facilitated by the nursing department. The scope of managerial roles of nurses in hospitals ranges from the staff nurses on the patient-care units to the director of nursing practice; managerial functions of nurses range from direct patient care to management of the entire nursing department. Intermediate management roles in-clude those of supervisors, or their equivalents, and head nurses. The pattern of organization used in a given nursing department is per-sonified by the management roles.

THE HEAD NURSE

Head nurse is the traditional title for the person who is responsible for managing nursing care on a particular patient-care unit. New titles and positions are being developed in certain instances, but the tra-ditional title is used here. The head nurse usually has a 24-hour responsibility for the patient-care unit, but may be responsible for the unit for a given shift, such as a day head nurse. All activities that take place on the patient-care unit fall into the realm of the head nurse's management. The head nurse sets the tone for relationships among people within the unit. Head nurses have a variable amount

of latitude in management of the patient-care unit, but they are usually responsible for developing patterns of patient care, policies, procedures, and rules that are specific to a given patient-care unit, and for following individual prerogatives for giving patient care.

The amount of latitude that the head nurse has in management prerogatives for the patient-care unit depends on the way that the entire nursing department is organized, on the director's interpretation of management roles in the organization, on the types of middle management positions in the nursing department, and on the head nurse's management competencies and perception of his or her own management functions. The head nurse's management style directly affects how staff nurses are expected to function on a given patient-care unit because the head nurse directs all staff and all patient care on the unit.

In addition to the direct patient-care responsibilities, the head nurse participates in providing supporting services to patients. In many instances the head nurse is the liaison person between the patient-care unit and other professionals or other departments. In this regard the head nurse has a coordinating function and establishes networks of communication between the patient-care unit and other departmental personnel. These networks may or may not be formalized in an organizational chart. Head nurses participate in the selection of nursing staff who are employed for the patient-care unit, and in some hospitals they work directly with the personnel department.

THE SUPERVISOR

The supervisory role, like the head nurse role, is a middle management position. The management roles of persons in these intermediate positions are sometimes interchangeable or overlapping. In some hospitals, the head nurse does not report to a supervisor since the head nurse, if knowledgeable, mature, and motivated, needs a minimum of direction. In these hospitals, head nurses often form a peer group for purposes of problem-solving and planning to develop improved methods for giving patient care and to have a source of support.

If there are supervisory positions in the hospital, the supervisor is usually in a pivotal position between the head nurses of several patient-care units and the director of nursing practice or that person's assistant. The supervisor is responsible for management of patient care on a given number of patient-care units, and this person may be

more or less directly involved in the processes of giving care. This variance results from different interpretations of the supervisory role among both individual supervisors and different hospitals.

In some hospitals, supervisors manage the operational and mechanical details of the patient-care units, such as arranging for patient services from dietary, laboratory, or x-ray departments. In other hospitals, the supervisor may be a consultant in matters of patient care and is responsible for staff development of head nurses and staff nurses. In yet other hospitals, the supervisor may be a clinical specialist who coordinates the clinical components of patient care. As mentioned previously, the traditional supervisory position may not be found in certain hospitals. When these supervisory positions have been deleted, lay managers or unit administrators are usually employed to take care of management of the operational aspects of the patient-care unit.

THE DIRECTOR OF NURSING

The director of nursing is responsible for the entire nursing department. This person may have an associate or an assistant who performs some aspects of management functions for the department. The scope of the director's managerial role includes definition of the philosophy of the department, formulation of policies that guide all patient-care activities for nursing, establishing working relationships among nurses within the department and between the nursing department and other hospital departments, and ensuring that the department is staffed and that patient care is given within the economic and quality standards of the department. The director interfaces with other management personnel in administrative positions and with community representatives who are involved in hospital functions. Through these contacts, the director interprets nursing to the rest of the hospital personnel at the level of hospital policymaking.

The placement of the department of nursing in the total hospital structure varies. In some hospitals the director has the title of Vice-President for Nursing, a title that implies that the director has a role and responsibility in the central core of the hospital's administrative functions. In other hospitals, the director may be appointed Department Head and may report directly to an administrator of the hospital. Some directors have the title of Clinical Chairman of the Department of Nursing; this title implies that the organization views nursing as a clinical entity on par with other clinical departments

such as surgery or medicine. Placement of the department and of the director's role influences not only how nursing is perceived by others in the organization, but also the scope of nursing functions in the organization.

As discussed in Chapter 1, the type of organizational structure influences the management roles of personnel. In a tall, traditional bureaucratic structure, the locus of control for decisions made in the department of nursing tends to be at the level of the director. In flat, decentralized structures, the control is disseminated throughout the nursing department. The responsibility for decision-making tends to follow the lines set forth in the organizational structure, but it can be delegated or not according to the director's philosophy and management style.

The director's philosophy of nursing is demonstrated in several ways. How the director defines the expectations of nurses, determines the criteria for effectiveness of patient care and for nursing staff performance evaluations, clarifies nursing functions, and initiates projects for nursing development, all reflect the director's philosophy. The director interprets nursing roles not only to nurses but also to other hospital personnel. Since the director is accountable for all patient care given by nurses, the director's beliefs will determine what he or she considers important in implementing plans that ensure accountability.

One of the director's functions is to determine the boundaries for nursing practice in the hospital, which in turn establishes the working relationships of nurses in the hospital. The structure or pattern of interaction that the director establishes reflects his or her concepts about nursing and management style. In practice, most directors use different management styles according to the requirements of a particular situation. The director's use of management styles affects the way that all nurses in the department adapt to different situations, since there is a tendency for people to manage as they are managed. The three major types of management styles discussed in the traditional literature include authoritarian, democratic, and laissez-faire.

AUTHORITARIAN MANAGEMENT

An authoritarian management style implies that the manager makes all of the decisions or maintains control over decision-making. The authoritarian manager often expects each person to comply with policies, procedures, and rules and tends to employ people who

respond well to structure and who will comply with directives. Some characteristics of an authoritarian manager can be gleaned from the following description of a nursing-department director.

Mrs. Jones believes strongly that if she is to be responsible for the nursing department, she must make the major decisions that relate to nursing. She holds weekly meetings with the head nurses and informs them of plans and activities she expects them to conduct on their units. Every other day, Mrs. Jones meets with the supervisors to discuss problems. Following these meetings she decides which problems require action and makes decisions accordingly. These decisions are usually announced at the following meeting. She handles problems efficiently and is able to give clear and concise directions. When you talk to her you feel that she really listens, but you know she is sorting out your comments and will do something only about the problems she thinks are important.

DEMOCRATIC MANAGEMENT

The democratic management style implies that decision-making extends throughout the organization. The democratic style involves others in identification of problems, in analysis of alternative courses of action, and in making decisions. The democratic manager communicates openly with the staff to ensure that decisions are in keeping with the organizational and departmental goals.

The democratic manager tends to work with groups in carrying out management functions. Group process is used to involve staff members, to facilitate their growth, to give them the opportunity to control their own activities, and to increase competency through participation. An outcome of working in groups to make decisions is that all group members have a chance to provide input and to work through problems, thereby increasing their understanding of decisions and giving them an opportunity to make a commitment to these decisions.

LAISSEZ-FAIRE MANAGEMENT

The laissez-faire management style is associated with an easygoing approach to management in which staff members have the freedom to make their own decisions. The person who uses the laissez-faire management style gives people latitude to follow their own prerogatives in determining their working relationships and in formulating policies, procedures, and plans. This type of management usually results in a loosely organized department and is beneficial when the manager wishes to stimulate creativity and innovation.

APPLICATION OF DIFFERENT MANAGEMENT STYLES

Managers often shift from one management style to another according to different situations, although the manager may have a predominant style. In order to apply management styles effectively, the manager assesses the staff members' needs for direction and evaluates the situation in which the managerial decisions are being made. Since the director sets the tone for the entire nursing department, the director can be perceived as beginning a chain reaction of relationships among employees through use of management styles. A supervisor or head nurse has similar influence on people they manage, just as a staff nurse influences relationships of others depending on the way that management styles are applied.

An example of the way that different management styles can be applied by the same person is given in the following notation.

Mrs. Green, Director of Nursing, has three major goals in mind for her staff. The first is development of criteria for evaluation of quality patient care. The second concerns formulation of policies for cooperation of hospital nurses with the Visiting Nurse Association in the community. The third is to develop an innovative pattern of organizing the department.

Each week Mrs. Green meets with the supervisors and the head nurses to explore methods for developing criteria for evaluation of care. The group first identified the value of developing the criteria and are now absorbed in establishing a survey of what actually happens on the patient-care unit. Thus far Mrs. Green has not intervened in group decisions, but she often clarifies alternatives in procedures when necessary. She has given the group complete control of definition of their own methods.

For several weeks Mrs. Green has been meeting with representatives of the Visiting Nurse Association to determine how they might establish a cooperative relationship with the hospital for referral of patients. She has worked with the director of the Visiting Nurse Association to develop a set of guidelines that she plans to present to the supervisors at their weekly meeting. At that time she will define the guidelines, explain their rationale, and outline a plan for initiating referral forms on all the units.

For the third goal Mrs. Green has formed a special committee of nursing personnel, representative of all management roles. This committee has been given complete freedom to develop new and different plans for organizing the nursing department. Mrs. Green does not attend the meetings unless invited and has assured the group that their final plan will be presented to the group of supervisors and head nurses when it is completed by the committee.

In the first instance Mrs. Green is using a democratic management style to establish criteria for evaluating the quality of patient care. She

chose this style for the specific purpose of obtaining the support of the staff through their involvement and participation in the planning stages. She believes that this involvement is a requisite of effectively conducting a project to evaluate patient care because the staff must understand the criteria if they are to apply them effectively to the work situation.

She has chosen to use the authoritarian management style in establishing a relationship with the Visiting Nurse Association. Factors which led to this decision were the personality of the director of the Visiting Nurse Association and the fact that all details inherent in the decisions were administrative in nature. The director of the Visiting Nurse Association appreciates authority and functions better in a one-to-one situation than in a group when plans are being discussed. In time, both directors plan to involve their staffs in this planning, but both wish to work out the details before presenting a project to their staffs.

Finally, Mrs. Green has chosen to use the laissez-faire method of management for the committee that is developing an innovative plan for establishing methods of care. She has done this because she believes that the staff will be more creative and innovative in a loosely organized structure. She sincerely desires to initiate an innovative plan and believes that the staff members who are directly affected by the pattern of care on the patient-care unit will consider factors she would not have thought of.

THE STAFF NURSE

A staff nurse's functions are concerned with management of a group of patients and sometimes with the management of other staff nurses and nonprofessional personnel. All of the other managerial personnel in the nursing department serve to support and facilitate the staff nurse's function. Staff nurses are crucial in nursing management since patient care is the central purpose of the nursing department, and staff nurses give patient care. The staff nurses' functions are not only supported by managerial personnel in the nursing department, but also by the entire organizational structure of the hospital.

Patterns for organizing nursing staff on a patient-care unit have changed over the years through a process of evolution. The present methods used in hospitals for organizing nursing staff differ and often reflect major characteristics of patterns that have been popular in the past. These patterns are changing continually. Projections for future

patterns can be made by evaluating the best features of those used in the past. The following descriptions of major patterns used in hospitals over time indicate how stages of development have occurred to the present time.

Organization of Nursing Services

Historically, patterns of organizing nurses in the United States have paralleled changes in the country's social climate. Each era has influenced the development of change in the next era. The changes have occurred gradually and at different rates in different hospitals. For this reason it is possible to find features representative of each era in present organizational patterns.

SCHOOLS OF NURSING

Organization of nursing services in this country can be traced back to its founding. However, the first major development that continues to affect today's nursing began with the establishment of nursing schools in hospitals in the 1870s. At this time the Victorian era was on the decline, and women were becoming actively involved in providing service to others through organizations. Some of the first schools of nursing in the country were initiated by groups of women who cooperated with others in their communities to improve care for hospitalized patients.

These early schools brought young women into hospitals to learn the practice of nursing. The learning process was a combination of a few classes concerned with the basic elements of patient care and much clinical practice. For the most part, the students learned nursing by providing patient care under the supervision of graduate nurses. The students actually staffed the hospitals, and following graduation they were usually employed by families as "private-duty" nurses. Some nurses remained in hospitals to assume the roles of administrator, executive overseer, and teacher. These people formed the management structure for the nursing department.

Perhaps the greatest contribution to nursing resulting from the establishment of schools of nursing is the fact that students proved the value of having trained nurses provide care in hospitals. By proving their worth for improving patient care, they established a need for nursing in hospitals that has increased throughout the years. Today we assume that nurses are essential for the care of hospitalized patients.

The Case Method

The next era of change in organizing nursing patterns came about as a result of the depression of 1929. Few families could afford a live-in nurse during the depression, and many graduate nurses returned to the hospital to seek employment. From necessity they agreed to work for room and board. The influx of graduate nurses led many hospitals to close their schools because students were no longer needed to staff the hospital.

Nurses at this time were accustomed to using the case method for giving care. Practice in homes reinforced their concept that they should care for the complete needs of the patient. The large numbers of nurses living in the hospital made it possible for them to continue using the same method. This meant that every nurse was responsible for giving complete care to her own patients. Today this method is still used by students in schools of nursing. The student focuses attention on meeting the complete needs of a patient who is usually representative of a particular type of patient needs that the student is studying in class, A recreation of the case method is used increasingly in current practice and is termed primary nursing. It was formerly thought that this method was very expensive in terms of professional nurse salaries, but current data indicate that primary nursing is an economical pattern of care delivery.

The case method remained the most prevalent pattern for giving care in the hospital until World War II. In the interim, medical care gradually increased in complexity. The growth of private and public health insurance plans in conjunction with development of medical technology led to increasing numbers of patients entering hospitals for treatment. Increased use of hospitals ensured the continuing employment of nurses.

During the period prior to World War II the role of nurses expanded. The focus of nursing has always been to provide patient care. Nurses in early schools were concerned with providing comfort and a safe environment for patients. Care consisted of providing a clean environment with proper ventilation, bodily comfort, and nu-tritious diet. Nurses were responsible for the total scope of such activities as bathing patients, preparing and serving food, and clean-ing the patients' rooms.

As medical diagnosis and treatment became more complex, nurses retained their environmental care and comfort functions and took on new functions such as taking blood pressures and body temperatures and assisting in surgical procedures. The increasing sophistication of

patient care created a need for medically related areas of practice for provision of special patient services, such as x-ray and laboratory procedures.

Nurses gradually assumed increasing responsibility for coordinating the patient care provided by all medical personnel. This coordination required channeling patients to other departments of the hospital, requisitioning services and equipment, reporting to increasing numbers of personnel, and coping with desk work. The changes in patient care also broadened the supervisor's function of coordination of services, leaving less time for working with staff or direct patient contact.

The Functional Method

World War II provided impetus for the next major change in organizing nursing staff. Many nurses left hospitals to care for soldiers at the battlefront, and hospitals were staffed with volunteers, aides, and graduate nurses who remained at home. The numbers of graduate nurses were increased through plans, such as the Cadet Nursing Program, that enabled many young people to enter nursing.

To ensure better utilization of the large numbers of personnel with different educational preparation then employed to provide patient care, and to cope with the rapid expansion of the nurse's role due to medical developments resulting from the war, the functional pattern of organization was developed. In this method, functions were assigned to staff members in accordance with their preparation and abilities. The professional nurse assumed the functions of communicating with physicians, carding orders, giving direction to subprofessional staff members, administering medications, and giving treatments. Nurse's aides performed more technical care measures, such as taking temperatures and giving baths. Assigning tasks according to ability and education provided for efficiency during the time when professional nurses were scarce.

In the 1940s Licensed Practical Nurses achieved formal recognition so that there were legally two levels of prepared practitioners: the professional nurse and the practical or vocational nurse. Patient needs continued to be categorized in terms of functions of the nursing staff. In addition to being an efficient method, the functional pattern also ensured that personnel performed the tasks for which they were prepared with supervision from professional nurses.

The functional method is still employed in some hospitals, espe-

cially in situations in which there is a lack of professional staff. Some hospitals may use a different pattern for staff organization during the day shift, reverting to use of the functional pattern for the evening and night shifts.

One result of the functional pattern of assigning duties has been fragmentation of patient care. It is reasonable to assume that when staff members concentrate on meeting specific and segmented patient needs they become task-oriented. An example of a task-oriented nurse is the "medicine nurse" whose role is administering medications to all the patients day after day. When giving the medications, this nurse focuses on expediently carrying out the task rather than on the complete needs of the patient. When the functional method is used, efforts must be made to stimulate staff to develop a perspective of total patient needs rather than a limited view that relates only to their specific function.

The Team Method

Team nursing emerged as a solution to the problem created by fractioning patient care. The basis for the team pattern is the concept of democracy. Through the team, the talents and skills of nurse's aides, licensed practical nurses, and registered nurses are united in a group. Members of the group share in the care of a number of patients. Participation in group activities gives members an opportunity to develop their abilities to provide patient care.

RESPONSIBILITIES OF THE TEAM LEADER

Organization of staff members in the team pattern places great responsibility on the team leader. The leader must be able to influence members of the team and must be secure in the knowledge of patient care and in the ability to work with groups. The leader is responsible for planning and evaluating the patient care provided by all team members while simultaneously identifying and developing their nursing skills through group activities. Team members depend on the direction and guidance of their leader. It is most important that the leader have a concept of teamwork because this concept is a requisite for the effectiveness of the team pattern for organizing staff.

TEAM ACTIVITIES AS MANAGEMENT TECHNIQUES

The team nursing method includes a series of activites that are conducted with groups of team members. These activities are management techniques that enable the leader to provide for guidance

and growth of the team members. They include assignment conferences, patient-centered conferences, and development of nursing-care plans. Each has a specific purpose.

Assignment conferences provide an opportunity to impart information about patient care and can also be used as planning conferences in which staff members make decisions about how they will work together. Patient-centered conferences give staff members an opportunity to express feelings and attitudes, discuss patient needs, and define solutions to patient-care problems. Nursing-care plans provide for continuity of care. They are written statements of goals and objectives for care and summarize nursing measures that are used by all who care for patients. All team members participate in designing nursing-care measures appropriate to specific patient needs.

These management techniques promote communication among staff members and involve them in learning more about patient care through participation in planning and evaluating patient care. The differences in educational preparation and experience among staff members are minimized through group participation. The knowledge and skills of the professional nurses on the team are shared with subprofessionals through cooperation in giving care and through continued exchange of ideas.

These management techniques can become routines when used by a leader who does not incorporate the concept of teamwork in relationships with staff members. If staff members perceive them as nonproductive experiences, conducted only because it is so prescribed, they lose their value.

TEAM NURSING AS AN ATTITUDE
Team nursing is perhaps more an attitude than a method. This attitude is one of "participative democracy" in achieving goals. The following excerpt from a team leader's diary affords insight into the thoughts and feelings of the leader:

7:00 A.M.   Attended report given by the night nurse. We made rounds for the sickest patients, and the night nurse demonstrated use of the new chest suction apparatus for Mr. T.
7:30 A.M.   Updated assignments made yesterday—changed the assignment for Mrs. X., the nurse's aide, because the RN should take care of Mr. T., the new patient with chest tubes . . . I think I really made sure that team member's abilities were matched with patient needs.

8:00 A.M.	Conducted assignment conference. The new nurse's aide is getting the idea—she actually told me what she planned to do for Mr. J. today. I was pleased with the depth of her thinking! Also with the way she and the RN spontaneously planned how they would cooperate in caring for their patients—it is true that each needs the other's help. Everybody discussed specific goals for patient care for the day. . . . Also posed the problem: how can we better care for Mrs. S.? Such a difficult patient! Set time for a conference to discuss her care. Hope all the team members were well informed and stimulated. Made rounds—observed care given and talked to patients, to doctors, to therapists. Revised nursing-care plans!! Helped NA with Mrs. S. Talked with Mr. J. about his new diet. Helped LPN get Mr. R. up for the first time. Must decide what to do about Mrs. M.—gave her a bath as a way to evaluate her condition more fully and to get to know her.
11:30 A.M.	Lunch with the NA—had to find out what she thinks about her responsibilities! She hasn't really participated in a conference yet.
12:00	More patient care—little Mrs. S. is a challenge. Gave advice, clarified-taught-evaluated. Had to change the RN's assignment—admitted a *very* sick patient this afternoon. Helped NA write new ideas on Mrs. S.'s care plan.
2:00 P.M.	Had a good discussion about Mrs. S. at patient conference. Will explain the use of the new disposables tomorrow. Have to prepare a conference about continuity of care for next week—also have to dream up a project for the team. Maybe the group should do the dreaming!
2:20 P.M.	Mrs. S. again—hoped to get her settled—talked with her son and think he understands her care better now. Made out assignments for tomorrow—got organized for report too. One final check to make sure that everything is O.K.
3:00 P.M.	Gave report—P.M. nurse has some good ideas about Mrs. S. Together we will cure her. Our motto is continuity.
3:30 P.M.	End of a busy day—the team spirit is improving.

DIFFICULTIES RELATED TO TEAM MANAGEMENT

From this excerpt you can get an idea of the scope of the team leader's activities. Because of the many demands on the team leader's time, some of the management techniques, such as conferences, seem to be extraneous to the immediate needs of patients. When the team leader finds it difficult to conduct group activities, the team method loses some of its meaning for the staff.

Other potential drawbacks of the use of the team method for providing patient care are related to staffing. When the team leader

and team members change from day to day, the benefits of team nursing cannot be realized because team members must work together for a period of time if the concept of team nursing is to be useful. Have you heard nurses say, "How can you have a team with only two staff members?" or "The staff turnover rate is so great that the same nurses rarely work together," or "How can I conduct a conference when I'm supposed to admit all of those new patients and then give reports?"

OTHER PATTERNS FOR STAFF ORGANIZATION

The team concept can be applied to almost every pattern of staff organization. Other, similar patterns have been developed on the same basic premise as team nursing—that group interaction is beneficial for giving patient care. Some of these patterns are referred to as group care or cluster care. Like team nursing they organize groups of staff, including nurse's aides, licensed practical or vocational nurses, and registered nurses, for the purpose of providing patient care. The mix of nursing staff can vary in group or cluster care patterns. These patterns are different from team nursing in that the numbers of staff in a group or cluster are fewer and the numbers of patients are also reduced.

Primary Nursing Care

Primary nursing care, initiated at the University of Minnesota Hospitals in Minneapolis, Minnesota, is emerging as an organizational pattern for giving nursing care that meets criteria of quality care and job satisfaction. Primary nursing care is most similar to the case method in that it emphasizes the nurse's involvement in meeting the patient's total care needs. This pattern of care enables the primary nurse to form an in-depth relationship with the patient in providing care that involves the patient in decision-making.

THE PRIMARY NURSE ROLE

The underlying philosophy of primary nursing care is that the primary nurse provides comprehensive care that is continuous throughout the patient's stay in the hospital and during the phase immediately following hospitalization. The primary nurse has a caseload of primary patients and is autonomous in application of clinical nursing knowledge and skill in their care. The primary nurse is accountable for the processes and the outcomes of care for assigned patients. Patients are assigned to primary nurses on the basis of their needs

and the primary nurse's competencies. The primary nurse has 24-hour responsibility for these patients and the related needs of their families and is assisted in their care by associate nurses.

Among the activities included in the primary nurse's role are taking a nursing history on admission and sometimes conducting a physical examination. On the basis of data collected in this assessment and from the physician's plan for medical care, the primary nurse initiates the patient's nursing-care plan. The primary nurse cares directly for the patient during one shift and is assisted in the patient's care during the other two shifts by designated associate nurses. These associate nurses follow the nursing-care plan initiated by the primary nurse and contribute to it as needed. Assignments are consistent so that the same nurses care for the patient during his or her hospitalization. The primary nurse makes decisions about the patient's nursing care and coordinates the patient's care with other hospital personnel who contribute to the care. Primary nurses maintain a colleagueship with physicians in which the medical plan of care and the nursing plan are integrated. The primary nurse is directly responsible and accountable for the patient's care, and directs and coordinates care given by the associates.

ASSIGNMENTS IN PRIMARY NURSING
The types of assignments used for primary nursing vary [11, 12]. In some instances, the primary nurse has five or so primary patients. In other situations, the nurse may have two or three primary patients and may be an associate nurse for two or three other patients. Sometimes only selected patients have primary nurses. When this is the case, the remainder of the patients are cared for in groups by groups of staff, using a modified team or cluster care approach. Modular nursing has been developed in some settings to bridge the gap between team nursing and primary nursing [1, 8, 14].

MODULAR NURSING: A BRIDGE TO PRIMARY NURSING
Modular nursing is a modified form of team nursing in which a registered nurse and either a licensed practical nurse or a nurse's aide form a module to take care of a group of eight to ten patients. The licensed practical nurse or nurse's aide is assigned to the registered nurse, who plans, implements, and evaluates the patients' care and directs, guides, and supervises the care given by the LPN or aide. The ratio of patients for each module varies according to the acuity of the patient's condition and the shift time. Usually the ratio is higher during the night shift.

JOB DESIGN FOR PRIMARY NURSING MODELS

Primary nursing models incorporate principles of effective job design. Because primary nurses are able to follow through with all steps of the nursing process personally in caring for their patients they develop a sense of "ownership" or territory in their patient assignments. This pattern of care presents the nurse with a personal challenge to be competent, to apply knowledge and skill, to grow in clinical expertise, and to be accountable and responsible for the process and outcomes of care. The feedback from evaluation reflects directly on the care that the primary nurse has given.

Research conducted to determine effective job designs for professionals supports the importance of job challenge and accountability. Hall and Lawler's study of professional research and development personnel [5], for example, indicates that these professional workers considered working in-depth on a small number of projects to be more challenging than working on a number of different projects. The challenge and responsibility associated with in-depth involvement in a small number of projects led to high levels of job satisfaction, which in turn served to motivate the professionals to achieve high levels of performance. The results of this study illustrate why nursing staff members respond favorably to the primary nursing model.

Hall and Lawler also found that job pressure could be related to challenge. They define pressure as "experience of a particular force," which is different from conflict. Conflict is defined as "opposition of two or more pressures." The pressures they studied included internal pressure to be competent exerted by the professional and external pressure from the organization to produce quality performance. They considered these to be positive pressures since there was congruence between the internal pressure in the individual and the external pressure from the organization. The pressures these researchers found to be positive included not only satisfying needs but also dealing directly with budgetary control and relating directly with the client.

Hall and Lawler believe that the job design for the professional who has high needs to achieve and to be successfully competent should provide for stretching the employee's capabilities. The job design has to allow the professional to demonstrate competence, to visibly influence the environment, and to grow in professional competence. They postulate that when the professional is successfully competent, his or her needs are satisfied and this satisfaction leads to

continued effort. Hackman [4] writes that core job dimensions in job design are variety in skills, identity with the tasks, significance of the tasks, autonomy, and feedback. He has developed a model in which these job dimensions are shown to be related to the employee's "psychological state" in creating job satisfaction. The variety, identification, and significance of the work are related to the meaningfulness of the work for the individual while autonomy is related to the responsibility a person feels for the work. Knowledge of results of one's work or feedback is necessary for continued satisfaction. Primary nursing fulfills the criteria for meaningful work by providing for variety in giving care. When a nurse is assigned a caseload of primary patients this nurse identifies with the care given and believes that this care is significant. The primary nurse has more autonomy than team members, and also receives more direct feedback about the results of the work because of the direct nurse-patient relationship.

Nurses have a reputation for short tenure in staff nurse positions and for high mobility, which is possible because they can be employed in hospitals throughout the country to perform similar nursing-care functions [10]. Although nurses who are employed by hospitals are dependent on the hospital environment for supporting services and for the environment for giving nursing care, they do not necessarily have to have a strong identification with any given hospital to function. Because of the high costs of orientation and of turnover [9], efforts to make staff nursing positions more satisfying to nurses are worthwhile fiscally. If the performance of the staff nurses increases in quality, the organization benefits from their increased productivity and from the increased satisfaction of patients.

Primary nursing care has proved to be an effective job design for increasing staff nurses' satisfaction. It has also been demonstrated that primary nursing care increases patient satisfaction. Daeffler [3] demonstrated that patients perceived that they gained more information about their care, were taught about their care more fully, and experienced fewer omissions in care when the primary nursing care design was used. There are also many reports in the literature that substantiate these findings [1, 8, 12, 14]. In many instances, patients who have experienced primary nursing care have requested their primary nurse on return admissions to the hospital. These patients perceive that primary nursing care provides them with a care-giver who is also a teacher, a counselor, an advocate and a liaison between the patient and other health services and community health-care

agencies during hospitalization and following discharge. In some settings, the primary nursing model includes an extended care function for the primary nurse, who makes home visits and who maintains contact with the patient for solving care problems following discharge.

Organizational Implications of Primary Nursing

Primary nursing care has implications for the total hospital organization. To be effective, this model requires that the staff be professional. Some hospitals have phased out employment of nurse's aides when changing to primary nursing care. Marram [12] found that nurses who gave higher quality care were more idealistic and professional. This finding has also been demonstrated in other studies concerned with evaluating the effectiveness of primary nursing care.

CLINICAL NURSING EMPHASIS

Another implication primary nursing care has for the organization is that it focuses nursing activities on clinical nursing. Primary nursing care changes the head nurse's function, and it also changes the role of the head nurse and of staff nurses in procurement of supplies and services. Many authorities cite that it is important that there be a position such as a unit administrator or unit secretary to take over this type of function so that the nurses are free to give patient care. In the primary nursing care model, the primary nurses report to the head nurse, who is responsible for the delivery of all nursing care given on the unit. The head nurse is most effective in the primary care model if he or she is a competent behavioral model for primary nurses. A clinical specialist or a person with clinical expertise [1, 12] appears to be the most effective behavioral model.

PROFESSIONAL GROWTH

Primary care nurses become increasingly involved in developing their own clinical expertise. This motivation to continue learning requires that the head nurse assume a major role in day-to-day staff development and that continuing education programs based on a needs assessment of the nursing staff be provided. Increased involvement with patients and their families or significant others stimulates primary nurses to upgrade clinical knowledge and skills in interviewing, communication, methods for integrating families in patient care, patient teaching, and assessment. These nurses can

concentrate on clinical nursing care rather than on spending their time performing tasks or directing and supervising the care given by nonprofessional nursing staff.

COST EFFECTIVENESS

An important consideration in change implementation represented by the development of primary nursing care is the cost effectiveness of the new model. A number of studies have been conducted to compare the costs of primary nursing care with the costs of team nursing or of functional nursing [1, 11, 14]. There is increasing evidence that primary nursing care models do not cost more than the other two models. Even though primary nursing care requires increased numbers of professional nurses, savings can be realized because of many factors. Corpuz [1] cites the inefficient use of time by nurse's aides, whose functions are restricted to specific tasks; the costs of orientation, training, directing, and supervising nurse's aides by professional nurses; the associated overextension of professional nurses, who are responsible for both patient care and for directing and supervising care given by nonprofessionals; and the tendency of nurses to be task-oriented rather than patient-care oriented in the functional and team methods as reasons why primary nursing care is cost-effective.

PROFESSIONAL INNOVATION

Primary nursing care stimulates innovation by professional nurses because these nurses tend to identify with and "live" in the patient's world. As a result, the primary nurses are more aware of the patient's problems and assume an advocacy role in helping the patient to use health-care services effectively and to assume an active role in his or her own care. The primary nurses are not distracted by tasks or functions that are not directly related to their patients' care. The primary nursing care model is a form of decentralized organization in which decision-making is disseminated throughout the organization. For many nurses, changing from a bureaucratic organizational structure in a nursing department to such a decentralized structure is difficult. Techniques of change implementation discussed in Chapter 8 are usually necessary when the change to primary nursing care is made in a hospital. Many of these nurses not only have to change their fundamental role concept of nursing, but they also have to learn many of the human behavior skills that are required by the one-to-

one nurse-patient relationship that is the locus of primary nursing care.

EFFECTS OF CHANGE ON THE ORGANIZATION

When changing the pattern of care to a new one such as primary nursing care, it is necessary to involve others in the organization in the change. The administrators of the hospital, for example, often have to adapt to the primary care model by changing methods for supplying the patient-care units and for maintaining the patient-care unit environment. If these changes are to be made and made effectively, administrative personnel should be knowledgeable about the goals, methods, benefits and needs that primary nursing care will initiate.

Primary nursing care can be a stimulus to the development and maintenance of professional attitudes in a nursing department. To be effective, nurses have to accept the responsibility, accountability, and authority implied by primary nursing care. In addition, these nurses have to be supported by the organizational structure. There is a potential for conflict between the professionals and the organization, since innovation is an aspect of professionalization but not of bureaucratization [2, 6]. R. H. Hall [6] states that professionalization can take place within a bureaucratic structure if the structure provides for coordination and communication that facilitates the professional's performance. The potential for conflict between the two arises from differing interests in regard to the professional's goals, application of knowledge, the complexity of professional tasks, and the professional's need to control resources. When the organization allows professionals to perform complex tasks according to their specified body of knowledge and code of ethics, there need not be conflict.

Thus far the primary nursing care model has proved to be effective in many hospitals. As with any pattern of organization or job design, the specific requisites of the primary nurse's role vary among hospitals. It could be speculated that one of the reasons for the effectiveness of primary nursing care is that both nurses and patients are gaining more recognition. Nurses who are changing to the primary nursing care model gain recognition through the "halo" effects of the stimulation of being involved in change (Chap. 8). Patients receive greater recognition through the improved performance of the primary nurses that results from their increased motivation to be competent. These effects are desirable, since they promote innovation and increased quality.

EFFECTIVENESS OF VARIOUS CARE PATTERNS

There is, at this time, no universal "most desirable" pattern for giving nursing care because of the diversity in hospitals and the differences in availability of professional nurses in various regions of the country. All nurses can, however, use the best aspects of all patterns of care to devise a pattern that suits their situation. Primary nursing care, for example, uses some of the management techniques that are also part of team nursing activities, such as nursing-care plans, patient-centered conferences, and measures for continuity of care. Modular nursing also uses some of the concepts of team nursing, such as group interaction. It differs in the span of control for the leader; the modular leader relates to fewer staff and patients and thus concentrates on patient care more than on staff direction. These are two examples of how components of different patterns of care can be recombined to form new patterns.

Many nurses have become accustomed to working in groups through their experiences in team nursing, group nursing, or cluster-care patterns. There are certain advantages that can be gained by employees through group participation in care. Some of these will be discussed in the following chapter. There are also advantages to practicing nursing in an autonomous fashion with associates, such as in primary nursing care. Hackman has written that ". . . as yet there are no simple or generally accepted criteria for a well designed job . . . and it is not clear whether work should be structured to be performed by individuals or by a group of employees working together" [4]. How nurses best work together changes with their role perceptions and with the changing normative expectations of the times. One of the current changes taking place in nursing is the increased educational level for nurses who are becoming clinical specialists. This development, associated with expansion in nurses' roles will probably have a great impact on the future developments of patterns of giving care in hospitals.

Specialized Nursing Care

The expansion of the nurse's role has gained momentum since World War II. Because patient needs have become more definitive through rapid growth of specialized medical knowledge, nursing has become increasingly complex. New developments in organizing patient care in health-care agencies are evolving in relation to specialization in medical care and the rapid growth of medical technology.

Efficient hospital administration involves grouping similar services together in a common geographic location. Services can be categorized in several ways, such as according to phases of illness or types of disease. Progressive patient care categorizes services by phases of illness including intensive care, intermediate care, convalescent care, self-care, and home care. This is an example of arranging hospital services according to the special needs of patients. The establishment of care units for patients with specific phases of illnesses fosters specialization of nursing skills. Categorization of patient needs according to phases also enables nurses to specialize in care for patients with acute or chronic illnesses. Special care units give nurses the option of developing competencies in a given area of practice. Some nurses feel that this specialization generally results in personal involvement, growth, and job satisfaction.

Another way of categorizing patient services is by type or classification of illness. Coronary care, renal dialysis, and neurological care units are typical of special care units. These special units have given impetus to development of the nurse-clinical specialist who becomes knowledgeable about the medical technology and related nursing care in a specialty area. One can become a clinical specialist through experience in giving care on a specialized nursing unit or through advanced study of a clinical specialty in a graduate nursing program.

Job descriptions and interpretations of the roles of clinical specialists reflect variations in the way different nursing departments organize care. In some hospitals the clinical specialist serves as a consultant who guides and directs other nurses in giving patient care. In other hospitals the clinical specialist assumes management responsibilities similar to those of a supervisor. Yet other hospitals employ clinical specialists who concurrently give nursing care and teach students and those who care for patients only during the critical phases of illness or in periods of stress. These nurses' work schedules are often determined by the patients' needs for their expertise.

There are presently no universally accepted roles for the nurse-clinical specialists and no common patterns of care which include such specialists. The nursing profession is evolving in the development of increasing numbers of nurse practitioners functioning independently or in joint practice, in private practice, and in various types of health-care agencies. Future roles for nurses, while a matter of speculation, appear to be advancing toward more autonomous and professional expertise. Hall [7] illustrates this change in description

of new definitions of nursing practice in state statutes that regulate the practice of nursing.

Only recently have nurses begun to rid themselves of tasks inherent in the management of physical and material aspects on the patient-care unit. Ward secretaries are now trained to assist nurses by performing such tasks as transcribing orders, answering the phone, and relaying messages. Unit managers have been employed by many hospitals to take care of such management aspects of the unit as obtaining equipment and supplies and coordinating the functions of units with the total hospital operation. When these services are available, nurses are able to consider their roles in terms of managing direct patient care.

Nurses participate in activities for developing the changing health-care system in daily nursing practice. This participation requires that all medical personnel coordinate their efforts to prevent segmentation of care and to provide for continuous care. Nurses can become "change agents" in patient care and must control their own practice of nursing. This control must foster progressive change in patterns used to manage patient care.

Study Questions

1. A student gradually formulates a concept of the nurse's role when studying nursing. This concept is influenced by the instructor's expectations of students as well as by the behaviors of nurses who are practicing in the health-care agencies that employ nurses.
   a. Consider your own concept of nursing. How were you influenced by others in formulating your concept of nursing?
   b. How did patients and your friends influence your concept of nursing?
2. Compare the different methods of organizing the staff for giving patient care, drawing on your own experiences.
   a. Have you observed one particular method that seemed to work better than others?
   b. Compare this method to the pure methods of case, functional, team, or primary nursing. How is it the same? How does it differ? What factors in the hospital setting and what factors from the staff have contributed to the success of the method?
3. Interview four nurses from one patient-care unit about their philosophy of nursing practice. How does this philosophy affect patient care?
4. Describe changes in nursing practice that have occurred during the past five years.
   a. What forces created the need for change?
   b. How do you think individual practicing nurses respond to the changes?

5. Abstract three research studies that have been conducted about some phase of nursing practice.
   a. Do you think that practicing nurses have been influenced by these studies?
   b. Do you believe that these studies could be replicated in any nursing setting in a similar way to obtain the same results?
6. Describe four ways that you as a nurse-practitioner influence the organization of nursing service and the improvement of patient care.
7. Evaluate the following objectives:

Patients on bed rest will be provided with a clean, secure environment which protects the patient's safety and meets the patient's needs for comfort. This is accomplished by the following procedures:

(a) Use side rails or restraints (or both) for patients who are confused, comatose, or who have interferences with mobility.
(b) Place beds in low positions to reduce the danger of falling.
(c) Place clean towels, washcloths, soap, and powder in patients' bedside stands, and check the supply daily to ensure that supplies are readily available when needed.
(d) Give patients morning care, which includes elimination, washing hands and face, brushing teeth, combing hair, and other preparation the patient desires for comfort.
(e) Give baths when necessary.
(f) Give passive exercises to patients twice a day for complete range of motion unless contraindicated.
(g) Change patients' positions every two hours.
(h) Place a patient's belongings within reach and remove unnecessary articles from the bedside stands.

   a. Are these objectives clearly stated?
   b. Do these objectives specify a standard of nursing care?
   c. What level of nursing staff (RN, LPN, NA) will find these objectives most useful?

References

1. Corpuz, T.   Primary nursing meets needs, expectations of patients and staff. *Hospitals* 51:95, June 1, 1977.
2. Corwin, R. G.   Patterns of organizational conflict. *Adm. Sci. Q.* 14:507–520, Dec. 1969.
3. Daeffler, R. J.   Patients' perception of care under team and primary nursing. *J. Nurs. Adm.* 5:20–26, 1975.
4. Hackman, J. R.   The Designing Work for Individuals and Groups. In J. R. Hackman, E. E. Lawler, and L. W. Porter, *Perspectives on Behavior in Organizations.* New York: McGraw-Hill, 1977. Pp. 242–256.

5. Hall, D. T., and Lawler, E. E.   Job characteristics and pressures and the organizational integration of professionals. *Adm. Sci. Q.* 15:271–281, Sept. 1970.
6. Hall, R. H.   Professionalization and bureaucratization. *Am. Sociol. Rev.* 33:92–103, Feb. 1968.
7. Hall, V. C.   *Statutory Regulation of the Scope of Nursing Practice.* Chicago: The Joint Practice Commission, 1975. Pp. 11–35.
8. Hegyvary, S. T. (Ed.)   Symposium on primary nursing. *Nurs. Clin. North Am.* 12:185–186, June 1977.
9. Kase, S., and Swenson, B.   *Costs of Hospital-Sponsored Orientation and Inservice Education for Registered Nurses.* USPHS DHEW HRA (77-25) BHM, Division of Nursing, Nov. 1976.
10. Levine, H. D., and Phillip, P. J.   *Factors Affecting Staffing Levels and Patterns of Nursing Personnel.* USPHS DHEW HRA (75-6) BHRD, Division of Nursing, Feb. 1975.
11. Marram, G. D., Flynn, K., Abaravich, W., and Carey, S.   *Cost-Effectiveness of Primary and Team Nursing.* Wakefield, Mass.: Contemporary Publishing, 1976.
12. Marram, G. D., Schlegel, M. W., and Bevis, O.   *Primary Nursing: A Model for Individualized Care.* St. Louis: Mosby, 1974.
13. Nenner, V. C., Curtis, E. M., and Eckoff, C. M.   Primary nursing. *Superv. Nurse,* 8:14–16, May 1977.
14. Werner, J.   The Evanston story: The primary nursing story comes alive. *Nurs. Adm. Q.* 1:9–50, Spring 1977.

Suggested Reading

Abel-Smith, B.   *A History of the Nursing Profession.* Atlantic Highlands, N.J.: Humanities Press, 1975.
Anderson, B. E.   *Nursing Education in Community Junior Colleges.* Philadelphia: Lippincott, 1966.
Bartels, D., Good, V., and Lampe, S.   The role of the head nurse in primary nursing. *Can. Nurse* 74:26–30, March 1977.
Bliss, A. A., and Cohen, E. D. (Eds.)   *The New Health Professionals.* Germantown, Md.: Aspen, 1977.
Brown, B.   The autonomous nurse and primary nursing. *Nurs. Adm. Q.* 1:31–36, Fall 1976.
Brown, E. L.   *Nursing Reconsidered: A Study of Change.* Parts 1 and 2. Philadelphia: Lippincott, 1971.
Bullough, B., and Bullough, V.   *Expanding Horizons for Nurses.* New York: Springer, 1977.
Campbell, E. B.   The clinical nurse specialist: Joint appointee. *Am. J. Nurs.* 3:543–546, 1970.
Davis, F.   *The Nursing Profession: Five Sociological Essays.* New York: Wiley, 1966.
Deloughery, G. L.   *History and Trends in Professional Nursing* (8th ed.). St. Louis: Mosby, 1977.

Drexler, A., Yenney, S. L., and Hohman, J.   OD: Coping with change. *Hospitals* 51:58–60, Jan. 1, 1977.

Drexler, A., Yenney, S. L., and Hohman, J.   OD: An ongoing program. *Hospitals* 51:89–92, Feb. 16, 1977.

Dubos, R.   *Man, Medicine and Environment.* New York: Praeger, 1968.

Ellis, B.   Nursing profession undergoes intensive scrutiny and adjustment. *Hospitals* 51:139–144, April 1, 1977.

Farrell, N. L., and LaCosta, C. J.   Unit administration updated. *Hospitals* 51:75–77, Feb. 16, 1977.

Felton, G.   Increasing the quality of nursing care by introducing the concept of primary nursing: A model project. *Nurs. Res.* 24:27–32, Jan./Feb. 1975.

Finer, H.   *Administration and the Nursing Services.* New York: Macmillan, 1952.

Georgopoulos, B. S., and Christman, L.   The clinical nurse specialist: A role model. *Am. J. Nurs.* 5:1030, 1970.

Goostray, S.   *Memoirs: Half a Century in Nursing.* Boston: Nursing Archive, Boston University Mugar Memorial Library, 1969.

Hall, M. B.   How do students learn on a primary nursing care unit. *Nurs. Outlook* 25:370–373, June 1977.

Hunnings, V.   If you've ever thought about being a nurse-practitioner. *R.N.* 40:35–38, May 1977.

Jennings, C. P.   Primary care and the question of obsolescence. *JPN and Mental Health Services* 15:9–17, Jan. 1977.

Jones, D. C., Cooley, P. C., Miedema, A., and Hartwell, T. D.   *Trends in RN Supply.* DHEW Publication No. HRA 76-15, Bethesda, Md., March 1976.

Lawrence, R. R.   How to deal with resistance to change. *Harvard Bus. Rev.* 1:4, 1969.

Levine, E.   What do we know about nurse practitioners? *Am. J. Nurs.* 77:1799–1803, Nov. 1977.

Littlejohn, C. E.   From staff nurse to supervisor: A plan of development. *Nurs. Outlook* 24:618–621, Oct. 1976.

Mackay, C., and Ault, L. D.   A systematic approach to individualizing nursing care. *J. of Nurs. Adm.* 7:39–48, Jan. 1977.

Mackenzie, R. A.   The management process in 3-D. *Harvard Bus. Rev.* 6:67, 1969.

Mager, R.   *Preparing Instructional Objectives* (2nd ed.). Palo Alto: Fearon Publishers, 1975.

Miller, M. H., and Flynn, B. C.   *Current Perspectives in Nursing Social Issues and Trends.* St. Louis: Mosby, 1977.

Notter, L. E., and Spaulding, E. K.   *Professional Nursing Foundations, Perspectives, and Relationships.* (9th ed.) Philadelphia: Lippincott, 1976.

Oda, D. S.   Specialized role development: A three-phase process. *Nurs. Outlook* 25:374–377, June 1977.

Ojeda, M.   Primary nursing for shortened stay surgical patients. *Superv. Nurse* 7:42, Sept. 1976.

Olesen, V. L., and Whittaker, E. W. *The Silent Dialogue.* San Francisco: Jossey-Bass, 1968.

Redman, B. K. *The Process of Patient Teaching in Nursing* (3rd. ed.). St. Louis: Mosby, 1976.

Rosen, G. *A History of Public Health.* New York: M.D. Publications, 1958.

Schweer, J. E. *Creative Teaching in Clinical Nursing* (2nd ed.). St. Louis: Mosby, 1972.

Simon, H. A. *Administrative Behavior.* New York: Macmillan, 1957.

Sulz, H. A., Zielezny, M., and Kinyon, L. *Longitudinal Study of Nurse Practitioners, Phase I.* USDHEW PHS HRA (76-43), March 1976.

Survey of perceived relationships between chief operating officers and directors of nurses. *Hosp. Top.* 55:38–40, March/April 1977.

The status of continuing education—voluntary and mandatory. *Am. J. Nurs.* 77:410–416, March 1977.

Vollmer, H. M., and Mills, D. L. *Professionalization.* Englewood Cliffs, N.J.: Prentice-Hall, 1966.

Walker, V. H. *Nursing and Ritualistic Practice.* New York: Macmillan, 1967.

Winstead-Fry, P. The need to differentiate a nursing self. *Am. J. Nurs.* 77:1452–1454, Sept. 1977.

4. Group Leadership in Nursing Management

All nurses are managers by virtue of their professional status. They manage patient care wherever they work—as school nurses, as industrial nurses, or as hospital staff nurses. Whether the nurse works alone or with others, the dimension of management is present in the work situation. The nurse works in a social climate in which both the care process and the management process require leadership and working with groups. Both of these topics, leadership and working with groups, will be explored in this chapter.

Leadership in the Organizational Structure

Health-care agencies vary considerably in the way nursing staffs are organized. Nurses are often given management responsibilities that include management both of patient care and of personnel with less educational preparation, such as licensed practical or vocational nurses and nurse's aides. In some agencies this dual role is well defined for the nursing staff. In others there may be no definite structure that delineates the scope of managerial responsibility.

Consider the patient-care units in hospitals you are familiar with. Do these units have appointed team leaders or their equivalents? Or do the units have rotating team leaders so that the responsibilities of managing are given to different persons on different days? Are management functions the sole responsibility of the head nurse? Or are clinical specialists given responsibility for managing patient care? You may be able to cite different organizational structures among different hospitals and in the same hospital.

Functions required of nurses for managing people are determined to some extent by organizational structures, the number of nurses employed to care for a given number of patients, by the qualifications (both experience and education) of the staff members, and by the supporting staff employed for a unit, such as ward or unit managers.

True management of patient care by a leader is possible only if he or she fills an appointed position. This management implies working toward long-term goals. In order to achieve the goals of patient care over a period of time, one must work consistently with people and

the resources through a process of growth and expansion toward achieving. Demands for creative and innovative nursing can be met only by continual application of the management process.

What happens if there is no designated manager in the organizational structure? When nurses rotate in management positions, the staff expends energy adapting to the style of management employed by each different person. Managers tend to focus on events that occur during their time as managers. When this period is just one or two days, it is difficult not only to determine long-range goals but also to concentrate on achieving such goals. The short-term manager places emphasis on daily events rather than on the growth of staff members over time. The manager by the day is actually a troubleshooter rather than a progressive planner.

DEVELOPMENT OF THE STUDENT NURSE AS A MANAGER

The variability among health-care agencies and their expectations of nurses makes it confusing for a beginning nurse to define clearly what a nurse-manager's role ought to be. The beginning nurse is also going through one of the most difficult career transitions—that of becoming a manager. Although student nurses gradually assume the stature required of nurses for managing patient care in their educational programs, they often find that functioning as an employee in the work situation is quite different from being a student in a guided learning experience.

Students first learn management through learning how to organize the very basic aspects of patient care, such as giving baths, ambulating patients, providing for proper diet, and giving medications. As the student progresses through the educational program, more complex functions are mastered so that eventually the student can successfully care for a critically or chronically ill patient, managing many different but related events which affect the patient. Educational programs are developed sequentially to broaden the nurse's scope of knowledge about patient care. During the educational process the student becomes increasingly confident of his or her ability to handle difficult situations. And yet, it is normal for a student to feel confident about student experiences but insecure about the expectations of employment as a registered nurse. Despite the fact that the basic expectations of patients for nursing care are no different for the student than for the graduate, the student often perceives that this scope of functions has changed overnight following graduation.

A "first job" as a registered nurse is a new and different experience. A beginning nurse perceives employment as a challenge or test of competency. The challenge can be met with either anticipation, apprehension, or both, depending on one's degree of self-confidence.

One major difference between being a student and being employed is that the beginning nurse is expected to assume a leadership position in the work situation and to interact with all personnel as a professional nurse who influences the behavior of others. Responsibilities in this interaction are inherently different from those required of a student. The student usually focuses on the health care of a particular patient or a small group of patients; as an employee, the graduate nurse is part of an organization and must focus on both patient care and working with the staff.

LEADERSHIP ABILITIES

What is the difference between being a leader and being a manager? Leadership is closely associated with management. Every manager does not necessarily have to be a leader. In nursing, however, where the work is accomplished by working with people, leadership is emphasized as a necessary qualification of nurse-managers. Defining leadership as the ability to influence the behavior of others is an oversimplification because leadership depends on the leader, the group being led, and the situation in which leadership takes place.

Compare two leaders: Mary is a good nurse who can be described as essentially task-oriented—that is, she pays attention to detail and is precise in carrying out the tasks of nursing; she likes structure and functions best in a well-defined situation with definite tasks to perform. Jane, on the other hand, is restless and thrives on change; she also is a good nurse and prefers situations which are unstructured so that she can make decisions that are flexible. Each of these leaders presents a different personality. Mary will be a successful leader in a structured situation that defines her role, whereas Jane would not be a successful leader in a structured situation—she would probably try to change the structure to meet her need for variety and change. Similarly, Mary would not be considered a good leader in an unstructured situation.

FACTORS AFFECTING SELECTION OF A LEADER

As you can see, leadership is effective if the leader's personality and abilities are matched to the requirements of a given situation. Be-

cause health-care agencies are variable in their philosophies, structures, and concomitant expectations for nurses, what constitutes a good leader for one might not for another. For this reason, the leadership abilities of a given nurse must be considered in relation to the needs of the situation.

Because leadership is so important to management in nursing, the choice of an appointed manager often depends on an individual's leadership abilities. These abilities can include the nurse's knowledge of patient care, natural or acquired leadership abilities, and familiarity with the organization. The importance of each of these factors in choosing a manager depends on the particular situation. Let us explore each separately.

Knowledge is often called a corollary of power. In nursing, knowledge enables the nurse to make decisions that other staff members may not be qualified to make or may be hesitant to make for themselves. The nurse with the most nursing expertise tends to be recognized by the group as a natural leader in matters related to making decisions about patient care. This is evidenced when staff members who need support or assistance in giving such care seek help from the nurse with the most knowledge. This nurse is often appointed to a formal leadership position when expertise is the most important criterion.

Natural or acquired leadership abilities are usually evidenced by the nurse's ability to work cooperatively with other staff members. This person tends to emerge as a natural leader because he or she can influence the behavior of others through personality. This type of leader can make others feel understood and important, usually has a good sense of humor, and can make other people feel satisfied with themselves and accepted by the group. The ability to work well with others is an important criterion for selection of a leader when group cohesiveness is a primary factor in the choice.

Familiarity with the organization is important for a leader in situations that require knowledge of the organization's policies and procedures. Although nurses adjust to the expectations of an organization at different rates, they are usually not secure in their understanding of the working relationships in an organization until they have worked there for some time. In situations in which the leader must be familiar with the operating policies of the organization, the nurse with tenure is usually appointed to the leadership position. Some organizations traditionally promote from "within the ranks" rather than selecting people from the "outside" for leadership positions.

INTERACTION WITH GROUP MEMBERS

Another, perhaps more complicated way of exploring leadership of nurses centers on the role of the nurse in interaction with all persons involved in giving patient care. These people include the patient, family or friends, the nursing staff, and other medical personnel, who contribute to patient care. The nurse-manager's interaction influences the effectiveness of patient care, which depends on coordination of the efforts of many persons. Being able to influence a group is a function of leadership.

CLASSIFICATION OF INTERACTING GROUPS

Fiedler [1] has classified the leader's interaction with group members according to the amount of power and influence a leader exerts in an organization. His classification of interacting groups includes three factors: (1) position power, (2) the structure of the task, and (3) the interpersonal relationship between the leader and group members. His theory can be adapted to nursing leadership.

Position Power. The first factor cited, position power, can be related to the nurse's sanctioned role for giving patient care. The knowledge which qualifies the nurse to become a professional gives the nurse the authority to be a leader in the nurse-patient relationship. If the patient accepts the position power of the nurse, it can be said that the nurse has high position power. However, if the patient's perception of the status and role expectations of the nurse negates the nurse's authority, the nurse has low position power in the nurse-patient relationship.

An appointed manager is given a legitimate position in an organizational structure. When a nurse is appointed to the position of team or modular leader, for example, that nurse is given authority for leading a group of staff members by the organization. This appointed position gives the nurse power to guide, direct, and control the activities of staff members. The amount of power given the leader to control staff activities affects the interaction between the staff and the leader. The group tends to comply with the leader's direction when the position is supported by organizational authority. For example, if the staff knows that the leader's evaluation of a staff member's performance is important when salary increases are considered, that leader will probably have high position power.

Position power in an organization must also be associated with the leader's ability to gain the group's cooperation. A leader's position power is visibly lower when staff members do not accept the leader.

Position power can give only formal authority. In an organization this formal authority can be negated if informal leaders exert more influence on the group than does the appointed leader.

Structure of the Task. When a group of people are involved in performance of work, the second factor in the classification system, the structure of the task, is important. The total task of administering patient care can be viewed as all of the work that must be accomplished to achieve the purpose of health care. The work of giving patient care is often divided among the many leaders. Tasks assigned to leaders encompass defining goals, organizing care, activating the care plans, controlling care given, and evaluating the work. Because these tasks are broad and general, they are complex and unstructured.

In comparison, nurse's aides are assigned the technical aspects of patient care that are well defined and can be structured. The need for task structure decreases as the staff member's knowledge, experience, and sanctioned authority increase. Tasks for a licensed practical nurse require less structure than those for a nurse's aide. A registered nurse requires less task structure than the licensed practical nurse. The ability to understand concepts and to make decisions are important criteria in determining the structure required for group members.

In nursing, the leader's tasks vary according to the capabilities of staff members. If the staff includes nurse's aides, licensed practical or vocational nurses, and a few professional nurses, the leader's tasks will include making detailed, clearly stated, and well-structured assignments. These assignments must be more definitive and must be accompanied by support and guidance because the needs of the staff members are more specific. The leader in this instance assumes the major responsibility for defining and helping others work toward achieving long-term goals.

When the nursing staff comprises more professional nurses than subprofessionals, the tasks must be assigned so that the professional nurses have an opportunity to use their conceptual abilities for defining and directing patient care. Tasks for professional staff members are broader, more general, more flexible, and unstructured. In this instance, the leader's tasks also are unstructured and complex, and would probably revolve around provision for continuing growth for staff members, development of methods for group decision-making, and participation in defining and achieving long-term goals for improvement of patient care.

Interaction of the Leader with Staff Members. In both situations just described, interaction is important. When working with nonprofessionals, the interaction depends on the leader's ability to define expectations in specific terms, to give specific directions, and to provide support, encouragement, and assistance in giving patient care. In comparison, the leader's interaction with a professional staff is based on the leader's ability to allow each person freedom to practice nursing autonomously according to his or her prerogative for giving care while coordinating the efforts of all staff members for achieving goals of patient care.

These differences in interaction stem from the fact that professionals share a common knowledge of patient care and have the same social sanction and legal authority for giving care. The major difference between professional nurse staff members and the professional nurse-leader is the leader's organizational authority. Professionals do not depend on the leader to direct the giving of patient care. When working with professionals, therefore, the leader must exert a positive influence toward their work satisfaction and development as practitioners. The leader of a group of subprofessional staff members must exert positive influence toward their growth and satisfaction but also exerts more control over the activities of the group in the performance of the work. Certain aspects of nursing care can be broken down into procedures and routines that can be assigned with specificity and that can be performed effectively by persons who do not fully understand the implications of their work. However, this can be accomplished only if the leader provides professional direction and makes decisions about care.

Acceptance of the leader by the group is paramount. The leader who is appointed to a position and who is capable of handling the complex tasks required of a leader must also be accepted by group members to be effective. Acceptance by group members is augmented by the formal appointment of the leader by the organization, because it implies that the organization will support the leader's authority by defining the role expectations of the leader and by supporting the leader's decisions as he or she functions in the designated role.

Recognition of this authority is sometimes demonstrated by patients who ask for the head nurse or supervisor when they have questions because they know that these persons have more authority than other staff members. These patients believe that the head nurse or supervisor has more knowledge and more power to "get things done." In a similar manner the physician might tell a modular leader

about a specific patient's care because the leader has the responsibility and authority to direct other staff members in the patient's care. The physician believes that the leader will make sure that the staff understands the communication. Communications directed to the leader from all sources in the work situation increase the leader's information and understanding of events related to patient care so that decisions will be more effective. This information is necessary for coordination of staff members' work.

Can you remember the first time you were a team or modular leader? Did staff members tell you about the progress of their patients' care and about the problems they were having? Did you find that as an appointed leader you were the recipient of much information you might not have received otherwise? Because of this flow of information to the appointed leader, one often hears the comment "I really like to be leader because I get to know what is going on," or "I did not realize that being a leader was so involved." These comments demonstrate the fact that people in an organization tend to follow patterns of behavior and prescribed pathways for communication. They accept appointed leaders because they have definite role expectations of appointed leaders.

LEADERSHIP STUDIES

The fact still remains that some leaders are more effective than others. What are the attributes of successful leaders? Over the years, many people have attempted to define leadership, but a clear definition of leadership remains elusive. Early leadership studies were concerned with attempts to isolate characteristics or traits that leaders have in common. One of the problems of using this approach is that the findings of one study often cannot be replicated in others. Leaders who have been studied do not demonstrate common or consistent traits or characteristics. However, a few characteristics do seem to be applicable to most leaders. For example, studies conducted by the University of Minnesota indicate that leaders are highly motivated, tend to be more educated than others, and are more intelligent [8]. Ghiselli [2] has recently found that leaders tend to be independent, be involved in activities, like intensive thinking, enjoy working with others as leader, and take some risks. It is interesting to note that people can have many different types of personalities and yet still have these characteristics.

Studies that approached leadership from the aspect of leader behaviors followed early research concerned with leadership traits. The

classic Ohio State University studies [7, 9] were concerned with defining the types of leadership behaviors and their effects on workers' performance and level of satisfaction. Two independent factors of leader behavior that were found to increase both performance and satisfaction are consideration and initiating structure. Consideration behaviors include trust, respect, friendship, and warmth. Initiating structure behaviors refer to the leader's ability to define and to accomplish the work through others.

Another classic set of studies was conducted by theorists at the University of Michigan [6]. Results of these studies indicate that the higher producing leaders spend more time planning and less time conducting task operations and that they give workers more latitude. Two of these theorists, Katz and Kahn [6], also demonstrated that supervisors used different styles, close supervision and general supervision. General supervision, in which workers are allowed more latitude, was thought to be more effective. Other research studies have indicated, however, that close supervision can also result in increased productivity in certain situations.

A number of studies have been conducted to investigate the influence of the situation on leadership. These studies include Fiedler's contingency theory [1]. This theory was developed retrospectively from accumulated data, and some experts feel that this method is not highly credible. The contingency theory developed by Fiedler is useful, however, in describing leadership. The contingency theory indicates that the effects of leadership are contingent on group outcomes. The leader behaviors are effective if the worker's performance achieves the desired outcomes. In this theory, the leader's needs, the nature of the work group, and the situation are considered to be interrelated in determining the effectiveness of the leader in achieving performance outcomes.

The path-goal theory of leadership initially authored by House [4] is somewhat similar to Fiedler's theories. This theory was also developed from retrospective evaluation of data. The path-goal theory includes four major styles of leadership: directive, supportive, participative, and achievement-oriented. The leader is viewed as one who supplements the work environment by providing aspects such as guidance, support, and rewards that are not otherwise present in the environment. This theory takes into account the nature of the situation, the worker's needs and goals, and the leader's ability to use power and to stimulate motivation.

The path-goal theory of leadership is based on the concept that

workers will be motivated to accomplish the work if they believe that their efforts will lead to rewards and that rewards will be given for effort. The basis for the worker's motivation includes a number of factors: the worker's internal satisfactions, which are related to self-actualization; the external satisfactions provided by the organization, such as status and pay; the clarity of goals that indicate what is expected; and clear statements of the rewards that will be achieved. An effective leader "clears the path" to goal achievement by removing impediments in the worker's path, by clearly defining the path, by providing rewards throughout the work cycle to foster continued worker motivation, and by ensuring that effort is rewarded as the worker expected by giving rewards for achievement.

Another approach to the study of leadership is to define the functions of leadership that are required to maintain the workers and to promote productivity. Two types of functions, expressive and instrumental, have been defined. Expressive functions are geared to the social and emotional aspects of the workers' interaction and are geared toward "maintaining" the workers. Instrumental functions are task-oriented, such as providing resources and defining tasks that are necessary for production of work. It has been postulated that one person cannot always perform both instrumental and expressive functions effectively since the focus of these two functions is quite different. It could be that one person is required to maintain the work group and another to ensure performance.

As studies of leadership have evolved, there is increasing evidence that organizational behavior is complex and that different types of leaders can be equally effective. Since there is no clear definition of leadership, the beginning leader often develops a leadership style through trial and error, learning through experiences. The beginning leader will probably be most effective if he or she accepts the role of "leader" and then develops a style of leadership that is an expression of his or her personality.

Working with Groups

There are many instances in which certain types of work in nursing are accomplished in groups. Participation in groups enables people to use their leadership talents through interaction with other group members. The leader who works with groups can use this interaction to develop competency of group members and to stimulate their motivation to produce. Gibb [3] has written that ". . . viewed in

relation to the individual, leadership is not an attribute of the personality but a quality of his role within a particular and specified social system." When people become involved in groups they take on roles within the group. These roles are factors in the effectiveness of the group interaction and personalities of members are subsumed to these roles. In the following section we will explore some characteristics of groups in the work situation.

PURPOSE AND PROCESS OF GROUP INTERACTION

Groups of people work together in organizations to accomplish work. In nursing, certain patterns of care delivery, such as team nursing or modular nursing, use job designs in which groups are an integral part of the design. Groups are also used in management for a number of different purposes. Task forces and project groups are examples of specially assigned groups that serve a particular purpose. Committees are another example of how groups are used in organizations to coordinate effort and to promote communication. These committees can be standing committees or ad hoc committees that deal with matters important to the organization.

Nurses also work in groups to give patient care. These groups may include other nurses, medically related personnel such as doctors and therapists, and the patient, family, or friends who participate in the care-giving process. These people may meet in conferences to plan care, evaluate care, solve operational problems, coordinate functions of a number of different people, and develop new ideas about care delivery. Groups may be used for providing instruction for staff or for patients. Interaction of people in groups is an aspect of working with others in an organization. Groups provide a medium through which some of the work of an organization is accomplished.

Groups can have many different purposes, but the processes of group interaction follow a sequence: developing strategy, setting goals, working out problems, defining methods for achieving goals, implementing the group decisions, and terminating the activity. Every group is different not only because purposes are different, but also because the group membership is different. To be effective in leading a group, the leader clearly defines the purpose of the group, determines the qualifications and concomitant contributions of the members, and applies concepts of group process to developing effective interaction among members.

Let us consider some concepts of group process that can be applied to working with a group of staff nurses. If the group works together

continuously, group process can be used to promote learning so that staff members increase knowledge and competency in giving patient care through group interaction. A stable and cohesive group of staff members can promote growth through continuous participation in progressively more complex group activities. This growth is enhanced by stability of group membership. When staff members shift from group to group, long-term group activities are thwarted. Have you experienced attending a group meeting one week in which the members organized, defined purposes and goals, and approved group decisions, returning the following week to find new members whose ideas completely changed decisions made at the first meeting? This experience illustrates how shifting group membership thwarts progress toward goal achievement by group members.

Groups deal with both content and process. The content is the purpose of the group or the group's task structure. The process is the way that the group members interact with each other in dealing with the content. Staff members often use the group process to meet individual needs, and the leader who recognizes these individual needs can foster group interaction that enables members to meet their own needs while also accomplishing the group tasks. The leader's task is to prevent loss of effort expended in process so that the group will be productive in accomplishing its tasks.

MOTIVATION TO JOIN A GROUP
An initial activity that helps the group leader recognize individual needs of members is to find out why each member has become part of the group. Answers to questions such as Why is Betty working as a nurse's aide? or Why does Bonnie travel an hour each day to work when she could be employed as a licensed practical nurse in a hospital much closer to her home? or Why has Rita elected to work in this particular unit? often give the leader clues to the staff member's basic motivation to working in the organization. This motivation influences the level of the worker's involvment in the staff's group activities for improving patient care.

The leader uses this information about the staff member's motivation to structure group tasks. If the staff is highly motivated to achieve the group purposes, the leader can immediately structure the tasks to achieve these purposes. If the members are not highly motivated to achieve group tasks, however, the leader structures the group tasks in such a way that the members' personal interests are challenged. Initial tasks for this group can be centered on improving

some aspect of the work situation that involves all of the members. Successful completion of a task such as arranging coffee-break times helps the group members to develop a sense of "ownership" for group membership that will help the leader introduce tasks geared to improving patient care.

Forming a cohesive group contributes to the productivity of a group. Ivancevich, Szilagyi, and Wallace [5] cite factors that increase group cohesiveness as "(1) agreement on group goals, (2) frequency of interaction, (3) personal attractiveness, (4) intergroup competition, and (5) favorable evaluation." Common goals serve to bind the group members together and frequency of interaction also promotes a feeling of closeness. When group members enjoy working with one another, are in competition with other groups, and when they perceive that their performance as a member of a group is rewarded, cohesiveness is increased. On the other hand these authors cite "disagreement on goals, large groups, unpleasant group experiences, competition within the group, and domination of one or more group members" as factors that decrease cohesiveness. The group leader can also develop a sense of trust among group members by clearly defining their roles. The leader outlines the boundaries of group decision-making and informs the members of the degree of authority and freedom they have in developing group activities. This authority and freedom stem from the organizational policies and structure, as well as from the capabilities of the group members. In defining the latitude for decision-making, the group leader must discern the level of task that the group members can realistically handle. Definition of roles and of the latitude the group has for decision-making reduces confusion and helps the group focus on the group tasks.

Acceptance of Group Members. Another way the leader contributes to group members' security is through acceptance of each person in the group. Acceptance can be demonstrated when the leader seeks information and opinions from group members and then visibly uses the information. Courtesy and respect for others can be sensed by group members, and this influences their response to the leader. Thus, the leader sets the tone for group interaction. Members usually want to be accepted not only by the leader but also by others in the group. Positive relationships among group members contribute to the effectiveness of the group. Knowledge that members accept an individual, even though that person's ideas are not always accepted, enhances the member's security in the group.

Group members' needs to achieve vary, and their requirements for help from one another when giving patient care also vary. Staff members can attain need satisfaction by participating in group activities and can share expertise and assistance in giving care with other group members.

EFFECTIVE GROUP INTERACTION

The need for acceptance by others may have to be dealt with before an individual can participate in a group. The leader's recognition of individual differences, encouragement of freedom of expression, and support for all staff members set the tone for interaction. How does the leader accomplish all of this? How do group members contribute to this? Let us consider a group:

Mary, Ruby, Bonnie, and Sam are meeting to discuss a particular patient's care. Mary cannot concentrate because she is bothered by the way Bonnie slumps in her chair. Mary finally tells Bonnie that her "slumping posture" bothers her. Mary then feels better, even though Bonnie may not change her position. Bonnie can react to Mary's comment in a number of ways. If she is secure in the group, she may respond with a laughing comment. She may even attempt to sit up. If she is not secure, she will probably react with a defensive comment, or she might withdraw from participation in the group.

In the situation just described, the leader may intervene by commenting that Bonnie may slump, but she really knows a lot about the particular patient's medications. More secure members of the group may also intervene. They may in a future meeting make a point of talking openly about individual differences in an effort to demonstrate to Mary that other members are accepted despite their personal idiosyncrasies. Openness about individual differences can be an adjunct to group participation. Familiarity with an object or a person, unless that object or person is continually fear-provoking, usually increases one's security.

Encouragement of Free Expression. Understanding of one another also fosters free expression for group members. The leader who allows free expression can determine how staff members perceive nursing and how they view their roles in giving patient care by interpreting what they say. Expressing ideas gives group members an opportunity to get acquainted with one another and with the leader. How does the leader allow free expression?

First of all, the leader must be both a good listener and patient. Let us say that in a group meeting Ruby makes a statement that the leader knows is incorrect. Instead of saying, "No, Ruby, you are wrong," the leader should wait to hear what other members of the group say. Mary, for example, may agree with Ruby, but Sam and Bonnie may explain why the statement is incorrect. When the correct definition emerges from group discussion, this definition is accepted more readily by all group members. Usually, if given freedom, the group will arrive at the right definition, because people can change their opinions and ideas through discussion. The leader should intervene only if the group does not correct Ruby's statement, or if asked by the group to intervene.

If the leader responds by saying, "No, Ruby, you are wrong," the group will probably be affected in a negative way. Ruby may be very hesitant to speak again. When others see what has happened to Ruby, they also may guard their comments so that they say what the leader will accept. The group members assume important roles in helping the group achieve through their interaction.

Individual Roles in the Group. Roles of group members are usually naturally assumed. Mary, for example, may have a natural facility for expanding ideas. Sam may excel in clarifying what the group is saying. Bonnie may be the accepted information giver, and Ruby may stimulate the group to stay on the topic. The members' responsibility for the group then fits with the personality and abilities of each. Through group interaction these roles are accepted so that the group is really controlled by its members.

Some of the roles that group members assume include initiating, information seeking, information giving, clarifying, summarizing, gate-keeping, standard setting, and mediating. The initiator is one who introduces new concepts or ideas. The information seeker questions group members about facts or data that relate to the group's task. The information giver presents these facts or data. Clarification is the role of the person who interprets the ideas of group members and who tends to intervene when there is confusion. The person who summarizes synthesizes ideas presented to lead to a conclusion. The gatekeeper is one who encourages free participation of group members, and the standard setter focuses the group members' attention on the goals or standards to be achieved. The mediator attempts to resolve conflict or disagreement and intervenes when tension among group members develops. These roles are

aspects of group behavior that allow the group members to deal productively with both the processes of their interaction and the task to be accomplished.

Peer Group Pressure. When belonging to a group becomes important for staff members, the norms of the group help to control behavior of those who tend to impede group process. This is called peer group pressure. A person who finds that deflating another's ego is met with group rejection will usually cease such action. A person who might ordinarily try to block the group discussion will try to cooperate if belonging to the group is more important than the personal need to be an obstructionist.

Peer pressure can be facilitating or detrimental to a group. The established behavioral norms of group members affect not only the members' interaction but also the types of choices that the group makes. When dealing with tasks, the group determines strategies that represent the choices of the group members. When the function of the group is to develop innovative approaches to patient care, the behavioral norms of the members may hinder consideration of new or different ideas. This is particularly true when group members have fixed ideas about patient care that have not changed over time. These members may be unable to choose strategies for the group task that are representative of current or changing nursing practice. The group leader must make an effort to help the group members develop new behavioral norms and endeavors to guide the group to the level of the most competent member. When the group leader is working to change behavioral norms, group effort is used in process activities that lead to development of new concepts and ideas. This process may necessarily precede actively working on the task, thereby lengthening the time required to accomplish goals.

COMMON UNDERSTANDING OF GOALS

As stated earlier, the group interaction is the vehicle for achieving group purposes. Once the group determines its working relationships, it can define and accept the purpose of work to be accomplished. A group of nursing staff members is a continuous group because its purposes are never terminated. Therefore, it is important that the leader organize group tasks so that segments of each task can be completed while also ensuring that there is always something new to work toward. Why? Because completing something gives satisfaction, but having no purpose leads to disinterest. Without a purpose

the group may consider staff meetings a waste of time. The leader must stimulate interest by continually stretching the group to new challenges.

How does the leader determine where to begin in defining a group purpose in the maze of problems that can be recognized in almost every nursing situation? Members will become involved more readily in a group if its activities are relevant to their personal concerns. If group members are given the opportunity to discuss problems they consider important, the leader can focus their attention on the most prominent problem. Group activity can then center on working for something definite that is pertinent to group members.

When discussing pertinent concerns of group members, the leader should understand that a common understanding of goals depends on a common definition of words used to express these goals. The processes of clarifying, interpreting, and expanding ideas are continuous as the group works together. Most words can be interpreted in numerous ways. For this reason, definition of terms should emerge from interaction among members so that everyone in the group has a common understanding.

DETERMINING REALISTIC GOALS

Knowledge about the staff members' abilities and capabilities and about the goals for patient care helps the leader determine realistic goals for the group activities. The leader with a predetermined plan for the group's function will be more likely to achieve desired results, even if the predetermined plan is changed by the group. This predetermined plan helps the leader maintain direction and provides task structure for the group's interaction. Considerations for developing this plan include the knowledge and experience of group members and their capability for organizing their thoughts for planning. New, inexperienced nurse's aides need to be given well-defined problems for solution if they are to participate effectively in the group, whereas experienced aides who are familiar with nursing terminology and care probably need less structure. Defining problems for group interaction that the members can solve prevents frustration for both the members and the leader.

For example, a group may be totally overwhelmed if the leader presents an activity such as writing objectives for patient care. The leader must present the activity to the staff members in terms that are understood and in a form that the staff members can handle. Instead of asking the staff to write objectives, the leader might ask them to

consider what they would list as important for patient care if they were the patients. The leader can then translate the ideas expressed by the staff into statements of objectives. The leader actually supplements that portion or segment of the activity that the staff is not able to accomplish.

GROUP PROCESS IN MANAGEMENT

In order to determine what segment of an activity the staff is able to accomplish, the leader must have a concept of all components of a given activity. This is comparable to the way a leader assigns care according to the abilities of staff members. When ideas come from the staff members, the leader must determine their feasibility and, if they are relevant, put them to use. Sometimes the leader may incorporate an idea into an already existing plan or into channels that will be acceptable for the organization. A leader sets limits for exploring ideas so that staff members can use their energies to make plans that will be workable and acceptable to eveyone affected by the idea and its implications. If the idea means a change in the way services are coordinated in an existing plan, the leader must "clear the idea" with other personnel involved.

Following clear definition of the work the group is to accomplish, the group must consistently work for results. A guide to activities which lead to results through group action is outlined as follows. Notice how ideas can be translated into group activities.

I-dentification of problems.
D-efinition of goals for patient care.
E-ngrossment in resource information, facts, principles, concepts.
A-nalysis of information.
S-ynthesis of ideas for formulating a plan which can be activated and evaluated.

This demonstrates how the group can become involved in the management process. When staff members participate in formulation of methods for improving patient care, they need support and encouragement from the manager. Throughout the group process of working out problems and reaching a conclusion to activities, the leader helps the group realize that progress must be planned, that it takes effort, and that sometimes results are achieved slowly. When group process is used in management, members of the group need to be continually informed of their progress, and they will be increas-

ingly motivated to participate if results are achieved. The support of the leader must also be continuous. Knowing when to intervene in group interaction by making an authoritative statement, and how to intervene in matters external to the group that affect its progress are management responsibilities.

CONCLUSIONS

If the group works effectively, the leader can expect to find that group members become increasingly sensitive to one another, that they are more accepting of individual differences, that they learn by sharing information and ideas, and that the group is capable of achieving results that each person would find difficult to achieve by working alone. An objective of management is to help workers achieve their potential by growing through performance of work. In nursing, when staff members continually grow, they give better patient care.

Study Questions

1. Susan is a personable, attractive nurse who is sensitive to other people's feelings. She has a good sense of humor which enables her to help other nursing personnel relax. Susan is well liked, and she is always able to get other staff members to help her with her work. Mary is an efficient nurse who has worked in the agency for six years. She always knows answers to questions about policies, where to get equipment and supplies, and whom to call when problems arise. Joseph is often called a "walking encyclopedia" by other nursing personnel. He knows what to do in unusual or emergency nursing situations. His ability for making diagnoses is superior to that of the other nurses, and he is often called on as a consultant by other nurses. Choose one of these nurses and explain why that person would be the best leader.
2. Consider the nurses you know. Choose the one you think is the best leader.
   a. Explain why you think this person is the best leader.
   b. What outstanding qualities does this person have?
   c. Describe the situation in which this person leads.
   d. How does this person influence other people?
3. Describe your own style of leadership.
   a. What types of nursing situations do you prefer?
   b. How do you work with other personnel?
   c. Are you able to influence others?
   d. Is your knowledge of nursing sufficient to allow you to work with other personnel as a leader?
   e. Is your knowledge of nursing good enough to allow you to be creative in planning patient care?

Group Session

1. Meet with your group members and talk about the major problems you recognize in giving patient care. (This should be a brainstorming session which is free and open for all members.)
2. Record the most frequently mentioned problems. Analyze them to determine whether they are related problems and whether the group can realistically become involved in solving them.
3. Identify how these problems are influenced by:
   a. The patients
   b. The staff
   c. The organization of nursing care
   d. The health-care agency organization
4. Check your summary of expressed problems with what actually happens on the unit by recording the major problems which occur each day for four consecutive days. Do the problems expressed by the staff occur consistently? How do the working relationships of staff members contribute to these problems?
5. Choose the problem you feel is outstanding, and work with the group for its solution. Define the limits of the group and of the problem so that group members know what is expected of them.
6. As the group works together consider the following:
   a. Do group members accept one another?
   b. Do group members express their thoughts freely?
   c. Does the group define terms for common understanding?
7. Observe each group member's interaction and describe the roles that each person assumes.
   a. Initiator
   b. Information seeker
   c. Information giver
   d. Clarifier
   e. Summarizer
   f. Gatekeeper
   g. Standard setter
   h. Mediator

References

1. Fiedler, F. E. *A Theory of Leadership Effectiveness.* New York: McGraw-Hill, 1967.
2. Ghiselli, E. E. The validity of management traits related to occupational level. *Pers. Psychol.* 16:109, 1963.
3. Gibb, C. The Principles and Traits of Leadership. In C. G. Browne and T. S. Cohn (Eds.), *The Study of Leadership* (2nd ed.). Danville, Ill.: Interstate Printers and Publishers, 1958.
4. House, R. J. A path-goal theory of leader effectiveness. *Adm. Sci. Q.* 16:321, 1971.
5. Ivancevich, J. M., Szilagyi, A. D., and Wallace, M. J. *Organizational Behavior and Performance.* Santa Monica, Calif.: Goodyear Publishing, 1977.

6. Katz, D., and Kahn, R. L.   Leadership Practices in Relation to Productivity and Morale. In D. Cartwright and A. Zander (Eds.), *Group Dynamics.* Evanston, Ill.: Row, Peterson, 1960.
7. Lowin, A. E., Hrapchak, W. J., and Kavanagh, M. J.   Consideration and initiating structure: An experimental investigation of leadership traits. *Adm. Sci. Q.* 14:239, 1969.
8. Luthans, F.   *Organizational Behavior* (2nd ed.). New York: McGraw-Hill, 1977. Pp. 434–466.
9. Schriesheim, C., and Kerr, S.   Psychometric properties of the Ohio State leadership scales. *Psychol. Bull.* 81:756, 1974.

Suggested Reading

Barrett, J.   *The Head Nurse and Her Changing Role* (3rd ed.). New York: Appleton-Century-Crofts, 1975.
Behling, O., and Schriesheim, C.   *Organizational Behavior Theory and Research Application.* Boston: Allyn & Bacon, 1976.
Bowers, D. G.   *Systems of Organization.* Ann Arbor: University of Michigan Press, 1976.
Browne, C. G., and Cohn, T. S.   *The Study of Leadership* (2nd ed.). Danville, Ill.: Interstate Printers and Publishers, 1958.
Claus, K. E., and Bailey, J. T.   *Power and Influence in Health Care: A New Approach to Leadership.* St. Louis: Mosby, 1977.
Day, R. C., and Hamblin, R. L.   Some effects of close and punitive styles of leadership. *Am. J. Sociol.* 69:499, 1964.
Ginzberg, E.   *The Development of Human Resources.* New York: McGraw-Hill, 1966.
Grissum, M., and Spengler, C.   *Womanpower and Health Care.* Boston: Little, Brown, 1976.
Gruendemann, B. J.   Preoperative group sessions part of nursing process. *AORN* 26:257–262, Aug. 1977.
Hackman, J. R., and Morris, C. G.   Improving Group Performance Effectiveness. In J. R. Hackman, E. E. Lawler, and L. W. Porter (Eds.), *Perspectives on Behavior in Organizations.* New York: McGraw-Hill, 1977.
Herzberg, F.   One more time: How do you motivate employees? *Harvard Bus. Rev.* 1:53, 1968.
Likert, R., and Likert, J. G.   *New Ways of Managing Conflict.* New York: McGraw-Hill, 1976.
Mager, R. F., and Beach, K. M.   *Developing Vocational Instruction.* Palo Alto: Fearon Publishers, 1967.
Maier, N. R. F.   *Problem Solving and Creativity in Individuals and Groups.* Belmont, Cal.: Brooks/Cole, 1970.
Merton, R. K.   The social nature of leadership. *Am. J. Nurs.* 12:2614, 1969.
Nelson, M.   Building a better team. *Nursing '77* 7:65–68, July 1977.
Pollak, G. K.   *Leadership of Discussion Groups.* New York: Spectrum Publications (Wiley), 1975.
Roche, W. J., and MacKinnon, N. L.   Motivating people with meaningful work. *Harvard Bus. Rev.* 3:97, 1970.

Stevens, B. J. (Ed.) The delicate art of nursing supervision and leadership. *Nurs. Dig.* 5:9–13, Fall 1977.

Szilagyi, A. D., and Sims, H. P. An exploration of the path-goal theory of leadership in a health-care facility. *Acad. Manage. J.* 17:622, Dec. 1974.

Webber, R. A. *Management: Basic Elements of Managing Organizations.* Homewood, Ill.: Irwin, 1975.

5. Management for Quality Patient Care

Controlling is a management process that incorporates all other processes associated with management. Controlling can be viewed as the essence of management since it is concerned with ensuring that an organization is productive. In this chapter we will explore some basic issues of controlling and will describe two of the mangement processes used to control the productivity in an organization, quality assurance programs and budgeting.

Organizational Control

Current health-care literature contains much information about quality assurance programs. Such programs are evolving as a result of the federal government's involvement in health care. Laws such as Medicare, Medicaid, and the PSRO legislation (PL 92-603) contain provisions for measuring certain aspects of care. The PSRO legislation mandates that there be both certification of need on the patient's admission and continued review of care, evaluation of medical care, and analysis of the patient profile, the hospital, and the practitioners. Health care in the United States is plentiful, but it is not distributed equally, nor is all health care of equal quality. One issue that these laws deal with is reduction of the inequities in both distribution and level of quality of health care. Another is controlling the cost of health care.

Because hospitals and other health-care agencies are a part of the larger health industry, the single organization is influenced by trends in the industry as a whole. Likewise, since each health-care agency is part of the broader industry, the sum total of the industry's effectiveness is determined to a large extent by the effectiveness of each agency. Quality assurance is an overall goal to control the industry, as well as a goal for control within each organizational entity. Quality assurance incorporates issues of accessibility to care, the effectiveness of care, and continuity of care, as well as cost containment. Practitioners who provide the care and consumers who receive it are the people who activate the system for quality assurance and who exercise control.

ACTIVATING THE PROCESS OF CONTROL

Controlling in an organization is multifaceted. For purposes of discussing organizational control, it is useful to think of control as a process that is activated by people. The process of control is activated by both practitioners and consumers who use material resources and who are influenced by environmental factors. Clinical effectiveness of patient care, the purpose of the health-care agency, depends on how people interact in admitting patients, providing care measures, teaching, referring, counseling, and ensuring the continuity of care. Quality care is often spoken of in idealistic terms, but the values assigned to these terms are sometimes different. Quality is actually demonstrated in the actions of the "controllers" of care, and these actions are determined by the different value systems of people. Family values, genetic traits, cultural and religious values are a few of the variables that influence decisions made by both the consumers and the practitioners who are involved in health care.

EXTERNAL SOURCES OF CONTROL

Organizations are dynamic and thus are changing continually in response to many factors, such as changes in society, changes in the technology of care, and new insights into the interpretation of health care. Today's issues in health care include how hospitals and other health-care agencies can change and adapt to increasing public demands and governmental regulation for quality and cost containment. Both have far-reaching implications in health-care organizations. These implications range from questioning the basic values of the health-care providers to changing specific methods used in organizations for such things as collecting data, keeping records, providing services, and generally accounting for the organization's activities. Hospitals and medical-care providers have not previously been accustomed to "outside" surveillance or to external controls to the extent being encountered at this time. Therefore, coping with external controls is becoming a predominant concern of administrators and health-care professionals.

To adapt to the increasing external control of health care, administrative and provider professionals are going through a stage of exploration and of learning how to cope with the demands for quality and for cost containment. Institutional practices are being questioned, as well as the value of certain care procedures and practices. In the processes of adapting and changing, professionals of all types who are involved in health-care agencies are learning and con-

sequently developing new methods and new approaches for rendering health care in organizations.

ADAPTATION TO CHANGE IN ORGANIZATIONS

An article written by Argyris [1] provides some useful insights into the ongoing process of organizational learning and adaptation to change. Argyris describes organizational learning as a process of detecting and correcting error. He speaks of the tendency for norms to develop within organizations. In some organizations employees are afraid to "get into trouble" and consequently hide their errors so that a "network of camouflage and deception" develops. To counteract this, he suggests that a system for obtaining valid information be developed in which employees make a commitment to choice and to constant monitoring of implementation of the organization's work. To create this climate, he suggests that internal assumptions made within the organizations should be based on attitudes that power derives from having reliable information, from competence, from responsible employees, and from continual monitoring of the effects of decisions. Managers, to create this climate, develop a support system of advocacy for employees and establish relationships that both encourage inquiry and tolerate confrontation.

ENCOURAGING PARTICIPATION IN CONTROLLING

Controlling is often interpreted as use of power at the expense of other people. Argyris proposes that information is the source of power and controlling is a process through which people grow and develop by participating in decisions, by evaluating the effects of behaviors, and by taking corrective action. Argyris describes some of the dilemmas of people who have the power to control; these include the need to be a strong manager yet being open about the existence of dilemmas, being able to be open and yet not controlling, being an advocate and at the same time encouraging confrontation, being able to respond effectively to employees who are anxious even though the manager may also feel anxious, and finally being able to manage one's own fear and at the same time help people to overcome their fears.

These thoughts are pertinent to managers, particularly to those who are just beginning a career that entails management responsibilities. There are always problems and issues that managers must deal with. In the health-care system, solving these problems and issues involves not only the personnel who work within the organi-

zation, but also the consumer or recipient of health care. Providers of care are sometimes reluctant to solve these problems in groups that involve participation of consumers. They feel that the problems are professional ones and that involving consumers in their solution can hinder the trust that is basic to the consumer-professional relationship in health care. Consumers (patients) do, however, participate in health-care processes and can provide input that can be used to improve health care. Joint discussions of the health-care problems can be productive—consumers and practitioners often have common concerns about events.

The Role of Professionals in Controlling

Consumers of health care are participating increasingly in formal groups, such as committees or regulatory bodies that evaluate health-care quality and expenditures. But the consumers, while confronting issues of quality in health-care systems, still rely on the judgment of professionals in matters of professional knowledge and use of medical technology. The professional then has the prime responsibility in any quality assurance program or other type of controlling process in health care.

VALUE SYSTEM

Let us consider the role of the professional in controlling. The basis for control of any human effort is the value system of those who provide care and of those who use this care. Values influence what people consider to be important, necessary, or desirable when making choices. The choices that are made in organizations about what to control represent the values of the people, both consumers and professionals, who are making decisions. Consumers may participate in making these decisions, but they often rely on professional expertise to evaluate or to guide the direction of the decisions. It is an aspect of professionalism that the professionals will actively take the lead in controlling health care.

ETHICAL DECISION-MAKING

Basically, control processes begin with each professional. Organizational control is an aggregate of "professional control," and controlling in an organization is an interactive process that is subject to interpretations and to actions of people. The care choices made by practitioners are often ethical choices—determining whether an ac-

tion is good or bad or right or wrong. Making choices is essentially decision-making. This ethical decision-making involves knowing the circumstances of a situation, knowing about one's freedom in making choices, evaluating and analyzing the alternative actions, determining the nature of the action (whether the person has a choice in the action), and judging the action according to principles or guidelines that will promote the most good.

The professional who is "in touch with his or her own reality" looks at care decisions as voluntary choices that have good and bad or right and wrong values. The health-care practitioner learns the principles or guidelines for making such judgments in a basic professional educational program and continues to update knowledge throughout the duration of practice. Values become clarified and firmed up through practice, and professionals become increasingly aware of their own values in making the difficult decisions about matters that arise in the course of a lifetime of practice.

SELF-CONTROL

Making decisions intentionally is an element of self-control. A system activated by human action is largely controlled by each person in the system. Control of the quality of health care—a broad endeavor—is accomplished in many ways, but the self-control exercised by knowledgeable workers who give health care is an important underlying element. Consistency in making decisions despite the pressures and stresses of daily events requires self-control. The consistency comes from inner sources—the person who is committed to a value system and who voluntarily makes decisions based on the values felt intuitively, as well as those known and expressed, can maintain consistency in behaviors. This consistency is viewed as control that is exercised when a person uses knowledge in making judgments that affect not only the person but also the person's use of resources and the behaviors the person exhibits when dealing with others in the care arena.

PROFESSIONAL SELF-REGULATION

Self-control is also applicable to a professional group. Self-regulation is an attribute of a profession. The regulation exercised by professionals within their group has ethical applications. A profession has a code of ethics that serves as a guide to professional judgment. Professionals provide a service that society requires and sanctions. They have a body of knowledge that is unique to the profession and

that is applied in making judgments when providing the professional service, in accord with the code of ethics. Peer review is a technique used for professional self-regulation that reinforces self-control in individuals. The ability of a professional group to regulate its actions is an expectation of the society that sanctions the profession. This self-regulation is a basis for trust that individuals develop in their expectations of quality service provided by the professionals.

CONTROL BY AN AGGREGATE OF PROFESSIONALS

When several different professionals form an organization there is an aggregate of professional values. While the health-care professionals such as administrators, doctors, nurses, and others have a common interest in providing quality care, their functions may differ. The values inherent in these different functions may seem to conflict because each professional group has a different knowledge base and a different function, uses different terminology, and has a different perspective. Nurses, for example, approach patient care from the point of view of nurturing the patient in order to control illness or disease and maintain health. Doctors approach patient care from the perspective of diagnosis, treatment, and preventive measures. Administrators approach patient care from the perspective of using resources effectively and containing costs so that the organizational operations that support patient-care processes will be efficient.

DEVELOPMENT OF A COMMON TERMINOLOGY FOR CONTROL

Nurses may perceive conflict in values when their terminology for describing quality patient care does not harmonize with the terminology of budget management that is important to the administrator's function. Administrators take courses in finance, accounting, and systems management. Nurses take courses in nursing process and care of the patient. An ability to translate nursing process and patient care into fiscal management terms is a process of "enlightenment." Current emphasis on the development of quality assurance programs is providing a medium for professionals to work together to determine how their aggregate of functions can be blended for effectiveness and efficiency in patient care.

Nurses involved in quality control programs are learning how to phrase their idealistic sounding or broad terminology of patient-care goals in statements of standards that are becoming increasingly specific and consequently more adaptable to translation into the terminology of other health-related professional groups. One of the

goals of quality assurance programs is to actualize a health-care delivery system that clearly delineates care values that can be related directly to efficiency values such as cost containment.

The Control Process

Professionals activate the control process. This process can be narrowly viewed as measuring outcomes. Examples of this approach are using predetermined standards to evaluate whether a cake is satisfactory after baking or whether a painting is satisfactory after the paint has dried. The process of control can also be viewed as measuring the means to achieve the outcomes as well as the final result. Traffic controls exemplify this approach. A speed limit is set as a standard of behavior: 20 mph in a school zone, 30 mph in normal city traffic, 55 mph on the highway. These speed limits represent a standard for safety in the designated category of area. In a school zone, 55 mph is an unsafe speed, and 20 mph is an unsafe speed for highway driving. The speed limits are the standards used to control the outcomes, in this illustration, public safety, which can be measured by the outcome goal of no traffic accidents.

Once the standard has been determined, there is an enforcer (a policeman) who measures vehicular speed. This person measures the speed of vehicles and compares the actual speed to the standard to reveal the differences, if any, between the vehicular speed and this standard. The enforcer controls by regulation—by stopping the noncomplying driver and giving a speeding ticket. The enforcer is implementing a plan of "corrective action." The principle of this corrective action is that knowledge of the regulation is well known by drivers, since to be licensed they must pass an examination that tests their knowledge of traffic laws. The driver also knows what the consequences of failure to comply will be. The speeding ticket is designed to make an impact on the person who does not comply—it serves as a force for behavioral modification so that the driver will comply with the standard in the future. If the driver repeatedly fails to comply, there are further corrective actions that can be used, such as loss of license or mandatory participation in driving classes.

CONTROL BY THE HEALTH-CARE PROFESSIONAL

The manager applies the components of the control process to the patient-care situation. Although speed limits are more easily translated into standards than are nursing-care measures, the same com-

ponents apply. In nursing, both the methods used in giving patient care and the outcomes are important for the patient's safety and welfare. The processes of care or events that take place throughout the patient's health-care experience can be delineated and can be controlled. The outcomes of care can also be defined and controlled.

Measuring quality care is a complex matter. Consider the patient-care process from your nursing perspective. There are certain aspects of care that are confined to the discrete relationship between the nurse and the patient. You and the patient could interact to implement these aspects of care in any setting: in the patient's home, in the hospital, or in a waiting room or conference room. Such nursing process components that are interactive in nature are teaching, counseling, emotional support, and history taking for assessment. Other aspects of the patient-care process require materials, supplies, and a controlled environment. Surgery, for example, is conducted in an aseptic environment and requires sterile equipment, specialized operating room equipment, monitoring devices, and sterile supplies. In order to assure quality patient care in these types of situations, not only the care processes, but also the environmental and operational processes that support care must be measured. The care processes include not only nursing functions, but also the specialized professional functions of others.

CONTROL BY THE PATIENT

In addition to the control exercised by people in the organization, patients can also exercise control in the health-care system. Patient's behaviors are often measured in quality assurance programs. Because the patient does not have to comply with care measures and is not a part of the organization, controversy can arise about whether these behaviors are actually a measurement of the quality of care given. Consider, for example, that people have a right to health care. Such rights or interests are provided for by law, and health-care providers have a duty to respect and provide these rights. A right implies, however, that an individual may choose to exercise the right or not, according to personal wishes. Providers have a duty to provide care, but patients have the right to accept or not to accept care. A provider may, for example, prescribe the correct medication for a patient's condition, but the patient does not have to purchase or take this medication. This explanation is an oversimplification of rights and duties, but it serves to describe the relationship between a health-care practitioner and a patient.

It is important that the practitioners perceive patients' rights for health care as interests that the patient controls. A patient does not have to comply with health care. When a given patient exercises this right to noncompliance, he or she is making a value judgment. As with professionals, the patients' values are the basis for their decisions about how they will participate in the health care. The professionals may provide all the necessary care processes and operational requisites for quality care, but the patient influences the outcomes by choosing how or whether to comply with treatment measures. To measure the outcomes of care in terms of patient's compliance with care is complex because noncompliance does not always imply that the health-care practitioners did not give "quality care." On the other hand, one of the professional duties is to develop methods through which patients can learn how to comply with their health-care measures on the basis of understanding the importance of the care for their ongoing health.

Quality Assurance Programs

Quality assurance programs conducted by nurses involve a process of self-regulation that demonstrates how nursing behaviors affect patient progress. These programs are related to the entire spectrum of quality assurance activities being conducted within the health-care industry. In this industry there are several factors that are considered in determining the quality of care. These include accessibility to care (which can be limited by distance, lack of transportation, limited hours, inability to pay, organizational barriers that cause delays in appointments or admissions, and obstructive behaviors by health-care personnel) and the beliefs and attitudes of patients about their health care. These factors tend to be measured by evaluating the patient's delay in obtaining and receiving care, the patient's failure to follow up with prescribed care, and the health-delivery system's use by people in a geographic location.

Another dimension of quality assurance is the structure of health care. This is defined as the organizational structure of health-care agencies, methods of financing care, and personnel staffing of the organizations. The process of care is yet another dimension and is defined as the professional-patient contact. Professional competence, which includes both technical and interpersonal skills of the health-care providers, is a common factor used to measure the process of care. Outcomes of care represent another dimension of

quality assurance. These outcomes include the patient's ability to function as a result of health care and the patient's satisfaction with the health care. Outcomes can also be measured by evaluating the health status of a population.

Professional nurses are concerned with self-regulation within this health-care system. An important point made by Davidson in a non-health care related article applies to nurses. He states that "professions devote themselves to public needs defined by the public but also have developed their own institutions for serving needs defined by their own parochial conception of the public interest" [3].

Quality assurance programs are concerned then not only with professional behaviors and with structural dimensions of the health-care system, but also with the patients' expectations of health care. One of the complex issues in quality assurance programs is defining the relationships between professional standards of care and the patients' expectations of care. Evaluation of quality must also include determining the relationships among the structure, the process, and the outcome dimensions of health-care delivery. Information about these relationships is important to determine how to improve the system. Thus far, research efforts have not revealed any clear relationships among structure, process, and outcomes [4].

UTILIZATION REVIEWS

One way of evaluating care is through the utilization reviews required by Medicare and Medicaid. The utilization reviews include appropriateness of the patient's admission to the hospital, the patient's length of stay, and the number of services used in the care of the patient. Utilization reviews can be conducted concurrently with the patient's hospital stay or can be done retrospectively by evaluating the medical records following the patient's discharge.

AUDITS

An audit is another commonly used measure to determine the effectiveness of care. The audit consists of developing a plan in which pertinent questions are answered: (1) What is the standard of quality to be achieved? (2) Why should the standard be achieved? (3) Where, when, by whom, and how should the standard be implemented in the health-care system?

Design of the audit procedure and forms used for auditing are based on the answers to these questions. The design of the audit

program specifies what is to be tested in the audit, the standard for measurement, comparison of what actually happened with this standard, and evaluation of the degree of conformity that has been achieved in attempts to meet the standard. The time frame for conducting the audit is also part of the design and can include all of the activities that take place from the time that the patient is admitted to the hospital to the time of the patient's discharge.

Assessment of the patient's status at the time of admission provides the data used to determine the baseline for evaluating changes that take place during the hospitalization. (Certificate of need required by PSRO legislation is designed to document the patient's status at the time of admission.) Once the patient is admitted, the processes of care are evaluated to determine what nursing actions took place. The end result of the patient's care is measured by the assessment completed at the time of the patient's discharge. Evaluation of this flow of care can be the basis for interpreting the effects of the hospitalization, but this interpretation must take into account factors that were not controllable by the patient, the professionals, or the structure.

An audit is most effective if it is related to the overall goals of the nursing department in the health-care agency. To conduct such an audit voluntarily is indicative of professional accountability and represents how organizations can learn, as described earlier. Audits can be designed to measure any number of aspects of patient care; those aspects selected for audit represent the value system as defined in the nursing organization's goals. One effect of audits is that they bring attention to the aspects of care being measured. It is important to develop measures that assess both what nurses consider to be important in patient care and what patients consider to be important in order to gain the most relevant feedback that can be used to improve care.

Professional groups have different perspectives about the importance of different aspects of patient care. Greene [4] cites that the dimensions of priorities for quality assurance vary for government, consumers, and professionals. He states that governmental priorities are efficiency and effectiveness. Consumer priorities are accessibility and acceptability. Professional priorities are provider competence and effectiveness. Greene states that there is overlap among these dimensions. A long-range goal to be achieved is to determine whether all of these priorities can be related to one another in developing methods to improve the quality of health care. The

current state of the art is early-stage development of measures of quality. Because audits are often used to measure the quality of nursing care, we shall examine the audit procedure.

THE AUDIT PROCEDURE

An audit is application of the control process. The basis for an audit is determination of the standard of care. This standard is written prior to conducting the audit and is stated specifically so that it can be measured against actual practice. Conducting an audit requires a decision about "what" is to be measured. This means that the standard of care should be written with criteria similar to the speed limit example. One of the concerns of the auditor is making choices about which standards to measure that will "test" or compare what actually happened with what should have happened. Following the measurement or test, there is the need for corrective action if discrepancies have been found. This corrective action is the mechanism through which future events are controlled for quality.

To be meaningful, the standards of care selected for audit have to be an index of quality. What standards are measurable? By what criteria? How do these standards measure quality? Patient care is complex and, if comprehensive and holistic, is difficult to measure. How do you know if a patient's emotional needs for preoperative support were adequately met? How do you know if counseling sessions for a patient achieved any results? How do you know if your teaching of a patient was effective? Which standards of care can you select for measurement to gain adequate information about the quality of care given?

In many instances, standards of care are determined by groups of nurses who are giving care. The group determination of standards is a developmental process that uses the concept of the value of group participation. The value of the use of groups as the vehicle for determining standards of care is that a consensus can be reached about what standards ought to be. Nurses who participate in determining what standards ought to be apply their cognitive knowledge of nursing to statements of criteria about what events determine quality in the care process. Awareness of the importance of these events serves to help nurses translate the words into actions when giving care. This developmental process is an exercise that in itself is a control device that heightens the practitioner's awareness of assessment factors, procedures, techniques, and methods of care. This heightened awareness colors the nurse's actions since it focuses the nurse's attention on these standards when giving care.

Written Standards. Written standards of care are valuable in the control process. These written standards are a consistent and retrievable data base for "testing" care actually given. They are also a reference for nurses who are giving care. Such references enable the nurse to "stabilize" care processes. When one considers the vast amount of knowledge applicable to patient care, the numerous interruptions the nurse is subject to in the course of a day, and the great demand to relate to patients and personnel at all levels of communication, references are invaluable in stabilizing the direction of actions. Nurses "think on their feet," but they are human, and when overloaded with sensory input, they cannot always think of all the important aspects of care for every patient without assisting devices.

Another purpose of written standards is that they serve to inform nurses (employees) of the expectations of their work. Knowledge of what is expected in performance and feedback about the effects of performance are important in motivation. When performance is visibly related to a tangible measurement, one can obtain feedback necessary for continued motivation. The process of developing and writing standards clarifies the expectations of the nurse in the employment setting; it also clarifies the role of the nurse for others.

The process of determining and writing standards has another advantage—those who participate in the process broaden their perspectives of care. A standard has to have a basis in fact, in theory, or in some background information that substantiates and validates the standard. To investigate an area of care implies that the committee or group classifies, categorizes, and conceptualizes and then derives tangible criteria from the data. What is generally present or true, what happens in most cases, and what determines whether this care process is effective for patients with this classification of illness or disease are questions that committee members must answer.

Relationships among events become more clear when writing standards. Consider the following example:

If a patient has _____, the patient will experience emotional and physiological responses of _____ that require _____ intervention. The patient is subject to _____ complications and can be expected to progress toward wellness or advance through the phases of _____. The patient requires _____ information or assistance to regain or retain maximum health consisting of _____.

Filling in the blanks directs attention to developing normative expectations of care for patients with certain categories of problems. By

viewing these patients in a classification or category, one's perspective is generalized and therefore broadened.

Determining Realistic Standards. Where do the data for these generalizations come from? Some sources include information from books and other media about pathophysiology; about treatment and therapies to determine what interventions restore, correct, or supplement the disrupted physiological mechanisms; about patients' responses to determine the normal course of events when certain physiologic or emotional disturbances occur; and about the complications that can occur as a result of the original disturbance, the treatment or therapies, or patients' responses to them. Standards based on theory and on observations of actual practice are more likely to be realistic and possible to achieve; these are both important factors in measuring such standards. The ANA standards of care can also be used as professional normative guidelines for developing standards.

Why should standards be realistic and possible to achieve? The importance of realism in standard setting has many implications. From a performance point of view, the standards or expectations must be attainable. Being expected to carry out performance standards that are beyond the ordinary capabilities of practitioners is frustrating. With such high standards, the practitioner could well react with the attitude, Why try since it's impossible? To engender motivation to perform well, standards must be perceived as attainable.

Another reason why standards should be attainable is that they must be accepted by practitioners if they are to become part of that person's repertory. The person makes a commitment to achieve standards, and this commitment implies agreement with and capability for carrying out the standard. People need to be successful in carrying out commitments to fulfill their own feelings of need satisfaction. A self-actualizing person has needs to achieve, and these needs are thwarted when the standards are not realistic or if only "supernurse" could attain them.

Written standards not only commit the practitioners to a level of performance, but they also commit the organization to that level of performance. A written standard can potentially be used in a legal action if a patient brings suit. The same test used in audits of comparing the standard to the actual events is used to determine "what should have happened" in legal actions. The standard then

becomes a "duty" that the nurse has to patients. One way of managing this use of standards is to clarify in writing that they are guidelines for practice or goals to be developed through continued assessment and improvement. Standards are not actually normative in nature until they are studied over a period of time and data from the studies are measured statistically on the basis of actual performance to find "normative" ranges of practice. It should also be mentioned that the written standard of care cannot be applied equally to all patients' care because of the variability among patients in their motivations for care and for cure, their responses to treatment, and other intervening variables. The normative standard that applies to a patient's condition is always subject to change according to the patient's condition and progress.

Conducting an Audit. The process of implementing an audit has both developmental and organizational implications. It is developmental in that the people who conduct the audit and those whose actions are being audited can learn from the feedback derived from the audit. It has organizational implications since the audit may reveal deficiencies in policies, procedures, rules, or methods of operations used to support patient care. The use of feedback from the audit, if validity in measures is ensured, is an impetus to evaluating the total patient-care situation. Audits are, however, made on the basis of chart documentation and have the potential for measuring expertise in charting rather than what actually happened in the care process.

It is important that everyone who participates in the audit process be informed about the procedures being used so that input and learning can be a part of the process from the outset. The audit is a procedure that is conducted by specified people, but it measures the effects of nursing actions in general and every attempt should be made to ensure that the feedback gleaned from auditing will be relevant. The audit itself is conducted according to specified conditions. An audit is a controlled evaluation. It is controlled, just as a scientific experiment is controlled, to ensure that measurement will be reliable and valid.

There are several approaches to conducting an audit. The method of the Joint Commission for Accreditation of Hospitals uses criteria for outcomes, 24 hours prior to discharge. Patients' charts are reviewed according to these outcome criteria but in retrospect, that is, after the patient is discharged. The review criteria are stated in terms of expected outcomes that should have occurred 24 hours prior to

discharge. Complications are indications that these expected outcomes were not met. If complications have occurred, the chart is examined to isolate factors that may have influenced development of the complications. Assessment, treatment, therapy, and other process factors are evaluated to determine if care was given according to process standards for prevention of the complications. This evaluation indicates whether the complications could have been prevented and whether they were detected and managed appropriately. Decisions are then made about the data so that remedial action can be taken.

Another commonly used system is the Medicus System. This system uses both process and outcome criteria. The criteria used include admission data, events that took place during hospitalization called interim data, and outcome data taken at the time of discharge.

Selection of charts for audit is usually based on the most frequently occurring category of patients. Not every patient chart is audited. Instead a representative sample is selected to evaluate care during a stated time frame—one month, three months, six months. Factors that influence the audit include the number of patient-care units represented, the staff turnover, and the number of patients within a given category. Patient charts are selected according to diagnosis, the reason for hospitalization, or other criteria selected for standards in the audit. Often patients have multiple health problems, but the diagnosis for the current hospitalization is the "primary diagnosis" used for an audit of events during this time period. In the patient charts the auditors check the nursing notes, the progress notes, measurement graphs for TPR or blood pressure, and medication chart forms. A summary of the audit results is distributed according to procedure, and the results are coded to protect the unit or staff identity, to maintain objectivity. The data are retrievable, however, to isolate factors that have contributed to the care.

A summary report of the audit includes the category of patient audited, the time of the patients' admission and discharge, the number of patient charts reviewed, the reason for the sample selection method, the age and sex of the patients, the number of patient-care units included, and the names of the auditors. The findings of the test for criteria, the data collected for each criterion, the percentage index of compliance, and other data that might be included are recorded by patient-care area. These findings are used as feedback to analyze the reasons for noncompliance present at the time the patients were in the hospital.

Analysis of Audit Results. The process of evaluation begins with analyzing the audit findings. If noncompliance in a given area is demonstrated, the reasons for noncompliance are investigated. Possible reasons are multiple. One may be that charting documentation was inadequate, another that staff turnover temporarily influenced the quality of care. Other reasons may include a large number of new orientees, problems related to use of equipment or supplies, environmental deficits, problems in communication networks, deficits in nursing knowledge, or inadequate staffing. The documentation of problems is the basis for corrective action. To be pertinent and relevant, corrective action must be directly related to the "root" problems identified. The type and duration of corrective action are based on the nature of the problem, and usually the solution is not as simple as giving a traffic ticket. Staff development activities, for example, may require a course or a series of workshops to remedy problems. Revision of the charting system may be another remedy, as are such activities as establishing better communication networks, improving charting, or working with other hospital personnel to improve delivery of supplies.

The analysis of audit results is usually conducted by a committee. This committee examines the results to interpret their meaning. Situational factors mentioned earlier, such as professional to nonprofessional nursing staff ratios, are explored in relation to the audit results. Review of situational factors is important in determining the causes of deficiencies or discrepancies. Interpretation of the data is basic to developing plans for corrective action.

Use of audit committees to interpret data is practiced in industries other than the health-care industry. Lovdal [5] studied thirteen New York Stock Exchange companies and found that the most effective results of audits were the results of deliberations of audit committees. Some of the practices he cites that were found to augment the effectiveness of audit committees are balanced membership of the committee, a flow of complete information to the committee, independence from the executive officer, and periodic self-assessment of the committee.

The purpose of an audit committee is to review the data in terms of changes in current practice that could be made to improve care. The data must be evaluated according to situational factors to prevent errors in interpretation. It is also important that the audit committee base the interpretations on fact, principles, and theories as much as possible to prevent inappropriate judgments. Many factors can create

dissonance in interpretation of audit data among individuals; changes in norms of the standards of care, new rules and regulations relating to federal and state laws, new technology, organizational practices, and changes within the health-care delivery system in a community can all influence interpretation of data.

Corrective action taken on the basis of audit data, if viewed in the broader perspective of the organization, has many implications. Interpretation of audit data can be the impetus for change in nursing-care practices that in turn can have impact on the organizational operations or on relationships among people in the organization. The overall goal is to improve patient care. Improvements suggested must be rational and cost-effective if they are to be implemented.

Qualitative Versus Quantitative Data

Quality assurance programs are designed to measure "qualitative" data. This is an effort that not only is difficult to define with any degree of universally accepted specificity, but that also taxes the imagination and the creativity of the evaluators. These programs are expensive, and some types of measurements, such as audits, are more expensive than others. The effort of measuring quality is useful and worth the expenditure only if it results in improved patient care.

Qualitative data are nominal and difficult to standardize, while quantitative data are much more amenable to measurement since they involve collecting information about tangible and visible aspects of care. Qualitative data are concerned with factors such as the effects of treatment and medication measures evaluated by the progress in the patient's cure. Quantitative data measure factors such as how much of what kind of medication was used, how many dressing packs were used, and how much nursing time was spent with the patient performing care activities. Nurses are becoming increasingly sophisticated in their knowledge of the importance of both qualitative and quantitative data. The remainder of this chapter will explore some of the issues and methods used by nurses to use quantitative data in control of patient care.

The Budget

A budget is a plan of how an organization will allocate its money resources in a given period of time for the purchase of other resources necessary to function. The processes of planning budgets and

of quality assurance programs are similar in that both are based on value judgments about health care. In quality assurance programs the judgments are made in planning standards of care to be measured. In budgetary planning, the value judgments are made in planning how to allocate institutional resources according to the health-care services that are needed or desired. Both budgets and quality assurance programs are concerned with efficiency and equality in health-care services, but they approach these concerns from different perspectives.

EQUATING QUALITY WITH COST

Quality assurance programs attempt to identify the effectiveness of health care from the perspective of qualitative standards. These qualitative standards sometimes are not easily applied to specific tangibles such as costs for manpower or the amount of space or supplies required for quality care. The budget is an attempt to identify how limited organizational resources can be allocated throughout the organization to provide the most effective health care. The specific and tangible resources such as cost of manpower, space, and supplies are equated with standards of care offered through health-care services in the organization. The issue of how to translate qualitative standards into quantitative measures of cost is central in both budgetary planning and in quality assurance programs. The different perspectives in approach for each of these control processes make them seem dichotomous or even incongruent. It is perhaps an oversimplification to state that the two different types of control measures have the same end goal because the perspectives of each differ. Grave questions such as, Can we assign a dollar value to human life? or on the other hand, Can we determine what level of quality in health care is affordable given limited dollar resources? are underlying the issues of effectiveness and equality in health care.

PHILOSOPHY OF BUDGETING

This introduction to budgets is designed to help you consider budgetary planning in the broad perspective of total organizational planning. Philosophies and values may seem tangential when you are actually planning a budget because numbers don't look like concepts such as quality or human life values. It is useful to think of budgets in terms of philosophy and values to overcome the constraining aspects of budgeting and to emphasize the strategical aspects of the budget process. In this process of budgeting, one considers how to get the

best value from limited dollar resources. The idea of best value for dollars spent is one you probably deal with every day in decisions you make. If you are hungry, for example, and you have a quarter to spend for food, should you buy an orange or a package of cookies? This decision requires knowledge of available choices and is made on the basis of value judgments, your feelings, attitudes, and habits, as well as knowledge of the nutritional value of foods and body needs for nutrients.

BUDGETING LIMITED RESOURCES

You can identify with the concept of limited dollar resources in your own life. You earn a specific amount of money from which you determine your expenditures. You are limited in your purchases of goods and services by the amount of your income. An organization, such as a health-care agency, also has to function within the limitations imposed by resources available. Money is one of these resources, and money is used by the organization to purchase other necessary resources. Decisions have to be made about how to allocate the money available to the agency for these other resources: people, supplies, and equipment. These decisions are crucial in determining the scope of patient-care services that the agency will provide.

A Budget as a Future Plan. The purpose of a budget is to make rational decisions about how much money you need and about how you will spend your money. In formulating a plan for income and expenditures, you think of your goals for the budget period just as an organization plans a budget according to goals. Because the immediate and long-range future is full of unknowns, the organization forecasts future events in the budget period just as you try to think of all the upcoming expenditures that you must meet or that you will desire to make in the future.

A Budget as a Control Device. A budget is a control device because it allocates expenditures and this allocation serves as a "standard" for the actual expenditures that are made throughout the budget period. When more money is spent than was allocated for certain items, corrective action is taken. This corrective action is based on evaluation of the reasons why the budgetary standard was not followed. Reasons might include finding that unnecessary expenditures were made, that the projected costs of items was unrealistic or that costs had increased after the budget was planned, or that not all costs for a given activity were planned for in the initial budget.

In planning a budget, it is necessary to project costs as accurately as possible. The allocation of expenditures in an organization is made according to some type of framework, and there is usually a format or guide for making out the budget that is followed by all persons involved in budgetary planning throughout the institution. Budgets for organizations are usually separated according to departments, programs, or special projects.

ALLOCATION OF ORGANIZATIONAL RESOURCES

The manager who is planning the budget for a specific department or unit within a department follows the organizational format for planning. When all departmental program or project budgets have been completed, the entire organizational budget can be prepared. Using a common format enables the central budget committee to prepare the master organizational budget more easily since a consistent approach has been made by all planners. After developing the entire organizational budget from the separate budgets, it may be necessary to decrease amounts in certain areas to comply with total organizational dollar resources. Budgets submitted by people from various departments are approved following total organizational review and revision of projected income and expenditures.

Types of Costs Included in Budgets. Budgets usually include different types of costs: those that occur consistently, those that vary, and major expenditures for equipment or for building projects. The consistent costs, called fixed costs, include items such as plant maintenance, salaries, supplies, and equipment rentals that are made on an annual basis. Fixed costs remain stable despite the amount of use or volume of services. Costs that change with the amount of use or volume of services are called variable costs. An example of a variable cost for a patient-care unit is supplies such as dressings or pharmaceuticals that are used as patients require. If the census of the patient-care unit includes 15 patients who require dressing changes in one week and only 5 patients who require dressing changes in another, costs for supplies will vary, being greater when there are 15 patients using them than when there are only 5.

Capital Expenditures. Major expenditures for equipment are capital expenditures. These capital costs include purchases of equipment that is expensive but that is expected to be used for many years. The capital equipment costs are figured over a lifetime of expected service. An x-ray machine, an examining table, or an auto-analyzer are

examples of capital expenditures. Equipment that is less costly is called minor equipment and includes such items as small tape recorders and sphygmomanometers. Minor equipment items may be included in operating costs or in equipment costs.

Operating Costs. Operating costs are those expenditures necessary for maintaining the ongoing services or day-to-day functions throughout the budget period. Operating costs are "what it costs to operate the service unit." These costs differ from capital expenditures in that the capital expenditures are made for items that maintain value during the item's lifetime. An automobile, for example, is a capital expenditure that you might make. It has a continuing value that depreciates over time. The items required to maintain the function of your car, such as gasoline, oil, and antifreeze, are operating costs. If you always drive your car the same number of miles each day, these operating costs are consistent or "fixed." If you drive your car a different number of miles each day, the operating costs are variable and depend on the amount of use. The license plates and insurance for your car are fixed costs.

DATA BASED BUDGET PROJECTIONS
You can estimate the costs for your automobile from your past experiences. Your previous bills for gas, oil, and other maintenance costs provide you with data to use in projecting future costs. Data are also the basis for forecasting organizational budgets. These data are obtained from review of past costs, from comparison of costs throughout the organization, and from evaluating methods of operations that have taken place in the past. Data must be analyzed to determine whether there might be a better and more efficient way to operate. It is not sufficient to say that past costs are an indication of future needs. Data can also be used to evaluate real costs over a period of time to determine which costs have remained stable and which costs have changed or fluctuated. The reasons for fluctuations can then be evaluated to determine the internal or external factors that influence costs.

Analysis of Data. Analyzing data to determine factors that influence costs is used in budgeting to develop strategy. The effects of changes in patient census, the mix of patients according to acuity of illness or diagnostic categories, the mix of staff (RN, LPN, or NA), the methods used to accomplish work, and the types of services rendered are

some of the major areas that can be analyzed to develop strategies for spending organizational dollars more effectively. Strategic aspects of budgeting are most challenging. Developing strategies for budgeting includes not only evaluation of material resources but also the potential of employees for functioning. Because health-care agencies are generally labor intensive, the function of employees is the central focus of many strategic plans.

EVALUATING THE COSTS AND BENEFITS OF RESOURCES

There are several ways to approach an evaluation of the potential of employees for functioning when developing strategies for budgeting. One approach is to evaluate what types of material resources the employees need to carry out their functions. A nurse who is carrying out teaching plans for patients with chronic illness needs printed materials and other forms of media as teaching-learning resources. Administering medications requires medicine cups, syringes, medicine carts, chart forms, requisition slips, inventories of medications, and other such material resources. In budgeting, expenses are planned according to the materials and people necessary to fulfill the roles specified by the operational activity. The benefits of the activity must justify the cost.

Manpower Resources. Another approach to developing budgetary strategy is to evaluate the capabilities of employees. The use of material resources requires decision-making by employees. The types of decisions made may require special educational preparation or particular talents. A registered nurse, by virture of education, can make decisions about the use of resources in giving patient care that a licensed practical nurse would not be expected to make. The licensed practical nurse, in turn, makes decisions not expected of a nurse's aide. In addition to educational preparation, the unique talents and the experience of employees also contribute to their capability for management of resources. The capability to use resources effectively is one of the criteria that are considered in promotion of employees to management positions.

Mode of Operation. Another approach to developing budgetary strategies is to analyze the mode of operation used to accomplish work. Often more effective and economical ways of operation can be determined. To introduce changes in the way that people function together in an organization, whether the change involves use of a

new technology, new equipment, or a new method of procurement of supplies, involves orientation or educational programs. Therefore, when making such changes it is necessary to forecast the types of problems that the employees may have in making the changes. The type of change being made may involve a role change for certain employees, or it may involve adapting to a new method for communicating with people in another department. If the change involves a redefinition of roles or functions, an educational program and development of support systems to help people adapt to the change must be included in the cost of the change.

Costs of Change. Costs that might be incurred in making operational changes are numerous. These costs may include rewriting and printing new procedure manuals; holding orientation meetings to introduce the employees to the new methods; writing, printing, and disseminating materials to employees to explain the new procedures and the reasons for their implementation; training sessions to learn about a new and sometimes complex technology; or continuing education programs or travel to other institutions to learn about different methods for accomplishing some particular function or to teach people about the conceptual rationale for changing. Continuing education costs may also be required to teach new content about a given area of professional practice that is required to implement the change in methods of operation. The capacities of the personnel and their needs for both training and development are integral parts of strategies developed in budgetary planning.

LONG-TERM EFFECTS OF A BUDGET
Many of the strategies developed in the budget process have long-term effects even though a budget is usually planned from year to year. Both the immediate future, which is the next year's budget that is being developed, and the long-range future are considered in developing any budget. Some programs may be expensive to initiate, but their costs are often figured over the long term if the change will effect savings over the long run. Going through the process of developing a budget for the coming year helps the personnel plan organizational activities and modes of operation in terms of what must be done to accommodate to changes in the organization, in professional fields, and in the expectations of the people who use the health-care services. These changes are ongoing, and an organization such as a hospital has to speculate about the future when planning

strategies for the present. You can understand, therefore, that a budget has far-reaching effects in an organization.

COMMITMENT TO FUTURE ORGANIZATIONAL GOALS

The understanding that the future of the organization is considered in the present budgeting process is important. A budget is often perceived as a constraining force by personnel, and in a way it is. Making commitments to a plan of action in the budgeting process involves planning for allocation of resources in the future. The processes of "budgeting now" to accommodate future changes determine a direction that the organization will take in the programs and services offered. For this reason, it is difficult to make changes that are not included in the budgetary planning because any change may also change the direction of goals to be achieved and may require a different set of income and expenditure figures. The master budget may be planned so that changes are difficult to make unless there is an even exchange of costs, income, and benefits for one type of activity for another, or unless the new activity will earn as much as it costs. As a professional employee of an organization, you should consider your function in terms of the future and provide input for the budgeting process so that changes you perceive to be necessary can be considered at the time of budgeting.

TYPES OF BUDGETARY PLANS

Budgets are plans that assign dollar values to programs and services of the institution. There are several different ways to go about planning for the budget. *Incremental budgeting* is a method in which the previous year's budget is used as the basis for developing the new budget. *Zero-based budgeting* is a type of planning that emphasizes evaluation of programs and services in terms of the mission of the institution. In this process the specific department or budget area must justify its purposes. The planners prepare a description of the functions and intended purposes of the activities and then assign costs to these functions. A number of different ways for accomplishing these functions are planned, with costs for personnel, materials, and space determined for each of the plans. The costs and benefits of each plan are compared to finalize the area budget.

A *program budget* is similar to zero-based budgeting in that the costs of the program are evaluated in terms of its intended purposes. All of the costs that will be incurred in implementation of the

program are evaluated in terms of the program goals. In program and in zero-based budgeting the master organizational budget is planned by evaluating the importance of each activity in view of the organization's goals. Priorities are made according to value systems, data available about patients' expectations of services, projected needs for services in the long run, professional standards, and the type of income or other benefit to the organization.

Budgets are often prepared according to line items. In the *line item budget* income and expenses are categorized into classes; this provides for data about specific types of costs. Differentiation of items enables the planner to forecast all the different types of expenditures that will be incurred and then to evaluate actual expenditures according to type. The line item budget is particularly useful if the different types of costs are appropriately defined for a given activity. When the budget in any line item is exceeded during the budget year, the reason for the overage can be pinpointed. If, for example, the budget for the line item maintenance of equipment is exceeded, one can immediately begin to evaluate why the equipment maintenance costs increased.

THE BUDGET AS AN EVALUATION TOOL

This brief description of the line item budget is included to demonstrate how a budget can be used to evaluate activities. As a manager, you are responsible for efficient and economical use of resources. If your expenditures in any one area, such as maintenance, exceed the amount planned for in the budget, you must investigate the cause. You may find that the equipment is old and cannot withstand wear. In this event, you would include purchase of new equipment to replace the worn-out equipment in the following year's capital budget. You might find that the personnel using the equipment do not know how to use it correctly. In this event, you would develop a plan for orientation or teaching to rectify misuse. Your evaluation might indicate that the equipment was recently used more frequently because a specific type of patient need had increased or because personnel were employed who use the equipment more frequently than past employees. In this case, your evaluation of the equipment involves analyzing the types of services that require its use. This evaluation may lead you to determine that the activities involved might be conducted in another way. You might find that the procedures or functions could be carried out more effectively and economically through different processes or by using a different type

of equipment. In this event you would not simply replace the existing equipment with a similar type, but would redesign the function.

The Budget as a Source of Information. As with any control device, analysis of the budget provides information that is used as the basis for evaluation of activities in an organization. Spending more or less money than was allocated indicates that the manager needs to evaluate the differences by isolating problems that are being encountered. Likewise, when income differs from the amount projected, the services producing the income must be evaluated. The manager uses the budget as a source of information for future planning. The budget is a useful tool that helps the manager understand the effects of people, the workplace, and resources on each other. When used as a tool for management, the budget is not constraining, but serves as a guide and as a reminder of plans made for functions throughout the budget period.

THE BUDGET AS A TOOL FOR COMMUNICATION

A manager can learn to use budgets for many purposes. The purposes of budgets in planning have been described. It should be emphasized that budgets are one type of plan that is recognized as important by everyone in the organization. Budgets provide a common language for communicating with people in different professional groups and can be used as a medium of communication by the nurse-manager. Because budgets are common to the entire organization, planning the budget for a specific department and having this departmental plan reviewed by the budget committee that plans the organization's master budget serve to communicate programs and purposes. In many respects, acceptance of a departmental budget by a master planning committee implies acceptance of the department's purposes and goals by the organizational hierarchy.

The Budget as a Goal. Budgets are total organizational plans that quantify the organization's purposes and goals. Personnel in each department or program manage a part of the total organizational budget, and through this management fulfill broad organizational purposes. The budget then provides a direction for operation for all persons in the organization. It is theorized that when people in various departments are actively involved in the processes of budgetary planning, these people make a commitment to achieving the goals set forth in the budget. When this is the case, the process of

budgetary planning and evaluation can be a source of motivation for employees.

The Budget as a Tool for Organizational Coordination. Analysis of budgets provides data that are used to evaluate the organization's activities. The data gleaned from budgets are useful not only to managers in specific departments but also to those who manage the entire organization. Budgetary processes, then, provide for coordination of activities within an organization. If maintenance costs have increased throughout the organization, for example, the spectrum of activities that take place in the organization and the types of external services purchased for maintenance are evaluated. This evaluation may lead to a change in plans made for the maintenance of equipment. Just as people in a specific department can evaluate their functions according to budgetary data, the administrators of the organization can evaluate activities in the entire organization from budgetary data.

THE BUDGET AS A TOTAL ORGANIZATIONAL PLAN

It is important, therefore, to consider that a budget is a plan for use of the organization's total resources. Everyone who is employed by the organization is accounted for in the budget through the inclusion of salaries and fringe benefits. In addition to these personnel costs, everyone who is employed uses the space and materials in the organization. Efficient and economical use by employees of all supplies, space, and equipment is necessary to control expenditures. Very small items, such as pens and paper products, can be large expenditures in the overall budget. Being careful in the use of material supplies is similar to saving pennies. Have you ever collected pennies in a jar for one month? And were you surprised to find how much money you had saved in just one month's time? As a manager, you are responsible for "saving pennies" in the way that you work with other people and in the way that you expect them to use materials and resources. You can better control costs in the area of your management responsiblity when you make every person fiscally responsible.

The Role of Nurses in Cost Containment

Nurses constitute the largest percentage of hospital employees. The productivity of nurses in providing patient-care services is therefore important in cost containment. Measurements of nursing produc-

tivity are not well defined. While a physician who sees patients in an office charges them for services rendered, nurses employed by hospitals are usually not paid directly by patients, nor are patients usually charged for specific nursing services. Nursing care has not previously been considered a cost center on the basis of services rendered in most hospitals. (A cost center is one in which separate accounting is made for a specific type of cost.)

DIFFERENTIATED NURSING-CARE COSTS

Stevens [6] and Bauer [2] suggest that nurses should determine methods for charging patients according to nursing-care needs. Stevens proposes that patients should be billed according to the level of care received, based on a patient classification system. If costs for nursing-care measures were specified, patients could be given information about the price of different services and could choose to use the services they are willing to pay for. Bauer proposes a nursing-care price index to measure and evaluate the costs of nursing services. By using a nursing-care price index, changes in costs could be more accurately measured in a given organization. A standard formula for a nursing-care price index could also be used to compare nursing-service costs in organizations that differ in size.

MEASURING NURSING PRODUCTIVITY

As a manager you are evaluated by your productivity, and you also evaluate other personnel according to their productivity. To measure productivity, one often relies on intuition and on evaluation of general performance. The nurse who is well organized, who is competent, who uses resources well, and who can complete care effectively and in sufficient quantity is generally termed "productive."

Nursing productivity is not easily defined in budgetary terms. To explore some of the facets of productivity one must consider the capabilities of the individual professional nurse, the organizational behaviors that have an impact on the nurse's function, the standards of nursing care on which evaluation of accomplishments is measured, and environmental factors that influence the nurse's practice. How the nurse perceives patient care, the role of the nurse and the profession influences how that nurse will give patient care on a day-to-day basis. Management factors, including organizational structure, management practices, leadership, and incentives, also influence a nurse's practice. The state of professionalism in nursing care in a given organization, including the type of facilities and equipment, the levels of staffing, and supporting services, are

influential in how the nurse functions in a given setting. The manager's role is to evaluate factors that influence productivity of nurses and to work toward achieving an environment in which nurses can apply their knowledge effectively.

Summary

Health-care costs are a matter of concern not only to patients but also to all professionals involved in health-care systems and to the public in general. Controls of costs in the health-care industry can be exerted by governmental forces, by community forces, and by people who work in health-care agencies. Professionals are accountable to their clients, and they are also autonomous in the practice of their selected profession. In this chapter you have been introduced to some of the basic concepts of budgeting and quality assurance. As a manager and a professional you can use this information to develop your expertise in exercising voluntary control over your own practice. This voluntary control is an aspect of professionalism that encompasses not only fiscal control but also control of the quality of services rendered.

Study Questions

1. Interview at least five different nurses, asking each to define quality nursing care. Compare the responses using the following as the basis of comparison:
   a. Terminology used.
   b. Descriptive examples or words used to explain the meaning of terminology used.
   c. Perspective. Did the nurse describe quality nursing care from the perspective of the nurse, the patient, or others?
   d. Similarities and differences in the content of responses.
2. In a group of three to five people, have one person collect data about one patient's hospital bill, including diagnosis, treatment, and costs for hospitalization; if appropriate have another person collect data about the budget of the patient-care unit where the patient was admitted by interviewing the head nurse or by other appropriate means; and have the third person investigate issues of third-party payers in terms of problems encountered in health-care insurance. After compilation of the data, meet to discuss findings and isolate three major issues that you might encounter in budget control when caring for the patient.
3. Conduct a "mini-audit" as a class experiment in which the group writes standards of care to be audited for a selected category of patients. The audit should be limited in scope to one or two aspects of nursing care, and the time frame of the audit should be developed in accordance with situational requisites of the care environment.

4. You have been charged with developing three different plans for setting costs for nursing care given to patients on a medical-surgical patient-care unit. Present your plans to a group, outlining the rationale for each, the costs of each, and the benefits you think would be derived from each plan.
5. Select one procedure or operations method that you have experienced in giving patient care in a health-care agency. Evaluate the procedure or operational task in terms of its efficiency in supporting patient care given by nurses and in terms of cost. As you investigate the procedure, analyze each step to determine whether a different approach would be more efficient or economical.
6. Obtain the staffing schedule for a patient-care unit in a hospital for a period of one month. Evaluate this staffing schedule in terms of:
   a. The mix of nursing personnel
   b. The average number of patients cared for
   c. The types of diagnoses of patients cared for
   d. The acuity of the patients' illnesses
   e. Absenteeism of the nursing staff
   f. Staff turnover (resignations and new employees)

References

1. Argyris, C.   Double loop learning in organizations. *Harvard Bus. Rev.* 55:115–125, Sept./Oct. 1977.
2. Bauer, J. C.   A nursing care price index. *Am. J. Nurs.* 77:1150–1154, July 1977.
3. Davidson, H. M.   The top of the world is flat. *Harvard Bus. Rev.* 55:89–99, March/April 1977.
4. Greene, R.   *Assuring Quality in Medical Care.* Cambridge, Mass.: Ballinger, 1976.
5. Lovdal, M. L.   Making the audit committee work. *Harvard Bus. Rev.* 55:108–114, March/April 1977.
6. Stevens, B. J.   What is the executive's role in budgeting for her department? *Hospitals* 50:83–86, Nov. 16, 1976.

Suggested Reading

Brown, B. (Ed.)   Quality assurance and peer review. *Nurs. Adm. Q.* 1:9–50, Spring 1977.
Brucker, M. C., and Reedy, N. J.   Quality assurance—an overview. *JOGN Nurs.* 6:9–14, May/June 1977.
Byrd, J. M.   Peer review for quality charting. *Superv. Nurse* 8:25–27, July 1977.
Chalef, M. N. (Ed.)   *PSRO Journal Articles.* Flushing, N.Y.: Medical Examination Publishing, 1977.
Clark, B. B., and Lamont, G. X.   Accurate census forecasting leads to cost containment. *Hospitals* 50:43–48, June 1, 1976.

Cohn, S. S.   Audit enhances patient's environment. *Hospitals* 51:61–62, May 1, 1977.

Curtin, L.   Human rights and professional responsibilities. *Update On Ethics* 1:1, Aug. 1977.

Davidson, S. V. S.   *PSRO Utilization and Audit in Patient Care*. St. Louis: Mosby, 1976.

Davis, A. I.   Measuring quality: Development of a blueprint for a quality assurance program. *Superv. Nurse* 8:17–26, Feb. 1977.

Doughty, D. B., and Mash, N. J.   *Nursing Audit*. Philadelphia: Davis, 1977.

Froebe, D. J., and Bain, R. J.   *Quality Assurance Programs and Controls in Nursing*. St. Louis: Mosby, 1976.

Fuller, M. E.   The budget. *J. Nurs. Adm.* 6:36–38, May 1976.

Gosfield, A.   *PSROs: The Law and the Health Consumer*. Cambridge: Ballinger, 1975.

Holle, M. L.   Retrospective nursing audit—is it enough? *Superv. Nurse* 7:234, July 1976.

Housley, C. E.   Budgeting at the supervisor's level. *Hosp. Top.* 54:6, March/April 1976.

Jelinek, R. C., and Dennis, L. C.   *A Review and Evaluation of Nursing Productivity*. DHEW PHS, HRA, BHM, Division of Nursing. DHEW Publication number (HRA) 77-15, Nov. 1976.

Lachner, B. J.   The cost accountability of the CEO and board. *Hosp. Prog.* 58:60–63, Aug. 1977.

Laros, J.   Deriving outcome criteria from a conceptual model. *Nurs. Outlook* 25:333–336, May 1977.

Lohmann, G.   A statewide system of record audit. *Nurs. Outlook* 25:330–332, May 1977.

Longest, B. B.   *Management Practices for the Health Professional*. Reston, Va: Reston, 1976.

Marram, G.   The comparative costs of operating a team and primary nursing unit. *J. Nurs. Adm.* 6:21–24, May 1976.

Marriner, A.   Budgets. *Superv. Nurse* 8:53–56, April 1977.

McNally, F.   Nursing audit: Evolution without pain. *Superv. Nurse* 8:40, June 1977.

Nelson, C. W.   The administrator's role in quality assessment and control. *HCMR* 2:7–17, Winter 1977.

Pearson, B. D.   Nursing implications of what price health care? *Nurs. Dig.* 4:51, Winter 1976.

Phaneuf, M. C., and Wandelt, M. A.   Quality assurance in nursing. *Nurs. Dig.* 4:32–35, Summer 1976.

Proceedings: Conference on Professional Self Regulation. USDHEW, PHS HRA, DHEW Publication No. (HRA) 77-621, June 1975.

Schaefer, M. J.   Forecasting and resource allocation in educational administration. *Nurs. Outlook* 25:256–270, April 1977.

Schulz, R., and Johnson, A. C.   *Management of Hospitals*. New York: McGraw-Hill, 1976.

Singer, J. P.   Flexible budgeting techniques provide tool for cost control. *Hospitals* 51:45–49, July 1, 1977.

Thompson, J. D.   Curriculums must address issues in practice milieu. *Hospitals* 51:73–76, Oct. 1, 1977.

Wallace, R. F., and Donnelly, M.   Computing quality assurance costs. *Hosp. Prog.* 56:53–57, May 1975.

Watson, A., and Mayers, M.   Evaluating the quality of patient care through retrospective chart review. *J. Nurs. Adm.* 6:17–21, March/April 1976.

Whittaker, A. C., and Holmes, S. L.   Man hour budgeting: A refinement of managerial control. *Hosp. Top.* 54:14–16, Jan./Feb. 1976.

II. The Challenge of Management

The preceding chapters serve to give the reader a cursory view of factors that influence nursing management. This view enables the nurse to form a perspective of the implications of management. Involvement in thoughtful practice of management expands this perspective so that the nurse eventually accumulates a fund of knowledge and experience that gives greater meaning to this cursory view.

When one accepts the commitment to manage patient care, one simultaneously accepts a challenge. This challenge is to participate in developing nursing practice in accord with the social and economic requisites of patient care. Because nursing practice in hospitals is structured, beginning staff nurses are tempted to accept the security of the structure. It is possible to perpetuate the structure in vogue at the time of initial employment through formation of habits and familiarity with secure routines. This perpetuation is not always compatible with sound management practices in a changing environment.

The wide spectrum of patient needs, ranging from acute care to maintenance of health, requires flexibility of nurses. The scope of abilities of nursing staff members also demands flexibility. Therefore, managers must continually question the relevance and practicality of their actions. Management is a continuous process of adaptation.

What seems fixed or stable in nursing today may not be appropriate in the future. The challenge of management is multifaceted and involves answering questions such as:

How should patient care be defined today? In the future?

How should the nursing staff be organized for best advantage?

What tools can be devised to assist nurses?

Your challenge is to become a realistic manager who can deal with the priorities of the present while forging ahead into the future.

The following chapters offer the reader concepts and principles of management that can be employed to ensure that staff members get the job done while experiencing job satisfaction.

The first chapter in Part II deals with motivation. Managers face dual challenges for motivation. They must motivate themselves and nurture the motivation of staff members. As with management,

motivation is a continuous process. People need stimulation to improve their abilities, and they vary in the degree of independence they assume. Managers set the tone for staff attitudes by making sure that all staff members have positive experiences in which they are successful in giving patient care. If the staff is successful, the manager is also.

Additional chapters emphasize concepts and principles that can be utilized to ensure staff member job satisfaction and management's goal of quality patient care. Skills in delegating, communicating, interviewing, appraising, teaching, introducing change, and disciplining are presented in a form easily adapted to any nurse-patient setting.

6. Motivation

In order for the nurse to guide and direct staff members, the nurse must first understand the nature of human behavior and understand why people act as they do.

To understand another person, we must know how he feels about himself. His self-image will influence his behavior. A person's self-concept is acquired from childhood experiences and from the feedback he receives from his achievements. A person's behavior is purposeful, and the manager needs to be perceptive in understanding why the staff members are behaving as they are. The successful leader learns the reasons behind the behavior and takes the necessary steps to correct undesirable behavior.

Individuals attempt to fulfill their wants, drives, and needs. The word *motive* implies action to satisfy a need. Further discussion of these concepts follows.

Maslow's Hierarchy of Human Needs

The psychologist A. H. Maslow has developed a theory of human motivation that has been widely accepted [6]. According to Maslow, our needs can be arranged according to priorities into a hierarchy, with physical needs being the "lowest" and most basic, followed in ascending order by security, social, egotistic, and self-actualization needs, as illustrated. In this hierarchy, a higher need does not motivate until the lower, more basic needs are first satisfied, but once a lower-level need is satisfied, it no longer motivates.

Thus, once our need for food, shelter, clothing, and protection from danger is met, we become relatively more concerned with higher needs. Once our desired standard of living is attained, our social needs are motivators, followed by our needs for esteem and respect. The highest need—that which motivates after all other needs have been met—is the ultimate form of accomplishment, self-actualization, which has been described as total fulfillment of the self in making the most of one's potentials. A person moving up the hierarchy may reverse direction and move downward if his lower-level needs are threatened. Once the need is satisfied it no longer serves as a motivator of behavior.

This hierarchy serves as a framework to many contemporary theo-

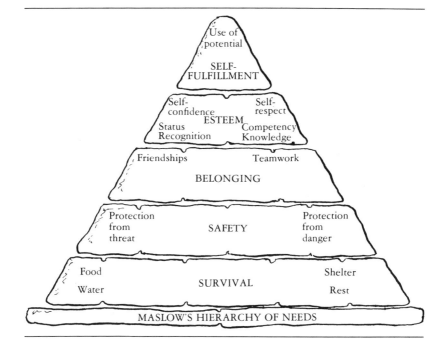

ries of motivation. It can be further illustrated by the following discussion.

SURVIVAL NEEDS

At the base of the hierarchy are the needs for survival. These are the biological needs of all men for food, water, protection, and rest. These are the lowest-level needs but become the first in importance when threatened.

Most of us have secured these basic needs. Our patients, however, may have these needs thwarted. Hunger can have a dominating influence on a patient's behavior after a day or more of being without food. A patient with chronic renal failure who is on a strict fluid restriction often finds thirst to be such a strong drive that he seeks extra water, even though he knows that it is harmful.

SAFETY NEEDS

Safety needs are fear-based needs for protection against danger, threat, or being deprived of something considered necessary. In the working situation this need may be manifested in workers' demands for tenure, saving and retirement plans, or forms of insurance. A

nurse may feel threatened when she does not feel qualified to care for a complex patient. A patient may feel threatened and insecure when placed in an involuntary dependency relationship or when faced with a frightening diagnostic test such as a sternal bone marrow biopsy. A nurse's aide in training may feel psychologically threatened when faced with something new, unfamiliar, or unknown.

Safety needs usually do not become a dominant motivator unless the individual is seriously threatened or endangered, but then they may take over completely. We have read of panic during fires when many people unreasonably attempt to satisfy their individual safety needs at the same time.

BELONGING NEEDS

Once survival and safety needs are satisfied, they cease to motivate behavior. People are social animals and are motivated by the need to belong and to be liked and wanted. They want friendship and often associate with others for companionship. An employee who has an unsatisfactory home life may find that the relationships with fellow employees provide a large part of the social-need satisfaction. Workers who belong to small, integrated work groups often have higher morale than those who work alone. Teamwork helps to build morale. Most people like to help others and to be helped by others when they need it. An individual usually adjusts his behavior to meet the norms of the group.

The Hawthorne studies [8] initiated in 1927, which were conducted on 20,000 workers, pointed out dramatically that the need to be accepted and liked by one's fellow workers was at least as important as and perhaps more important than economic incentives in determining how the individual performs on the job. The workers restricted their production output (to their own detriment from the standpoint of financial gain and promotion) in order to gain acceptance from their fellow workers. The studies also showed how workers resist being put into competition with their fellows and tend, consciously or unconsciously, to band together to resist anything from management that might appear a threat to the individual.

A nurse may be confronted with a group of aides who find greater satisfaction in meeting their group norms—for example, taking extended coffee breaks—than in being more productive in their nursing functions. Greater work output by one of the aides may result in that aide's being rejected by the other aides.

ESTEEM NEEDS

Once the social (belonging) needs are met, esteem needs become the motivators of behavior. These needs include the desire for self-confidence, independence, self-respect, achievement, competence, and knowledge. Esteem needs also include a desire for status, recognition, appreciation, and respect from others. These needs are rarely fully satisfied, and an individual will continue to seek indefinitely for greater satisfaction of these needs. For many people, the need for respect and recognition from others is more important than the need for self-respect.

This fourth level of needs is especially prominent among successful managers, professionals, highly skilled workers, and those with a high need for achievement.

SELF-FULFILLMENT NEEDS

The highest need at the top of the hierarchy is self-fulfillment or self-actualization. These are the needs for fulfilling one's potential, for continual self-development, and for being creative in the broadest sense of the term. Maslow describes the self-actualizing person as one who has the following qualities [5]:

1. Superior perception of reality
2. Increased acceptance of self, of others, and of nature
3. Increased spontaneity
4. Increased problem-solving ability
5. Increased detachment and desire for privacy
6. Increased autonomy, and resistance to enculturation
7. Greater freshness of appreciation, and richness of emotional reaction
8. Higher frequency of peak experiences
9. Increased identification with the human species
10. Changed interpersonal relations
11. More democratic character structure
12. Greatly increased creativeness
13. Certain changes in the value system

All the needs overlap and the lowest needs never disappear. We must always eat, sleep and take refuge from the weather, and no one can think of self-actualization if worried about belonging. These levels are interdependent and overlapping, each higher need level emerging before the lower needs have been satisfied completely. In

our society, most people tend to be partially satisfied in each need area and partially unsatisfied. Most individuals tend to have more satisfaction at the lower need levels than at higher need levels.

ADDITIONAL MOTIVATING FACTORS

In addition to basic needs, a person is strongly motivated by the interests, attitudes, and values that he has acquired. Even within the same social milieu there is considerable variation in the abilities, attitudes, and temperaments of people. People react to praise, criticism, promises, and frustration very differently. One assignment may challenge one individual but frustrate another individual. As managers we can be alert to notice and remember the wishes and preferences of our staff. Attitudes, biases, and prejudices should be understood and taken into consideration in nurse-patient contact, as illustrated by the following examples.

1. A nurse's aide was especially interested in caring for patients with colostomies; thus, she was motivated to give good care when assigned to a colostomy patient.
2. A strained, uneasy relationship existed between an Arab doctor and his Jewish patient that prevented the patient from feeling that the physician was genuinely concerned about his welfare.
3. A nurse who was very opposed to alcohol or common law marriage was very judgmental in giving care to a patient who was married by common law to an alcoholic.

Other Theories of Motivation

In addition to the widely accepted theory of Maslow's hierarchy of needs, there are three other important theories of motivation. One has been formulated by psychologist Frederick Herzberg [3]. It is a theory of work motivation rather than a general human motivation theory. Herzberg's researchers asked workers to tell them about events at work that resulted in improved job satisfaction and about events that decreased job satisfaction. When the results were tallied, the factors resulting in increased job satisfaction were labeled as *motivators* because they were effective in motivating the individual to superior performance and effort. These factors were achievement, recognition, work itself, responsibility, and advancement. Another group of factors labeled *hygienic* or *maintenance* factors focused on

discontent with the work situation. These included environmental factors (such as working conditions), company policies, administration, supervision, salaries, and interpersonal relations.

The hygiene factors are preventive. If the organization provides them, it will prevent the workers from getting sick of work. But to get the workers to do creative, satisfying, responsible work, the organization must provide them with the motivators.

The healthy worker likes a balance of both hygiene and motivator factors. He wants a pleasant environment, but at the same time he needs to accomplish and create.

If the hospital concentrates on supplying hygiene factors and neglects the motivators (interesting work, responsibility, on-the-job growth, self-improvement opportunities, recognition), then the hospital workers are going to seek the hygiene factors.

Another helpful way of classifying needs for application on the patient-care unit is to categorize needs according to the way they can be satisfied. We can place them into three categories:

1. Needs satisfied away from the hospital
2. Needs satisfied in the hospital environment
3. Needs satisfied through giving patient care

When the hospital administration stresses vacation days and bonus checks, it is attempting to satisfy employees' needs away from the hospital. The hospital that provides coffee on the unit for the nurses is attempting to satisfy needs in the working environment. This helps to make the environment pleasant, but it does not provide direct motivation in rendering patient care. It is the third category, that of satisfying needs through the giving of patient care, that should be emphasized if managers wish to provide positive motivation to staff to work harder. Basically, the physical and security needs are satisfied off the job, social needs are satisfied through personal contacts around the job, and egotistic needs are chiefly satisfied through the job.

David C. McClelland [7], a Harvard psychologist, has investigated the achievement motive in people. The subjects for his experiment were shown pictures and were to tell a story about each picture. This technique revealed what the subjects thought about when they were not required to think about anything in particular. If one spends time thinking about doing things better, psychologists say he has an achievement orientation (*n Achievement*). If one spends time thinking

about family and friends, he has an affiliation orientation (*n Affiliation*). People with a strong need for power (*n Power*) want to command attention, get recognition, and control others. Most people possess some of each, but there are people who lean more in one direction.

McClelland's research has shown that achievement-oriented people tend to translate their thinking into action. They place great demands upon themselves, are persistent, realistic, and believe in moderate risk-taking. Evidence suggests that high achievers have come from parents who set moderately high achievement goals but who were warm, encouraging, and nonauthoritarian in helping them reach these goals. McClelland points out that individuals who score high in achievement motivation are motivated by the love of accomplishment, interest in their work, and by success itself.

No matter how high a person's need to achieve may be, he cannot succeed if he has no opportunities, if the organization keeps him from taking initiative or does not reward him if he does.

The third theory is behavior modification. B. F. Skinner [9] is a leading proponent of the behaviorist school of psychology, which holds that behavior is caused primarily by externally induced stimuli. He thinks that man and his environment are the focus for behavior and that all behavior is shaped and maintained by its consequences. A person does something because of the reinforcement he received the last time he behaved in a similar way. If the outcome of his action pleases him, he is likely to repeat the action. A reinforcer is something that increases the probability of a behavior's occurring again.

There are three types of reinforcement:

1. Punishment reinforcement
2. Extinction or neutral reinforcement
3. Positive reinforcement

Punishment is used to decrease the behavior. Skinner argues against punishment. Extinction consists of applying a neutral stimulus after the behavior occurs. Positive reinforcement is the most recommended by Skinner since it increases the likelihood of a desired response. Informing staff members of how they are doing is a form of reinforcement. Positive reinforcement may consist of a smile or a nod of approval. It should come as soon after the behavior as possible.

Morale and Productivity

Recent research shows that there is no simple correlation between morale and productivity. There can be high morale with low productivity or low morale with high productivity. Morale can be defined as the total satisfaction a person derives from his job, his work group, his boss, the organization, and his environment. It is affected by the person's personality and pertains to the feeling of well-being, satisfaction, and happiness.

Rensis Likert [4] claims that the relationship between morale and productivity for complex and varied work tends to be moderately high. When the job performance depends upon the individual or team, then those workers who like their job are more likely to be motivated to produce. Much recent behavioral research has demonstrated that when the leader and the team are highly work motivated, then team members' satisfactions and attitudes are often positive.

The ideal system of work motivation is to provide opportunities for need-satisfaction through doing the job itself. This necessitates developing staff commitment to the objectives of the health-care agency. Ideally people will exercise self-direction and self-control in working for objectives to which they are committed. This emphasizes openness and trust, supportive supervision, and participation in decision-making.

IMPORTANCE OF TASK

How can the nurse provide satisfaction to the staff in the category of providing patient care? Let us look at some of the dimensions of the egotistic needs. One of man's strongest needs is the need for a sense of accomplishment—that the work is important. Therefore, the importance and value of the task to be done must be emphasized. If the aide who is to give a patient an enema is told that the enema is an important preparation for an x-ray that is of diagnostic value for the patient, the aide will be better able to see the importance of the task. Prevention of skin breakdown should be stressed in helping an aide see the importance of keeping the incontinent patient clean. There are many unpleasant tasks in nursing that nurses must do; understanding their value helps promote a feeling of satisfaction when the task is accomplished.

SENSE OF ACHIEVEMENT

Staff members also need to feel a sense of achievement in their tasks. They need some way of measuring their progress. Everyone wants to know, How am I doing? People like feedback even when

there is no reward or penalty attached to failure or success. We generally receive feedback from our patients. For example, a patient might say, "That backrub feels so good," or "I feel much more comfortable now that I have had my medication." Other patients, however, are unable to tell the staff how they feel. It may be an aphasic patient or a very withdrawn patient that the staff is caring for. In these cases it is important for the professional nurse to apprise the staff on how they are meeting the patient's needs.

SENSE OF CREATIVITY
Another egotistic need is that of enjoying the sense of creativity that springs from doing something well, from being "on top" of the job. People like to imagine that their jobs require unusual skill and as a consequence tend to exaggerate the job's importance. If you have ever observed one hospital maid showing a new hospital maid her job, you will probably have seen her stressing its complexity. The professional nurse should acknowledge the skills of those doing jobs of less status than her own. The maid may be pleased to have cleaned four rooms to be ready for the new admissions of the day; the orderly may tell you that he has helped ambulate ten patients; and the maintenance person may be pleased to announce that the side rail on bed A in room 303 is now fixed. All of these employees like to feel that their job is important, that they have done it well, and that they had special skills that made it possible to complete the task. Managers must not fail to use the creative abilities of the staff, for they like to use their initiative and imagination.

Motivation and Productivity
Generally, people in our society have a genuine desire to work and to be productive in their employment. Then why do we see employees who loaf and at times go out of their way to avoid working? Usually such behavior indicates that the individuals are dissatisfied with their job, with their supervisor, or with the work place, or feel that they have been treated unfairly. It is important to identify the underlying problem that is keeping a staff member from being a productive member of the team and attempt to correct it.

SATISFYING HIGHER-LEVEL NEEDS
As previously stated, a satisfied need is no longer a prime motivator of behavior. This must not be overlooked in nursing. For example, consider the aide who was interested in caring for colostomy patients.

Her interest might have stemmed from the intense desire to learn as much as possible about colostomy care. If she is assigned time and time again to the colostomy patients, however, she may have her need met, and it will no longer serve as a motivator. She must now be provided with opportunities to meet higher-level needs. If her higher-level needs are ignored, she will feel deprived. This can be manifested by frequently taken sick days or decreased effectiveness on the unit.

Managers cannot provide staff members with self-respect or esteem, but they can create conditions that foster rather than hamper the satisfaction of these needs. Managers need to know in which situations an individual staff member seeks recognition. To tell an aide that she gave an enema well when she has given fifty enemas well may mean little to her. Managers need to recognize the areas that are a challenge to the aide and then must praise the performance of the task that was difficult to accomplish.

As mentioned earlier, the professional nurse sometimes encounters an unproductive staff member. Staff members are motivated not so much by what you want them to do as by their own desire to get along as best they can in the situation they perceive. It may be that you are overmanaging staff members by too narrowly defining anticipated behavior and making too many decisions for them. By making minimal and confining demands on staff members' abilities and by placing all decision-making in the leader's hands, managers provide little opportunity for responsibility, self-reliance, or independence. Staff members need a sense of pride and accomplishment from their work, not a childlike role that is neither stimulating nor dignifying.

GELLERMAN'S THEORIES OF POSITIVE MOTIVATION
Dr. Gellerman [2], a noted manager, has written management theories describing three methods which have been found to have a positive motivational effect. They need to be applied selectively, as they may not be effective in all cases.

One method is called *stretching;* this is the assignment of tasks that are more demanding (in difficulty level, not necessarily in terms of time or effort) than you believe your staff capable of handling. This enhances the likelihood that staff members will use more of their potential to experience the satisfaction of achievement and will develop a desire for more of it. This method should be used sparingly and infrequently. It must not be used as a continuous motivational method.

A second method is *management by objectives;* that is, giving the staff members rather broad direction as to how they perform a task, provided they accomplish the end goal.

The third method is *participation;* that is, seeking the staff's comments and suggestions prior to making significant decisions affecting their work. Research seems to indicate that the power of participation to motivate persons stems primarily from its capacity to give a feeling of personal worth through the recognition that the individual receives from others in the group.

OTHER MOTIVATIONAL CONSIDERATIONS

Dr. Mortimer R. Feinberg [1], an industrial psychologist and personnel consultant, states that the best way to motivate subordinates is to show them that you are conscious of their needs, ambitions, and fears and recognize them as individuals. In other words, identify what level of needs staff members are attempting to satisfy before conversing with them, and then plan your interaction with them to be in tune with their level of needs. This will show them that you recognize and understand what is important to them.

There are actions to be avoided if you are concerned about motivating the staff. Do not belittle a staff member. You may have had a teacher in school who belittled students if they gave a wrong answer, and before long the students stopped volunteering answers. Do not criticize a staff member in front of others. Do not get so preoccupied with your thoughts that you fail to listen to your staff members with undivided attention. Do not play favorites or make exceptions because of personal preference for a staff member. Other staff members will resent it and lose motivation. Do not vacillate in making a decision. Being wishy-washy shows your lack of confidence, and staff members will then lack confidence in you.

There are positive actions the manager can cultivate in order to motivate staff. Communicate to the staff your standards so that they have a goal and a guide. Be consistent in these standards. Recognize your own biases and prejudgments in order to prevent them from altering your objectivity. Keep staff members informed of their performance and inform them of changes that may affect them. Go out of your way to help the staff to develop, and take responsibility for the staff members. If one of them fails, you, too, fail in part. You have probably heard the remark "Oh, that happened on the evening shift" as a response to a reprimand by a physician that a patient's need was not met. In contrast, the head nurse who assumes responsibility for patient care around the clock must have nurse leaders who

assume responsibility for actions of their group members. Encourage staff members to be independent by encouraging them to solve problems, show initiative, think creatively, and ask pertinent questions. Be willing to learn from others; acknowledge ideas, suggestions, and proposed changes that are brought to you. Demonstrate confidence; if you have doubts about your head nurse, your nursing supervisor, or the director of nurses, review them alone. Do not review them with subordinates. Exhibiting doubts to staff members disheartens them and tends to lessen their confidence in you. Allow freedom of expression. Staff members should be allowed to make their jobs interesting by doing it their own way as long as the principles are followed and the desired results attained. Be tactful and courteous.

There are many factors that motivate individuals. To be an effective leader, one needs to understand individual staff members' needs and to help them attain satisfaction in their work. Provide them with more interesting work, more responsibility, and the opportunity for achievement. Managers need to tap the staff's valuable resources in planning and carrying out patterns of patient care.

Study Questions

1. Choose a staff member with whom you are well acquainted to illustrate what types of things the leader needs to understand about the staff member in order to promote motivation.
   a. Can you give an example of how well you understand one of the staff members by describing the member's interests, wants, and needs?
   b. What happens when those needs go unsatisfied?
   c. How can you create conditions that will encourage this staff member to attain satisfactions on the job?
   d. What specifically can you do to make this staff member's job more satisfying?
2. Staff members have the following needs. Discuss how you can manage staff members to see that these needs are met. Give specific examples of what you can do.
   a. Belonging needs.
   b. Sharing in planning the group goals.
   c. Attaining meaningful goals.
   d. Knowing clearly what is expected so as to work confidently.
   e. Challenging duties and responsibilities that are within range of abilities and that contribute toward reaching the goals.
   f. Seeing that progress is being made toward the goals that *we* have set.
   g. Keeping informed. What the staff is not *up* on, it may be *down* on.
   h. Confidence in the leader, based upon fair treatment, of recognition when it is due, and trust.

3. As a group exercise, relate to one another the specific things that motivate you as an individual. What do you respond to?

References

1. Feinberg, M. R. *Effective Psychology for Managers*. Englewood Cliffs, N.J.: Prentice-Hall, 1965. Pp. 122–142.
2. Gellerman, S. W. *Motivation and Productivity*. New York: American Management Assn., 1963. Pp. 105–121.
3. Herzberg, F. *Work and the Nature of Man*. Cleveland: World Publishing, 1973. Pp. 91–111.
4. Likert, R. *The Human Organization*. New York: McGraw-Hill, 1967. Pp. 53–77.
5. Maslow, A. H. *Toward a Psychology of Being* (2nd ed.). Princeton, N.J.: Van Nostrand, 1968.
6. Maslow, A. H. (Ed.) *Motivation and Personality* (2nd ed.). New York: Harper & Row, 1970. Pp. 35–58.
7. McClelland, D. *The Achieving Society*. Princeton, N.J.: Van Nostrand, 1961. Pp. 36–62.
8. Roethlisberger, F. J., and Dickson, W. J. *Management and the Worker*. Cambridge: Harvard University Press, 1939. Pp. 511–524.
9. Skinner, B. F. Where Skinner's theories work. *Business Week,* December 2, 1972, pp. 64–65.

Suggested Reading

Axne, S., Boniger, G., and Dodson, D. Staff motivation through a self-help design. *Superv. Nurse* 7:65, Oct. 1976.

Chopra, A. Motivation in task-oriented groups. *Nurs. Dig.* 5:80, Fall 1977.

Ford, R. N. *Motivation Through the Work Itself*. New York: American Management Association, 1969.

Gellerman, S. *Motivation and Productivity*. New York: American Management Association, 1963.

Gellerman, S. *Management Motivation*. New York: American Management Association, 1968.

Herzberg, F. One more time: How do you motivate employees? *Harvard Bus. Rev.* 46:53, Jan./Feb. 1968.

Holloway, R. C. Management can reverse declining employee work attitudes. *Hospitals* 50:71, Oct. 16, 1976.

Livingston, J. S. Pygmalion in management. *Harvard Bus. Rev.* 47:81, July/Aug. 1969.

Mager, R. and Pipe, P. You really oughta wanna or how not to motivate people. *Nursing '76* 6:65, Aug. 1976.

Marriner, A. Motivation of personnel. *Superv. Nurse* 7:60, Oct. 1976.

McClelland, D. C., and Winter, D. J. *Motivating Economic Achievement.* New York: Free Press, 1969.

Nusinoff, J. R. How to motivate your employees toward more effective patient care. *Hosp. Top.* 54:50, Mar./Apr. 1976.

Roche, W. J., and MacKinnon, N. L. Motivating people with meaningful work. *Harvard Bus. Rev.* 48:97, May/June 1970.

Skinner, B. F. *Beyond Freedom and Dignity.* New York: Knopf, 1971.

7. Development of Staff

In the majority of hospital nursing situations, the nurse cannot meet all the patient needs alone. Limited time and energy prevent the nurse from being all things to all patients. Professional nurses most frequently provide patient care with the assistance of subprofessional nursing personnel and paramedical personnel. Thus, the nurse becomes involved in delegating aspects of patient care to others. Before the care can be delegated, the nurse must know that the tasks can be performed well by the staff. Often, this involves informal teaching and training to perform tasks.

The objective of this chapter is to discuss management principles used in helping people to develop their potential in the working environment. The reader will be presented with behavioral and environmental aspects affecting learning, principles of learning, teaching techniques, problems that may prevent development of staff, and forms of adult education.

The influence the professional nurse has on a staff member depends upon their relationship as individuals. Emotional attitudes of the teacher and student are extremely important. The nurse needs to be trained to recognize and deal with normal emotional factors that prevent learning from occurring. The nurse needs to be aware of staff needs in order to identify and communicate with staff members and must show confidence in the staff's capacity to perform. They, in turn, must respect the nurse as a person with ability and integrity, worthy of authority. They must believe that their leader has the knowledge and skills of a professional nurse and represents model conduct. This does not mean they need to be friends, or even that they need to like each other. We like people for social reasons; we can respect people, however, for their honesty, their courage, and their ability.

The Helping Relationship

Carl Rogers defines a helping relationship as one "in which at least one of the parties has the intent of promoting the growth, development, maturity, improved coping with life of the other" [8]. This definition of a helping relationship can apply to the nurse-manager's relationships with staff members.

From research done on students at the Massachusetts Institute of Technology [3], we find some very helpful principles in understanding the dynamics of helping relationships. These principles can be broken down into five key areas:

1. The *task* or problem around which the helping relationship develops
2. The helper's *motivation* (achievement motivation—n Achievement; power motivation—n Power; affiliation motivation—n Affiliation) and his *self-image*
3. The *receiver* of help and the receiver's motives and self-image
4. The *environment* and *psychological climate* in which the helping activities occur
5. The information *feedback* which occurs during the helping process

THE TASK
The task can be placed on a scale. At one end of the scale the receiver of help takes a passive, uninvolved role. At the other end of the scale is education. The helper avoids using his special skills and knowledge to solve the task and instead works with the learner's frame of reference to increase the learner's ability to solve the problem. This method can help the learner the most but may cause frustration if the learner wants an immediate solution to the task.

THE HELPER AND RECEIVER OF HELP
The personal characteristics of the helper and learner are very important in the helping relationship.

The power motivation of the helper and the learner determines how much they will attempt to influence and control each other. The helper needs to deal with a tendency to feel "superior." The learner needs to overcome feeling weaker or dependent. These feelings must be dealt with in order for a helping relationship to develop.

The affiliation motivation of the helper and the learner determines how much they will be concerned about intimacy and understanding. The helper needs to know how the learner understands and perceives the problem. A lack of affiliation puts them in two different worlds. Too much affiliation can produce pressure toward conformity and sympathy, which may result in the helper's losing perspective on the problem and the learner's losing respect for the helper's expertise.

The achievement motivation of the helper and the learner deter-

mines how concerned they will be about accomplishing the task or solving the problem. The two need to agree on a mutually acceptable goal.

There is an interaction among motives in any helping relationship. If the power motivation is too high, the helper and learner can get preoccupied with controlling one another at the expense of understanding each other or accomplishing the task. High achievement motivation can cause the helper and learner to orient themselves to accomplishing the task without giving attention to the interpersonal aspects of influence and understanding needed for the learner to solve the problem on his or her own. "Here, let me help you" may result in the helper's pushing the learner aside, thus leaving the learner nearly as ignorant as before in regard to solving the problem. High affiliation motivation can result in the accomplishment of the task's taking a back seat to intimacy and understanding between the learner and helper.

Thus, for helping relationships to occur, moderate levels of achievement, affiliation, and power motivation in the helper and learner are necessary. The dynamics of the helping relationship are such that influence, intimacy and understanding, and a concern for task accomplishment are all necessary for effective help to take place; yet excessive concern in any one area can lead to deterioration of an effective helping relationship.

The self-image and attitudes of the helper and the learner are also important to the helping relationship. The learner must see himself as capable of improvement and must be willing to receive help. The helper must see himself as capable of helping without being a "know-it-all." The helper must be willing to influence and at the same time have empathy for the feelings of the person he is helping.

THE ENVIRONMENT AND PSYCHOLOGICAL CLIMATE
Behavior is a function of both the person and the environment. Comfort of surroundings, freedom from distraction, and the individual's perception of the environment all influence the learning process.

FEEDBACK
The last factor in the helping relationship is information feedback. Two aspects of information feedback are important. First, there is the source that controls information. Feedback can be controlled by the task, as in the case of programmed instruction, or by the receiver of

help, as in self-research methods, or by the helper, as in traditional teaching methods.

The other important aspect is the nature of the feedback. Most learning theorists have concluded that in the long-run reward is more effective than punishment. Carl Rogers, in his concept of unconditional positive reward, places heavy emphasis on the importance of positive feedback to the learner. "I find that the more acceptance and liking I feel toward this individual, the more I will be creating a relationship which he can use. By acceptance I mean a warm regard for him as a person of unconditional self-worth—of value no matter what his condition, or his feelings. . . . This acceptance of each fluctuating aspect of this other person makes it for him a relationship of warmth and safety, and the safety of being liked and prized as a person seems a highly important element in a helping relationship" [8].

EFFECTIVE HELPERS, INEFFECTIVE HELPERS, AND NONEFFECTIVE HELPERS

An effective helper is one who, in an environment where giving help is appropriate, attempts to help others, while the others see this help as significant and important to them. The ineffective helper attempts to give others help, but these others do not regard the help as important. The nonhelper does not attempt to help. The MIT experiment showed that ineffective helpers scored much lower on n Affiliation than did effective helpers or nonhelpers. Ineffective helpers scored much higher on n Power than did effective helpers or nonhelpers.

As far as self-image is concerned, the nonhelpers are different from both the effective and ineffective helpers in that they describe themselves as more passive, democratic, not cynical, submissive, followers, guarded, quiet, timid, not influential, inarticulate, self-conscious, and preferring to listen. The general picture is one of an accepting, democratic person who lacks the self-confidence to influence others.

Ineffective helpers describe themselves as organized, impatient, open, and superior. These adjectives summarize a person extremely self-confident with impatience and lack of interest in others.

The effective helpers consistently place themselves between the ineffective and nonhelpers. They are self-confident without being overbearing, and they score moderately in achievement, affiliation, and power.

These results focus on the two types of help that are doomed to failure—the brash, overconfident, superior approach, which places the learner on the defensive, and the timid, hesitant, passive approach, which may raise questions about the helper's qualifications and lead to a lack of confidence in the helper. The results of the research also showed that the effective helpers gave more positive feedback and ineffective helpers gave more negative feedback.

To summarize the experiment, the helping relationship is best viewed as one involving a complex interaction of at least three motives—n Achievement, n Affiliation, and n Power. Effective helpers appear to be those individuals who score moderately on these three motives. Similar moderation appears in the self-image of effective helpers. They are not as brash and overconfident as ineffective helpers nor as timid and self-conscious as nonhelpers. The feedback that is received from effective helpers tends to be more positive and less related to control issues than feedback from ineffective helpers.

Understanding Viewpoints of Others

Effective communications are of paramount importance in the nurse's relationships with staff. However, a common problem frequently exists in our communications with others. We have a natural tendency to evaluate, to judge, to approve, or to disapprove the expressed opinions of the other person. The primary reaction is to listen to another's expressed opinion and evaluate it from one's own point of view [7]. An example could occur during a patient-care conference when a nurse states that a patient seems to be exaggerating his discomfort. Almost invariably your reply will be approval or disapproval of the attitude expressed. This tendency to evaluate another's opinion can be a major barrier to interpersonal communications.

Rogers [7] states that we can solve this problem by avoiding the evaluation and instead seeing the attitude or idea from the other person's viewpoint. This is not as easy as it may seem. A way to test your ability to understand rather than to evaluate is to try the following experiment. The next time you have an argument or heated discussion with a friend or with a group, institute this rule: You may speak your opinion only after you have restated the last speaker's opinion to his satisfaction. This means you must achieve his frame of reference.

Too many managers fail to listen intently when communicating

with staff. Do you tap your fingers on the desk, allow yourself to answer the phone, or fidget when a staff member is talking with you? You need to hear the staff's feelings as well as their words. Feeling has its source in emotions, and emotions are the most potent catalyst of action. Feelings, if not allowed to escape, can develop into forces of anxiety and frustration that erode morale and efficiency and produce incompetency.

Asking Staff for Opinions

How do we know if our perceived attitudes foster suggestions from the staff? Are you listening only for what you want to hear? Are you making patient-care decisions without the opinions, counsel, and assistance of the staff? If you do more than half of the talking at a patient-care conference that includes a group of staff members, it is a good bet that you fall into this category. Are you really interested in getting the advice or suggestions of staff members? The risk involved in not getting counsel from the staff is that you are failing to provide them an opportunity to develop. Another important risk is damage to morale. Patient care is the end product at stake. A good rule to follow is to seek staff's counsel on major patient-care decisions. If a decision has already been made, solicit advice on how to implement it.

The relationship the leader has with staff members depends upon the leader's attitudes and feelings toward them. If the nurse accepts and respects them as individuals and has a positive and helpful attitude, a nonthreatening environment is promoted in which staff can learn and develop. This can be termed a "climate of confidence." The staff members must feel that they are approved of as individuals, that their strengths and weaknesses are recognized, and that they are important persons doing an important job.

Candor with Staff

If you promote an open atmosphere, your staff will not feel inhibited about talking freely with you. Frankness, honesty of opinion, and forthrightness are the key words. This means being honest with them when you do not know the answer to their questions. Tell them you do not know rather than brushing off the question or giving a feeble reply. It means tolerating their questions about your decisions. They should sense that you do not become defensive when questioned. It means openly accepting criticism of your behavior. It may be better

to hear things that hurt from time to time than not to get the true feelings of the staff. This is difficult behavior to develop for the leader who lacks self-confidence and for the autocratic leader. Perhaps such an attitude is difficult for the most competent leader at times. It is a goal, however, toward which all should work.

Here, again, make a self-check. Next time you are in a conference discussing a controversial subject, make a note of how often ideas contrary to your own are advanced. If they come up rarely, or not at all, you probably have failed to create an open environment.

Influence of Manager's Expectations

What a manager expects of staff members and the way they are treated largely determine their performance. Staff members, more often than not, do what they believe they are expected to do [5]. This is similar to other patterns of human behavior. We have seen the relief of pain from placebos. The patient's response was related to what was expected. In a series of scientific experiments, Robert Rosenthal of Harvard University has demonstrated that a "teacher's expectation for her pupil's intellectual competence can . . . serve as an educational self-fulfilling prophecy" [9]. An experiment conducted with 60 preschoolers of equal ability compared the performance of pupils of teachers who had been led to believe their students were slow learners to that of pupils of teachers who had been led to believe their students had rapid learning ability. Pupils of the second group learned much faster.

Staff members can usually sense the leader's attitude toward them; they know whether or not the leader believes they can meet expectations. Too frequently, however, managers are unaware of the feelings they transmit to others. The nurse's standards of patient care are revealed by the example the leader sets. If the nurse gives thorough skin care to patients, for example, staff members will be inclined to give the same quality of care. Nurse-leaders therefore transmit their expectations by their behavior as well as by what they say.

An important aspect of the ability to transmit high expectations is the leader's self-confidence in the ability to motivate and develop the staff. If the leader has doubts about the ability to stimulate the staff members, the leader will expect less of them. An executive has been quoted as saying, "Your administrative success will be in direct proportion to your subordinate's belief of your belief in him" [6].

Managerial expectations have the greatest effect on new em-

ployees who have not yet formulated their attitudes on how well they can perform in a nursing situation. This is very significant when one thinks of the generally high turnover rate of nursing personnel. One can see the importance of having new personnel placed under the leadership of a nurse with high standards and high expectations of staff. The staff members' self-confidence will grow, their capabilities will develop, and they will be more productive as a result of good leadership.

Principles of Learning

Teaching is another necessary part of developing staff members to their fullest work potential. Every contact you have with staff can be an opportunity to teach. Some attention to the principles of learning is helpful. Most of these have been formulated by psychologists [2, 4, 10].

Learning can be defined as that human process by which skills, knowledge, habits, and attitudes are acquired and utilized in such a way that behavior may be modified. Psychologists, primarily through experimentation, have developed a number of important principles of learning. These are equally pertinent for application by training directors who administer programs, classroom instructors who teach employees, and supervisors who train employees on the job.

MOTIVATION

The individual must be motivated to learn. He needs to be aware of the inadequacies of his present behavior, skill, or knowledge and have a clear idea of the behavior he needs to attain.

Adequate motivation is essential to the success of any learning experience. People are goal-oriented in their behavior. They will exert themselves to fulfill a felt need. Learning is effective when the trainees perceive that they can satisfy some goal through participation in a training program. The staff members must see the need to improve their abilities and job performance in order to benefit from attempts to develop their potential.

Both rewards and punishment play a powerful role in motivation to learn. A reward for a desired response serves to stimulate a repetition of that behavior. Mild punishment is effective if it is immediate and if the learner understands the reason for it. This must be handled very judiciously, for punishment may cause the learners to resent or fear the instructor so much that they cannot concentrate upon learning the work.

Generally, people will learn to behave in a desired way if they understand the reasons for the desired behavior and if they are rewarded for such behavior.

Leaders can help motivate the staff by giving new and challenging assignments, by delegating authority, and by rotating tasks. Assignments should be planned so that they are meaningful to each individual.

REINFORCEMENT

Related to motivation is the need for reinforcement. For learning to take place, the individual must receive some encouragement or reward. In many cases the reward need not be tangible. The learner needs to experience some feeling of progress, either through the leader's comments or through self-observation that the job was well done. Praise for progress is more effective than punishment for mistakes made. Most people have only limited tolerance for failure. Learners must be made aware of their failures, but the ability to tolerate failure should be a function of the success achieved and the degree to which correct behavior has been reinforced.

FEEDBACK

In order for reinforcement to be effective in improving performance, there must be feedback, or knowledge of results. Research experiments have demonstrated that people learn faster when they are informed of their accomplishments. Such knowledge should be automatic, immediate, and meaningfully related to the task at hand. The learners need to know how their performance measures up to the desired standard. When learners have made a mistake, they need to recognize why and how they went wrong and how close they came to doing it correctly. All too frequently positive feedback is not given. The feedback you give should be given in a nonthreatening environment if possible. In other words, do not correct your staff in the presence of the patient or others unless it is absolutely necessary for patients' well-being. Praise, too, should usually be given in private. When criticizing, criticize the action, not the individual. Feedback should be provided as soon as possible after the performance is observed.

LEARNING BY DOING

Learning is most efficient when the learner is actively involved rather than passively listening to a description. The most economical and practical training method should be selected for the type of desired

learning. Much patient-care related training has taken place on the job under the direction of the employee's or student's immediate supervisor. Simulated learning experiences and modern technology are now being used to develop the learner's active involvement in developing competency. Motor activity directly stimulates the higher mental processes, such as learning [1]. The greater the number of senses involved, the more effective the learning. Doing rather than just seeing or hearing also means that the individuals are more likely to devote more of themselves to the task; they become more involved in the learning process. The difference between knowing a principle and making it work must be learned by performing. Permit mistakes to be made when they will cause no harm. Mistakes are then corrected, and the correct behavior reinforced.

SPACED REPETITION

Many experiments have shown that learning periods distributed through time are more efficient than single, sustained attempts. Repetition serves to inhibit forgetting. Without practice, learned skills gradually disappear.

LEARNING BY PARTS

Learning is enhanced when the total process or skill to be learned is divided into small segments, each of which can be mastered in a sequence until the total task is learned. Whether or not this is possible depends on what is to be learned. For example, the nurse's aide in training may have three weeks to master the skills of giving a patient morning care. The skills involved may include taking the patient's temperature, pulse, and respirations, giving the patient a bath, making a bed, and helping the patient with ambulation and with the use of a bedpan. If each of these tasks can be taught separately rather than attempting to teach them all at once, learning can be enhanced.

LEARNING BY MASTERING LARGE SEGMENTS

Learning is inhibited if the segments to be mastered are too small. Integrating fragments into a whole activity as a smooth, continuous process becomes extremely difficult. Whenever possible, the learner should try to master as a single unit all those activities that must be performed in a smooth, continuous sequence, as a complex pattern cannot be learned until all its parts are practiced simultaneously. Separate practice of the parts can improve the learner's skill in each

one, but it cannot teach the learner the total pattern. An example of this principle would be teaching a practical nurse how to insert a Foley catheter. The procedure encompasses principles of asepsis, cleansing techniques, anatomy, positioning, and assembling equipment. All these aspects of the total procedure need to be practiced in a smooth, continuous sequence.

PROVIDING THEORY

Learning is faster and can be better applied to new situations if the learner understands the principles involved. In nursing situations the employee who knows the "whys" behind the skill is better able to transfer knowledge to new situations. If the staff is to develop insight into new problems that arise during the course of rendering patient care, a more basic understanding of activities than that provided by "this-is-how-you-do-it" training needs to be achieved. Logical training is more effective than rote training in nursing. Therefore, staff members should be taught sufficient theory to understand the principles and reasons underlying their work and to cope successfully with the general types of problems they may encounter.

GEARING LEARNING TO THE INDIVIDUAL

All human beings can learn. The effective teacher sees that each learner has different needs and abilities and so must be taught in a different way. The learner must secure satisfaction from the learning. In other words the training must seem useful to the learner. Teachers have a strong inclination to make people over into their own image. This temptation should be avoided and should be replaced by understanding that each learner must achieve results within the framework of the learner's personality and motivations.

When teaching, the nurse-manager must start at the student's present level. Do not assume that the learner knows or does not know something. To determine what the learner knows, ask a question that requires an explanation rather than one that must be answered by "yes" or "no." You waste your time and the staff's time explaining something they already know. Observation of the staff members working with patients and with fellow workers will give you insight and valuable information as to their level of performance.

We must not judge performance solely on results, with little or no consideration of how the results were obtained. The results do not always justify the means. You can observe the action directly or utilize questions to determine how the results were obtained.

LEARNING MOTOR SKILLS

If the skill to be taught is a motor skill, the instructor begins by showing and explaining the supplies and equipment needed. The activity is then performed by the instructor. If it involves steps, the procedure should be broken down into logical components and explained. Next the learners should practice the procedure. They should understand what they are doing and be able to explain the activity. The instructor should provide guidance and feedback. The learners must know if their performance is progressing properly or not. A rest period should follow the practice period. Distributed practice periods are more fruitful than prolonged and concentrated practice.

LEARNING CONCEPTS AND ATTITUDES

This process is much more complex than learning motor skills. There are many ways to learn ideas and attitudes. We can learn by trial and error, by personal experience, by reading and observing, or by listening and talking with others.

Preservation of Staff Initiative

It can be a temptation, when observing a staff member involved in patient care, to pitch in and take the initiative. For example, a staff member may be giving care to a comatose patient. If you want to help, refrain from initiating such care as turning the patient or giving range of motion exercises. When being aggressive in initiating care, you tend to stifle the initiative of the staff. Your help is very supportive, but refrain from "stealing the thunder" from your learner. The staff will derive much more satisfaction in initiating the plan of care and then receiving your help in carrying it out.

Exploring Problems Through Questions

The ability to ask good questions is essential in teaching. Good questions help the learner gain insight and understanding. You do not want your questions to seem threatening or authoritarian; rather, your intent is to explore the problem and in so doing bring greater understanding to the learner. The same holds true for questions brought to you. There is a temptation to derive personal satisfaction from being an authority and to exhibit your knowledge by answering

the question. This may be necessary in situations where an immediate answer is needed. If time permits, however, the question can be used as a learning process. By asking the learner questions leading up to a solution, the leader can help the learner determine the answer. For example, the staff may ask you, "Mr. Smith wants some milk. May he have it?" You can reply with questions such as: What kind of diet is he on? Is that included in a low-fat diet? Is he having any tests done today?

If a staff member comes to you with a solution to a problem that you believe will not work, do not answer with a "That will not work because . . ." This is not teaching by the use of problem-solving. Instead, attempt to get the staff member to explain how the solution was determined. You can ask questions such as: What are some advantages and disadvantages? or What alternatives did you consider, and why did you reject them? It is by answering these questions that problem solving is accomplished.

Demonstration

Skill in demonstration is another effective tool in teaching. Prior to the demonstration you should prepare staff members by discussing what is to be demonstrated. Here again, utilize questions to keep learners actively involved, to determine how much of the activity is already understood, and to find gaps in knowledge that will need special emphasis. The demonstration should be as lifelike as possible. For example, "Resusci-Anne," a training manikin, is a very lifelike tool for teaching heart-lung resuscitation. At the conclusion of your demonstration, have the learners demonstrate back to you, if this is feasible, and have them explain what is happening and why. Learning is reinforced when the learner repeats the procedure soon after it is learned, and retention is increased by repetition. It is useful to plan to have the learner perform the skill at the earliest possible opportunity, and have the learner explain to you how the procedure will be done just prior to doing it. The demonstration or return demonstration should be followed by an analysis and evaluation to ensure the learner's complete understanding. Guard against expecting the learners to repeat the demonstration exactly as you originally performed it. A grasp of the principles is more important. Let the staff members develop the methods most suited to their abilities and limitations.

Potential Impediments to Teaching Role

Some nurses hesitate to utilize these principles of staff development. They claim it is faster to do a job themselves than to show someone else how to do it. They believe there just is not enough time. Others fail in this management role because consciously (or unconsciously) they lack self-confidence or adequate nursing knowledge. Some nurse-teachers fail to disclose all their "tricks of the trade," fearing competition. Others cannot communicate with staff because of an age barrier or a personality clash—for example, when a new graduate nurse leads a group of employees who have been at the hospital five or ten years.

For several reasons the staff may not accept help from the professional nurse. The staff may feel knowledgeable and thus become very sensitive to suggestions and criticism. The staff may lack self-confidence in their ability to do the job, or the staff may fear the professional nurse. Poor communication often proves to be the reason for failure. Resistance to change also hampers development.

It is important to identify the preceding problems. Factors preventing development of individuals or groups rendering patient care have their effect on the quality of patient care given. Interest, ingenuity, and fresh approaches must be developed by the group to solve problems of patient care.

In-Service Education Programs

Hospitals with in-service education programs often provide a variety of adult education programs. Some hospitals provide employees with the teachers and time needed to complete courses for a high school diploma. Other hospitals offer special courses such as speed-reading. Employees of some hospitals are given an opportunity to take college courses with the hospital paying part or all of the tuition.

In-service education, a form of adult education, is a means of keeping staff members informed of the many advances and changes in medicine, nursing, and management. M. Shanks [11] writes that an in-service program has four components:

1. Orientation
2. Skill training
3. Continuing education
4. Leadership training

ORIENTATION

Although proper orientation is easily and often neglected, it is essential for ensuring that new employees get off to the right start. Orientation is the guided adjustment of the employee to the organization and the work environment.

Orientation programs are advantageous to both the hospital and the employees. The hospital administration seeks to create favorable attitudes about its goals, policies, and personnel. A well-run orientation program may minimize the likelihood of policy violation, discharges, resignations, grievances, and misunderstandings.

In most instances the employee is partially oriented to the hospital before starting work. Such orientation began with the employment interview and from the reputation the hospital has earned. After the employee is hired, the orientation progresses with both the personnel department and the nursing personnel playing key roles.

The personnel department needs to orient the newcomer by explaining the pay, pay increases, promotion opportunities, holidays, vacations, and benefit plans. It should also train the nursing personnel in the performance of their orientation responsibilities.

The role of the orienter (this may be the head nurse) is to make the newcomer feel welcome. This person should review the job description with the new employee, introduce the other staff members working on the unit, and conduct a tour of the patient-care unit and its facilities.

The following is a list of important content information and actions that may be included in an orientation program.

1. Hospital history, policies, practices
2. Hospital services
3. Hospital facilities
4. Organizational structure
5. Employee responsibilities to the hospital
6. Hospital responsibilities to the employee
7. Pay
8. Rules of conduct
9. Tour of the hospital
10. Work schedules
11. Collective bargaining agreement and union relationships
12. Benefit plans—life insurance, medical, hospitalization, pension, unemployment
13. Safety program

14. Training or educational opportunities
15. Promotion policy
16. Introduction to fellow employees
17. Establishment of a feeling of belonging and acceptance, showing genuine interest in new employee
18. Employee appraisal system
19. Work assignment

SKILL TRAINING

These programs serve to train the nonprofessional hospital employee. The nurse's aide, for example, needs to be taught the skills required in the hospital's job description. Referring to the sample job description on page 207, one sees that the nurse's aide must know how to do a variety of functions, including taking vital signs, giving enemas, hematesting stools, and collecting specimens. These skills should be learned and practiced under the supervision of the instructor either in a classroom or on the patient-care unit. To leave initial teaching and supervision of aides to staff members is unfair to both the aides and the staff members unless provision is made for a special "mentor system." The staff members' primary concern is the patient, whereas an instructor in the classroom can give full concern to the aides-in-training.

CONTINUING EDUCATION

Continuing education is either mandatory as a requisite for relicensure or voluntary in almost every state. In most states there are stipulations about the types of programs that qualify for continuing education. Some of the continuing education programs must be obtained from sources other than the institution that employs the nurse, but many employing agencies conduct programs that can be used to meet a portion of the total continuing education requirements.

Continuing education is also supported by the Joint Commission on Accreditation of Hospitals. The Nursing Services section of the Accreditation Manual published by the JCAH includes a requirement that there must be continuing training and educational programs for nurses in the hospital. Both the American Nurses' Association and the National League for Nursing have published information about continuing education. The American Nurses' Association publication *Continuing Education in Nursing: Guidelines for Staff Development* contains information about goals for staff development

programs, the organization of staff development departments, the roles of personnel, and evaluation of programs. Staff development terminology is also defined.

Some staff development programs include a continuing education component designed to provide learning experiences for nurses that include content and skills different from those learned in basic educational programs in nursing but that are general to the practice of nursing. Staff development programs also include learning experiences specific to the practice of nursing in a given health-care agency. The types of programs specific to an agency include orientation programs and in-service education. Orientation consists of an introduction to the role and expectations of nurses in a given agency. In-service education is designed to increase the knowledge and skills of nurses employed by an agency in relation to their roles and job descriptions in that agency. Continuing education in the hospital can be done in a wide variety of ways. For example, it may encompass a televised education program such as "Surgical Repair of an Aortic Aneurysm"; it may be an on-the-unit drill of the procedure for cardiac arrest; it may be a formal presentation by a guest or by a member of the medical or nursing staff; or it may be an informal lecture by a technician on the use of a new piece of equipment. The key to a successful continuing education program is to survey the employees to learn their wants and needs for the program. For example, to teach professional nurses how to make a bed might be folly; there would be no interest or need. A questionnaire may be used to gain suggestions from staff members for in-service educational programs. Once a program is scheduled, the nurse-leaders should encourage as many staff members as possible to attend. This may involve scheduling the program to be presented at different hours in order to reach nurses of the three shifts and to maintain nurses on the unit with patients during the program.

LEADERSHIP OR MANAGEMENT TRAINING
This aspect of in-service education is generally concerned with the preparation of professional nurses for leadership or supervisory positions. The authors believe that such training can be beneficial to all registered nurses.

Each patient-care unit not only can participate in the agency's in-service educational program but can also have an educational program on the unit. Staff members on an orthopedic unit may be interested in specific aspects of orthopedics that a delivery room

nurse might find less useful. Once a subject of interest is found among staff members, the subject can be studied in a variety of ways. One or more staff members can research the subject at the library and bring the information back to the others; a specialist in the subject can be asked to lead an informal question-and-answer discussion; or a film may be shown on the patient-care unit. It is also helpful if staff members can attend conferences and courses and share their information with those who did not attend. For example, the Hawaii Heart Association presents an annual three-day conference on cardiovascular nursing. Those nurses able to attend gain a great deal educationally.

With such a variety of means for continuing education, all staff members should be able to gain new knowledge. Not only should all levels of the nursing staff be considered, but also personnel on the evening and night shifts.

As M. Shanks states so well, "In-service education cannot force individuals to learn, but it can emphasize the need to learn and can be the stimulus for personal and professional development . . . It is rapidly becoming a successful method towards improving care for patients" [11].

Group Session

The following questions are written for group discussion. Get a group of classmates or friends together to discuss these questions if you do not have an opportunity to answer them in a classroom session.
1. Have two people role play a teaching situation. Have one assume the role of the professional nurse and the other the role of a nurse's aide. The nurse is to teach the aide how to get a paraplegic patient from the bed to the wheelchair. Have the other members of the group observe the interaction between the nurse and the aide and evaluate the teaching situation in terms of:
   a. Relationship between the nurse and aide
   b. Utilization of learning principles
      (1) Motivation
      (2) Reinforcement
      (3) Feedback
      (4) Learning by doing
      (5) Spaced repetition
      (6) Learning by parts
      (7) Learning by mastering large segments
      (8) Providing theory
      (9) Gearing learning to the individual

    (10) Learning motor skills
    (11) Learning concepts and attitudes
  c. Utilization of techniques in questioning
  d. Utilization of techniques in demonstrating

Additional situations that could be used are positioning a comatose patient, putting a patient through range of motion exercises, and feeding a C.V.A. patient.

2. Have members of the group reflect and share with the others two memorable events in their working experience: (1) What moment stands out in your memory as being the most satisfying experience? (2) What moment has been the most dissatisfying experience? Analyze why the experience was satisfying and why the contrasting experience was dissatisfying. What implications can you derive from this to apply to your role in developing staff?

3. Are any members of the group having difficulty with staff members who are not functioning at their potential? If so, describe the individual's behavior and attitudes to the group. Utilize this example to investigate the problem and to derive possible solutions. Have the group approve a strategy to be used in future interactions with the staff member. Have the nurse-leader utilize these suggestions and report back to the group on how effective the solutions were in the actual situation. This situation and others of similar types can be followed in as many group discussions as necessary until the problem is solved.

4. Select an emotional and controversial issue that members of the group can use to argue conflicting positions. Divide into opposing groups and begin to debate. At a given time, stop to analyze how much communication took place. Return to the debate, and this time utilize the suggestion of Carl Rogers as noted in this chapter, "You may speak your opinion only after you have restated the last speaker's opinion to his satisfaction." Were you able to see a difference in how much real communication took place?

5. Identify attitudes and habits that you have seen on your patient-care unit that are barriers to communication. What communication habits do you have that you would like to change?

6. Did your orientation program to the health-care agency or school communicate high standards? Was there one person in particular who stood out in your mind as a role model?

References

1. Allport, G. The psychology of participation. *Psychol. Rev.* 52:117, May 1945.
2. Hilgard, E. (Ed.) *Theories of Learning.* National Society for the Study of Education 63d Yearbook. Chicago: University of Chicago Press, 1964. Pp. 1–360.

3. Kolb, D. A., and Boyatzis, R. E.   On the dynamics of the helping relationship. In *Organizational Psychology: A Book of Readings* (2nd ed.). Englewood Cliffs, N.J.: Prentice-Hall, 1974.

4. Leavitt, H.   *Managerial Psychology*. Chicago: University of Chicago Press, 1964. Pp. 65–80.

5. Livingston, J. S.   Pygmalion in management. *Harvard Bus. Rev.* 47:81, July/Aug. 1969.

6. Myles, M.   *The Growth and Development of Executives*. Boston: Division of Research, Graduate School of Business Administration, Harvard University, 1950.

7. Otto, C. P., and Glaser, R. O.   *The Management of Training*. Reading, Mass.: Addison-Wesley, 1970.

8. Rogers, C.   *Carl Rogers on Personal Power*. New York: Delacorte, 1977. Pp. 3–27.

9. Rosenthal, R., and Jacobson, L.   *Pygmalion in the Classroom*. New York: Holt, Rinehart & Winston, 1968. Pp. 174–182.

10. Skinner, B. F.   *Science and Human Behavior*. New York: Macmillan, 1953.

11. Shanks, M., and Kennedy, D.   *The Theory and Practice of Nursing Service Administration* (2nd ed.). New York: Blakiston Div., McGraw-Hill, 1970. Pp. 248–264.

Suggested Reading

Chokrieh, A.   In-service education, leadership and management. *Nigerian Nurse* 8:37, July/Sept. 1976.

Munn, Y. L.   How to get it and use it in nursing today. *Nurs. Adm. Q.* 1:95, Fall 1976.

Nelson, M. A.   Building a better team. *Nursing '77* 7:65, July 1977.

Schaefer, M. J.   The knowledge worker. *J. Nurs. Adm.* 7:7, April 1977.

8. Introducing Change

Today's nurses are seeing many changes in the field of patient care and health-care agency management. New medications, new equipment, and new methods of treatment are being introduced to the health-care scene at a rapid rate. We like to think that we keep up to date in a field where last year's knowledge may be obsolete today. Some changes we may welcome readily—for example, lighter, easier to handle cardiographic equipment or computerized medication selection. But we tend to resist the changes introduced by management that affect our interpersonal and job relations. Why do we resist these? Because they tend to threaten the security of the patterns to which we have grown accustomed.

In order for health-care agencies to meet the increasing demands for patient-care services, changes in management of personnel must occur. The ability to introduce such changes with a minimum of resistance is a key managerial skill. This chapter deals with people's reactions to change on the job and how change can be introduced in an acceptable way.

Why Individuals Resist Change

Automation may make an employee feel that he will no longer be needed and may therefore lose his job. In hospitals we have seen automation in the transportation of food trays from the kitchen to the patient, in the use of the computer for staffing, and in the use of television to enable the nurse to visualize the patient in his room.

A worker may resist the change of assignment of duties. For example, a licensed practical nurse may be so accustomed to helping ambulate patients in the rehabilitation department that she resents a new job of planning recreational activities for patients that will require different duties. It does not take long for an individual to develop a routine in an everyday work situation. Learning new ways which have been brought on by change requires energy that individuals may resent putting forth. In other words, it is easier not to change.

Another factor in the worker's resistance to change is the uncertainty that change brings. The reason for the change may not be understood. The uncertainty may be helped by explaining the purpose for the change and answering the worker's questions.

Changing work procedures and systems and introducing new equipment may also upset the interpersonal relationships established prior to the new system. For example, two aides on the evening shift always divided the unit in half according to room numbers for their giving of patient care. When the student nurse-leader attempted to arrange assignments according to patient-care needs, she met with much hostility and resentment from the two aides. They had developed their own work pattern and resisted change that would affect their interpersonal work relationships.

Fear of failure may also cause resistance to change. Individuals may feel that they are doing their jobs well now and that the change will alter their ability to work as well.

Employees may view change as having to take orders. If the so-called orders come from supervisors who have little contact with the staff members or from a student nurse-leader who is not one of the regulars, the staff members may view and resent the change as coming from an outsider.

Unions are also likely to resist change unless management consults with them either formally or informally. More and more health-care employees are being organized into unions.

The Nature of Resistance

The key to the problem is to understand the true nature of resistance. What employees resist is usually not technical change but social change—the change in their human relationships that generally accompanies technical change. Resistance is usually created because the people introducing the change are so preoccupied with the technical aspects of the new idea that they do not see how the change will affect social relationships.

We need to think of change as having both a technical and a social aspect. The technical aspect of the change is the making of a measurable modification in the physical routines on the job. The social aspect refers to the way those affected by the change think it will alter their relationships to the organization. The nature and size of the technical aspect of the change does not determine the presence or absence of resistance nearly as much as the social aspect.

Therefore, nurse-managers need an in-depth, detailed understanding of the specific social arrangements that will be sustained or threatened by the change or by the way that it is introduced.

Many changes take place without resistance. People who work

closely together often swap ideas to make their work easier. Because they work so closely and because they initiated the ideas, these changes are not threatening.

By contrast, if the change is initiated by the agency administration or by someone higher up in the hierarchy who is not a part of the working unit, the changes are more likely to be resisted. We may sometimes wish that the validity of the technical aspect of the change were the sole determinant of its acceptability. The fact remains, however, that the social aspect is what determines the presence or absence of resistance.

Even after the plans for change have been carefully made, it takes time to implement them fully. Time is necessary even when there is no resistance to the change itself. If the staff members feel that they are being pushed and are not allowed enough time to implement the change, they will begin to resist it.

An attitude that may cause trouble is assuming that the change will result in resistance. Staff members will sense this attitude, and you will probably get the resistance you are anticipating as a result.

When resistance does appear, do not think of it as something that needs to be overcome. Instead, think of it as a signal that something is going wrong. Paul Lawrence [1] uses an interesting analogy. He says that signs of resistance in a social organization are useful in the same way that pain is useful to the body as a signal that some bodily functions are getting out of adjustment.

The resistance, like the pain, tells you something is wrong. You need to find out what is causing the pain. To take a pain killer or to try to stop the resistance without first finding out the cause of the pain or resistance will not take care of the basic problem. Therefore, when resistance does occur, you need to listen carefully to find out what the problem is.

It may be a technical reason that is causing the difficulty. More likely, however, the problem will be a result of threatened established social arrangements for doing work.

If efforts to create positive attitudes towards the change fail before the change is implemented, then the nurse-manager may decide to enforce the change regardless of the attitudes. The nurse-manager then relies on cognitive dissonance to dissipate the resistance. The concept of cognitive dissonance asserts that when a person is required to demonstrate a given behavior consistently, his or her attitudinal patterns are apt to become favorable to the enforced behavior [2]. In other words, as the person behaves in the required

way, he resolves the conflicts between his attitudes and his behaviors. By doing the required activity, the individual will soon rationalize that activity's desirability.

How We Get Staff Members to Accept Change

No change can be successfully carried out unless logical and psychological foundations have been established. Generally, the logical foundation is built well but the psychological aspect is less well designed. If the psychological foundation—the one concerned with staff members and their possible reactions to the proposed change—is not well designed, staff member resistance may follow.

A positive approach to building the psychological foundation for change has been outlined by Nathaniel Stewart [3]. He calls for the following measures:

Identification
Reassurance
Communication
Participation
Mutual interest
Follow-through

IDENTIFICATION
This refers to having the staff members themselves identify with the problem. Employees must first see and feel the need to change. For example, the Waterton Hospital administration decided that each patient-care unit should change from a verbal report to oncoming shifts to the use of a taped report. Prior to the change, 4 North, a hectic, disorganized floor, took an average of one hour to complete reports between shifts. The staff members considered this unsatisfactory and were eager to try the tape recorder to see if this would lead to better utilization of nursing time. Three North, however, was able to give a 20-minute report verbally that was prompt and complete. The staff members on 3 North, therefore, had difficulty identifying with the change introduced by the use of the tape recorder.

REASSURANCE
Industrial psychologists agree that employees will seek to protect the job satisfactions that exist and will be apprehensive of any proposal that may infringe on established satisfactions. This anxiety must be alleviated prior to acceptance of the change. The following situation

illustrates this point. The intensive care unit and coronary care unit functioned as separate units with separate staff members but were adjoining geographically at Waterton Hospital. A plan was devised for merging the staffs of the two units to achieve greater flexibility in staffing patterns. Prior to the change there were days during which the coronary care unit had three nurses caring for only one patient while the adjacent intensive care unit had three nurses caring for ten patients. The new plan would allow nurses to float between the two units when needed. The staff nurses in the intensive care unit were very anxious as they felt unqualified to interpret electrocardiogram monitor strips. The coronary care unit nurses were also anxious about the proposed change. These anxieties needed to be recognized and alleviated by those introducing the change. Fortunately, the nursing management of Waterton Hospital saw the need for in-service education to precede the change so that the nurses would have class preparation for new experiences in patient care. This was a necessary aspect of reassurance.

COMMUNICATION

If change is desired, it must be explained carefully and thoroughly. Important changes affecting staff members should be communicated face-to-face in a personalized way, not via an intercom or a printed handout. It is a must that the communications precede the change. Staff members need to be thoroughly informed and have their questions answered in advance of a proposed or pending change. Background and reasons for the change should be communicated to staff members. As health-care agencies grow bigger and more complex, the need to communicate in understandable language must not be overlooked.

Organizations have grapevines that spread news and rumors rapidly. To prevent unwarranted speculation from growing, management should keep staff members informed throughout the planning, introduction, installation, and follow-through of the change.

PARTICIPATION

Participation of staff in the management of change is a psychological and functional asset in management. It is helpful to solicit from staff members their suggestions, views, and criticisms of the proposed change. The communication pattern should be such that staff members talk to each other as well as to the person introducing the proposed change. It is important to encourage the staff members to express themselves. T. A. Wickes [5] points out that getting opinions

out in the open so that they can be examined and evaluated is an important, trust-building task. Ideas that get no hearing often seem better to their author than ideas that actually get used. During staff members' discussions, the leader should refrain from asking staff members to "stick to the subject." What may seem to be irrelevant tangents often contain personal and emotional elements that need to be brought out and discussed. Failure to do so may result in staff members dragging their feet instead of cooperating with the change.

Participation will not work if it is used as device to get others to do what you want them to do. Real participation is based on respect. Respect is acquired when the nurse-manager faces the reality that the contributions of the staff members are needed.

Ideas should not be solicited from the staff members if in fact there is no flexibility in the plans for change. Involving staff members deeply in a project and then incorporating nothing of what they had to offer in the plan of action may result in anger and frustration among those staff members consulted.

MUTUAL INTEREST

Proposed change should appear to solve problems at the patient-care unit level as well as in the overall management of the agency. It is helpful to identify how the new changes will benefit staff members as well as management in contrast to the existing system.

FOLLOW-THROUGH

Change often takes time. Time must be allowed for organizational, technical, and human change. Follow-through is needed in each of these areas to detect and correct any weaknesses or difficulties in the change. When playing tennis it is not enough to hit the ball. The stroke must continue past the moment of hitting the ball to the stage called follow-through in order for the ball to sail on target. So too with proposed change. Without follow-through the change may be sent out but may fall off course rather than landing on target. It is necessary to make certain that the solution is really suitable to the problem that prompted the change.

Techniques for Introducing Change

One of the most common and most difficult problems in introducing change is that of bringing in a new nurse to head an already established unit. If the former head nurse was well liked, the new one will

have to contend with the staff members' attitudes that the new nurse cannot be as good as the former head nurse. Staff members wonder what changes the new head nurse will make. They may resent the newcomer as an outsider and prepare themselves to reject everything the new head nurse does.

Let us examine this problem and how it was handled in a specific situation. Keep in mind that although the case discusses a new head nurse the same could apply to a new group leader or a new staff nurse who is a group member. The example will illustrate techniques that may be helpful in introducing change in a wide variety of situations.

Mrs. Bennett, head nurse in the intensive care unit, had developed warm relationships with her staff members. The nursing supervisor was afraid that Mrs. Bennett's departure from the head nurse position would have a bad effect on the morale of the staff members. Consequently, the supervisor prepared the way for Mrs. Bennett's departure with great care. The supervisor discussed the problem of a replacement with the registered nurses in the intensive care unit.

When the new head nurse, Miss Fischer, was selected, she was introduced to the staff members at a general meeting. The nursing supervisor announced that Mrs. Bennett would be leaving and went on to say how much she had meant to the unit. Mrs. Bennett spoke of her sadness in leaving and then introduced Miss Fischer, extolled her virtues, and asked the staff members to show Miss Fischer the same cooperation they had given her. Finally, Miss Fischer promised to do her best to follow in Mrs. Bennett's footsteps.

For the next few days Miss Fischer followed Mrs. Bennett around, getting to know the staff members and trying to learn Mrs. Bennett's routine and methods of dealing with people.

Although Miss Fischer decided that she would eventually make certain changes in the intensive care unit, she spent her first few weeks trying to follow the human-relations patterns established by her predecessor. Only after she was fully accepted by the group did she begin making changes.

What techniques were used here to win acceptance for the new head nurse? How might these techniques be used in other situations? Strauss and Sayles [4] outline the following points:

Consultation. The nursing supervisor involved the registered nurses in the selection process and thus substantially increased their acceptance of the final decision.

Introduction. The former head nurse was careful to introduce the new head nurse to all key personnel and to explain the customs of

the unit. This helped to prevent the new head nurse from making social faux pas, to integrate her into the social pattern of the organization, and to minimize the amount of disruption caused by the change in command.

Ceremony. The meeting at which the head nurse was introduced and a farewell party for the departing head nurse both served a ceremonial or symbolic function. They formalized the fact of change and helped the old head nurse pass on some of her prestige to the new. The use of ceremony is a public proclamation that, in spite of apparent change, the basic values remain the same.

Avoiding change until acceptance is assured. The new head nurse avoided making changes until she had developed informal social relationships with her subordinates. It is usually wise for new managers to wait before taking action until they know more about the organization and the people with whom they are dealing.

Building on the past. The new head nurse made it clear that she had no intention of throwing out past practices wholesale. As missionaries have discovered, it helps to learn the customs of the people with whom one works. Changes can be introduced more easily if an adjustment is made to the past.

Conclusions

In conclusion, you, the nurse-leader will be involved in changes that you or others in the health-care agency have introduced. Too often we concern ourselves solely with the technical aspect of change and fail to consider the human-relations problem that many changes generate. A seemingly small change may have profound ramifications. Staff members may have vested interests in the old ways; they may fear the uncertainties of the new. People seldom resist change just to be stubborn; they resist because it hurts them economically, psychologically, or socially.

Nurses helping to introduce change need to seek out the reasons for resistance to the change. They need to find out how the change will affect the people involved, and particularly how it affects their interrelationships.

The first step in dealing with resistance is to bring the problems out in the open with two-way communication. Objections and suggestions for modification should be carefully listened to. Some suggestions may not be realistic, but their airing brings them into the open for consideration. Some objections and modifications may be

useful, and their acceptance will improve the overall quality of the proposed change.

Group Session

1. How would you personally react to the following situation?

    You have spent considerable time Monday preparing your plan of care for patient A for Tuesday. This preparation included reading his entire chart, studying textbooks about his medical condition, and talking with patient A. On Tuesday morning, you find your assignment has been changed so that someone else is caring for patient A.

    a. What would be your initial reaction?

    b. What factors would help you to accept this change?

    c. What factors would hinder your accepting this change?

2. Analyze times in your life when you had to undergo change. Which changes went smoothly? Why? Which changes did not go smoothly? Why?

3. Which staff members on your unit adjust to change easily? Which ones adjust less easily? Is there a correlation between their adjustment and their needs? What levels of needs (Maslow's hierarchy of needs) are affected by change?

4. Give examples of recent changes introduced on your unit. What were the technical implications? What were the social implications? What were the various reactions by individual staff members? Could the change have been introduced in a way that would have promoted easier acceptance?

5. Plan a hypothetical change for your nursing unit. Outline the steps included in the change. If practical, implement the change on the unit and analyze the results. If this is not practical, role-play with a group the effects of the change. What follow-up measures would you use?

References

1. Lawrence, P. R.   How to deal with resistance to change. *Harvard Bus. Rev.* 32:49–57, May/June 1954.
2. Stevens, B. J.   Management of continuity and change in nursing. *J. Nurs. Adm.* 7:26–31, April 1977.
3. Stewart, N.   Nothing is as permanent as change. *Nation's Business* 47:33, 57–59, Aug. 1959.
4. Strauss, G., and Sayles, L. R.   *Personnel: The Human Problems of Management* (3rd ed.). Englewood Cliffs, N.J.: Prentice-Hall, 1972. Pp. 241–263.
5. Wickes, T. A.   Techniques for managing change. *Automation* 14:84–87, May 1967.

Suggested Reading

Aeschilman, D. D.   A strategy for change . . . the nurse practitioner must develop a workable solution, gain acceptance for the solution, acquire

negotiation skills, and develop the reputation as a successful innovator. *Nurse Pract.* 1:121, Jan./Feb. 1976.

Asprec, E. S.   The process of change. *Superv. Nurse* 6:15, Oct. 1975.

Bennis, W. G., Benne, K. D., and Chin, R.   *The Planning of Change.* New York: Holt, Rinehart & Winston, 1969.

Bunning, R. L.   Changing employees' attitudes. *Superv. Nurse* 7:54, May 1976.

Guerin, Q. W.   A functional approach to attitude change. *Manage. Rev.* 59:33, 1970.

Labovitz, G. H.   How to improve your management effectiveness in coping with change. *Hosp. Top.* 52:24, July/Aug. 1974.

Leary, P. A.   The change agent. *J. Rehabil.* 18:30, 1972.

Miller, B.   The manager—roadblock to change? *Manage. Rev.* 50:4–12, April 1961.

Mullane, M. K.   Nursing care and the political arena. *Nurs. Outlook* 23:698, 1975.

Nehls, D., Hansen, V., Robertson, P., and Manthey, M.   Planned change; A quest for nursing autonomy (Minneapolis, Minn. Univ. Hosp.). *J. Nurs. Adm.* 4:23, Jan./Feb. 1974.

Reinkemeyer, A. M.   Nursing's need commitment to an ideology of change. *Nurs. Forum* 9:340, 1970.

Smith, D. W.   Change: How shall we respond to it? *Nurs. Forum* 9:391, 1970.

Soltis, R. J.   A systematic approach to managing change. *Manage. Rev.* 59:2, 1970.

Stevens, B. J.   Effecting change. *J. Nurs. Adm.* 5:23, 1975.

Stevens, B. J.   Management of continuity and change in nursing. *J. Nurs. Adm.* 7(4):26, 1977.

9. Devising and Using a Plan of Care

The professional nurse uses a plan each and every day that patient care is assigned to the staff. This chapter discusses the nurse's role in the hospital in assessing patient needs, planning for these needs to be met by the members of the staff, and supervising and evaluating the patient care rendered. As the nurse formulates the plan for the day, the following questions should be considered, which will serve as a guide in the development of this chapter.

1. What are the general and specific needs of each patient?
2. What are the abilities, interests, and limitations of the staff working today?
3. What is the plan for the day?
4. How can the plan be communicated to the staff?
5. What method of follow-up should be used?
6. How can the effectiveness of the plan be evaluated?
7. What alterations may be necessary in the plan?

The General and Specific Needs of Each Patient

The need for the nurse to know well each of the patients on the unit cannot be overemphasized. The nurse can gain information by reading the patient's chart, by discussing the patient with the patient's physician, the nursing staff, and the appropriate paramedical staff, by talking with the patient's family and friends, and, most importantly, by talking with the patient.

ASSESSING PATIENT NEEDS THROUGH ROUNDS

One of the best ways of getting to know the patients is through nursing rounds. The term *rounds* in this context means seeing the patients for the purpose of assessment. More specifically, the goals of rounds may be to: (1) get to know the patient, (2) give the patient a chance to know the nurse, (3) inform and teach the patient, (4) serve as a liaison between the patient and hospital services, (5) evaluate patient care, and (6) improve communications between the staff and the patient.

Nursing rounds can be accomplished in a variety of ways for a variety of purposes. M. Melody and G. Clark [8] have written of a method of making rounds as an entire team. Their method of rounds takes place after the change of shift report. Rounds at this time are for the purpose of discussing plans with patients, refining preplanned assignments on the basis of changes in the patients' condition or patient preference. On other units the offgoing shift may make rounds with the oncoming shift during the report. The purpose and technique of rounds may also vary with the time of day. A nurse may want to make quick rounds immediately after report to check briefly the current status of all the patients and to make more careful observations of the patients with multiple or critical needs. The nurse may want to make midmorning rounds for the purpose of talking with each patient, to inform patients of tests, or to check how their morning care is progressing. As physicians visit their patients, the nurse may want to go along to communicate to the physician the status of the patient and to learn the physician's findings and plans for the patient. This gives the nurse the opportunity to hear what the physician says to the patient so that the nurse can clarify plans to the patient if necessary, and also helps to keep the goals of the nurse and the physician in agreement. The nurse may make rounds just prior to reporting to the next shift to see if needs have changed and if tests and care have been completed.

There is much information to be gathered during rounds. The position and expression of the patient can indicate how he is feeling. What the patient does or does not say may be an indication of what he is thinking. Equipment must be checked for correct functioning. The current status of dressings and wounds should be checked. The environment should be observed. Does the patient have water? Is the light shining in his eyes? You may need to utilize this time to consult with the patient on the patient-care plan for the day or to answer patient questions. As you enter each room, you should have specific objectives in mind as to what to observe, learn, or discuss while with the patient.

INTERVIEWING THE PATIENT

The nurse should be familiar with interviewing techniques when talking with patients. It is best to develop a system that is comfortable to you rather than using a cookbook recipe of "how to interview" that may result in artificiality. Your primary objective is to get the

patient to talk to you. This requires that you be a good listener. A good listener conveys understanding and interest in what the person is saying. A friendly facial expression and an attentive but relaxed attitude are important. You can also use phrases such as, "Uh-huh," "I understand," or "Could you tell me more?" You may need to steer the conversation tactfully to gain purposeful information about the patient. If you need to ask a question, avoid questions that can be answered with a simple yes or no. Avoid giving an indication that what the patient says pleases or displeases you. Also avoid giving advice; it is better to help the patient work through his own problems. The basic purpose of this nondirect approach is to enable the nurse to determine how the patients see the problem or situation and then to help them think and feel their way through to a solution. This text does not attempt to discuss interviewing in depth. The reader can study interviewing in greater depth by referring to authors [4, 10, 11] who utilize different approaches in the interviewing technique.

OBTAINING INFORMATION FROM OTHERS

Information about the patient can be obtained from the patient's family and friends. Such questions as, "Has he been confused before?," "What types of food does he like?", or "Do you have stairs in your house?" can be helpful in gathering information about a specific patient. Relatives are often relieved to sit with a staff member and talk about their concerns for the patient. By being supportive of the family, one indirectly helps the patient. Research in pediatrics has shown that if a mother's anxiety can be relieved, she in turn is less anxious with the child (who can sense the mother's feelings). The child relaxes as the mother relaxes. Therefore, family and friends can be of help to the nurse not only in giving information about the patient but also in being supportive to the patient.

Patient needs can be brought to the awareness of the staff through conferences. A patient-centered conference draws on the staff members' observations of the patient. Patient problems are identified, and solutions are discussed by the staff. The conference serves as an opportunity for members to share their information about a patient with the rest of the staff. T. Kron [5] discusses the team conference in depth.

In conclusion, one obtains information about patients in many different ways. Leaders must be aware of the various avenues for information and utilize them effectively. To misjudge a patient's

need negates the entire plan. Problem-solving must start with a correct definition of the problem. One must therefore *correctly* identify patient needs before proceeding with a plan.

The Abilities, Interests, and Limitations of the Present Staff

The nurse must know what each of the staff members is qualified to do. This should be spelled out in the hospital policy in the form of a job description for each level of nursing personnel. A sample job description is outlined at the end of this chapter. The Nurse Practice Act, which varies from state to state, and the American Nurses' Association's statement of standards are sources of general information. The most reliable information about the staff's qualifications is obtained from observing the patient care the individual staff members give.

This emphasizes the need for the nurse to have frequent personal contact with the staff in order to learn their interests, abilities, and limitations. The nurse may learn that Miss Cousins, RN, has developed a good rapport with the patient Mrs. Long and would like to continue caring for her. Mr. Monk, LPN, may work best with male patients. Miss Kahn, a nurse's aide, may not like caring for the unconscious patient. The nurse who does not yet know the staff well can get helpful information about them from the head nurse. If there are students or working-in-training personnel on the unit, their learning needs should be known. Discussions with the instructor and reading the students' course objectives are means of ascertaining what these students are allowed to do and what experiences would be most helpful for them.

Once this information is obtained, the nurse can continue on to the next step in planning patient care.

The Plan for the Day

We now know the needs of our patients and the abilities of the individual staff members who are to meet the patient needs. We now must arrange a plan for the interaction of patients and personnel to take place. Ask yourself the following questions:

1. What do you want to achieve today? What results need to be obtained?

2. What is the order of the priorities for the day? What can wait, and what must be done today?
3. Who is going to do it?
4. How should they do it?

UTILIZING TIME

Let us look at you, the leader, as a starting point. How can you best utilize your time? A good place to start is by writing a list of things to do in their order of importance and then crossing them out as they are accomplished. People always postpone the difficult, and that is why it is important to accomplish the high-priority items first. Why is this helpful? Because many people fall into the bad habit of wasting time by giving too much of their time to the things they like to do or find easy to do. The list helps you to stick with your goal.

A head nurse who makes unoccupied beds in her free time seems to be wasting talent that could be better spent with patients or staff. The nurse who grabs the phone when it rings rather than waiting for the secretary to answer is also losing valuable time. It helps to think of what your time is worth in dollars. If you are getting paid $8.50 per hour and the secretary is getting $3.00 per hour, then do a job worth the $8.50—not the $3.00 an hour job. Time is too precious to waste. If you have to wait at the end of the phone or for a staff member to appear, do not use the time idly. You can jot down observations of the day, make revisions in the plan, or be thinking of aspects of patient care.

One aspect of utilizing your time well is to know when a job has been completed. The vast majority of people let go of each task far short of the completion point. We need to look at the beginning and the end of each task. For example, we have encountered patients who put their call lights on at frequent intervals. If the nurse answers their verbal requests only and considers the job completed, the light may go on again. The patients may have additional needs to identify and meet. They may be fearful, angry, insecure, or uncomfortable. By the staff's not meeting patient needs the first time the light is answered, valuable personnel time and patient satisfaction are sacrificed. Partial completion of a task may result in having to go back to the patients over and over again.

BUDGETING TIME

Time should be budgeted. If a conference is scheduled to last 20 minutes, then conclude it at the end of twenty minutes. Do not allow

sidetracks to prolong it beyond the budgeted time. One management author [2] suggests a time budget that is arranged in four broad areas: routine work, regular work, special assignments, and creative work. The nurse may find that routine work includes checking that patient menus have been collected, that doctors' orders have been checked off, and that laboratory tests have been completed. Try delegating as much of this work as possible to a staff member. You should concentrate on doing your regular work—passing medications, going on patient rounds, meeting complex patient-care needs—in about two-thirds of your time. This would leave time for accepting special assignments and for doing creative work on the unit. For example, you may want to set up a new method for giving tracheostomy care, plan a conference with the physical therapy department on how a patient is progressing, or have a conference with a patient and the public health nurse.

The more systematic you are, the more effective you will be in the use of your time. You need to make a conscientious effort to avoid

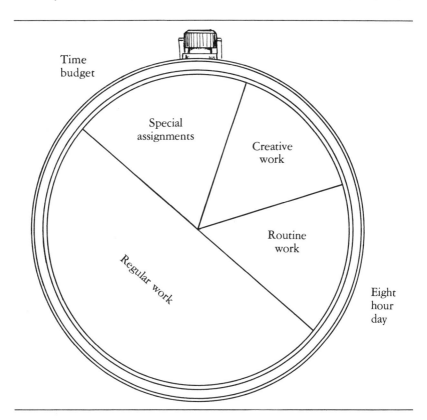

hopping from one job to another. Instead, whenever possible, complete one task before moving to another.

When budgeting your time, the kind or level of work you are doing must be considered as well as the amount of time you will have to spend. The creative things should be done when you are rested, whereas the routine tasks can be done when you are less rested.

IMPROVING PLANNING SKILLS

How can you sharpen your planning skills? The following points should be kept in mind when you devise your plan:

1. Have as complete a knowledge as possible of the patient care that needs to be done.
2. Think clearly and logically, and sort out irrelevant facts.
3. Have a mature sense of values. You must view the plan on your patient-care unit in relation to the hospital's goals, needs, and objectives. To propose a plan that helps your unit to the detriment of another department hinders the hospital's goals.
4. Have foresight. Foresee events that will affect your unit. Holidays, in-service programs, and other such activities will affect the plan.
5. Have a sense of timing. For example, do not leave the stool culture specimen for the evening shift to obtain if the lab closes at 5:00 P.M.
6. Look for training and development needs of staff. Foresee what your staff will need to know in the future, and help them to achieve it. If a patient is about to go to the operating room for a tracheostomy, now is the time to review tracheostomy care with the staff rather than waiting until the patient is back on your unit needing the care immediately.

Once you have devised the plan for the day, utilizing the preceding principles, it should be written clearly, in logical order, and be readily accessible to the staff. The written assignment should be supported by verbal review and clarification; this is the next aspect to be discussed.

How Can the Plan Be Communicated to the Staff?

The nurse who is assigning patient-care tasks to staff members must utilize the management principles of delegation and giving instruc-

tions. These two aspects should go hand in hand, for to delegate well means more than entrusting activities to staff. It means defining for each exactly what is to be done. We delegate to relieve our load of detailed responsibilities—in order to have time for other things and, secondly, to develop to the fullest possible extent the potentialities of the staff to whom we have delegated those responsibilities.

GUIDELINES FOR DELEGATION OF TASKS

To get the most from delegation one should proceed with certain guidelines. First, give staff members the proper send-off by specifically outlining what they are to do. Secondly, prepare and support them by indicating confidence in their ability, by giving them reassurance from time to time, and by emphasizing that they may come to you for help whenever they are in doubt. Finally, and most importantly, let them do the job. One of the main principles of modern delegation is that one does not just pass down the work, but that one also passes down to the staff the authority and freedom to handle the details on their own initiative. You may remember having been delegated a job at home such as cooking a meal or cleaning and had your mother give frequent suggestions as to how it could be done. If you felt capable of accomplishing the task alone, you may have been annoyed by the suggestions. Remember how this feels when you are about to interfere with someone else's job.

If the responsibility is new and large or difficult to handle, you may need to check the staff members; but if the staff is well prepared, you may be able to adopt a hands-off policy.

THE NATURE OF DELEGATION

Whenever you delegate, you must be clear in your own mind about the nature of the delegation, because even though a performance is entrusted to another, it is you who retains the ultimate responsibility. You, the leader, are responsible for the care given the patients by your staff members.

When an assignment is a *true* delegation, it has five implicit characteristics:

1. Responsibility is shared with the staff member giving the patient care.
2. Authority is passed along to help the staff member get the job done.
3. Decision-making is shared with or left largely to the staff member.

4. The staff member is given freedom to take actions that that person thinks are needed to reach the objective.
5. The individual accepting the assignment must be held accountable by the delegator.

The leader who perfects the ability to delegate will find it a staff builder because it produces three essential effects: It develops the staff members' sense of responsibility, it enlarges their general understanding, and it increases their job satisfaction.

EFFECTIVE VERSUS INEFFECTIVE DELEGATION

Can you think of units in the hospital in which effective delegation takes place? Can you think of units in which the head nurse holds all the reins of administration and does not delegate enough? As a staff nurse you will find it interesting to watch the return of the head nurse who has been off duty a few days. Some head nurses return with the attitude that the unit must have crumbled in their absence and that they must immediately put it back together again. If in truth things did not run smoothly in the head nurse's absence, the head nurse should start delegating so that the unit can function well in that person's absence. In contrast to this head nurse is the one who returns to the unit calmly after a few days of absence and knows that the staff can function alone. Much more credit is due to this head nurse, who has developed the potential of the staff nurses, than to the one who has been afraid or is unwilling to let go of the reins. The concept of team nursing has been obscured many times because the head nurse has not been able to relinquish to the group leader the authority to lead the staff members. Similarly, leaders who do not delegate well will find themselves flying around trying to do more than they are able to do well.

Delegation can also be carried to the opposite extreme—it can be overdone to the point where the leader relies entirely on the staff. We therefore cannot advocate any cut-and-dry rules in delegation; it remains an art. It should be a reciprocal process in which the delegator instructs the staff and they in turn report on their progress.

REASONS GIVEN FOR FAILURE TO DELEGATE

Managers most frequently give the following reasons for not delegating:

1. The staff members lack experience. I feel insecure about them and am reluctant to take chances.
2. I am too busy to explain things to them.

3. I am afraid their mistakes may harm the patients.
4. I am afraid of losing control.
5. I do not know how to organize my work around others.
6. I like to make all the decisions.
7. The staff members are too busy.
8. I can do it faster and easier myself.

Managers who are guilty of using any of these excuses should reexamine their own performance as leaders, for the ability to work through others is one of the hallmarks of success. Through others one multiplies one's own effectiveness. Managers then use their time to concentrate on those things that bring the greatest return.

EFFECTIVE COMMUNICATION OF PLANS TO STAFF
After you decide what to delegate you need to communicate the plan. C. A. Cerami [1] has made some valuable suggestions as to how to tell others what to do:

1. The simple and routine tasks should be assigned in a direct, straightforward, unapologetic fashion. Do not appear hesitant in your request, but make it clear exactly what you want done and when.
   EFFECTIVE: "Mr. James, I would like you to help Miss Wright ambulate Mr. Gregory and Mr. Williams."
   LESS EFFECTIVE: "Mr. James, I hope you will not mind too much helping Miss Wright, when you have some free time, to ambulate Mr. Gregory and Mr. Williams."
2. Do not confuse the staff with parenthetical thoughts, but keep your statements positive, clear, and courteous.
   EFFECTIVE: "When Mrs. Burn returns from the operating room, please check her urine output, vital signs, dressings, and intravenous fluids every fifteen minutes."
   LESS EFFECTIVE: "When Mrs. Burns returns from the operating room, I guess we had better check her vital signs every thirty minutes, or better yet every fifteen minutes. She may have a Foley catheter; if she does not, try to get her to void. Measure her urine output whether it is a Foley catheter or not. I am not sure what kind of dressing she will have but check it. She might have an intravenous running, but then again it may be discontinued by the time she leaves the recovery room. If she has one, let me know how fast it is running."

3. The assignment should be stated in a manner that will generate a desire to do the job well. In so doing you should convey your interest and enthusiasm for the job, make the job seem important, and convey your confidence that the staff can handle it competently. You may need to "sell" your idea by making it appeal to the other person's point of view.

   EFFECTIVE: "Mr. Shriner is to be ambulated for the first time today. It will be exciting to see how he does for he has really been looking forward to getting out of bed."

   LESS EFFECTIVE: "Mr. Shriner is to be ambulated today. He has been on bed rest two months so he will probably need considerable help."

4. There should be no overlapping of functions. For example, there should be no confusion as to who is to take a patient's blood pressure when he returns from the recovery room.

5. Each staff member should report to one and only one superior; in true team nursing the team member should report to the team leader, not to the head nurse.

6. When you assign jobs, you should indicate when they should be completed, how thoroughly the work should be done, and all the factors involved.

7. Usually some explanation of "why" is necessary in order to spell out precisely what is wanted. If the person receiving the order understands why something is to be done a certain way, or better still, the importance of its being done that way, there is a better chance of its being done correctly. Knowing why will help the staff members use their own judgment along the way. For example, if a nurse told the aide that Mr. Brown was allowed nothing by mouth (NPO) but did not tell her why, the following problem might occur: The aide goes into Mr. Brown's room and removes the water pitcher. He asks why, and all the aide can say is "You are not supposed to have anything to drink." It leaves the patient questioning, and if he wants to know why, the aide has to go back to the nurse to find out the reason for the order. How much more effective it would have been if the nurse had told the aide *why* in the first place!

CHECKING THAT INSTRUCTIONS ARE UNDERSTOOD

It is essential that you check to see that your assignment is understood. You can watch the staff member's face for expressions of doubt or of understanding. Do not ask, "Do you understand?"

because people often reply affirmatively rather than admit that they do not understand. Instead you can ask, "How do you plan to proceed?" or "Can you tell me what steps you are going to take?" or "What are your plans?" The leader can also verify the understanding by checking the progress the staff member is making in completing the assignment.

Sometimes instructions go afoul. The fault may be with the staff member. The staff member may not be listening, may not understand the assignment, or may fail to ask questions to clarify the assignment. The staff member may dislike the person giving the assignment. The simple omission of taking notes may result in an assignment's not being completed properly.

The leader may also be at fault. A *very common* cause of instructions' going afoul is an assumption by the sender that the receiver will understand. Incorrect terminology may be used, however, or the words understood by the sender may not be understood by the receiver. Other possible errors are that the assignment is vague, not positive, or that there is no explanation of why, whereby the receiver does not understand the importance of the assignment. There may be a lack of verification or feedback.

Another common error by the leader is failure to give instructions in a systematic way. The consequences of poor instructions may be that the assignment is not done correctly, completely, or on time; that the patient may be displeased or actually suffer from the lack of assigned care; and that the staff member may also suffer by knowing that the job was not done well. If this should occur, analyze where the breakdown in communication occurred. Once alerted to the possible problems in giving instructions, concentrate on giving them correctly as discussed in this chapter.

What Method of Follow-up Should Be Used?

For further verification that the patient-care assignment is proceeding satisfactorily, the leader uses a method of checking and supervising. The nurse-leader's effectiveness as a first-level supervisor will be measured in terms of the help given the individual staff members. In order to be effective as a helper, the leader must develop a good working relationship with the staff members. This relationship helps meet the needs of the group by providing an atmosphere of security and belonging that precedes job satisfaction.

The staff must view the leader as one skilled in giving patient care. The leader must behave in a manner that is accepted by the group and therefore should become familiar with the expectations of the staff as soon as possible.

CLOSE SUPERVISION

Strauss and Sayles [12] define two types of supervision: *close supervision* and *general supervision*. The *close supervisor* gives the staff member an assignment telling exactly how and in what sequence tasks are to be done. For example, take the case of Mrs. Wagner, the group leader. She is giving Miss Jones, LPN, her morning assignment. "Miss Jones, you are to care for Mr. Smith today. His TPR is to be taken at 7:30 A.M., his blood pressure at 7:45 A.M., his intake and output at 8:00 A.M., complete bath with back care at 8:15 A.M., up in a chair at 8:45 A.M." "He is to ambulate around the room." "Do that before putting him back to bed." "His slippers are in the closet." "He needs to cough deeply every two hours." "Do that after he has ambulated but while he is sitting." And on and on for the remainder of the day. Mrs. Wagner, team leader, does not acknowledge that Miss Jones has any initiative or judgment. Mrs. Wagner then proceeds to check up on Miss Jones frequently to make sure the instructions are being carried out. Miss Jones is not allowed freedom to do her work in her own way. Mrs. Wagner is so busy checking up on the staff members and working alongside them (for she feels she can often do the job better than they can) that her entire day is consumed with short-range problems. One can often find Mrs. Wagner busily performing tasks that could have been delegated to a staff member. Consequently she has no time for training and developing her staff members.

Close supervisors feel the need to hover over staff members to make things come out right. They do not trust their subordinates to do a good job. They are of the school of thought that believes the only way to get a job done is to do it yourself. They may be psychologically insecure.

GENERAL SUPERVISION

In contrast, the *general supervisor* sets goals, tells staff members what is to be accomplished, fixes the limits within which they can work, and lets them decide how to achieve these goals. Instead of rattling off a list of orders, the general supervisor is likely to communicate

helpful information or make suggestions. This supervisor explains "why" and points out how the staff's contribution fits into the goals for the day. If Mrs. Wagner were a general supervisor her assignment to Miss Jones might have gone like this: "Miss Jones, you are to care for Mr. Smith today. He had a pneumonectomy done yesterday for cancer of the lung. His vital signs, intake, and output are to be taken every four hours. He needs to be encouraged to cough deeply and to get out of bed to ambulate today to help expand the remaining lung. Our goals for his care are to get him up and about and doing as much as possible for himself in order to use the remaining lung fully, and to prevent development of atelectasis."

General supervisors know that the individual staff members will not perform an assignment in precisely the same way they would, but this does not bother them. They concentrate on objectives and results not details.

General supervisors seek to develop an atmosphere in which staff members feel free to bring their problems to them. The general supervisor has spent time training staff. Therefore, the staff has no need for detailed instruction. The general supervisor thus has time to concentrate on long-range rather than short-range problems.

CHOOSING BETWEEN GENERAL AND CLOSE SUPERVISION

Research [6] has shown that the general supervisor is more productive than the close supervisor. The reason for this is that the general supervisor has time for planning, improving staff relations, and coordinating activities with other departments. The close supervisor, in contrast, is doing the same sort of work as the staff members or may be concentrating on paperwork and short-term activities such as checking up on the staff or arranging for supplies.

Which type of supervisor would be most effective on the patient-care unit? There is some evidence [9] that general supervision is most effective where the job is challenging, where the work cycle is long, and where there is an opportunity for intrinsic job satisfaction. In contrast, where there is little opportunity for creativity and internalized motivation, employees are less likely to perform effectively when left alone. It is important to recognize which staff members find their jobs challenging and satisfying and which ones do not.

Another factor in choosing between close and general supervision is that there are substantial differences in the amount of responsibility people are willing to accept on the job. One person may flourish under supervision that another might find extremely restrictive.

Psychological research [7] provides evidence that the nature of a person's personality affects his attitude toward supervision. Some people have a high need for independence, whereas others prefer to be told what to do. Some employees have become so accustomed to the authoritarian approach in their culture, family, and previous work experience that they regard general supervision as no supervision at all. They may abuse the privilege of general supervision and refuse to accept the responsibilities it demands.

Consider the case of two hospital units supervised by two very different head nurses [3]. The first head nurse (Miss Kelly), though extremely courteous, is very strict with nurses. She insists that conversations be kept to a minimum, and she hands out detailed, unambiguous work assignments to her nurses. The second head nurse (Miss Rogers) has a much more informal, almost chummy relationship with the nurses. She consults with them about problems and changes and has developed a feeling of camaraderie on the floor. Which unit do you think nurses chose to work on? Both units are popular, but to different types of nurses. Some nurses like the security of Miss Kelly's unit where everything goes according to predetermined routine. The staff like having everything structured for them; otherwise they feel lost. They require close guidance. Other nurses prefer Miss Rogers' unit as she allows them independence. They have initiative and self-confidence and respond best when they can assert themselves and work on their own. It is probable that these nurses were permitted more freedom in the home environment and in their study of nursing than were the other nurses. Both types respond better to the style of supervision that fits their life-style.

The overall pattern of supervision is more important than any one aspect of it. A manager who delegates authority but neglects to train the staff to exercise it intelligently may well provide poorer nursing care than the manager who retains all authority.

Both the close and general supervisor must exercise authority. You, the leader, will need to make decisions on your own at times. If your goals are unmet, you must find out who or what was responsible.

RELATIONSHIP OF THE SUPERVISOR WITH STAFF
The supervisor's job is always complicated by the fact that people feel an ambivalence toward authority. People value freedom but may feel lost if they have too much. People like feeling safe, but do not like

interference. Most people like to be assured that they are performing well and that they will receive help when needed.

How can leaders exercise authority effectively, but without being restrictive? The kind of working relationship the leaders have, the way they give orders, their fairness, and the way they handle mistakes all affect the way staff members will respond to their authority.

The relationship the leader has with staff members has a lot to do with the way the staff members view their work. They need to feel that their leader approves of their work and of themselves as individuals. The leader can show approval by taking an active interest in staff members, by listening to their problems, by giving praise when it is justified, and by showing tolerance when mistakes are made. The existence of a feeling of approval indicates that the supervisor has demonstrated a personal loyalty to the staff. Because different individuals respond differently to supervision, leaders should adjust their behavior patterns to the staff members' individual personality needs.

Good informal relations on matters that are not directly related to the unit set the stage for better communications between the leader and the staff on problems related to work. Any social barrier will create a communications barrier. If the staff members feel free to talk to the leader about their social life or family problems, they will usually feel free to talk to the leader about problems on the unit. It is the supervisors who set the tone of the relationship, not the staff members. You set the tone by being available. Busy, hurried leaders are going to find staff members reluctant to approach them.

EXCHANGE OF INFORMATION AND IDEAS WITH STAFF

Research indicates that productive supervisors give their staff as much information as possible about what is expected on the unit and what is likely to happen in the future. Referring back to the two different head nurses: Some nurses on Miss Rogers' unit complained because they did not receive enough detailed instructions; and some nurses on Miss Kelly's unit felt insecure because Miss Kelly failed to provide enough information for them to make decisions on their own and had a habit of issuing unexpected and seemingly arbitrary orders.

Encouraging staff members to bring ideas and suggestions to you or to the other staff members also helps foster a healthy working climate.

Another factor in supervision is to avoid playing favorites. It is easy to be unconscious of doing this. You must be fair with all staff

members, and if you need to make an exception for one member it should be considered legitimate by all members of the group.

CORRECTING ERRORS OF STAFF MEMBERS

How you handle mistakes is another management skill. You do not want to encourage mistakes, but to insist that mistakes must never be made hampers staff members from assuming any real responsibility. Most nurses make a medication error sometime in their experience. If all medication errors were to be disastrous, either we would have few patients or we would have few nurses left to care for them. Actually, doing something wrong is often the most effective way of learning to do it right. For example, next time the nurse who made the error will read the label more carefully, check the dosage in the *Hospital Formulary*, and read the accompanying literature prior to giving the medication.

If you, the leader, overpunish the staff member who makes a mistake, staff members will avoid any task where a mistake is possible.

If you come into a patient's room and you see the LPN making a mistake, what should you do? If the LPN recognizes her own mistake and takes steps to correct it, then do not criticize. Save your criticism for instances when the staff member is unaware of the mistake or fails to correct the mistake. When a nurse makes a mistake, ask how it happened and then listen to the answer. If the explanation is weak, the nurse will recognize it and so will you. Then ask the nurse to tell you how the mistake can be avoided in the future. You may not agree with the solution, but by using this approach, you encourage staff members to accept responsibility for their actions.

CRITICIZING STAFF ERRORS

Most mistakes are due to ignorance or lack of skill and can be handled through training and without resort to criticism. If negligence is the cause, however, you must let the staff member know you are dissatisfied with the performance. Whyte [13] suggests some rules in offering criticism:

1. The criticism should be voiced in a matter-of-fact manner. Emotionalism will arouse defensive reactions.
2. Criticism should be focused on the error, not on the person.
3. After criticism is stated, it should be dropped, unless the mistake has not been corrected.
4. Criticism should be balanced by giving credit for good work.

How Can the Effectiveness of the Plan Be Evaluated?

The leader looks at the objectives for the day when assessing the plan. These factors can be considered in evaluating the objectives:

1. Did individual staff members complete their assignments on time?
2. Did any staff have excess time? If so, how was this time spent?
3. How did the staff members respond to their assignments? Did they appear to derive satisfaction from the day's work?
4. Were the patients content with the nursing care they received today?
5. Did you, the leader, complete the list of priorities to be accomplished for the day?

In evaluating the plan you may find ways to improve it.

What Alterations May Be Necessary in the Plan?

"The best laid schemes of mice and men often go awry" (Robert Burns). The patient-care unit, unlike the automobile assembly line, is subject to multiple changes. The unit can be besieged by many incidents that result in a change of plans. For example, it is Saturday morning. Two aides call in sick at 6:30 A.M., a patient with a head injury is admitted to the unit from the emergency room at 8:45 A.M., the linen supply is depleted at 9:00 A.M. due to a problem in the linen department, and a cardiac arrest occurs at 1:00 P.M. The leader must be flexible in altering priorities and in changing the plan. Inability to do so threatens the quality of the patient care. As changes are necessary, the leader must once again use the tools for communicating the changes to staff members. The completion of the altered plan must then be followed by an evaluation of its effectiveness.

Group Session

Questions 1–4 are written for group discussion. Get a group of classmates or friends together to discuss these questions if you do not have an opportunity to answer them in a classroom session.

1. Have one or more group members bring to the group the hospital's job descriptions for each level of personnel on the nursing unit. Also bring a description of the staff members and the patients on a given unit on a given day. Have the group work out a day's assignment for each of the staff members assigned to the unit.
2. If you have made assignments on a patient-care unit and have worked an eight-hour shift with this assignment, bring it to the group and discuss your evaluation of the assignment. What changes would you make if you could do it over again?
3. Role play the leader's interaction in the following situations:
   a. The nurse-leader is seeing Mr. Round for the first time. He has been admitted with the diagnosis of emphysema.
   b. The leader is making rounds in the morning and has been told in report that Mrs. Weather is one day postpartum.
   c. The nurse's aide comes to the leader to say that Johnny's mother is sobbing. Johnny is a three-year-old patient with hydrocephalus.
4. A new aide has the following patient to care for: Miss Black, age 28, with nephritis; on an 800 cc fluid restriction per 24 hours; 40 gm protein diet; no salt; accurate intake and output; up to bathroom with help. Role play how you would explain this assignment to the new aide.
5. The work load is heavy today. As you complete the assignments and explain them to the staff, the LPN says angrily, "I cannot possibly do all of that. It is not fair!" How can you, the leader, best handle this situation?
6. Discuss which of the staff members on your unit require close supervision and which ones respond better to general supervision. Under which type of supervision do you work best?
7. As you walk into a four-bed ward, you observe that the orderly has detached the patient's traction ropes to make the bed. What would you do?
8. During the assignment conference you told the aide to turn the patient every two hours. Since then you have been into the patient's room four times, and each time it appeared that the patient was in the same position as the last time you were in the room. What would you say to the aide? If she says she has been too busy to turn him, how would you respond?

Job Description: Nurse's Aide

A. The nurse's aide will be assigned to care for hospitalized patients in all areas of nursing practice except for special care units, including the coronary care unit, the intensive care unit, the recovery room, and the emergency room.
B. The nurse's aide will give basic nursing care as assigned and directed by a registered professional nurse.
C. Functions of nurse's aides include:
   1. Making patients comfortable
   2. Assisting the patients with special needs, such as combing hair
   3. Maintaining a safe and clean environment for the patients
   4. Assisting the patients' families and visitors when needed

      5. Observing patients for specific signs and symptoms directed by the registered nurse

      6. Reporting changes in the patients' behavior or condition to the registered nurse

      7. Assisting other staff members with patient care

D. The nurse's aide may perform the following procedures:

      1. Baths (complete, partial, shower, tub, sitz)

      2. Beds (occupied, unoccupied, postop, and circ-olectric)

      3. Cold applications (ice collar, ice bag, rubber glove)

      4. Pre- and postop care (shock, I & O fractions only, Foley catheter)

      5. Weighing patients

      6. Hematesting stools

      7. Collection of specimens (urine and stool)

      8. Safety measures, such as footboards, bed cradles, siderails, restraints, and posey belts

      9. Ambulating patients

     10. Transferring patients

     11. Admission, transfer, and discharge of patients

     12. Dietary care, including diet forms, giving nourishments, and feeding patients

     13. Giving enemas (soapsuds, tap water, oil retention, Travad, Fleets, or flatus bags)

     14. Taking vital signs, including temperature, pulse, and respiration

CONTROLS

The nurse's aide is ultimately accountable to the head nurse on the unit. The team leader is responsible for making out assignments for the nurse's aide and supervises the care given by the nurse's aide. The nurse's aide is responsible to the team leader for care assigned.

QUALIFICATIONS

The nurse's aide must be a high school graduate who has completed the nurse's aide course given at "X" hospital. The nurse's aide must be a dependable and responsible person who is interested in giving quality nursing care.

References

1. Cerami, C. A. How to tell others what to do. *Supervision Magazine* Aug. 1955.

2. Dewey, W. E. You can use your time better. *Factory Management and Maintenance* 111:84–89, Feb. 1953.

3. Hamilton, E. Delegation. In G. Strauss and L. Sayles, *Personnel: The Human Problems of Management* (3rd ed.). Englewood Cliffs, N.J.: Prentice-Hall, 1972. Pp. 158–159.

4. Kahn, R. L., and Cannell, C. E. *The Dynamics of Interviewing.* New York: Wiley, 1957. Pp. 233–252.

5. Kron, T. *The Management of Patient Care: Putting Leadership Skills to Work* (4th ed.). Philadelphia: Saunders, 1976. Pp. 135–148.

6. Likert, R. *New Patterns of Management.* New York: McGraw-Hill, 1961. Pp. 89–96.

7. McClelland, D. C. *The Achieving Society.* Princeton: Van Nostrand, 1961. Pp. 36–62.

8. Melody, M., and Clark, G. Walking-planning rounds. *Am. J . Nurs.* 67:771–773, April 1967.

9. Morse, N. *Satisfaction in White Collar Jobs.* Ann Arbor: Survey Research Center, University of Michigan, 1953. Pp. 55–67.

10. Richardson, S., Dohrenwend, B., and Klein, D. *Interviewing: Its Forms and Functions.* New York: Basic Books, 1965. Pp. 1–327.

11. Rogers, C. *Client-Centered Therapy: Its Current Practice, Implications and Theory.* Boston: Houghton Mifflin, 1951. Pp. 3–196.

12. Strauss, G., and Sayles, L. *Personnel: The Human Problems of Management* (3rd ed.). Englewood Cliffs, N.J.: Prentice-Hall, 1972. Pp. 139–162.

13. Whyte, W. F. *Leadership on the Work Team* (mimeograph), 1956. Pp. 12–13.

Suggested Reading

Clark, E. L. A model of nurse staffing for effective patient care. *Nurs. Adm.* 7:22, Feb. 1977.

Clark, J. Authority patterns in nursing managent structures. *Nurs. Times* 73:65, May 12, 1977.

Damos, V. R. Management skill: Objectivity. *A.O.R.N.* 25:195, Feb. 1977.

Gellerman, S. W. Supervision: Substance and style. *Harvard Bus. Rev.* 54:89, March/April 1976.

Grant, C. Future trends in health care management. *Ga. Nurs.* 37:2, June 1977.

Hill, B. S. Participative management: A valid alternative to traditional organizational behavior. *Superv. Nurse* 7:19, March 1976.

Holloway, R. C. Management can reverse declining employee work attitudes. *Hospitals* 50:71, Oct. 16, 1976.

La Monica, E., et al. Managerial decision making. *J. Nurs. Adm.* 7:20, May 1977.

Lewis, J. H. Conflict management. *J. Nurs. Adm.* 6:18, Dec. 1976.

Miller, N. How to succeed in nursing management. *Superv. Nurse* 8:18, Oct. 1977.

Munn, H. E., Jr. Measure your nursing supervisor leadership behaviors. *Hosp. Top.* 54:14, Nov./Dec. 1976.

Nelson, M. A. Building a better team. *Nursing '77* 7:65, July 1977.

Pellet, J. Are you making delegation work for you? *A.O.R.N.* 25:865, April 1977.

Stevens, B. J.   The delicate art of nursing supervision and leadership. The head nurse as manager. *Nurs. Dig.* 5:13, Fall 1977.

Treat, M., et al.   The delicate art of nursing supervision and leadership. The question behind the question. *Nurs. Dig.* 5:1, Fall 1977.

Vance, C. C.   How to enrich your management skills. *Nursing '75* 5:65, April 1975.

Veningia, R.   Interpersonal feedback: A cost-benefit analysis. *Nurs. Dig.* 5:54, Fall 1977.

Volante, E. M.   Mastering the managerial skill of delegation. *Nurs. Dig.* 5:33, Fall 1977.

Watkin, B.   Nursing Forum. Do we manage to care? *Nurs. Mirror* 141:48, Oct. 2, 1975.

White, R.   Management of the nursing service. *Nurs. Mirror* 143:67, Oct. 28, 1976.

Zorn, J. M.   Nursing leadership for the 70s and 80s. *J. Nurs. Adm.* 7:33, Oct. 1977.

10. Appraising Staff Performance

Managers must judge continually the contributions and abilities of the staff members. Certain individuals are more adept at doing one type of work than another, certain ones cannot be depended upon to carry through an assignment to completion, others show great initiative and reliability and can take on projects with a minimum of supervision.

Appraisal of staff performance serves primarily as a training device—to help staff members improve their performance. An effective performance-appraisal program also serves as a rational basis for determining who should be promoted or receive salary increases. It permits staff members on each level to be considered on the same basis as others on the same level. If ratings are linked to promotions, they can serve as a tool for motivation. Performance appraisals need not be limited to identifying those who should be promoted, receive pay increases, or obtain special attention. They can be the springboard for coaching and for helping individuals to set goals for their own development. Employees learn how effective they are and how they can improve and develop.

Performance appraisal is the systematic evaluation of individuals with respect to their performance on the job and their potential for development. Ordinarily the evaluation is made by the individual's immediate superior in the organization, and this is reviewed in turn by that person's superior. Thus, everyone in the organization who rates others is also rated by a superior.

Evaluation Procedures

Health-care agencies should have a well-defined program for the evaluation of personnel. Job descriptions can outline performance standards and should be discussed at the time of employment and again during the employee's orientation to the position. These standards then become the basis for evaluation. It is advisable to have ongoing evaluations at set intervals or whenever the evaluator feels they should be held or when the employee has questions.

A variety of evaluation procedures are used in health-care agencies. The traditional rating form is being replaced in some institutions

by a less biased procedure. Various types of evaluation forms will be explained in the following paragraphs.

RATING SCALES

The rating scale is the oldest and most widely used type of rating procedure, and it appears in various forms. Usually the individual doing the rating is given a printed form that contains a number of qualities and characteristics to be rated. This is usually done by the employee's immediate supervisor. An example of this type of form can be found in Appendix A at the end of the chapter.

DRAWBACKS OF TRADITIONAL EVALUATION

The traditional rating scale is subject to certain human errors. One is clarity in standards. Unless all evaluators agree on what terms such as "good" or "excellent" mean, their final ratings simply cannot be compared. For example, the rating scale in one agency includes excellent, very good, fair, satisfactory, and unsatisfactory. One evaluator might describe an aide's performance as very good, whereas another evaluator may describe the same performance as excellent.

A second human error in rating is that people differ in their standards of judgment. Raters may be unaware of their prejudice against staff members whose behavior, attitudes, or values are very different from their own. For example, a head nurse who is always punctual may be prejudiced in evaluating a staff member who usually arrives at work a few minutes late, but who does an excellent job once at work. Having more than one individual rate the employee will reduce the degree of subjectivity. This is exemplified by the Olympic diving championships in which a group of judges rate each contestant.

A third problem is that external considerations may result in easy or hard grading. An evaluator may hesitate to give a low rating to an LPN fearing that ill feelings may develop that will hamper their working relationship. Another evaluator may purposely rate a staff member low the first time in the hope that the next evaluation can be higher and thus show improvement.

A fourth tendency is for the raters to be inclined to give similar ratings on the various points on the evaluation scale. For example, an RN may excel in initiative. The evaluator may then mark additional traits excellent, even though they have not been demonstrated.

A more fundamental criticism of the traditional rating scale is that

personality traits rather than measurable objectives are often emphasized. Such traits as learning ability, loyalty, judgment, and enthusiasm are difficult if not impossible to measure. These are personality traits that are difficult to change and whose evaluation is of little value in helping a staff member identify areas for improvement.

NURSE'S DILEMMA IN
EVALUATING STAFF MEMBERS

1. What's the difference between good, excellent, and very good?
2. What's more important — excellent sterile technique or good rapport with patients?
3. If I grade low will he be so offended that our working relationship will suffer?
4. She's very neat, so does this mean she gives thorough nursing care?
5. How can I measure "initiative"?
6. The things that stand out the most in my memory are those that have happened recently.

As a consequence of the foregoing criticisms of traditional rating scales, personnel researchers have developed new rating procedures that are less affected by the raters' personal biases and are less concerned with personality traits. Two well-known forms are forced distribution and the critical incident form.

FORCED DISTRIBUTION RATING

Forced distribution requires the rater to distribute ratings in a pattern to conform with a normal frequency distribution. It uses the same principle as "grading on a curve." Staff members being rated by this technique would be compared to one another. Ordinarily, only one overall rating of ability is given, rather than a series of ratings on separate factors. This form alleviates the tendency to rate all staff members high or low.

This evaluation method also has its shortcomings. The staff members in an agency are a select group of people and do not necessarily have abilities that are distributed according to a normal curve. It is hoped that individuals who would be rated at the low end of the scale in the normal population would not be staff members to begin with.

CRITICAL INCIDENT RATING

The critical incident technique of rating begins with the formulation of critical job requirements or objectives. Once these have been determined, the evaluator looks for critical incidents or examples of the staff member's success or failure to meet the objectives. Schools

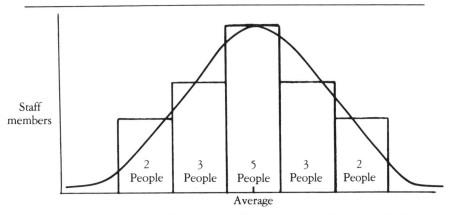

Staff members

| 2 People | 3 People | 5 People | 3 People | 2 People |

Average

Would you evaluate the staff members with the forced distribution method?

of nursing may utilize this method in planning course requirements, employing measurable behavioral objectives as standards for evaluation. Anecdotal notes of clinical experiences serve as examples of the student's ability or inability to meet the objectives.

In order for performance appraisal to be effective for coaching, teaching, and changing undesirable behavior, the staff member needs to know which behaviors are desirable, as well as which ones need improvement. Such incidents will be observed and recorded by the evaluator as they occur.

To keep these data useful, the manager needs to write down what happened or did not happen, the situation in which the action took place, and what was said to the staff member. This information forms a behavioral record, a critical incident report of which the staff member has already been informed and which is now in the staff member's record and is open to review.

The advantage of this rating method is its objectivity, because the anecdotal notes can be evaluated to determine patterns of behavior and progress toward goal achievement that have been going on over a long period of time. Use of the critical incident technique helps the manager who is preparing yearly evaluations from being influenced primarily by what has been observed during the past month. To ensure objectivity the specific incidents to be cited must be recorded promptly. Attempting to remember events that occurred 6 to 12 months earlier without written records would be much less objective. A recent event should not outweigh accumulated evidence. When unfavorable incidents are observed, the evaluator must tell the

staff member about it at the time and give the staff member a chance to explain how it occurred. This rating method requires the evaluator to pay close attention to the performance of staff members. The critical incident process compels evaluators to face staff members, a responsibility too many shirk.

When the time comes for the manager to have an evaluation conference with the staff member, the critical incidents will be reviewed. There should be no surprises for the staff member. These specific records are also helpful in cases in which an employee needs to be fired or a student failed.

This technique also serves as a form of coaching. If staff members receive feedback at the time incidents occur, they can be aware of any changes they need to make to improve performance. It will help correct problems before they escalate into larger ones.

When staff members receive continual feedback they can better assess their abilities, which can help them in deciding whether to stay with the current job or seek promotion. The employer too needs to know which employees are ready for increased responsibility and promotion.

FREE-FORM EVALUATION

Another form for evaluation is the free-form essay evaluation record. The free-form essay evaluation does not use scales, checklists, or any other devices. It simply requires the evaluator to write down impressions of the individual. The comments can, if desired by the employer, be grouped under headings.

If done well, this method requires a considerable amount of time from the evaluator. It is also true that the resultant appraisals often depend more upon the skill and effort of the writer-rater than upon the real performance of the people being evaluated.

MANAGEMENT BY OBJECTIVES

Management by objectives is a relatively new approach to performance appraisal that has been designed to overcome some of the problems associated with the traditional appraisal methods. The major elements of management by objectives are as follows:

1. The manager and staff member sit down together at the beginning of the appraisal period to establish measurable goals for the staff member to accomplish. They jointly agree upon and list the principal duties and areas of responsibility of the individual's job.
2. The staff member sets short-term performance goals in coopera-

tion with the manager. The manager guides the process to meet the needs of the patient-care unit.

3. They agree upon criteria for measuring and evaluating performance.

4. They periodically meet to evaluate progress toward the goals. The staff member makes an appraisal of what has been accomplished relative to the targets set earlier. It is substantiated with factual data if possible. The "interview" is an examination by manager and staff member together of the staff member's self-appraisal, and it culminates in a resetting of goals for the next period of time.

5. The manager is supportive through counseling and coaching in helping the staff member achieve the goals.

6. The manager is less the judge and more the helper.

7. The process focuses upon results accomplished and not upon personal traits.

In a nutshell, the manager can say, "What are your plans? How can I help?" At the evaluation interview the manager can ask, "What can you do for the patient unit that I have not given you a chance to do?"

There are many advantages to management by objectives. There is an ever-increasing body of data that clearly shows that when workers are given the opportunity to participate in establishing their own work rules, their performance is significantly improved. By the same criterion, the quality of performance appraisals will be improved if the staff member is given the opportunity to participate in setting work objectives and in evaluating performance against those specific objectives. This procedure would considerably decrease reliance on the single source of information and would tend to reduce the amount of bias.

A sample evaluation form using the principles of management by objectives is in Appendix B at the end of this chapter. This evaluation should include a list of objectives to be met during the coming year, the standards of performance to be met, and major improvements to be made. The items should be specific. For example, in the hospital setting, such a goal for an aide might be: (1) ensure that all patients who are NPO are instructed as to its meaning; (2) place a sign over these patients' beds designating that the patient is NPO. This type of appraisal is consistent with the psychological principle that people work better when they have definite goals that they must meet in specified periods.

A basic requirement for success with this method is that the

staff member be interested in the work and in the organization. The individual must have ideas and ambition.

Management by objectives may be difficult to implement in certain cases. The authoritarian manager might find this method difficult to use. The staff member might try to set easily attainable goals in order to meet the objectives. Generally, however, evidence shows that the appraisal-by-results method is superior to traditional appraisal systems.

An experiment contrasting the goals method to the rating scale was conducted by Morton, Rothaus, and Hanson [4]. First the subordinates were rated by the standard trait-rating scale. Then both the subordinates and superiors reported their feelings and experiences on a behavior-rating scale. Finally, the superiors and subordinates jointly participated in the goal method and again reported their feelings and experiences on a behavior-rating scale. The results showed that with the goal approach there was greater agreement between the supervisor and subordinate. There was also less resistance to suggestions, a friendlier attitude, a greater sense of responsibility by the subordinates regarding the area in which change was needed, a clearer view of the routes to improvement, and greater eagerness to change.

Management by objectives differs from traditional rating methods in that it shifts the emphasis from appraisal to analysis. The subordinates are examining themselves in order to define not only their weaknesses but also their strengths and potentials. One of the main differences of this approach is that it rests on the assumption that individuals know—or can learn—more than anyone else about their own capabilities, needs, strengths, weaknesses, and goals. The conventional approach, on the other hand, makes the assumption that the superior can know enough about subordinates to decide what is best for them.

The proper role for the manager is to listen and advise, guide, and encourage staff members to develop their own potentials, which will (1) lead to increased knowledge and skill, (2) contribute to organizational objectives, and (3) test staff members' appraisals of themselves. The knowledge and active participation of both manager and staff member are necessary components of this approach.

PEER REVIEW

As health-care professionals, nurses collectively monitor and evaluate the health care they provide, thus assuring quality care. Peer review is an essential component of quality assurance. The American

Nurses' Association [1] has written that peer review occurs when those people who deliver a specific type of care develop norms, standards, and criteria for review and carry out the review process for members of their own profession.

Peer review is currently being implemented in some schools of nursing and health-care agencies. Registered nurses with the same role expectation or job description or both are examining the nursing care given by their peers. Thus, operating room nurses give peer reviews to operating room nurses, and delivery room nurses review performances of other delivery room nurses.

The purpose of peer review is to measure the quality of care being given patients, to build on the strengths of the nurses being reviewed, and to identify the nurses' deficiencies or limitations to assist them in improving the quality of patient care given. The results of the peer review may be used in determining advancements and salary increases.

Peer review is based on nursing standards. If peer review were to be implemented on an obstetrical unit, for example, the first step to be taken would be to identify the quality of care to be given an obstetrical patient. The nurses being reviewed would be evaluated on their ability to give the quality of patient care defined by the standards or objectives. These standards or objectives are observable and measurable.

An example of how peer review could be implemented is as follows: The nurses on a 35-bed postpartum unit were chosen to initiate peer review on a trial basis. This unit was selected because of its high standards of care, the cohesiveness and maturity of its staff, and the willingness of its staff to cooperate in the trial study. Whenever a change is to be initiated on a trial basis, it is helpful to start on a unit that has the greatest potential for success. The nurses were given time to discuss the implications of the change and what it would mean to them personally and professionally. The RNs on the unit researched and wrote out the standards of care to be given the postpartum patient. Twelve RNs were to be part of the peer review. Each RN had the opportunity to review and evaluate the performance of at least one peer and to be evaluated by two or three peers. The emphasis was on objectively judging the quality of patient care given, not on finding fault with the nurse.

The nurses had mixed feelings about the peer review, both desiring knowledge of how they could improve yet feeling defensive about their shortcomings being identified by their peers. Because the

12 nurses involved respected their colleagues, apprehension was kept to a minimum. The nurses doing the review had scrutinized the practice of the nurse they reviewed. Therefore, they were able to compliment the nurse on accomplishments as well as make suggestions on how to improve. It became a learning experience for both the reviewers and the nurses being reviewed.

Peer review is possible when nurses have trusting relationships and can work together to set standards for which they are accountable. Under this system nurses can continually grow and develop professionally to improve patient care.

Evaluation Conferences

In order for evaluations to be a tool for staff development, they must be shared with the staff members concerned. Some agencies have the manager hold evaluation conferences with new staff members at the conclusion of their third and sixth months on the job and yearly thereafter. Oftentimes, however, the evaluation conference is allowed to fall by the wayside. One head nurse told the author that she had never received an evaluation as a staff nurse, and therefore did not know how to evaluate the staff members.

Evaluation conferences give staff members a source of feedback about performance on the job and provide the opportunity for the manager to counsel staff members on ways to improve performance.

In addition to performance-appraisal discussions, interviews may be held for such purposes as correcting mistakes, gauging reactions to orders, settling disputes between employees, and helping resolve personal problems that affect performance on the job. Other important purposes are discipline and grievance handling.

DIRECTIVE AND NONDIRECTIVE INTERVIEWS

In the _directive interview_ the manager keeps the initiative and controls the conversation. The manager starts with a set of assumptions, asks direct questions to support or modify these assumptions, and then reaches a decision based upon them and whatever added information is gained from the questions. The directive interview has several disadvantages. Staff members may be put on the defensive or may say only what they think the manager wants to hear. It usually fails to reveal the staff member's true feelings.

The _nondirective interview,_ sometimes called the _counseling inter-_

view, is a much preferred method for getting staff members to express themselves freely, for improving understanding between people, and for working out solutions to problems. The principles and practices of nondirective interviewing were developed in the Hawthorne research at the Western Electric Company and by Carl Rogers and his followers [6, 7].

The four stages in the nondirective interview process are:

1. Development of rapport
2. Expression of feelings
3. Development of facts
4. Discovery of solutions

The manager adopts a friendly, patient, understanding attitude and tries to put the person at ease and to establish a feeling of rapport. Their past relationship determines in large part whether the individual feels free to speak openly.

The nondirective interview is essentially a listening one. Neutral rather than pointed questions are asked. Try to draw the other person out and refrain from moralizing, preaching, or admonishing.

After feelings have been expressed and understood by both, the next stage is to develop relevant factual information. The manager can ask such questions as "How did the difficulty arise?", "Can you tell me more about that aspect?", or "Why do you think it happened that way?"

Solutions to problems can evolve in many ways. Sometimes listening to and supporting staff members is enough to help them work out their own solutions. The manager may need to make suggestions but should avoid "masterminding" the solution.

DIFFICULTIES IN GIVING EVALUATION INTERVIEWS
Evaluation interviews are not easy. Most people have mixed feelings about being evaluated, both resenting it and seeking it out. They desire feedback on "where they stand," and yet assessment is a threat to independence and autonomy. Staff members often hope their strengths will be recognized and their weaknesses overlooked. Evidence suggests that staff members tend to rate their own performance higher than do their evaluators; consequently, the interview can be a deflating experience [3].

The informative and motivational purposes of appraisal cannot be served unless the staff member being evaluated desires and ap-

preciates constructive criticism. Substantial controversy exists as to whether staff members in fact want to know of their shortcomings. It is the position of the authors that if the criticism is timely, skillfully offered, and related to jointly determined standards, friction will not necessarily be the final result.

Most managers endorse performance appraisal in principle, but few would initiate an evaluation program on their own. Personnel specialists [3, 5] report that most managers carry out performance-appraisal interviews only when strong control procedures are established to ensure that they do.

Managers may be uncertain as to the consequences of negative appraisals. Most managers fear that negative appraisals, or even negative portions of an otherwise favorable appraisal, will discourage staff members rather than serve to motivate. If, as is usually the case, managers do most of the talking during the interview, then they are not doing much listening. If they are not listening, then they are not gaining any insight into staff members' problems.

Some managers "forget" about evaluation interviews. Others hand staff members the form in an embarrassed fashion without asking for comments or replies from the staff member. Even managers who understand principles of supervisory development feel uncomfortable when they have to criticize staff members. If the evaluation form is the traditional type, the manager may hesitate to "judge" the staff member or to "play God." People feel guilty when they criticize others and therefore fear appraising honestly. To avoid ill feeling, many evaluators avoid unpleasant truths. The result is an evaluation in name only.

Fortunately, there are group methods for relieving guilt and for helping managers understand the value of accurate evaluations. One method is to have a group of nurses at the same peer level discuss their problems in giving appraisals. In-service education could also set up a specific program as outlined by Levinson [2]:

1. Group discussion among peers concerning their feelings about appraising subordinates
2. Group discussion resulting in advice from each other on the specific problems that each anticipates in appraising individuals
3. Role playing appraisal interviews
4. Actual appraisals
5. Group discussion to review the appraisals, problems encountered, both anticipated and unanticipated, lessons learned, and skill needs that may have surfaced

GUIDELINES FOR EVALUATION INTERVIEWS

Some guidelines will be given for the nurse giving an evaluation interview or conference. In preparing for the evaluation, remind staff members of the time so that they too can prepare for it. Prior to the interview, they should have a copy of the form that is used and review their job description and any targets or goals that they are attempting to meet. If they have had an evaluation before, review what was written and refresh in your mind what has been discussed previously. Consider what questions they might have about such things as opportunity for promotion. Think of what you have done to help or hinder their development.

Decide what the goal is for the interview. You will probably want to stimulate them to greater effort, help them understand where improved performance is needed, let them know how effective they are, and help them work out specific steps for their own improvement and development.

Plan what you are going to say. The primary emphasis should be on helping them to improve their work results. In so doing you can explore why better results were not obtained in certain areas, in what respect improvement is needed, and what the employees might do to get better results in the future. In planning what you say, try to put yourself in their shoes and think what your reaction would be if these things were said to you.

Plan to tell them what they are doing well, but also ask them about the things that they are not doing especially well. Frequently they will know best what their shortcomings are. Do not dwell on past errors if you discussed them at the time they occurred (as you should have). Have specific suggestions for methods of improvement. Remember that you are evaluating the work, not the person. Avoid words that sound critical or antagonistic, such as "faults," "mistakes," and "illogical." Do not compare them to other staff members.

It is important for the evaluator to have a helpful attitude—not the attitude of a judge or a superior talking down to an inferior. You can ask yourself:

1. Do I feel genuinely friendly to the staff members?
2. Am I interested in them?
3. How can I be helpful to them?
4. How can I encourage them to express themselves?
5. I may be wrong. Can I admit it?
6. How can I express the evaluation so that they will try to do better?

7. Am I thinking of my feelings more than their feelings?
8. If we disagree, will I argue?

Allow a private, comfortable setting for the interview. You should have ample time set aside free from interruptions. Make the staff members comfortable and begin by stating the purpose of the interview and by assuring them that you want to get their views.

The secret of success is putting yourself in the staff members' place and seeing things from their point of view. Do not jump to conclusions or assume you understand, but get them to express their thoughts and ideas. Refrain from dominating the discussion with your own ideas. Let them talk, and as they do, be a good listener. Avoid talking about your own experiences.

During the discussion amplify points with specific facts and occurrences. For example, the statement "Uses good judgment" should be expanded with examples such as "Notified the module leader promptly when patient's urine output suddenly decreased." Give credit for accomplishments, and review goals not accomplished or areas in which improvement is needed. Explore why and how. Notice what they do not say.

Some questions that are helpful to ask the person you are evaluating are:

1. Are aspects of your job defined adequately?
2. Are you challenged?
3. Do you feel your work is appreciated?
4. Do you feel supported?
5. Are you informed and consulted when necessary?
6. Do you have opportunities to use your initiative?

SOME PROBLEMS THE EVALUATOR MAY ENCOUNTER

Occasionally the interview runs into snags. Sometimes you find that staff members will not open up. They answer direct questions briefly but do not enter into the conversation freely. You do not know if they are nervous, angry, or if this is their nature. You can try to discuss something other than the evaluation just to get them to talk. Once they begin talking, they may then talk about the evaluation. Show a special interest in what they say.

Occasionally the persons being evaluated become angry even though you have been tactful. If this should occur, be a good listener as they may be expressing feelings of insecurity, disappointment, or

resentment. When they calm down, be sure they understand you will not hold this against them. Go out of your way to be friendly to them in the next few days.

Another problem in interviewing is the employees' agreeing too quickly with everything you say. It may be that they do not understand, but more frequently they want to avoid criticism. Be sure to emphasize strongly the areas that need improvement and outline how you intend to follow up on these plans.

Long-term employees need special treatment. They often need reassurance, and their pride may suffer when they are being evaluated by a younger person. They will probably be highly appreciative of recognition of their judgment and skill.

In closing the interview, review the points on which you have agreed and encourage the staff members to come to you if they have questions or suggestions. The evaluator has the responsibility to follow through to see that staff members are achieving the goals discussed.

OUTLINE OF EVALUATION INTERVIEW

The following outline is an example of how an interview could be conducted:

1. The head nurse tells staff members the purpose of the interview and that it is designed to help them do a better job.
2. The head nurse presents the evaluation, giving the strong points first and then the weak points.
3. The head nurse asks for comments on the evaluation, anticipating that defensive or hostile feelings may be expressed about the negative points. Staff members are allowed to blow off steam. Resenting what is said, defending oneself, or "putting them in their place" gets the evaluator emotionally involved and may stop people from expressing their feelings. Find out why staff members do not agree instead of trying to prove they are wrong.
4. The head nurse asks staff members to discuss the progress they are making, what areas need improvement, and methods for improvement.
5. The interview concludes with the head nurse and staff members discussing the direction for improvement. Both how the staff members can improve and how the head nurse can assist are discussed.

PROVIDING OPPORTUNITIES FOR STAFF MEMBERS
TO EXPRESS VIEWPOINTS

The manager should accept any criticism from staff members without argument. If this is poorly handled, the conference can lead to hostility rather than understanding.

Some managers start the interview with "Tell me how you think you are doing." This has the advantage of letting the staff members express their viewpoints first. Some individuals would rather point out their weaknesses to the manager than have the manager point them out. Others, however, feel that they do not want to expose their opinions until after they have read what their manager has written.

VARYING OBJECTIVES ACCORDING TO THE INDIVIDUAL

The objectives of the interview vary from one person to another. For example:

1. If a weakness is difficult to correct, such as shyness in an aide, or a speech difficulty in an LPN, there is no point in discussing it at all.
2. If the weaknesses are correctable, it is often better to wait for staff members to bring them up when they see fit.
3. If performance is so unacceptable that staff members may be discharged, they should receive a warning. To be genuinely helpful you should face the problem at the earliest possible date, while there is some hope of helping the employees.
4. If employees have done an outstanding job, you may want to help these individuals use their abilities to fullest advantage. This may result in a better job.
5. If employees have not improved, it is best to be frank and direct as to whether they are in the right job. Some nurses may really dislike nursing but have yet to face up to the fact. They might be much more successful at a different job.
6. If employees are just sliding by, it is helpful to find out how they feel about their job. Are they happy in their work?

Performance Appraised: Conclusions

In conclusion, the primary objective of performance appraisal is to encourage and support development of an employee toward meeting the objectives of the institution. Providing for evaluation of employees at all levels emphasizes the expectations of everyone to

progress in position, be it at the top, bottom, or middle of the organizational chart. To progress rather than regress, an organization must help motivate its personnel to continuous development. This substantiates the need to comment on weaknesses when they exist; to avoid this denies the purpose of performance appraisal. For criticism to be beneficial, however, it must be accompanied by constructive suggestions for improvement. The likelihood of keeping the evaluation objective will be enhanced if the evaluator's goal is to help the employee rather than to justify the appraisal. There must be leveling, honesty, and helpfulness.

The advantages of a systematic appraisal system to the health-care agency are that: (1) employee strengths and weaknesses can be routinely assessed, (2) it can provide evidence to terminate employees who have had unsatisfactory achievement, (3) it can reveal areas of need for in-service education, and (4) it can serve as periodic feedback to employees.

Study Questions

Questions 1 and 2 are written for group discussion. Get a group of classmates or friends together to discuss these if you do not have a classroom opportunity for discussing them.

1. Miss Walker, RN, age 22, started working on your unit three months ago. She is an extremely enthusiastic worker with lots of good ideas. As a leader, she is short on patience with the staff members. She is constantly pushing them and is annoyed when she finds them taking a break. The staff morale suffers when Miss Walker is leader. During conferences, she has excellent suggestions, but she dominates the discussion. You are concerned about the animosity developing between her and some other staff members. As a head nurse this is the first evaluation you have given Miss Walker.
    a. What should your strategy be in handling the evaluation interview with Miss Walker?
    b. Role play this interview. Miss Walker is sure her ideas are good, and she is pressing for a head-nurse position in the hospital.
2. Miss Saunders, age 25, is an LPN. She is best described as dumpy, quiet, and withdrawn. She often asks the team leader questions that she should be able to answer for herself, given her LPN background. Miss Saunders lacks initiative and needs detailed instructions. Team members ignore her, and she is a loner. Self-confidence appears to be lacking in Miss Saunders. She never says a word in a team conference unless asked a question directly, and then the answer is brief. How would you interview Miss Saunders for her three-month review?
    a. What will be your strategy?

   b. Role play this interview. Miss Saunders responds minimally during the interview.

3. What evaluations did you find most helpful in nursing school? Did any serve as a motivation for change? Which were least helpful? Why?

4. What were your feelings prior to an evaluation conference, during the conference, and after the conference when you were the one being evaluated?

5. Which staff members would you be most reluctant to evaluate in a conference? Why? Which person would be easiest to evaluate? Why?

6. Is it possible for individuals to identify for themselves areas of weakness and areas of strength?

Appendix A
Evaluation Form for Nurses' Aide

Place a check mark in the appropriate column; comments may be added

	Excellent	Very Good	Average	Poor	Unsatisfactory	Comment
	A	B	C	D	E	
1. Technical Skills						
a. Quality of work (Performs procedure correctly, completely)						
b. Quantity of work (Finishes assignments adequately)						
c. Ability to observe (Makes thorough observations of patients)						
d. Emotional support to patients (Recognizes patient needs and acts accordingly)						
e. Reports (Reports accurately, thoroughly, promptly)						
f. Practice of safety (Observes safety in care of patients and equipment)						
2. Group Member						
a. Follows instructions						
b. Cooperates with staff members						
c. Communications (Communicates effectively with patients, visitors)						
d. Contributions (Makes suggestions for improving patient care)						
3. Attitudes						
a. Adaptability (Accepts change; adjusts smoothly)						
b. Etiquette (Is polite, thoughtful, and kind)						
c. Responsibility (Is responsible for work; is concerned for welfare of others)						
d. Initiative (Sees tasks to be done; volunteers)						
e. Supervision (Willingly accepts directions, assignments, constructive criticism)						
f. Interest (Asks questions; appears to enjoy work)						
g. Self-improvement (Tries to improve)						
h. Learning ability (Learns easily)						
4. Personal Hygiene						
a. Is neat, clean, and well groomed						
5. Attendance						
a. Reports on duty promptly; no excessive absences						

Appendix B
Performance Appraisal

The person being evaluated and the evaluator should prepare for the evaluation conference by individually completing the following form. The conference should include a review of both persons' expectations, and the discussion should focus on determination of realistic objectives and standards for the work of the person being evaluated. Each person should keep a copy of the corrected form. This can then be used to check progress during the year and to compare accomplishments with the objectives at the end of the year.

Objectives for the Year. (Determine goals for work to be accomplished and list them in an order of priority.)

Standards. (Outline specific plans for what ought to be achieved during the year. Include information about materials, supplies, human resources, and assistance needed to achieve the objectives stated above. Standards should incorporate quality as well as quantity statements to facilitate measurement.)

Plan for Personal Growth. (Outline specific plans you have for improving your abilities, knowledge, and skills. This can include formal and informal educational plans as well as personal objectives for improving the effectiveness of your performance.)

Year-End Evaluation. (Compare objectives with actual accomplishments. Identify reasons for differences in results, and determine how the desired results can be obtained in the future. Again, both the person being evaluated and the evaluator should prepare their thoughts individually in advance of the conference.)

Objectives Achieved

Objectives Not Achieved: Analysis of Reasons and
Plan for Future Improvement

Results of Plan for Personal Growth: Plans for the Future

References

1. American Nurses' Association. Philosophy of Peer Review, Peer Review Guidelines (pamphlet). American Nurses' Association, Nov. 1973.
2. Levinson, H. Appraisal of what performance? *Harvard Bus. Rev.* 54:44, July/August 1976.
3. Meyer, H. H., Kay, E., and French, J. P. P., Jr. Split roles in performance appraisal. *Harvard Bus. Rev.* 23:123, 126, Jan./Feb. 1965.
4. Morton, R. B., Rothaus, P., and Hanson, P. C. An experiment in

performance appraisal and review, *J. Am. Soc. Train. Direct.* 15:19, May 1961.

5. Parker, J. W., Taylor, E. K., Barrett, R. S., and Martens, L.   Rating scale content: Relationship between supervisory and self-ratings. *Pers. Psych.* 12:49, 1959.

6. Roethlisberger, F. J., and Dickson, W. J.   *Management and the Worker.* Cambridge, Mass.: Harvard University Press, 1939. Pp. 270–291.

7. Rogers, C. R.   *Counseling and Psychotherapy.* Boston: Houghton Mifflin, 1942. Pp. 115–128.

Suggested Reading

Cain, C., and Luchsinger, V.   Management by objectives: Applications to nursing. *J. Nurs. Adm.* 8:35, Jan. 1978.

Carroll, S. J., Jr., and Tosi, H., Jr.   *Management by Objectives.* New York: Macmillan, 1973.

Dau, G. J.   The appraisal process. *Superv. Nurse* 7:39, Aug. 1976.

Fleishman, E. A.   *Studies in Personnel and Industrial Psychology* (rev. ed.). Homewood, Ill.: Dorsey Press, 1967. Section 2.

Haar, L. P., et al.   Performance appraisal: Derivation of effective assessment tool. *Nurs. Dig.* 5:38, Fall 1977.

Hamric, A. B., Gresham, M. L., and Eccard, M.   Staff evaluation of clinical leaders. *J. Nurs. Adm.* 8:18, Jan. 1978.

Humble, J.   *Management by Objectives in Action.* New York: McGraw-Hill, 1970.

Kellogg, M. S.   *Closing the Performance Gap.* New York: American Management Association, 1967.

Koontz, Harold.   *Appraising Managers As Managers.* New York: McGraw-Hill, 1971.

Lasagna, J. R.   Make your MBO pragmatic. *Harvard Bus. Rev.* 49:64–68, Nov./Dec. 1971.

Levinson, H.   Appraisal of what performance? *Harvard Bus. Rev.* 54:30, July/Aug. 1976.

McGregor, D.   An uneasy look at performance appraisal. *Harvard Bus. Rev.* 50:133, Sept./Oct. 1972.

Meyer, H. H., Kay, E., and French, J. P. P., Jr.   Split roles in performance appraisal. *Harvard Bus. Rev.* 23:123, Jan./Feb. 1965.

Oberg, W.   Make performance appraisal relevant. *Harvard Bus. Rev.* 50:61, Jan./Feb. 1972.

Odiorne, G. S.   Management by objectives: Antidote to future shock. *Nurs. Adm.* 5:27, Feb. 1975.

Patz, A. L.   Performance appraisal: Useful but still resisted. *Harv. Bus. Rev.* 51:74, May/June 1973.

Rieder, G. A.   Performance review—a mixed bag. *Harvard Bus. Rev.* 51:61, July/Aug. 1973.

South, J. C.   The performance profile: A technique for using appraisals effectively. *J. Nurs. Adm.* 8:27, Jan. 1978.

Stevens, B. J.   Performance appraisal: What the nurse executive expects from it. *Nurs. Dig.* 5:48, Fall 1977.

11. Discipline

Discipline is necessary to all organized working units. The staff members must control their individual urges and cooperate for the common good of the health-care agency. Individual employees need to conform to the code of behavior established by the agency administration.

Skill in achieving discipline in the work place is an important qualification for a manager. Leaders also need this skill in working with staff members.

Positive discipline involves creation of an attitude whereby staff members conform willingly to the agency's established rules and regulations. It is achieved when the nurse-manager applies principles of positive motivation, when sound leadership is exercised by supervision, and when the entire agency is managed efficiently. The staff members, both as individuals and as a group, adhere to the desired standards of behavior because they understand, believe in, and support them.

Self-Discipline

The best discipline, of course, is self-discipline. Most people want to do a good job and do their share by the rules established. Once people understand what is expected of them, they generally can be counted on to do their job correctly.

If the rules established are viewed by the staff members as fair, they will generally observe them without question. They obey the rules because the rules are reasonable, rather than because they fear punishment. Rules such as coming to work on time, carrying out patient-care assignments, reporting to the nurse-leader, and not stealing agency supplies are viewed by staff members as reasonable and a necessary condition of work.

Group Norms and Discipline

A norm is a group-established standard of expected behavior. People do not behave as isolated, independent individuals. Instead, their behavior is strongly conditioned by the pressures, norms, and culture of the groups to which they belong. The social groups on a work unit

frequently exercise very strong control over the behavior of their individual members. These group-established standards of behavior are not written down, but are often expressed orally. The group enforces its standards by social pressure.

Most work groups exercise a stabilizing effect upon the conduct of their members. If the nurse-manager has good relations with the staff members and if the staff members respect the rules of conduct established by the nurse-manager, then this group discipline works in support of management's objectives. The successful manager is one who understands the nature of group forces, who is perceptive to group action, and who can blend group goals with those of the organization.

If the nurse-manager has built a cohesive, loyal work group, then its members will adhere generally to the manager's disciplinary efforts. The nurse-manager can lead discussions covering agency rules and regulations, as well as the need for them. The staff members can discuss how these rules apply to them in their own work situation. If the group as a group understands and believes in the rules, it will often exert social pressure upon its members to ensure that they live up to them. This also applies to unofficial rules and standards accepted by the group. For example, one patient-care unit has an unwritten agreement that any staff member is to answer any patient's light. For a staff member to say, "That isn't my patient," and not answer a patient's light is unacceptable to the group.

Most staff members are tolerant of an occasional infraction of their written and unwritten rules. If Mrs. Jones had a late night celebrating her tenth wedding anniversary and is slow on the job the next day, this can be overlooked if she does her part the rest of the time. But staff members resent seeing someone else "get away with murder" while they are doing a full day's work. As one nurse's aide said, "We're all here to do our job. It really bugs me when I'm working hard and the other aides are goofing off in the lounge while I'm answering all the patients' lights." Lax performance by some may result in lowering the level of performance by all. Thus, enforcing the rules strengthens the group's informal efforts at correction.

Responsibility of the Nurse-Manager
COMMUNICATING RULES
What is the nurse-manager's responsibility in ensuring good discipline? All rules and policies should be communicated to the staff

members. A new staff member should receive information concerning agency policy in a written pamphlet and in an orientation session. In orienting a new person, expected work performance should be explained, as well as what help is available in achieving it. New rules or policy should be communicated to staff members in a written memo to be placed on the bulletin board or added to their policy book. It helps if someone can explain the reason for and background of the policy to the staff members. Before you penalize staff members they must know the rules they are accused of having violated. The rules introduced should seem reasonable to the staff members if they are expected to be followed. For example, a policy stating that all requests for vacations must be submitted one year in advance would seem quite unreasonable. Such a policy might breed "hate and discontent."

FIRM ENFORCEMENT

Rules and policies serve to draw the lines of limitations and freedom for staff members. Therefore, rules must be enforced firmly and fairly. L. Cassels [3] writes that the average worker's natural inclination to obey the rules can be dissipated by lax or inept enforcement policies. Staff members can develop contempt for nurse-managers who allow regulations to be disregarded. Numerous attitude surveys have shown that staff morale is highest in organizations whose members are conscious of being held to a high standard of performance. Reflect for a moment. Would you be happiest working with a nurse-manager who is firm but fair in expecting staff members to give high quality of patient care; or, in contrast, with one whose standards and leadership are lax and staff members do as they please when they please? To achieve constructive discipline, the manager must set a good example.

FAIR ENFORCEMENT

Rules need to be enforced fairly. Is it fair to reprimand an aide for arriving at work 30 minutes late while ignoring the fact that an RN is also 30 minutes late? The rules should apply to everyone and be enforced 24 hours a day, seven days a week. Consistency of treatment is an important principle and one that is easily ignored. Inconsistency can occur because managers in different areas have different standards of what they expect and different tolerance levels when staff members deviate from the standards.

The best way to achieve consistency of treatment and application

of the rules is through supervisory training courses and by consistent action by higher management on a day-to-day basis as cases are brought up.

The need for consistency does not mean that two persons committing an identical offense must always receive identical penalties. The background and circumstances of each case may call for differential treatment. But consistency does require that both employees know that they have violated a rule. You must not condone the infraction by one and not the other, but the punishment should fit the offender as well as the offense. If the aide mentioned previously has been 30 minutes late six times in one month and this was the first time the RN was late, genuine fairness requires that each be treated differently. The RN needs to be corrected but does not deserve a harsh punishment.

The basic aim of disciplinary action is to encourage adherence to the rules in the future rather than to punish passing infractions.

Types of Penalties

What are the penalties for wrongdoings? Obviously, penalties must be tied to the gravity of the offense. Some offenses require immediate and final discipline (such as stealing or drug abuse). Many organizations have a progressive system; this means that there is a sequence of penalties from less severe to more severe. Ordinarily it includes these steps outlined by G. Strauss and L. Sayles [5]: (1) oral warning, (2) written warning, (3) disciplinary layoff, and (4) discharge.

The oral warning is given according to the principle presented in a previous chapter about correcting an error promptly. If the aide is 30 minutes late to work, she should be corrected promptly—not six months later during an evaluation conference. The written warning is psychologically more severe than the oral warning since it goes in the employee's record.

Disciplinary layoffs are next in severity. The employee is sent home for several days or weeks without pay. Discharge is the most severe penalty. It is hard not only on the employee, but also on the organization. An RN who is fired must look for a new job and may have difficulty gaining employment. The agency too suffers, for it must hire and orient someone to replace the RN.

Avoiding Resentment

Enforcing discipline puts you, the nurse-manager, in a difficult position. You work with the staff members on a daily basis and want to

be regarded as a source of help. Disciplining a staff member is painful for you as well as for the staff member. How can you do it without generating resentment? When you reprimand a staff member, tell (1) what was done that was wrong, (2) why it was wrong (the rule that was violated), and (3) what will happen if it is done again. Then quickly, while it is still fresh in your mind, write a memo on how you handled the situation and what you told the staff member. The written memo becomes part of the staff member's performance record.

The "Hot Stove" Rule

An old but well tested rule for discipline called the "hot stove" rule was advocated by Douglas McGregor [5]. His rule says that when you touch a hot stove, you are burned:

1. Immediately (Your hand gets burned as soon as you touch the stove.)
2. With warning (You knew what would happen if you touched it.)
3. Impersonally (It burned you because you touched it, not because it was you.)
4. Consistently (If your neighbor touched it, it would burn him too.)

The hot stove discipline emphasizes that the act was wrong—not the person.

Let us look at what happens when the principles for discipline are not followed:

Mrs. Slow, RN, has a bad tardiness record. She comes in 30 minutes late but thinks the head nurse is too busy to notice. The head nurse says nothing. By noon, Mrs. Slow assumes that she will not be reprimanded. At 3:15 P.M. the head nurse explains to Mrs. Slow that she has filed a written warning that will be put in her record.

Mrs. Slow is angry with the head nurse and the discipline. She feels that the head nurse was pretending not to notice the offenses until enough were gathered to result in disciplinary action. If the head nurse had followed the hot stove rule, the discipline would have been *immediate* and Mrs. Slow would have seen the act of tardiness disciplined rather than experiencing the discipline as a personal affront.

In order to maintain discipline in the work place, the staff members need to understand what offenses will lead to discipline and what the discipline will be if the offense occurs. For example, a policy

states that 30 minutes will be allowed for lunch. The manager has not enforced it, and some staff members take 30 minutes for lunch one day and 40 minutes another day. No one expects the manager to rigidly enforce the rule since it has not been enforced in the past. If the manager were to suddenly choose a staff member to punish for infraction of the rule, it would be without warning. If the manager wanted the rule enforced, the better method would be to announce that infringements would not be tolerated. This would serve as the *warning*. The nurse would also need to explain what disciplinary action would result if an infraction of the rule occurred.

If on Monday you require staff members to ambulate patients at least twice during the day, you should be *consistent* and expect the same performance on Tuesday unless extenuating circumstances intervene. You must also remember consistency when you would rather overlook disciplining some rule breaker. This aspect of consistency is hard to maintain; it means not playing favorites by disciplining some and not disciplining others.

Impersonality is another rule. C. Argyris [2] states that discipline is most effective and has the least negative effects on individuals if the individual feels that the behavior at the particular moment is the only thing being criticized and not the total personality.

The Disciplinary Action

When disciplinary action becomes necessary, attempt to keep communication lines open. You want to learn the basic reason for the incorrect behavior, not the excuse for it.

Incorrect: RN: Miss Watkins, according to Mr. Write you have not been into his room for three hours. Didn't I tell you yesterday that he needs hourly measurements of intake and output and needs turning every two hours?
Correct: RN: Miss Watkins, Mr. Write tells me you haven't been in to check him for three hours. Can you tell me why?

Once you decide what discipline is appropriate, impose it quietly, impersonally, and in private.

Once you have disciplined a staff member, there is a natural tendency to avoid or to act differently toward the individual. Make a conscious effort not to do either of these, as your relationship with the staff member may be impaired. By treating the staff member the same as you did prior to the incident, you are showing that it was the act, not the person, that was punished.

Common Mistakes

Mistakes are common in imposing discipline. The nurse may either be apologetic in handing out discipline or may bawl the offender out. The following serve as examples of each:

Apologetic Discipline

NURSE-MANAGER: I hate to seem like a meany, Miss Hanson, but the nursing supervisor expects me to enforce the rules. I'm really sorry that I have to do this.

STAFF MEMBER (*thinking to herself*): Miss Hag thinks the rule is dumb, *or* Miss Hag doesn't have much backbone, *or* Who does she think she's kidding?

Personal Bawling Out

NURSE-MANAGER: I'm getting pretty tired of your slack standards. I've told you repeatedly to keep your IVs on time. What kind of a nurse are you anyway? You certainly aren't the kind of nurse I want working on this unit. You had better start shaping up if you want to keep your job.

In the second example, the discipline is much too personal. There is no need to rub the staff member's nose in dirt. Instead, correct the behavior, assume that the staff member will improve, and write a memo.

Grievance Handling with Union Personnel

In 1974 an amendment to the Taft-Hartley Act made nonprofit health-care facilities subject to the national labor laws. Hospital employees were thus allowed to become unionized.

Generally employees join a union when they feel that they are not being satisfied by the employer. Employees who feel that they are not being treated well by management seek out unionization as a form of power in dealing with management. Because more and more hospital employees are being unionized, the nurse-manager needs knowledge of the ramifications of managing unionized staff members.

Through collective bargaining at the local level the union and hospital administration agree on a contract which specifies wages, hours, work rules, and other conditions of employment. This contract is a legal document about which the nurse-manager needs to be fully informed. In-service education programs or the personnel de-

partment should provide nurse-managers with the details of the contract.

It is understood by union and management alike that the signing of a labor contract does not automatically take care of all labor-relations problems that may arise. A grievance procedure, which is part of the contract, provides one means of settling difficulties. The contract states how complaints are to be resolved between union members and the health-care administrators. Most grievances are filed against management.

An example of how a grievance procedure might work is as follows: Mrs. Sherman, an LPN, is upset with the schedule she will be working during the next month. She feels that it is less desirable than the schedules the other LPNs will be working. Her first step in the grievance procedure would be to talk with her manager informally. If this fails she could ask the steward to intercede. The stewards police the labor contract and ensure that managers do not violate its provisions [1]. It is through stewards that formal complaints or grievances are made against management. The steward would attempt to correct the problem by talking with the manager. If this fails, the steward writes a formal complaint to be given to the next level of management, which could be the nursing supervisor. If this also fails, Mrs. Sherman could request that a committee made up of union and management representatives review the grievance. If the results continue to be unfavorable to Mrs. Sherman and if the union officials feel further grievance procedure to be appropriate, the problem is presented to an arbitrator. An arbitrator is a neutral person who hears the case presented by labor and management and resolves the problem by offering a solution which is binding to both.

Agency administrators also need protection against inappropriate actions by unionized subordinates. A portion of the contract is devoted to guidelines on discipline. In the contract there will be a list of inappropriate acts and their associated penalties, and there will be an explanation of due process [6]. The nurse-manager needs to document everything in accordance with procedures in the union contract.

P. King [4] gives seven common laws against which all arbitrators seem to check all discipline cases. They are as follows:

1. Make the rule reasonable.
2. Stay out of private lives.
3. Don't keep rules in your hat.

4. Correct—don't punish.
5. Make the punishment uniform.
6. Don't double up on punishment.
7. Grant the benefit of the doubt.

The grievance procedure is a valuable protection for the employee. The nurse-manager needs to read and fully understand any union/management contract so that the rights of union members are protected and the hospital is not subject to lengthy and costly labor disputes.

Common Disciplinary Problems

Let us look at some of the more common disciplinary problems that we find in nursing situations:

1. *The Absentee:* You have probably had staff members who are chronically absent from work. Equally aggravating are the staff members who neither come to work nor call to say they will not be at work. Weekends especially can be notorious for absenteeism of staff members. What can be done about this problem? A procedure should exist, be known to employees, and be enforced that spells out: (1) when to call, (2) whom to call, and (3) what happens when there is no call. A policy needs to be written as to how many days of absenteeism is unreasonable. The chronic absentee who is away from work unreasonably should be discharged. Warning the employee of probable discharge should precede the discharge.
2. *The Loafer:* Staff members who are present at work but are not doing their job are another common problem. Night nurses may even work with staff members who sleep on the job. Here, again, a policy should exist and be enforced. The wrongdoer must be corrected and warned. The manager can keep a record of the offenses to back up the cause for any additional discipline.
3. *The Staff Member Working Under Par:* A job description must exist for each category of employee. If a staff member does not work up to the standards spelled out in the job description, and training and constructive criticism have failed, then the nurse-manager must show where poor performance exists. Once again written memos of examples of behavior are helpful in substantiating your charge against the staff member.

4. *The Rebel:* Occasionally we encounter staff members who refuse an aspect of their assignment. For example, an aide may refuse to admit a patient or take care of a particular patient. Find out the reason for the refusal. If the reason does not "hold water," then disciplinary measures are needed following the principles stated earlier.

Conclusions

Basically, discipline is a form of training. Failure to keep staff members informed may be the cause of the disciplinary problem. It takes more than one-way communication, however. Staff members need to regard the rules as acceptable. Managers must initiate discipline by winning acceptance of the standards.

For discipline to be accepted, the rules must be known to all the staff members, and penalties for disregarding rules must be consistent. Discipline helps staff members recognize their job requirements and if done impersonally can build a stronger group that renders better patient care.

Group Session

1. What occurs when the nurse-manager is inconsistent in handling disciplinary situations?
2. What happens when two head nurses on two different units handle similar disciplinary problems in completely different ways?
3. Why have you failed as a manager and leader if you do not maintain discipline on your unit?
4. Do a relatively few individuals cause most of the disciplinary problems in your school or agency? Why? What characteristics do they have in common?
5. What happens when the nurse-manager overlooks that Miss Jones, NA, stays away from work three days without calling in to inform the manager?
   a. What effect does this have on Miss Jones?
   b. What effect does it have on the other staff members?
   c. How does this decrease the nurse-manager's effectiveness?
6. Suppose an RN has been making frequent small mistakes. Is it better for the manager to: (1) discuss each mistake separately as it occurs, or (2) discuss the RN's overall performance with her from time to time?
7. What are the established "rules of conduct" in your school or agency? Who formulated them? Do the managers or instructors know what they are? Do all the staff members or students know what they are?
   a. How do they know?

b. What steps have been taken to ensure that they understand the policies?

c. Are they enforced? If not, why not?

8. Does your school or agency have an established disciplinary policy? Does a procedure exist for implementing it?

9. What are the criteria for dismissing an employee or student in your agency or school?

a. Do you know?

b. Do the employees or students know?

c. Is there a chance for appeal? To whom is the appeal made?

References

1. Alexander, K. G. Union structure and bargaining structure. *Labor Law J.* 24:164, 1973.

2. Argyris, C. *Executive Leadership*. New York: Harper & Row, 1953. P. xiii.

3. Cassels, L. Discipline: Key to high morale. *Nation's Business* 47:82–91, Nov. 1959.

4. King, P. Tips to successful discipline. *Factory Management and Maintenance* 116:78–87, June 1958.

5. Strauss, G., and Sayles, L. *Personnel: The Human Problems of Management* (3rd ed.). Englewood Cliffs, N.J.: Prentice-Hall, 1972. Pp. 264–282.

6. Werther, W. B., Jr., and Lockhart, C. A. *Labor Relations in the Health Professions*. Boston: Little, Brown, 1976.

Suggested Reading

Anderson, M., and Farran, C. We are accountable. (#16-1626) New York: National League for Nursing, 1976. Pp. 147–168.

Bennett, R. and MacRobert, R. Building skills in discipline and grievance handling. Part 1—*Hosp. Top.* 53:8, Jan./Feb. 1975. Part 2—*Hosp. Top.* 53:50, March/April 1975.

Bryant, Y. Labor relations in health care institutions: An analysis of Public Law 93-360. *J. Nurs. Adm.* 8:28, March 1978.

Davis, K. Steps toward a more flexible disciplinary policy. *Personnel* 38:52–56, May/June 1961.

Hamil, E. M. Conflict management . . . flight, fight, negotiate. (#52-1677) New York: National League for Nursing, 1977. Pp. 1–6.

Herron, I., Nash, P., Roberts, L., Lewis, L., and Bishop, A. Labor-management issues in the health care fields. (#21-1624) New York: National League for Nursing, 1976. Pp. 1–59.

Knutson, K. E., and Robertson, P. The disciplinary conference letter. *Superv. Nurse* 7:10, March 1976.

Marriner, A. Discipline of personnel. *Superv. Nurse* 7:15, Nov. 1976.

Petersen, D. J., and Halstead, E. G. The arbitration of cases involving improper professional conduct in the health care industry. *A.A.N.A. J.* 45:189, April 1977.

12. Communication

Communication is the integration process of management. Every chapter in this book deals with theories and techniques of management, and you will find that they all involve relating to other people. In this chapter some of the basic communication tools important to effective management are isolated and their application to working relationships is explored.

Communication Skills

A manager fills many roles. Among them are ambassador, consultant, innovator, boss, disciplinarian, and practitioner. All these roles require communication skills. Managerial communications encompass all types of communicating. The manager must listen, read, write memos and notes, fill out forms and requisitions, and talk to others. The manager is actually in a pivotal position in an organization and must articulate not only the purposes of the organization to the staff but also the needs and problems of the staff to the organization's administrative personnel. Let us examine some of the communication skills inherent in the manager's many roles.

An ambassador must be able to listen, to know what to say and when to communicate. This knowledge stems from understanding people and events so that communication will be effective for each situation. Nurse-ambassadors have to know how to phrase their communication so that patients and staff members will understand what they are saying. Managers have to know how to interpret what is being said to them so that their responses will be appropriate. Tact and diplomacy are criteria for communicating to personnel from other departments, patients, families, and staff members. These characteristics enable the nurse-managers to develop common understanding and cooperative relationships among all those with whom they work.

Innovators often have ideas that are new and different. Therefore, managers who are also innovators must be able to channel the thinking of others along their line of reasoning. This requires that innovators develop acceptance of innovative ideas by being persuasive, logical, and patient. Communication must reflect these characteristics. In nursing, it is sometimes difficult to gain the nursing staff's

acceptance of new ways of doing things, because the tried and true method seems to work well. Innovators in this situation must lead people to understand the purposes for change and to become involved in the growth process. Communication is very important in this process.

To be boss and to be disciplinarian require that managers be able to express themselves with sincerity and directness. The communications required of a boss and of a disciplinarian are related. The boss must be able to give clear, meaningful directions. The nurse-manager, for example, must succinctly outline the care a nurse's aide is to give a patient so that the aide understands what has to be done. The disciplinarian must be able to cite definite and pertinent events that define an individual's personal responsibility for doing or not doing what should have been accomplished. The nurse's aide, for example, must be told why the manager is not satisfied with the patient care given through the use of specific examples if the communication is to be meaningful. Both the boss and the disciplinarian roles require that the manager assess events and performance of workers through listening as well as observing. Both roles require a constructive approach in communication so that improved performance will result. Both require that the manager be open in communication so that the workers feel that even though their performance requires improvement, they are supported and understood by the manager.

Use of terminology in nursing is important in fostering common understanding in the specialized field of health care. The professional nurse must be able to articulate needs and goals of patient care to other professionals in the hospital and community in a way that fosters acceptance, respect, and cooperation. A common language among the health-related professionals is the basis for common understanding and cooperation. In addition, nurse-managers must be concerned with proper use of terminology peculiar to the particular organization in which they work. The managers must be able to use and interpret standard forms, requisitions, and memos for communicating with other departments. It is important to understand and recognize the nuances of communication peculiar to the organization—the unwritten policies and the accepted routes for communicating used within an organization which have their basis in the way people work together rather than in formal policy. All these organizational communications serve to integrate the work of employees in an organization.

Communication Networks

In an organization networks of communication are delineated by the general organizational structure. The networks are established to channel the continuous flow of information. This flow is contiguous with coordination of efforts and cooperation. Generally, the networks are formed on the basis of who needs what information. People in the organization relate to the networks in two major ways—they impart information and they receive information.

Numerous methods can be used to transmit information in an organization. When the information can be consistently categorized, a stable format can be devised to provide a means for "automatic" communication. The format may be a report form, a checklist, or any procedure that outlines necessary information. The networks are used to channel this information according to which persons need it and when they require it for their work.

Information that cannot be categorized, such as that concerned with solving problems, planning, and developing new ideas, takes place through personal contacts, conferences, and through written memos. In this instance the networks of communication serve to define which persons should be involved in these activities.

The major networks (which are often overlapping) with which the nurse-manager is involved in a health-care agency usually include the following:

Nurse-patient
Nurse-staff member
Nurse-supervisor
Nurse-other hospital employees
Nurse-doctor
Nurse-family and agencies in the community

All communication that takes place through these networks is concerned with the work of the organization and with the workers' needs to communicate. Managers in various positions determine how these networks can be used, what methods best suit transmission of specific information, and what they will do with the information they receive. A major management responsibility then is making sure that communication flows along the networks and that the information received is made useful.

Communication is important to workers in an organization. Those who impart information should consider that what is heard, under-

stood, and believed by other persons is determined to a large extent by the receivers' systems of thought. The person who imparts information realizes that if the information is necessary for work, it must also be valid and pertinent to that work and should be obtained by the receiver at an appropriate time. By the same token, those who receive information must make an effort to understand and interpret what has been communicated.

Nurse-Patient Communication

Let us consider some of the techniques of communication that are appropriate to specific communication networks in the nurse's realm of management. In your study of nursing you have discovered that patient care requires sensitivity to patient needs and thoughtful planning to meet the needs assessed by the nurse. Among the techniques used by nurses to accomplish this are interviewing, reading, discussing patient care with others, conferring with the doctors, the patients, and the patients' families, and imparting information through explanations of pamphlets, brochures, films, slide-tape presentations, and other illustrations or diagrams that can be used for teaching patients.

Through your study of nursing you have also learned that many factors are involved in any given communication. You learned, for example, that communication takes place through the written word, verbally, and through nonverbal communications such as bodily position, facial expression, and gestures. You gradually gained skill in looking beneath the surface of any communication for meanings and implications because you increasingly became aware of the fact that superficial communication is sometimes misleading. True therapeutic communication is concerned with "crawling into another's skin," reaching the depths of the other person's reactions, and supporting that person in adjustment and adaptation.

Just as nurse-patient communications must have depth to be effective, so do nurse-staff communications. Social amenities are not sufficient for interaction among a manager and staff members when they are working toward progress and goal achievement. They are also not sufficient for developing innovative methods for giving health care or for facilitating growth of staff members. Therefore, nurse-managers should apply all the knowledge and skill they have gained in nurse-patient communications to their communications with staff members.

Nurse-Staff Communication

Leaders have great power to shape how others interpret information they receive and how they analyze events that occur. The major way leaders influence others is by their own "transmissions." Leaders of groups bear the responsibility for integrating all communication pertinent to the group so that it is indeed useful to the work. They place this integrated information in context for group members; the way the leaders communicate, the attitudes demonstrated, the way information is organized, and the methods used to present information all affect how the communication will be received by the staff members. Staff members' interpretation is colored also by the way they perceive that leaders want them to react to their communication.

SENSITIVITY TO STAFF

Attitudes are extremely important in shaping the morale of staff members. Cooperation is enhanced if the leader of the group remembers some nonacademic but basic facts. First of all, no individuals like to hear negative things about themselves: Do you? How do you react when someone tells you that Mrs. X thinks that you don't listen, are not efficient, or that you are lazy? Another fact is that all people want their efforts and abilities to be appreciated—feedback is needed to support one's self-concept. Although staff members may believe that they are doing a good job, they need to know for sure. When those in authority or those whose opinions staff members value also think they are doing a good job, then they are supported in self-knowledge. For example, in preceding chapters it has been stated that people, when allowed to participate in decision-making, are more likely to be committed to carrying out the decisions because they accept and understand them. Basically, the manager who allows others to participate in decision-making and who then uses their decisions is recognizing staff members' worth, intelligence, and capabilities.

The third point to remember is that everybody wants to be "in the right." Making errors is considered inappropriate behavior that can exclude an individual from a group. The manager who communicates effectively reduces the probability of errors' being made because of misunderstandings about what is expected or through misinterpretations about what has been said.

Personality conflicts among staff members occur—in fact, some think that they are inevitable. The manager must realize that when

they do occur, conflict can be localized to those most directly involved. The manager can support the staff in working through conflicts and can act as a mediator in conflicts by being positive about each person and by demonstrating respect for them and for their work. However, the manager must remember that each person has the most intimate understanding of his or her own feelings and problems and must accept and work through relationships in a personal way.

ASSESSING COMMUNICATION NEEDS

Managers have to be sensitive to the staff members and must assess their needs for communication. The network of manager-staff relationships relates to the work as well as to the staff's personal needs for communication. Managers should examine the total scope of information that the staff members need to do their jobs and then should devise definite methods or formats suitable to impart this information. In addition, nurse-managers have to consider what kind of information they need from the staff and then must similarly devise methods to obtain this through the communication networks.

Beginning managers are sometimes reluctant to tap this network's potential because of basic uncertainties about their ability to fill the managerial role. A study conducted in Pillsbury installations [1] demonstrated the importance of the leader's communication and revealed that good communications contribute to favorable employee attitudes. Employees indicated that good communication involved providing them with the information they wanted, quickly and through channels they preferred. The majority of employees preferred to get information from their own supervisors. We can apply the findings of this study to nursing management. How do you relate to the staff members? Do you provide information to them when they need it? Do you communicate enough?

If the manager of a group does not provide members of the group with adequate information, they will find their own. This means that group members will be susceptible to rumors about their work and about their status. If they do not know "how it actually is," they will decide for themselves which of the rumors are true. Similarly, if rumors are not available, the staff members will posit "how it is." They will consider what they think is happening according to the information they have. The result is often a misconstruing of information to far more negative conclusions than even the most punitive of managers could entertain. People tend to be hard on themselves when they are speculating about matters that affect them personally,

and they often conjure up unrealistic problems and feelings through their speculation. Because of this, the manager who finally does communicate information will have to work through all the rumors and speculation before the staff members will understand and accept what is being said to them.

Communication with Individual Staff Members

Managers must talk to their staff members regularly and must make each communication meaningful in order to achieve a continuous development of common understanding and interpretation between themselves and the staff members. As the common understanding grows, the communication becomes more effective, and eventually the manager can more easily and correctly discern what is on the employee's mind while the employee can just as easily determine what is on the manager's mind. Have you ever experienced this type of common understanding with members of your family or with friends?

Much has been written in previous chapters about how to delegate work, how to give directions, and how to evaluate the performance of others. All these activities can be considered one-to-one relationships between the managers and the staff members. Managers should remember that in conducting all these activities they must talk to the other persons, not around or through them. Have you ever received direction from a group leader through someone else rather than from that manager? Or have you ever talked to some other people, all the while thinking that they were uninterested in what you were saying—and perhaps did not even hear you? A building relationship between manager and staff member can be maintained by referring to previous communication and achievement and by leading up to the next step in every interaction.

A BUILDING RELATIONSHIP

Such a building relationship is illustrated by the story of Jane Abel, a new nurse's aide. The group leader, Carol Inlow, had a short conference with Jane when she first came to work. In this conference she asked her what she expected from her job, what she wanted to accomplish, and how she could help her the most. At first Jane was reluctant to answer, saying that she did not yet know enough about the work. Eventually, Carol found that Jane was particularly uncom-

fortable about what to say to patients and about how the other staff members would treat her. Carol planned for Jane to spend the first week of orientation to the unit with a nurse who was particularly adept at communication skills and who understood Jane's needs to be oriented to the group and to patient care on that unit.

Each time that Carol gave Jane her assignment, she would be particularly careful to tell her human-interest anecdotes about her patients. When Jane reported to her, she would ask her to relate her feelings about the patients and to describe what she had learned by working with the experienced nurse. Carol made a point of discussing patients' reactions with her and also supported the positive things she had accomplished by complimenting her, both alone and in group meetings. As a result, Jane felt that she could talk to Carol, that she was learning how to communicate better, and that when she questioned her own interaction, Carol would help her determine what she should have said or done, without indicating that she should have known better in the first place. In this instance the group leader created a situation in which she and the staff member were free to communicate about a personal problem, because the climate had been set for learning.

WRITTEN RECORDS OF COMMUNICATION

The manager should keep a written record of interaction with staff members. For example, Carol kept notes on Jane's daily progress in improving her communication skills. From the last month's notes she found that Jane was less fearful of other staff members, noting that she increasingly had asked for help, initiated group activities on three recent occasions, and offered to help others consistently during the previous week. Carol's notes also indicated that Jane communicated more easily with people who were older or younger than she, but that she had the most difficulty with those in her own peer group. Carol might have been able to "feel" that these things were so by remembering what Jane did. However, with good notes she could point to specific incidents that objectively supported her feelings.

Communication with Staff as a Group

THE STAFF CONFERENCE

Perhaps the most common technique used by managers to work with staff members collectively is the staff meeting or the conference. When staff members are assembled for a conference, the manager

has to make sure that they know why the conference is being held, that they feel comfortable in participating in the conference, and that the conference is useful to them in their work. A conference usually progresses through phases of climate setting, of orientation, of participants' expectations for the conference, information sharing or collecting, group participation in planning priorities for action, and determination of how to follow up on what has been discussed or decided.

GUIDELINES FOR CONDUCTING CONFERENCES

The conference or meeting is one of the best opportunities for a manager to ascertain what staff members are thinking about and how they are relating to one another. Some pointers about conducting successful conferences follow:

1. Inform staff members about the purpose of the conference in advance so that they will be prepared.
2. Set a definite time for the conference as well as a time limit, and make sure that the conference starts and ends on time.
3. Be prepared for the conference. If you are holding a conference to impart information, think through your approach to the topic, your presentation of the information, and your conclusions about how the information should be used. Do not expect the staff to apply the information, especially if it is new, after just hearing a presentation of facts. You must explain how they should apply the information if you want them do draw the same conclusions that you have drawn.
4. Arrange materials for demonstration or for illustration in advance and make sure that any equipment you are using is in working order. Graphics are helpful in presenting complicated information, and an explanation of new equipment is more meaningful if people can actually see how it works.
5. If you are having a conference for the purpose of problem-solving by the staff, you must be prepared to speak on the topic as a consultant for the group. This requires just as much preparation as actual presentation of material does, if not more.
6. Solicit participation from group members. Ask them what they think about the topic, listen to what they say, and use the information they put forth in your comments.
7. Each conference should be summarized at the end. The summary should include comments made by participants to demon-

strate the value of their contributions, as well as a summary of what has been accomplished during the conference.

8. If the conference is one of a series conducted for the purpose of developing plans or special projects, begin each session with a review of what happened previously. At the end of the conference the summary should indicate what is to happen next in order to establish goals for the next session.

9. Plan the meetings or conferences to meet definite needs of the staff for doing work better. If the topics are relevant to the workers, they will contribute more effectively to the conferences. Refer to discussions, solutions to problems, or plans that have been made in the conference when it is appropriate in performing daily work activities. This helps staff members appreciate the importance of the conferences and makes them part of the work rather than extracurricular activities.

10. If conferences are being held to develop a project or plan, provide staff members with an assignment so that they can contribute to the sessions in a positive way. Merely talking about a topic for problem-solving soon exhausts the staff's ideas. They must bring new input to the conferences if they are to be "growth" sessions.

11. When assignments have been given for conferences, allow sufficient time for staff members to complete the assignment before the conference is held. Sessions should be close enough together to provide motivation for doing the assignment while it is fresh. Otherwise staff members tend to rationalize about doing the "homework" because there is plenty of time and it can always be done later.

12. Keep minutes or notes about each meeting or conference. In this way you can remember what has taken place and staff members can refer to notes if there are questions about decisions that have been made by the group. Keeping good notes prevents staff from belaboring the same points over and over again; minutes also help staff members maintain consistency in applying what has been learned in the conferences. A written record of meetings and conferences is also helpful to demonstrate progress, or lack of progress, toward accomplishing the goals of the sessions. Managers have many interruptions in their train of thought during the course of one day and deal with a myriad of different problems over a span of time. Notes help the manager remember what has happened; by reviewing notes objectively, the manager can determine patterns in behavior and

in events. This review serves as an evaluative measure to provide input on which future decisions can be based.

COMMITTEES

Many of the concepts that apply to conducting and to participating in conferences also apply to committees. Committees are used for decision-making, to gain employee acceptance of new ideas, and to promote communication among employees, or to establish or maintain relationships with consumers or community agency representatives. You may be a member of a committee comprising nurses, or you may be appointed to a committee comprising many different types of health professionals. In some instances you may be the only nurse on the committee. Organizations typically have many different kinds of committees; some may be temporary (ad hoc) and others may be standing committees with changing or rotating appointment of members. The standing committees are often a part of the organizational structure and may have operational responsibilities.

Committees serve to coordinate efforts in an organization and to elicit cooperation among employees through participation in committee decision-making. Productive and active committees can be a mechanism for challenging employees and for stimulating motivation. Committees are groups, and their effectiveness is therefore determined to some extent by the expertise of the members, by the members' ability to use group process to work constructively together, and by the usefulness and applicability of the committee's activities to the organization's work.

Members of committees are often selected from among employees for a purpose. You may be selected for a specific committee because that committee needs a nurse-representative. As a member of a committee you often represent a group of employees—a group of nurses or the group that composes the staff of your unit. Initially you may feel uncomfortable if you are appointed to a committee made up of people you do not know or of employees who represent administration or other professional groups such as doctors. It is important for you to realize that you have an important role as a member of the committee and that your contribution to committee activities is of value. In addition, your particular nursing expertise on committees with "mixed membership" ensures that the nursing point of view is considered in committee decisions.

To participate effectively in such committees, it is necessary that you do your "homework" and that you know the issues involved and how those issues impact on nursing. It is prudent for a committee

member to discover how others in the organization feel about the committee's activities and to learn from others how to deal with interaction among committee members. Participation in active committees can be a valuable learning experience that serves to broaden your perspective by sharing ideas and concepts with others. Through committee membership, you will find that you meet people you would not have known otherwise. You can learn from these people, just as they can learn from you.

Written Communication

All the other networks of communication in the nurse-manager's realm are similar to the nurse-patient and nurse-staff interactions. The major differences are that the farther the network is removed from the immediate nursing-care unit, the more predesigned formats for conveying information are used. An example of a format is a referral form that the nurses might use for the Visiting Nurse Association. This form includes basic questions that are important for continuity of care. The necessary information can be written in a uniform manner. Usually it includes information that is common to all patients; this can be presented in the form of a checklist. Other portions of the form require information specific to the given patient. These forms supplement oral communication and can be retained for the patient's record for future reference.

EFFECTIVENESS OF YOUR WRITTEN COMMUNICATION

When completing referral forms, or in preparing written communication, there are some simple questions that you can use to evaluate the effectiveness of your communication. First, is it readable? Is it thoughtful? Have you included the most important facts about the patient? If you were reading these comments without previous knowledge of the patient, could you form a clear picture of the patient's needs? Are your comments appropriate for the situation? Are they objective? Are they realistic? Is the information you have given correct? Can specific information be checked if necessary? Could you have written your comments in fewer words while still retaining the meaning?

VALUE OF WRITTEN COMMUNICATIONS

Writing memos, explanations, or narrative statements requires the art of conciseness and clarity. All the previous questions are applica-

ble to anything that the manager writes for other people's use. It is important to note that everything committed to writing forms a record that can be retained. The record can serve as a check to see if work has been accomplished, as a means for evaluating whether something should or should not be done, or as a source of ideas that state your problems or position about a given topic. Writing is a valuable tool in an organization because of the great number of demands upon people's time and energy. Although it is sometimes easier to call and discuss a problem with someone on the phone, the written memo serves as a reminder that could jog memories. There seems to be a natural tendency for people to respect the written word, so that if you wish to make a greater impression you are more likely to do so in writing.

THE REPORT

A common means of communication in organizations is the report. This may be written or verbal. Many reports are verbal and can be recorded for information retrieval. Staff members report to their managers, the managers report to their managers, and so on along the scalar chain.

A good report includes an introduction to the topic, succinct discussion of events and related problems, and presentation of facts in logical sequence. Uniformity of order when giving a report helps the listener clarify what is being said. The report should be given clearly without distortion. This means that the speaker's voice should be audible and that extraneous information should be deleted. The latter is important to prevent information overload for the listeners.

Two major types of information are important in reporting: (1) information gleaned from observations and (2) information that can be documented. The person reporting should differentiate between the two so that the listener knows which information is subject to differences in perception and which information is fixed and definite. Again, reports are developed to give the listener the information needed to accomplish work and to provide for continuity.

REVIEW OF FORMATS OF WRITTEN COMMUNICATION

Formats used to facilitate communication should be reviewed periodically to ensure that they continue to fulfill their functions. Everyone involved in use of the format should be included in the evaluation review to make sure that all opinions about the effectiveness of the communication for all persons along the network are

considered. Subtle changes are continually taking place in organizations because new employees use different methods and have different styles; therefore, ideas that were in vogue yesterday may not be stylish today, and new methods may have been initiated because of external factors such as legislative requirements for some organizational activity. These are a few of the reasons why periodic review is necessary.

DEVELOPING EFFECTIVE PERSONAL COMMUNICATION

When nurses are involved in changing the health-care system, either through development of their particular role in an organization or through group interaction with persons from related disciplines, they must learn to identify and to articulate their thoughts in a sophisticated way. This means that nurses must first of all be well informed about current events in nursing and related health-care activities. They must be cognizant of the issues inherent in the planning, and they must draw independent conclusions about the meaning of all this information. Nurses should go through the process of information analysis before attending meetings so that their contribution to the meeting will be meaningful.

One of the best ways to clarify thoughts is to participate in discussions. Sometimes merely saying something out loud helps one realize what it means. Have you ever changed your mind or clarified a thought in midsentence? For some people writing out ideas is even better than talking. Try writing out your thoughts concerning a specific activity you deal with in patient care. Write down the purpose of the activity, the methods used to accomplish the purpose, and the results of the activity. Place what you have written in a secure place and let it cool. Then go back a week later and read it. How does it sound to you one week later? How would you change what you have written? This process is helpful not only in thinking through an idea but also in forming a sense of objectivity.

A good question for the nurse-manager is How can you explain the results of your staff members' work? Try telling someone what you have achieved during the past month. Can you remember events you were most proud of? Or those that bothered you the most? Are certain events clouded in your mind? A written diary of your evaluation of the results of each day's activities is of considerable help in defining results over a period of time. From it you can identify a pattern of good and bad performance. As you read, question: Is there uniformity in the way people behave at work and in the way you

manage? Can you identify consistency in successes or problems? Are the activities you have described appropriate to the needs of the situation? Could you have avoided some difficulties with better planning? How could you improve?

Effective communication incorporates a sense of curiosity with a sense of propriety. Managers will acquire information if their minds are open and questioning. Managers should keep in mind a saying the author once read: "Keep your mind open, something might fall into it." The sense of propriety serves to ensure that the communication networks are used to best advantage in the most appropriate manner. Essentially, this is part of the ability to get along with others. If you, as manager, respect others' needs for information, they will in turn respect your own needs.

Conclusions

Communication is essential to stability in the organization. Staff members do not like to feel that they are in a vacuum; they need to know that they will be listened to and that they will receive information. Effective communication helps workers feel confident in their working relationships. This in turn helps workers feel secure about themselves and about their work. When people are confident and secure, they can better meet the challenges for progressively improving their abilities to do their jobs.

Study Questions

1. In a group of students identify all the techniques and tools that are used in the nurse-manager's network of communication. Examine all of these tools to determine:
   a. Their purpose
   b. Their value for communicating
   c. Results of their use
2. Outline a series of topics for meetings that you wish to conduct with your staff for the purpose of:
   a. Imparting information
   b. Sharing information
   c. Improving patient care
3. Keep a diary of all your communications as a manager for a period of one week. Classify these according to communication:
   a. About direct patient care
   b. About staff members' needs and problems
   c. With the administrative staff

d. With the doctors
e. With other departments
f. With patients and their families
g. With other agencies
Within each classification determine if the communication was effective, if it took unnecessary time, and if it could be better organized. Evaluate whether the communication you imparted and that you received was adequate.

4. Isolate one patient and draw the networks of communication you were involved with in caring for the patient, placing yourself in the middle of the communication networks. Include communication that you initiated and communication you received.
5. Evaluate how communication networks in an organization might be illustrated in:
   a. A bureaucratic organizational structure
   b. A decentralized organizational structure
   c. A matrix organization

Reference

1. Gefland, L.　Communicate through your supervisors. *Harvard Bus. Rev.* 48:101–104, Nov./Dec. 1970.

Suggested Reading

American Nurses Association Clinical Conference, 1969, Minneapolis/ Atlanta.　New York: Appleton-Century-Crofts, 1970.
Coffin, R. A.　*The Communicator.* New York: American Management Association, 1975.
Egan, G.　*Interpersonal Living.* Monterey, Cal.: Brooks/Cole, 1975.
Egan, G.　*The Skilled Helper.* Monterey, Cal.: Brooks/Cole, 1976.
Hemalt, M.D., and Mackert, M. E.　Factual medical records protect hospitals, practitioners, patients. *Hospitals* 51:13, July 1, 1977.
Kron, T.　*Communication in Nursing* (2nd ed.). Philadelphia: Saunders, 1972.
Matson, F. W., and Montagu, A. (Eds.)　*The Human Dialogue: Perspectives on Communication.* New York: The Free Press, 1967.
Price, E. M.　*Learning Needs of Registered Nurses.* New York: Teachers College Press, Columbia University, 1967.
Redman, B.　*The Process of Patient Teaching in Nursing* (3rd ed.). St. Louis: Mosby, 1976.
Ujhely, G.　*Determinants of the Nurse-Patient Relationship.* New York: Springer, 1968.
Wiley, L.　Communications: Understanding the gravity of the situation. *Nursing '76* 6:4, April 1976.

III. Case Studies

This section contains cases that are designed to give you practice in managerial thinking. Management is complex and requires synthesis of many different theories and principles as they apply to a given situation. In working through these cases you can develop a perspective of the manager's role in analyzing situations. You can define priorities, develop plans for action, and make decisions that are based on the theories and principles presented in the first two parts of this book. These cases can provide you with a model for defining and analyzing the situations encountered in the work situation. Management of patient care in an organization involves working through many similar "cases" that are full of challenges and problems to solve. Your experiences in management can be considered cases that require thoughtful decision-making and that allow you to reflect on the impact that you can make through application of management theories and principles.

The case studies presented in this section have been designed to provide you with situations you might encounter in the work situation. Each of the case studies included has been developed to emphasize one component of management theory, but, as with real-life situations, their solution is not limited to a discrete aspect of management. Instead you must synthesize the theories and principles of management in solving these cases. As with most management situations there are no right or wrong solutions. Solving the cases depends on developing a rationale for action based on determination of the dynamics that are taking place in each situation. You can become familiar with managerial roles in solving these cases.

Practice in management gives you an opportunity to develop a perspective of a manager's role and behaviors. One of the most difficult adjustments you may make as a newly graduated nurse in a first job is in becoming a manager in the context of an organization. Your previous experiences in management may have been limited to direct patient care. Even though you may have completed patient-care experiences in a variety of health-care agencies, you may not have belonged to the organization as an employee. In your first position you become part of the organization and must learn to function within that organization in a managerial role. These cases, and others that you may develop from your own experiences, will help you to develop the broadened perspective necessary for assuming your new managerial role.

Amerton Hospital Case

Amerton General Hospital is a 350-bed hospital located in the city of Amerton, which has a population of 95,000. The majority of patients served at Amerton General are self-supporting and have hospitalization insurance. About five percent of the in-patients are on welfare. The salaries of the majority of hospital personnel are slightly below the average income within the community. Both professional and other employees of the hospital are largely recruited from Amerton and the nearby towns. Amerton General is the larger of two hospitals in the area.

Four North, which is one of the 11 units at Amerton General, has 36 patient beds and comprises four private rooms, eight semiprivate rooms, and four wards of four beds each. It is primarily a general thoracic surgery unit. The average length of stay for a patient is 12 days. Usually one preoperative day is used for tests, one day for operation, and the remaining days for intensive postoperative care and convalescing care.

Mrs. Webster, Head Nurse

The unit's leader is Mrs. Webster, aged 47, who is the head nurse. She has held this position for five years. She had worked 10 years as a staff nurse prior to and between the births of her three children. Mrs. Webster takes pride in being neat and precise. She enjoys her position of authority and relates easily to physicians and those of equal and superior positions in the hospital hierarchy. She sees her role as that of a manager and devotes the majority of her time to making out time schedules, keeping supply rooms stocked and orderly, attending meetings, and promoting smooth functioning between 4N and other hospital units and departments.

On occasional holidays and weekends, when only one other registered nurse is working on the unit, Mrs. Webster functions as team leader for 18 patients. As a team leader, she passes medications to patients and delegates all other aspects of patient care to team members. She does very little follow-up to see that assignments are completed, but when she reports to the next shift, she almost always knows what tests have been completed and what changes have been made in the patients' treatments. During the week, when Mrs. Webster makes "rounds" on the patients, they are primarily social in

nature. At times patients express problems to her, some of which she occasionally follows through to solve.

Mrs. Webster believes in team nursing and is especially interested in team conferences. Occasionally she enjoys presenting nursing or medical knowledge to the team at a conference. For example, Mrs. Webster often conducts conferences for teaching team members about a subject, such as cancer of the larynx.

Mrs. Webster is known to others as being somewhat egotistical, but she is well liked as a person. Her actual expertise at nursing is difficult to evaluate as she rarely becomes involved in direct patient care.

Patients are generally pleased with the care they receive on 4N. Mrs. Webster is well known in the community, and people associate her self-confidence with a well-run patient-care unit. In contrast, some of the other units in Amerton General have reputations for being disorganized or sloppy.

Staff Members

On a typical day on 4N the following events transpire. At 7:00 A.M. the night nurse gives a report to the day shift. There is a total of 36 patients on the unit today. Mrs. Webster has divided the staff into two teams:

Team 1	*Team 2*
Team Leader: Mrs. Kent, RN	Team Leader: Mrs. Crawford
Miss Winter, RN	Mrs. Evans, LPN
Mrs. Cooper, aide	Mrs. Green, LPN
Mrs. Taber, aide	Miss Allen, aide

TEAM 1: PERSONNEL

Mrs. Kent is very pleasant to work with. Her nursing care is good but could be more complete. She enjoys chatting with the team members and visitors and allows herself to be away from the patients for 30 to 45 minutes at a time while she chats socially. Mrs. Kent is four months pregnant.

Miss Winter was graduated from nursing school two years ago and has worked on 4N since graduation. She enjoys nursing and gives thorough nursing care. She prefers caring for a group of patients rather than being a team leader. Mrs. Cooper, nurse's aide, is energetic and pleasant, but her nursing knowledge is limited. Her observations of patients are incomplete, and she lacks common

sense and judgment. She generally asks questions when she does not understand. Mrs. Taber seems lazy and gets by with doing as little work as possible. She is a mother of six and needs to work to help support her family.

TYPICAL DAY: TEAM 1

Mrs. Kent, team leader, begins her day by checking medication cards, pouring and preparing medications, and passing medications to patients. She sees her first patient at 8:30 A.M. She chats briefly with patients as she gives them their medications. Both Mrs. Cooper and Mrs. Taber have taken patients' temperatures and have started giving patients their morning baths and getting them ready for breakfast. Miss Winter, RN, is giving care to an unconscious patient.

After passing medications, Mrs. Kent stops to make herself a snack of crackers and peanut butter. She sits on a stool in the medicine room and chats with anyone who comes in. By 10:30 A.M. Mrs. Cooper and Mrs. Taber have completed the morning care for their patients. Miss Winter is still giving patient care. The patients on Team 1 have received essential physical care only. There has been no patient teaching, patients who need help in ambulation are still in bed, and treatments that are to be done two times on the day shift have not been done once. Blood pressures have been taken.

At 10:30 A.M. Mrs. Kent makes rounds on her team, using Kardex as a guide. She notes that one patient's IV is 100 cc behind schedule and that another patient's Foley catheter is leaking. Three patients ask her for the bedpan as she is making rounds. The aides are nowhere in sight. Mrs. Kent gives the patients the needed care. She makes a list of things that need to be done for the patients and goes to find the team members. Miss Winter is talking with a physician. Mrs. Cooper and Mrs. Taber are taking a coffee break in the conference room. Mrs. Kent asks Mrs. Cooper to do a few things when she finishes her break. Mrs. Cooper agrees pleasantly. When Mrs. Taber is asked to do a few things for patients, she replies, "I'm going to soak Mr. Black's foot just once today. He is such a baby about having the dressing removed. Mrs. Smith won't cough and deep breathe for me. I told her she'd get pneumonia if she didn't. I'll get to that other stuff later." Mrs. Kent does not pursue the issue.

The afternoon finds the team members accomplishing the patient treatments once, ambulating the patients one time each, and doing their charting. It has been a typical day. No one has been rushed to complete her work. The patients seem content and none have complained about their care.

TEAM 2: PERSONNEL

Mrs. Crawford was graduated four years ago from a university nursing program. She worked three years at a medical center hospital in a different state before coming to Amerton. She expects perfection of herself and the team members in meeting patient-care needs. Mrs. Crawford often finds herself upset with the slack standards she observes in team members. She feels that much more could be done to improve the quality of care the patients on 4N are receiving.

Mrs. Evans, LPN, works hard most of the time. She is not consistent, however. She may do an excellent job one day and a poor job the next day. She is moody and calls in sick about twice a month. Mrs. Green, LPN, is somewhat nervous and shows her irritability openly. She can do an excellent job or can loaf and accomplish little. She relates to Miss Winter particularly well and likes to be on the same team with Miss Winter. Miss Allen, nurse's aide, does what she is told in her assignment but never goes beyond those instructions. She resents having any tasks added to her original assignment. She frequently grumbles that her assignment is too heavy but is often observed taking extended coffee and lunch breaks.

TYPICAL DAY: TEAM 2

Mrs. Crawford takes extensive notes during report. Her assignment conference to team members is thorough and complete. Mrs. Evans, LPN, takes no notes during the assignment conference. She was on the same team with the same assignment yesterday. Mrs. Green has been off duty for three days. She seems more interested in telling Mrs. Evans and Miss Allen about what she did at home for three days than in listening to report. Miss Allen listens to report and assignment conference with half-interest.

Mrs. Crawford makes patient rounds immediately after report and assignment conferences. She spends about one hour making rounds and utilizes the time to meet patient needs and talk with patients. The highlight of patient-care needs on Team 2 is that one patient who was anuric postoperatively is receiving peritoneal dialysis. Mrs. Crawford has assigned this patient to Mrs. Evans, LPN, who has had this experience previously. Mrs. Green, LPN, has never done peritoneal dialysis. Mrs. Green's assignment consists of patient-care needs that are neither new nor particularly challenging. Miss Allen's assignment is relatively light today.

As the day progresses, nursing care is accomplished as planned due to Mrs. Crawford's close supervision. Rather than trying to find team members when something is needed by a patient, Mrs. Crawford

meets the need herself. Mrs. Crawford relieves Mrs. Evans, LPN, for lunch since the patient with peritoneal dialysis needs fairly constant care. When relieving her, Mrs. Crawford finds that the peritoneal cycles have been charted incorrectly. She corrects this herself. The patient also complains that she has not yet been bathed and that her skin itches. When Mrs. Evans returns from lunch, Mrs. Crawford says, "Your patient needs skin care; do you remember the special technique we are using for her?"

Team 2 concludes its day with nursing-care objectives met.

An Evaluation Conference

Mrs. Webster has spent most of the day off the unit attending meetings. She returns at 2:00 P.M. and decides that she has enough time to have an annual evaluation conference with one of her staff members. She decides to have one with Mrs. Taber, nurse's aide. Mrs. Webster quickly fills out the rating form and asks Mrs. Taber to come into her office for a few minutes. The evaluation conference goes like this:

MRS. WEBSTER: Mrs. Taber, I have completed your yearly evaluation and thought you would like to read it over. You can sign it at the bottom.

MRS. TABER (*after reading it*): You have me marked below average on "attitude." What's wrong with my attitude?

MRS. WEBSTER: There's nothing wrong with it. It's just that you have a tendency to be sullen at times. Now I know you don't do this often and, as you can see by the other markings, you've really done a good job on 4N. Do you have any questions?"

MRS. TABER: No.

MRS. WEBSTER: Good. Please sign that you've read it. (*Mrs. Taber signs the evaluation and leaves.*)

It is now 3:00 P.M. and time to report to the afternoon shift. Another day shift has come to an end on 4N.

Study Questions
1. Identify the management problems on 4N.
2. What are possible solutions to each problem?
3. Which solution would you choose and why?
4. Considering the personalities of the staff involved, what difficulties would you expect in bringing about changes that might solve the problems?

Eight Hours in the Wardship Hospital Emergency Room

The Wardship Hospital emergency room provides emergency treatment in Wardship, a middle-class residential suburb with a population of 60,000. It serves an average daily census of 60 patients. There are five rooms, each with two beds. This case will describe the people involved and the events occurring on an eight-hour shift from 7:00 A.M. to 3:30 P.M.

Personnel

Miss Plain is the head nurse. Her name serves as a description, as she is quiet, nondynamic, and very mousy in appearance. She has served as head nurse for two months and was previously a staff nurse in another state. Mrs. Clark, RN, has worked in the emergency room for the two years following graduation from nursing school. She is efficient and skilled technically, but is frequently blunt and tactless in communication with staff members and patients. Miss Hambrick, RN, graduated from nursing school one year ago. Her approach to patients is both professional and kind. She uses good judgment in patient care and is interested in learning and helping others to learn quality emergency room nursing care. Two senior student nurses are assigned to the unit for two weeks. Their purpose in the ER is to learn emergency room policy and nursing care through giving patient care under the supervision of their instructor or the staff nurses. The instructor is responsible for five other student nurses scattered throughout the hospital and, therefore, is in the ER at occasional intervals. Both students have studied content about emergency room nursing care, but neither of the two students has been involved in a stressful or true emergency situation. An intern is in the ER 24 hours a day.

The Day's Activities

The day begins with the routine tasks of cleaning the rooms and checking the equipment. At 7:30 A.M. the first patient comes into the ER, with complaints of dizziness and faintness on the way to work.

He is a diabetic who skipped breakfast. After being given some glucose intravenously, he is asked to stay and rest for a few minutes. One of the student nurses was following this patient when the head nurse asked her to take another patient to the x-ray department. The diabetic patient left the ER unnoticed by the staff members before receiving any instructions or teaching.

A 40-year-old woman is admitted next with complaints of epigastric pain. After being seen by the intern, she is asked to wait for further tests and examination. She is apprehensive and uncomfortable. All the nurses peek in the door at intervals to see how she is, but none takes time to try to make her more comfortable. A patient with a broken finger and one with a twisted ankle are also seen before 9:00 A.M. They are treated and discharged.

At 9:00 A.M. the police bring a 70-year-old man who has been involved in a car accident to the ER. He was a driver involved in a head-on collision with another car. The two students and their instructor plan to follow this case. As neurosurgeons, general surgeons, and orthopedic surgeons take their turns with the patient, the students are busy and tense with assisting the doctors. No staff nurse offers to assist. The staff nurses are busy with patients in other rooms, and the head nurse is involved in ordering supplies and doing paperwork. The patient's wife sits alone in a waiting lounge. She is unaware that her husband's condition is critical and growing worse. Each of the specialists treating the patient is concerned only with his specialty. No one is viewing the patient as a total person except for the instructor who is helping the students and growing anxious as she sees the patient's condition worsening. She finds a brief minute to take the patient's valuables to the wife and to explain what is being done for the patient.

At 1:00 P.M. the student nurses and instructor are still with the car accident patient. At this hour he has a cardiac arrest that makes an already chaotic atmosphere catastrophic. The resident at the bedside is hyperactive and nonproductive as he jumps from one thing to another; the student nurses are nervous but functioning fairly well. The instructor is doing what she can to keep a proper perspective on the patient's needs. The head nurse opens the door a crack and makes a hasty exit. Mrs. Clark comes in and is efficient and helpful in getting equipment and drugs assembled. The patient does not respond to treatment and expires. The students, shaken by their first contact with death, assist in postmortem patient care, cleaning the room and equipment, and then welcome a chance to relax and

unwind. The instructor, who has not seen the other students for four hours, makes a hasty exit to make rounds. The head nurse begins to complete the death certificate.

At 2:00 P.M. a mother comes to the ER with her son, a one-year-old toddler. He may have swallowed some aspirin, but the mother is not sure. The doctor orders an emetic given and a blood test drawn for salicylate level. When Mrs. Clark attempts to give the child the emetic, the mother says, "Is that really necessary? I'm not sure if he took the aspirin."

Mrs. Clark replies curtly, "The doctor ordered this, but if you want to refuse treatment you can."

The mother says, "But I thought he would want to see the results of the blood test first."

Mrs. Clark replies, "That may take an hour to run, and meanwhile he should have this." The child starts to cry loudly, and the mother is visibly upset. The mother helps the nurse give the child the medicine.

At 3:00 P.M. the nurses, tired from a physically and emotionally traumatic day, complete their day's work in the ER.

Study Questions

1. Identify the management problems in the ER.
2. What are the possible solutions and alternatives to each management problem?
3. How could the solutions best be accomplished?
4. What are the needs for staff development?
5. If you were Miss Hambrick, how would you institute a change in policy?
6. Was this day a learning experience for the student nurses? Could the experience have been handled differently by the instructor and the staff nurses?
7. If you were to help Miss Plain with leadership qualities, where would you begin?
8. How do you think Mrs. Clark would respond to constructive criticism from Miss Plain? Role play an evaluation conference between the two.

Staff Nursing in Transition

Mrs. Healy, the head nurse on a 60-bed, medical-surgical patient-care unit, is an energetic woman who has actively participated in many community events related to her children's school life. She enjoys organizing and likes a flurry of activity, feeling satisfied when deadlines have been met. Mrs. Healy has been the head nurse on this patient-care unit for seven years and has initiated several innovations in nursing-care plans and team conferences. Recently Mrs. Healy has been a member of an advisory committee organized within the nursing department to evaluate the feasibility of initiating the primary care pattern of patient-care assignments.

Of all the committee members, Mrs. Healy is most enthusiastic about the concepts of primary nursing care. She likes the idea of nurses having 24-hour responsibility for patients and supports the involvement of the RN staff in direct care of patients. Because of her enthusiasm, she has volunteered to work with her staff to make the transition from team to primary care along with another head nurse. The second head nurse also has responsibility for a 60-bed, medical-surgical patient-care unit.

The two head nurses have decided to follow a similar methodology in making the transition. Mr. Estrand, the other head nurse, is a calm, soft-spoken person who expresses himself well. In contrast with Mrs. Healy's energetic approach, his seems to be reserved and conservative. In their discussion of methodology for introducing primary nursing, it is clear that the two head nurses prefer different approaches. Mr. Estrand would like to begin by conducting group conferences to engage the staffs of the two units in a study of primary nursing and discuss their expectations of the new pattern of care. Mrs. Healy feels that this approach is a delaying tactic and prefers to draw up guidelines for the new pattern that both head nurses could use.

Mrs. Healy's patient-care unit serves patients with short-term illnesses, many of whom are admitted for gastrointestinal and genitourinary problems. Some of these patients remain in the hospital for two or three days, being admitted for diagnostic procedures. Others have elective short-term surgery. Mr. Estrand's patient-care unit serves patients with cardiovascular and respiratory illnesses. These patients tend to remain in the hospital from six to eight days. The staffing for both patient-care units is similar except that Mrs.

Healy's has more nurse's aides, whereas Mr. Estrand's has more LPNs. Both have about the same number of RNs. Mrs. Healy believes that they should both change their staffing to an all RN staff in order to initiate primary nursing care successfully. Mr. Estrand does not agree. They reach a compromise in that each decides to manage staffing ratios independently and both will use the outline they have prepared to initiate primary care.

For the most part, this outline consists of a new job description for the RN, including a statement of the purpose of primary care, the responsibilities of the RN, and the expected benefits of changing from team to primary nursing care. Mrs. Healy and Mr. Estrand decide to present this outline to their respective staffs independently, and they plan to compare their impressions of the staff responses to determine how they can best support one another during the transition.

Two weeks after presenting the outline to the staff, Mrs. Healy receives resignations from three of the five nurse's aides and three registered nurses. She cannot understand why these people are resigning because her relationships with the staff have always been based on trust and mutual respect. During the two weeks since she initiated the new pattern of primary nursing, the staff has seemed to work effectively. The registered nurses indicate that they like the primary care pattern and state that they prefer being "peers" rather than having to rotate the position of being in charge of a team. Previously there had been three separate teams, each with a team leader, for the 60 patients. An aide and an RN worked with the team leader for each of the teams.

Mr. Estrand does not change staffing to primary care patterns all at once as does Mrs. Healy. Instead, he asks the RNs for volunteers to be primary nurses to "pilot" the transition for the patient-care unit. Only two RNs volunteer, but he thinks this number sufficient and retains the ongoing team nursing staffing pattern for two teams. He reduces the number of staff and patients for the third team to accommodate the primary care "pilot" staffing. Mrs. Healy thinks that his approach is too conservative and secretly wonders whether Mr. Estrand really wants to convert to primary nursing. The two nurses who volunteered to be primary nurses on his unit like their new role and demonstrate their interest by studying primary nursing care literature. Two of the RNs on Mr. Estrand's unit think that primary care will never work, but the remainder of the RNs are watchful.

Mary Smith and Jane Ellis are two of the nurse's aides on Mrs. Healy's patient-care unit who decide that they should resign. They have been checking the positions available that are posted by the personnel department and plan to interview for ward clerk positions. Susan Palmer, another nurse's aide, discusses their plans with them and also decides to resign. She plans to seek employment at a nursing home located near her residence, which is 20 miles from the hospital.

The three RNs who plan to resign from Mrs. Healy's patient-care unit ask to be transferred to other departments in the hospital. One asks for a position in the coronary care unit, so that she can advance her knowledge and experience. The other two are uncertain about what to do. One wants to investigate degree programs in nursing, and the other is thinking about applying for a job as a school nurse.

Mrs. Healy holds conferences with each of the six persons who are transferring or resigning. She challenges the registered nurses with the idea that they are finding primary care difficult and offers to assist them in developing a continuing education program to increase their knowledge. She thinks this approach is appropriate since two of the three RNs tell her that their desire to continue their education is the major reason for resigning. In the conferences with the nurse's aides, Mrs. Healy emphasizes their need for career planning. She hopes to help them find ways to upgrade their education. Although Mrs. Healy is distressed by their abrupt resignations, she is already formulating plans for revising her budget to employ more RNs and fewer nurse's aides. She does not mention her plans to change the budget to anyone.

One registered nurse and two nurse's aides actually terminate their employment at the hospital and are interviewed by the personnel representative in a routine exit interview. The RN tells this representative that she is leaving because the patients are being neglected with the new primary nursing care. She feels that the RN has too many patients in this new method and cannot "be everywhere at once." She says, "In the team method, someone was always free to see a patient or to answer a patient's call." Now each nurse is specifically assigned to certain patients and cannot be available to all the patients. This RN also expresses a feeling of loss about not getting to know all the patients assigned to the team and about not having the help of the aides.

The two nurse's aides who are leaving the hospital tell the personnel representative that they know they should resign because Mrs. Healy is "set on having primary nursing care and doesn't want

aides." They express high regard for Mrs. Healy personally, but feel that she has made up her mind and will forge ahead until she accomplishes her goal. They know that the hospital will support Mrs. Healy because primary nursing is the coming thing, and they "may as well accept it" and find something else to do.

Study Questions

1. Compare the approaches used by Mrs. Healy and Mr. Estrand to initiate primary nursing care.
2. Analyze the approaches used by Mrs. Healy and Mr. Estrand in terms of:
   a. The management theories that apply
   b. Reactions of staff members to change
   c. The motivation of each of the head nurses
   d. The possible effects on the patients' care during the transition period
3. Consider that you are applying for a staff nurse position and can select a position with either Mrs. Healy or Mr. Estrand. Which position would you select? Give the rationale for your selection.
4. Evaluate the effects of the six resignations from Mrs. Healy's patient-care area on the following persons:
   a. Mr. Estrand
   b. Mrs. Healy
   c. The staff nurses on both patient-care areas
   d. Other staff nurses working in the hospital
   e. Nurse's aides working on other patient-care units
5. What measures would you suggest that Mr. Estrand and Mrs. Healy take now that would facilitate the transition to primary care from the perspective of the:
   a. Staff nurses
   b. The advisory committee
   c. The Director of Nursing Service
6. Evaluate the potential for the success of the project to initiate primary care nursing staffing patterns in this hospital.

The Case of the Missing Tape Recorder

Walton Community Hospital is located in a community of 5,000 people. The hospital has five patient-care units including obstetrics, a convalescent care unit, and three medical-surgical nursing units. The hospital has an operating room, physical therapy and occupational therapy departments, laboratory and x-ray facilities, and an emergency room. Specialists come to the hospital from a nearby city for consultation and for special services requiring expertise in medical practice. Patients are referred to the larger hospital when their needs require health care services not available at Walton.

Many of the nurses employed by Walton are part-time nurses who fill in when needed for private duty or who work one to three days per week. The full-time staff is made up of a combination of older nurses who have resided in the community all their married lives, and young graduates who plan to work at the hospital for a year or two at most. There are permanent staff nurses for days, evenings, and nights—only occasionally does a staff member have to rotate shifts.

The director of nursing is a relaxed and pleasant individual who likes to become involved in patient-care activities. She knows all the patients, and hospital personnel are accustomed to seeing her in every department of the hospital, as she likes to know how the patients are progressing when they go to surgery, to the lab, to PT or OT, or when they are on the patient-care units. Personnel often comment that her name fits her personality, as she is Mrs. Gladden in her contacts with the patients.

Mrs. Gladden loves gadgets, and new techniques of caring for patients fascinate her. She particularly likes to discuss the "big city" hospital methods with the young graduates who come to Walton to work. Many of the staff members recognize that the director would like to be involved in a "progressive medical center" atmosphere like that of her student experience, but that her home and family ties keep her in Walton.

The five patient-care units are semi-autonomous in methods used to organize staff. The atmosphere of the hospital is informal and there are no supervisors. The title of head nurse has been discontinued and the title, "coordinator," is used instead. Mrs. Gladden had decided that the title "head nurse" was traditional and changed the

title to coordinator in order to emphasize the clinical leadership role of the nurse. There are no position descriptions for the coordinators. Two of the five coordinators are having difficulty deciding how to interpret the role of the coordinator because they do not perceive any significant changes in the behaviors of the other three coordinators. One of the two, Mrs. Caller, has been working at Walton for two years. She was formerly a head nurse in a larger hospital where the head nurses were supported and guided by supervisors. She was so accustomed to working in this situation that she finds it difficult to work at Walton as a coordinator, because there are no supervisors. The other coordinator, Mrs. Hill, was appointed to the position after working as a staff nurse at Walton for six months. Since she had never been appointed to a leadership position, she is not sure about what her job entails and does not know if she is "doing the right things" as coordinator.

The other three coordinators have been employees at Walton for fifteen or twenty years and have learned to manage their units in an independent fashion. The coordinator in obstetrics can rightfully boast that she has taken care of every child born in Walton for the last seventeen years. She knows everyone in the community and is often called upon for advice by mothers who are uncertain of what to do during the prenatal and postnatal periods. The doctors on the medical staff depend on her because she is a very capable nurse who knows obstetric theory and practice.

The two other "secure" coordinators are also knowledgeable about patient care and are able to make decisions about patient care. They know the doctors and understand their preferences for care. These three coordinators get along well and often share stories of their units. Other staff members, the newer staff included, enjoy hearing their tales of events of the past which involved some of the doctors currently on the medical staff as well as some of the patients who still come to the hospital.

A new graduate from a nearby school of nursing has recently been employed at the Walton hospital on Mrs. Hill's medical-surgical nursing unit. The graduate, Miss Melton, is alert and enthusiastic about patient care. She feels that Mrs. Hill does not exert enough influence in utilizing new techniques for patient care or for teaching staff. Her opinions were formed during the first weeks of employment when she did not receive an expected orientation to the unit and when most of her questions about what to do were answered with, "We . . . well, what do you think we should do?"

Staff members of the unit include two other RNs, an LPN, and

four nurse's aides, one of whom works four days per week, two on the day shift and two on the evening shift. These staff members find Miss Melton refreshing. They enjoy working with her because she has new and "efficient" ways of caring for patients that are sometimes different from the methods usually accepted as the way to do things by the staff. All the staff members have begun to ask questions of Miss Melton instead of the coordinator because she gives quick and definite answers to their questions. All the staff members, that is, except one—the nurse's aide who works two day shifts and two evening shifts per week.

This nurse's aide, Mary Parks, often finds Miss Melton's ways of doing things disconcerting because she never knows what is expected of her. Formerly, she could work days or evenings and know just what to do, but now things are always changing. Mary is considering asking to move to another unit or to work straight evenings, even though she knows that there is no position open on the evening shift.

One of the things that most bothered Mary was the care of a patient who had just discovered he had diabetes. Miss Melton had worked with other staff members to decide how to teach the patient about his diet. They had obtained a scale from the kitchen so that the patient could weigh his food for replacement. Miss Melton thought that if he weighed his food in the hospital, he would be better able to manage his diet at home. Mary had reacted strongly to seeing the scale in the patient's room because it got in her way. She was also upset because the patient asked her to check the accuracy of his weights and she did not know how to read the scale.

Now Mary is upset because the "new" Miss Melton has come up with another bright idea. Because so many personnel work part time, Miss Melton had asked Mrs. Hill if they could get a tape recorder to tape reports. That way she would not have to stop patient care to give reports at 9:00 A.M. and 10:00 A.M. to oncoming staff. Mrs. Hill had been reluctant to ask, but Miss Melton gained her permission to ask Mrs. Gladden for the recorder. As could be expected, Mrs. Gladden was delighted with the idea and immediately procured a tape recorder for the experiment.

Mary conveyed her dislike for Miss Melton and her new ideas to the evening charge nurse, Mrs. Sharp. Her comments were received with thoughtfulness because Mrs. Sharp has great respect for Mary's ability to care for patients. She is precise and pays attention to details in carrying out directions. Mrs. Sharp had misgivings about using the tape recorder anyway, because she felt very strange using a recorder for reports rather than telling the next nurse about the

patients in person. She did try the new method for a day or two and then decided that using a tape recorder took too much of her time. She also worried about the tape recorder's being left at the nursing station all evening because the staff was often busy with patient care during the evening, leaving the station unattended. Mrs. Sharp's solution to this problem was to lock the tape recorder in the equipment area. Soon after placing the recorder on a high empty shelf in the locked cabinet, Mrs. Sharp admitted a critically ill patient. In the hurry and stress of the evening she did not give the recorder another thought.

When the night nurse came at 11:00 P.M., Mrs. Sharp gave her a detailed report. The two nurses spent some time with the critically ill patient so that Mrs. Sharp could be sure that the night nurse knew what to do for the patient. The night nurse had been on vacation for the past two weeks and had to be oriented to all the patients very thoroughly. Mrs. Sharp was finally satisfied that the unit was under control and left at 2:00 A.M.

On the following morning Mrs. Hill could not find the tape recorder. The night nurse did not know about the new method and had no idea where the recorder was. After some searching Mrs. Hill determined that the recorder had been stolen. She was concerned because she knew that Mrs. Gladden would be upset about the loss—not only for the tape recorder but also for the apparent failure of the new method for giving reports.

Study Questions

1. How do you think this situation was handled by the following persons?
   a. Mrs. Gladden
   b. Mrs. Hill
   c. Miss Melton
   d. Mrs. Sharp
   e. Mary Parks
   f. The other members of the nursing staff
2. Identify the problems which are inherent in this case in reference to:
   a. The hospital organization
   b. The nursing-department
   c. The organization of the patient-care unit
   d. Relationships among staff members
   e. Needs of the staff for staff development
3. How would you have handled yourself in this situation had you been Miss Melton?
4. Outline the solutions for the problems identified. Be specific in determining a course of action for all the staff who play prominent roles in this situation.

Index

Index

Team Up With
Picture Publisher 4.0
The World's Best-Selling Image Editor For Windows

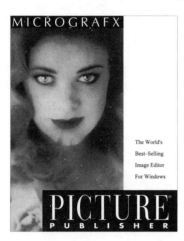

*Your
Picture
Here*

For faster service call:

1-800-733-3729 Or Fax 1-214-994-6475

Outside the U.S. and Canada – call 1-214-234-1769

Picture Publisher 4.0 Special 65%-Off Certificate

This certificate guarantees the owner of *Learn Desktop Graphics and Design on the PC*
a price of **only $199** on Picture Publisher 4.0 (regularly $595).

Payment Method: ❏ MasterCard   ❏ Visa   ❏ Discover   ❏ Amex   ❏ Check or Money Order

Order amount ($199/ea)	$ _____	
Shipping & handling	$ 10.00 Continental U.S. (Call for shipping outside the continental U.S.)	Name
Sales tax	$ _____ (AZ, CA, GA, IL, MA, MD, MI,	
Total enclosed	$ _____ NJ, NY, TX, VA, WA residents: Please add appropriate sales tax.)	Company

Cardholder _____ **Phone (_____)** _____

Card number _____ **Exp. date** _____

Signature _____

Address

_____

City   State/Province   Zip/Postal Code

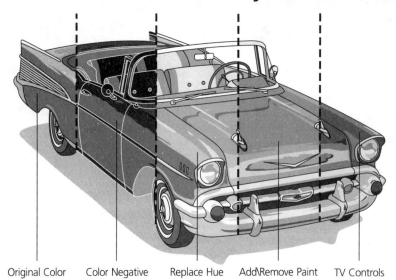